Damned for Their Difference

Damned for Their Difference: The Cultural Construction of Deaf People as Disabled

A Sociological History

Jan Branson
and Don Miller

Gallaudet University Press
Washington, D.C.

HV
2380
.B685
2002

Gallaudet University Press
Washington, D.C. 20002

© 2002 by Gallaudet University
All rights reserved. Published 2002
Printed in the United States of America

Library of Congress Cataloging-in-Publication Data

Branson, Jan.
Damned for their difference : the cultural construction of deaf people as disabled : a sociological history / Jan Branson and Don Miller.
p. cm.
Includes bibliographical references.
ISBN 1-56368-118-8 (cloth : alk. paper)
ISBN 1-56368-121-8 (softcover : alk. paper)
1. Deaf. 2. Deaf—Great Britain. I. Miller, Don. II. Title.
HV2380 .B685 2002
305.9′08162—dc21

2001056888

⊗The paper used in this publication meets the minimum requirements of American National Standard for Information Sciences—Permanence of Paper for Printed Library Materials, ANSI Z39.48–1984.

For our granddaughter, Jemima Krishnayanti
and for Kylie, Nick, and Tiffany-Jane

Contents

Preface ix

Acknowledgments xix

PART ONE
The Cultural Construction of "the Disabled": A Historical Overview

Introduction 3

1 The Cosmological Tyranny of Science: From the New Philosophy to Eugenics 13

2 The Domestication of Difference: The Classification, Segregation, and Institutionalization of Unreason 36

PART TWO
The Cultural Construction of Deaf People as "Disabled": A Sociological History of Discrimination

Introduction 59

3 The New Philosophy, Sign Language, and the Search for the Perfect Language in the Seventeenth Century 66

4 The Formalization of Deaf Education and the Cultural Construction of "the Deaf" and "Deafness" in the Eighteenth Century 91

5 The "Great Confinement" of Deaf People through Education in the Nineteenth Century 121

6 The Alienation and Individuation of Deaf People: Eugenics and Pure Oralism in the Late-Nineteenth Century 148

7 Cages of Reason—Bureaucratization and the Education of Deaf People in the Twentieth Century: Teacher Training, Therapy, and Technology 178

8 The Denial of Deafness in the Late-Twentieth Century: The Surgical Violence of Medicine and the Symbolic Violence of Mainstreaming 203

9 Ethno-Nationalism and Linguistic Imperialism: The State and the Limits of Change in the Battles for Human Rights for Deaf People 233

Appendix 255
The 1881 Survey of Methods Used in British Schools for the Deaf

Bibliography 259

Index 289

Preface

Over the last decade, the public has been growing more aware of the fact that deaf people have been discriminated against and that approaches toward the nature and use of sign languages lie at the heart of these discriminatory processes. The driving force in the cultivation of this growing awareness has been the rebirth of concepts of Deaf Culture, Deaf Pride, and the Deaf Way among signing deaf people throughout the Western world.[1] National dictionaries of sign languages have been developed,[2] sign languages have been included in school and university curricula, departments of sign language studies and deaf studies have been set up in universities, and the activities of the World Federation of the Deaf have caught the attention and imagination of governments and the wider public.

But little analysis has been done to determine why attitudes and behavior toward deaf people have been so discriminatory, why deaf people have been robbed again and again of their pride in their own sensibilities and languages. What analysis has been done has focused either on the textual and visual imagery of prejudice and discrimination—images in literature, the arts, and the cinema—or on somewhat narrowly focused histories of deaf education. Neither the textual studies nor the histories of deaf education place their analyses in their wider cultural, social, and historical contexts. The textual studies, often pursued in the context of cultural studies, fail to consider how these discriminatory texts about deaf people relate to wider discriminatory discursive processes with respect to ability, gender, race, ethnicity, or social class, and they rarely place their analyses in an historical context. The histories of deaf education similarly fail to place their histories in wider historical contexts to understand developments associated with the transformation of deaf education in terms of wider pedagogical and philosophical movements. In stark contrast to, for example, Foucault's histories of insane asylums, medical clinics, prisons, and sexuality, these histories of deaf education also do not consider their particular case studies of the history of deaf education in relation to the wider conceptual transformations of the societies in which they are set.

We will explore the cultural construction of deaf people as "disabled," the construction and marginalization of deaf people as a minority group, in both its current and historical dimensions by exercising what C. Wright Mills called a "sociological imagination," which involves the integrated study of social structure, history, and biography (Mills 1970). We will place significant people and events in their wider cultural contexts, proceeding through the book to examine the orientations toward and the treatment of deaf people, primarily in Britain, in the context of

- the new philosophy of the seventeenth century;
- the scientific rationalism and the middle-class thirst for reason through education in the eighteenth century;
- the "moral therapy" and missionary zeal of the educators of the poor in the first half of the nineteenth century;
- the professionalism and bureaucratization coupled with imperialism, evolutionism, and eugenicism that dominated the second half of the nineteenth century;
- eugenicism and the increasing alliances among professionalization, medicalization, and bureaucracy through the wars of the first half of the twentieth century;
- the rebellious and even revolutionary moves against the restrictions imposed on individuality and creativity through the 1960s and 1970s;
- the widespread deinstitutionalization through the 1980s; and
- the multiculturalism as well as the assertion of ethnic rights and identities through the 1990s.

The exploration of the concept of disability lays bare the contours of our society because the construction of a pathological population is at the core of the construction of every other person's "normal" subjectivity, as they define, understand, justify, and console themselves in relation to this embodied other. All peoples evaluate, all categorize, but the question we must ask is Why these categories in this society at this stage of our history? Deafness, lameness, blindness, myopia, autism are only labeled and signaled as disabilities if these conditions run counter to the sensory and physical expectations and demands of the society. In a Deaf community, a hearing person who cannot sign is disabled, handicapped. In a hunter-gatherer society, a myopic person is intensely disabled, more so than by deformity of limb, face, or speech. Depending on the society, to be hairless or hairy, pale or dark, fat or thin might be an intense disability, a barrier to marriage or to effective membership within society. Conditions categorized in our society as petit mal epilepsy, autism, and blindness may be associated in another society with intense spirituality and accepted as evidence of superiority. Appearances and behaviors are interpreted within cultural contexts. "The disabled" are not a natural but a cultural construction.

Although we concentrate on disabling processes in Western societies, we do not want to insinuate that the maltreatment of people judged disabled is peculiar to the West. The Dewa Agung, the supreme ruler, of the kingdom of Gelgel in southern Bali in Indonesia, is described in 1597 as having a "troupe of 50 misshapen dwarfs (their bodies deliberately deformed to resemble the grotesque figures of *kris* hilts)" (Hanna 1976, 9).[3] In a village in northwest India in 1968, a woman bemoaned the fact that her father had married her to a simpleton because no dowry had been required and so she could stay in the village and manage her father's house and land because he had no sons.[4] In a neighboring ward of the same village, a mother living in poverty despaired that she could never get a wife for her simpleton son, a wife who could come and help in the house, because no woman would marry him. In a village in southwest Bali in 1979, children took delight in mocking and purposely confusing the deaf brother of the household head. Unmarried because of his deafness, he could never become a whole person in the eyes of the village, and he would never inherit land or property. And yet across the mountains in north Bali, a hereditary deaf population live as an integral part of their village, marrying freely and participating as full members of their village through the use of a local sign language that is known and used by most villagers, hearing and deaf (Branson, Miller, and Marsaja 1996). And in villages throughout the north of Bali, hearing people readily use sign languages in their communication with deaf people (Branson, Miller, and Marsaja 1999).

This book brings together the many and varied strands of our struggles to understand, research, and teach about the puzzling process whereby some of our fellow citizens are classified as disabled and, thereby, are marginalized and oppressed. Much of the material discussed derives from our own primary ethnographic and archival research, particularly though not solely in relation to the past and current treatment of deaf people. In this book, we have given prime attention to historical processes in Britain. Most studies of the treatment of deaf people and of the development of deaf communities have concentrated on developments in America and France. The British situation has been summarily dealt with and, in the process, seriously misrepresented.[5] With respect to British histories of the education of deaf people in Britain, Hodgson's study (Hodgson 1953) provides excellent data for the first half of the twentieth century but is ill informed with respect to earlier history. McLoughlin's later study simply repeats Hodgson's errors and then continues from where Hodgson left off with an account of later developments, thoroughly biased in favor of oralism. These misrepresentations, in turn, have failed to appreciate Britain's historical links with France and America.

While writing this book, we have benefited from the recent sudden flowering of studies dealing with disabilities and, particularly, with deaf people. Baynton (1996), Davis (1995), Mirzoeff (1995), Harris (1995), Wrigley (1996), Corker (1997), and Lane, Hoffmeister, and Bahan (1996) all provide provocative analyses of the discursive construction of deafness. Mike Oliver (1996) has provided a succinct overview of his long-term engagement with disability; Sander Gilman (1991a, 1991b, 1995) has continued to provoke us to reveal and understand our deep-seated prejudices in relation to normality and pathology, and Ingstad and Whyte (1995) have provided access to what is the most coherent and sophisticated set of studies on disability and culture yet available. Whyte (1995), in particular, has opened to the Anglophone world a feast of non-English language sources on the discursive construction of disabilities.

We are by no means the first sociologists or anthropologists to theorize the cultural construction of disabling practices. Writers such as Ryan and Thomas (1987), Busfield (1989), Tomlinson (1987), Littlewood and Lipsedge (1989), Hirst and Woolley (1982), Fulcher (1989), Abberley (1987), Oliver (1986, 1996), Robert Murphy (1987, 1995) and Ingstad and Whyte (1995) all approach disabilities as culturally constructed and seek to understand aspects of those cultural processes. Our own theorizing of these processes as they relate to people who are disabled dates from the late 1980s (Branson, Miller, and Branson 1988; Branson and

Miller 1989a). Many theorists, however, remain more or less bound within the parameters set by the categories of our society or deal with only a section of those deemed disabled. But not one of them provides a sociological understanding that combines history and biography with the study of social structures and processes.

Of importance in developing the analysis presented here has been our contact with the work of sociolinguists dealing with the social, cultural, and particularly the educational effect of discrimination against linguistic minorities throughout the world. Above all, we have been influenced and stimulated by the joint and individual work of Tove Skutnabb-Kangas and Robert Phillipson on linguistic human rights, the right to bilingual education, and linguistic imperialism.[6]

Who Are "the Disabled"?

As we turn to explore the cultural construction of "the disabled," we must clarify the term that is central to our enterprise. Who are the disabled? The term *the disabled* must be understood as functioning on a number of levels:

as a colloquial category that able-bodied people in particular assume is embodied but that remains vague and undefined—an other;

as a collection of people who are defined as disabled by others for administrative purposes such as housing, education, income tax, and social services;[7] and

as a collection of people who consider themselves to be disabled and thereby share a sense of identity with others who are similarly defined.

The disabled, therefore, are not a tangible and unproblematic collection of people but, rather, a population that is assumed to exist, a category into which able-bodied people can slot others who pose a threat to their own normal view of the world and to those who inhabit it, and into which those who identify themselves as disabled can welcome those whom they see as suffering the same marginalization and oppression as themselves. The issue of whether signing Deaf people are a linguistic minority or are disabled, for example, has generated intense debate within both Deaf communities and among disability rights activists.[8] The problem of identity as being either Deaf or disabled derives from the way a disabled identity encompasses an individual's subjectivity in the same way as gender or race. Seeking to move beyond this essentialist view of identity, many Deaf people are seeking alliances with disability rights movements to counter the essentialist view that people with disabilities are inherently pathological.[9] Those people who are actively involved in the achievement of rights for people who are disabled refer to those who bask in their own normality as "TABs"—temporarily able-bodied.

What we are exploring is the discursive construction of a category with shifting referents and shifting significance, a concept that demonstrates par excellence that its meaning lies, in Derrida's terms, in "*differance*," in the establishment of meaning through the assertion of difference. No finite meaning is ever achieved, but meaning is constantly deferred as people manipulate it for their own strategic ends. The meaning of "the disabled" is elusive but dramatic, vague in its specificity, and destructive in its application as this label is applied to others and as "the disabled" are defined by difference, with the boundaries of their identity deferred. It is a label that threatens us all but one that is assumed by the majority of the population to be embodied in others.

This view of the discursive construction of meaning—as being dependent on the construction of difference but, at the same time, involving constant negotiation in a way that no finite meaning is ever established—is central to the ways this book explores the cultural construction of "the disabled." To a very large extent, this study is, in the tradition of Foucault's studies of madness and medicine, a historical sociology of the development of concepts and of their effect on social and cultural practice. It is about the concepts that influence the way people orient themselves in relation to themselves and others. The concept of sanity has no meaning without the realization of its opposite, insanity. The concept of being able-bodied is meaningless without the experience of its opposite, being disabled. For the rational society to experience rationality, it must experience, embody, the irrational.

The texts through which these concepts are accessed and analyzed are many and varied. Sometimes, they are conventional written texts, where concepts such as sanity and normality are overtly used, but often, they are the metatexts of human practice and of material culture—paintings, sculpture, and architecture: the elaborate, grandiose architecture of seventeenth- and eighteenth-century madhouses and nineteenth-century asylums for deaf people; the sculptures that stood at the gates of Bedlam at Moorfields in London; paintings and drawings of the mad or of the education of deaf students; the sideshows at town fairs; the methods of treating madness or other conditions deemed pathological. These cultural practices and products are all "texts" to be read, texts to be analyzed in terms of the concepts central to the messages they conveyed to the people of the time and in terms of the clues they give us about the way the discursive construction of discrimination and prejudice occurred.

In seeking to understand these processes, we focus on the social that is in us all but that the hard-toned individualism of the West tends to obscure. Despite the West's devaluation and even denial of "socialness," our behavior can be "collectively orchestrated without being the product of the orchestrating action of a conductor" (Bourdieu 1977b, 72). What we do has more meaning than we know. And so we delve below the threshold of consciousness to explore the unknown, the ignored, and the usually unintended social and cultural consequences of everyday behavior.

The perspective through which we will interpret the interweaving of history and biography does not focus exclusively on either structure or the individual. Theories that concentrate simply on synchronic structure fail to explain why and how certain sociocultural forms have developed. Phenomenological theories that concentrate on an individually centered, voluntaristic view of everyday life fail to appreciate the structural contexts and structuring effects of that behavior, particularly the unconscious and, often, oppressive effects. Our focus is on the discourses within which and through which we embody the concept of the disabled in our society, on not only what we say and do but also the way we say and do things.

In analyzing the effect over many centuries that changing ideas and practices have on the disablement of people who are deaf, we must draw eclectically on a range of theoretical approaches to the study of society and culture. Social and cultural theorists, like the people they study, are women and men of their times. Their theorizing is stimulated by the cultural atmospheres in which they write and the social situations they seek to understand, no matter how scientific they claim to be. Through our combined historical, anthropological, sociological, and linguistic experience, we seek to provide a contribution to deaf studies. Deaf studies is a multidisciplinary academic enterprise focusing on the development of a coherent understanding of the myriad social and cultural processes that have influenced and continue to influence the position and role of people who are deaf both within and beyond our own society. Deaf studies recognizes the effect of a Deaf identity on these processes. Like women's studies and black studies, deaf studies contributes, on the one hand, to exploring the way society has imposed an identity—in this case, "deaf"—which, thereby, has generated discrimination against the people so labeled and, on the other hand, to promoting a sense of pride and potential power in and through that identity, a Deaf identity. Like women's studies and black studies, deaf studies also involves the development of social theory that is adequate to and appropriate for the cross-cultural analysis of the structuring and reproduction of inequalities and associated discriminatory processes.

All research, whether in medicine, engineering, architecture, philosophy, anthropology, literary criticism, or veterinary science is oriented toward the improvement of the quality of life for somebody or something. So, too, is deaf studies. As we explore the history of the education of deaf people or the cultural construction of people who are deaf as "disabled," we are exploring the history and current ethnology of being deaf. Ultimately, we are exploring the historical, social, and cultural parameters of Deaf communities. In the West, where communal identities and responsibilities were sacrificed on the alter of capital accumulation, the effort to reestablish a sense of community through the development of a tangible and valid history is, indeed, in the interests of improving the quality of human life—especially among a people who for so long have been damned for their difference.

Notes

1. For a discussion of these identity issues in relation to Britain, see Harris (1995).

2. See Branson and Miller (1998a).

3. A *kris* is a short, elaborately decorated sacred sword.

4. The examples given for India and Bali were gathered by the authors during fieldwork in Indian and Balinese villages.

5. Nowhere is this more apparent than in a recent discussion of the education of people who were deaf in Britain during the seventeenth and eighteenth centuries by Safford and Safford (1996, 31–32). They heap scorn on the work and writing of John Wallis and then of Henry Baker, basing their interpretation on Bender (1960), which is entirely misinformed, and on Lane (1984), which, although providing a very well-researched coverage of the history of deaf education in France and then in America, is dismissive of the work of the British educators without basing his conclusions on a careful analysis of the data. Safford and Safford even claim to use Laurent Clerc as their source on Wallis and then Baker, again citing Lane (Safford and Safford 1996, 31 and 32), when, in fact, Lane simply uses Clerc as a figure through which to tell the history of deaf education.

6. See in particular Skutnabb-Kangas and Phillipson (1994) and Phillipson (1992).

7. For examples of formal definitions, see the *UN Standard Rules on the Equalization of Opportunities for Disabled Persons* (www.independentliving.org/STANDARDRULES/), and for further discussion of the terminology in such definitions, see Mitchell and Snyder (1997).

8. Since the 1960s, many deaf people who identify themselves as deaf in a culturally distinct way, especially those who see their use of sign language as marking them off as a linguistic minority, have used the term "Deaf" with a capital *D* to indicate that they belong to a Deaf community. The term "Deaf" will be used throughout the text where it is historically and culturally appropriate.

9. For discussion of these issues, see Ladd (1995), Woolley (1995), Finkelstein (1991), and Corker (1997).

Acknowledgments

Many people have helped us over the years as we have sought to understand the cultural construction first of "the disabled" and then of "deaf people as disabled." Paddy Ladd first led us into the challenging field of deaf studies. In Australia, our Deaf colleagues and students have been vital to our effective engagement with Deaf issues. Particular mention must be made of the late Graham Peters and of Jenny Toms and Brian Bernal, colleagues in Australia who also accompanied us around the world as we all sought to understand and contribute to the shape and parameters of Deaf history and of sign language studies. Our archival research in Britain, especially our research into the history of the London Asylum for the Deaf and Dumb in the Old Kent Road, benefited from the knowledgeable guidance and friendly assistance of Peter Brown and Jack Piggott. For her ongoing support in our seemingly neverending research into the education in Britain of deaf people, we also extend our sincere thanks to Mary Placket, librarian of the Library of the Royal National Institute for the Deaf in London. Of particular importance in our research into the education and treatment of deaf people through the ages, both in Britain and throughout Europe, has been the cataloging and annotation of The Farrar Collection of Books on the Education of the Deaf and Cognate Subjects in the John Rylands Library, Deansgate, in Manchester. We thank the staff of the John Rylands Library in Deansgate who patiently helped us find our way through the Farrar Collection. In particular, we would like to thank Anne Young, Alistair Cooper, Jean Bostock, Ann Crowther-Doyle, and Sarah Lucas, who all became intrigued by the collection as it emerged from the depths of the library and made the task both exciting and efficient. Dr. Peter McNiven gave our project his full support. We would also like to thank the staff of the following institutions in London: The Family Records Centre, The British Library, Somerset House, and the Geological Society. Our thanks goes also to the staff members of the West Yorkshire Archive Service in Wakefield, the Leeds Local History Unit in the Leeds Public Library, and the Local History Service in the Manchester Public Library. A very special thank you goes to the Reverend Malcolm Deakin, current minister of the Doddridge Church, Castle Hill United Reformed Church, Northampton, who not only gave us open access to the church's papers, including those of Thomas Arnold but also assisted us in tracking down the houses that Farrar had lived in with Arnold in Northampton. None of the British research would have been possible without family, without the generous hospitality of our mother-in-law Joan Scoles as well as Gill and Jeff Armishaw.

Our two months at Gallaudet University in Washington, D.C., in 1997 and, above all, the award of Powrie V. Doctor Chairs in Deaf Studies to us both in 1999 not only provided vital access to the Gallaudet archives but also provided the ideal environment for the final rewriting of the manuscript in 1999. We express our thanks to King and Linda Jordan. The dean and staff of the Graduate School and Research were a delight to work with and provided all the facilities we needed. We give very special thanks to Sally Dunn. For their companionship, especially during those Friday lunches, our thanks go to Michael Karchmer, David Armstrong, and Vic Van Cleve, and, for treasured memories, Bill Stokoe. Thanks, too, goes to Carol Erting and Joe Kinner. For their help in the Gallaudet archives, we extend our thanks to Ulf Hedberg and Michael Olsen. The librarian of the Volta Bureau in Washington, D.C., Judith Anderson, also provided open access to valuable archives. The text has benefited substantially from the comments on earlier drafts by press readers. Finally, we express our sincere thanks to our editors, Vic Van Cleve and Ivey Pittle Wallace, for their interest, their patience, and their editorial skill.

We dedicate this book to our CODA grandchild Jemima Krishnayanti, in the hope that she will eventually find in its pages inspiration to explore the complexities of her multicultural, multilingual environment, growing up as she is with two sign languages and one spoken language, and to our three children, Kylie, Nick, and Tiffany-Jane, for making it possible for us to spend so much time away from Huthnance Farm.

PART ONE

The Cultural Construction of "the Disabled": A Historical Overview

Introduction

Before we can understand the historically and culturally specific context that underlies how people who are deaf are conceptualized and treated as being disabled and before we can understand the violence, overt and symbolic, that these views and actions have wreaked on those damned by their difference, we must set the scene. We must understand how and why the current Western view of the cosmos came to rely on the conceptual division of humanity into the normal and the pathological, the able-bodied and the disabled. The cultural construction of the concept *the disabled* did not occur overnight but was formed and transformed by the peculiar cultural conditions associated with the gradual development of capitalist democracies. A society that asserts, on the one hand, that all people are born equal, that all individuals are equal before the law, and that all individuals are free to access the boundless resources of their society and yet, on the other hand, is characterized by enduring structured inequalities—of social class, gender, age, race, ethnicity, and ability—demands very complex ideological practices to ensure that its citizens continue to have faith in progress and in those at the helm. The concept of people who are disabled has been constructed as an integral part of that ideological practice.

We seek to unearth the themes that underlie the bewildering variations of history, to discover the conceptual unity in the diversity of cultural practice. Our historical overview, like the book as a whole, centers on the historical transformation of British culture and society. But politicians are the ones bound by the imagined community that is the nation, not intellectuals or, indeed, those entrepreneurs who drove the world headlong into modernity. Thus, attention will and must be drawn also to developments across the English Channel and, later, across the seas into colonies, the Empire, and the New World.

First, however, we must map the stage on which the actors in the emerging battle of the sciences developed new cosmologies, new views of the world and humanity's place in it. These new cosmologies emerged in conjunction with dramatic changes in the way people not only thought about one another but also interacted with one another. They are associated with the breakdown of societies based on communal identities and communal needs and the emergence of individualistic societies focusing on the accumulation of individual wealth.

The Feudal Community in the Middle Ages

Feudal society in Britain through the first half of the second millennium was made up of communities based on personalized, face-to-face relationships.[1] A person's identity was not individualized but bound to family and community. The responsibilities of master for servant, whether observed or neglected, whether kindly or ruthlessly exploitative, extended across generations and involved far more than payment for immediate services rendered. People were born no more equal than they are today, but the inequalities were assumed inevitable, a normal aspect of society. Without communal associations, a person had no socially sanctioned identity, no honor. To be cast out of the community was a fate worse than death itself. It was the death of self, condemnation to a terrifying individuality, expulsion beyond the boundary of the community—the town, the village, the fief, the monastery—into the wilderness.

The feudal lord used the labor of those bound to him to produce tangible products such as food, crafts, and military service. In return, he or occasionally she was expected to provide for the basic personal needs of those who served him or her, to provide housing, assistance with costs for ceremonies associated with life-cycle rituals (birth, marriage, death) and seasonal rituals (harvest, Christmas), and generally to provide support in time of crisis. Some lords were ruthless and cruel in the exercise of their authority and neglectful in the fulfillment of their obligations, but the general form of the relationship was recognized by all.

Although families were expected to care for kin whatever their condition, poverty was rife, and many families could not care for those who were unproductive. The fate of people who were crippled, deaf, blind, deformed, mentally retarded, or mentally disturbed depended entirely on the circumstances of their kin and of the community into which they were born. Although a crippled weaver might continue as a full and productive member of his or her family and community, a crippled farm laborer might be rendered destitute. Similarly, although in one situation people who were deaf and mute might labor effectively in the fields or engage in a wide range of other tasks—weaving, blacksmithing, carpentry—while communicating through signs, in other situations, their deafness and muteness might have resulted in rejection by the community, in possible banishment to the mercy of the church.[2]

The use of monasteries and nunneries as depositories for unwanted children was common.[3] These unwanted children became oblates and sometimes made up a large proportion of the monastery or convent community.[4] Boswell records that 85 percent of the monks in one English monastery between 1030 and 1070 had come to the monastery as oblates (Boswell 1990, 297). Boswell also quotes Jerome (a fourth-century monk and saint) as claiming "that parents dedicate to virginity those daughters who are deformed or defective in some way" (240–41) and Ulrich of Cluny as stating in the eleventh century that parents "commit to monasteries any hump-backed, deformed, dull or unpromising children they have" (298).[5] The presence of deaf children in monasteries is occasionally referred to over the centuries, and in many monasteries, especially those with silent orders, sign languages were used.[6]

Poverty rendered many people destitute, particularly those whose physical, sensory, or mental conditions made them in any sense unproductive and a burden on their families. Many were forced to beg to survive and were not considered members of their communities. Records from medieval times reveal occasional mention of deaf children begging at the doors of monasteries and abbeys (Saint-Loup 1993, 380n). Much of this medieval poverty was one of the terrible consequences of seemingly constant warfare. Disbanded rabbles returning from wars that left a ravaged countryside in their wake included lines on lines of those rendered blind, deaf, deranged, and mutilated in battle.[7]

Communities were also linguistic communities. Today, we conceptualize language as something apart from the individual and certainly beyond any individual community. We learn a language or we speak and write a language as though the language had a separate existence, something to be accessed. This abstract quality of language has been generated by a wide range of factors but, above all, by the development of widespread literacy, by the expression of language in tangible print on which we are to reflect. But feudal agricultural communities were nonliterate communities in which language was "a mode of action rather than . . . a countersign of thought" (Malinowski 1960, 296). People focused on ways of communicating.[8] In these environments, we can surmise that the use of signing often flourished when deaf people were present, a natural aspect of the communicative process. Certainly, this signing seems to have been the case in the Weald in Kent, at least, during the seventeenth century and is the case in communities in Bali, Indonesia, today.[9] The linguistic needs of people who were deaf, therefore, were often catered to as a natural aspect of the community's localized culture of communication.

The Breakdown of Feudalism and the Cultural Construction of the Disabled and Impotent Poor

The fifteenth century was an era of uprisings. The bubonic plague of the fourteenth century, or "black death" as it was known, had devastated the population. Twenty-five million people died in Britain and Europe. In the countryside and the towns, the whole productive system was thrown into chaos. Political chaos followed. Church rebelled against church, the state rebelled against the church, and the peasantry rebelled against church and state. People were increasingly forced to look outward, beyond familiar communal environments, to survive. At the same time, they were forced to look inward, to focus not on communal needs but on those of the immediate family and household. As communities broke down, so too did the processes whereby those who today are labeled disabled were integrated into community life—the adjustments to productive relations and processes as well as the use of communication forms that were suited to the specific needs of community members. Less and less were people members of coherent, long-term cultural and linguistic communities.[10]

Many of those who had survived the plague flocked to the towns in search of sustenance. The number of beggars on the streets increased dramatically. Poor and out of work through no fault of their own, the unemployed poor came to epitomize potential chaos. As early as 1359 in London, those people "able to labour and work," were distinguished from those "many poor folks, such as lepers, blind, halt, and persons oppressed with old age and divers other maladies" (Coulton 1919, 321). In the desperate struggle to survive, to find work, the "able-bodied" poor beggars had the advantage, driving the "disabled" further into poverty and the mercy of church and state. Although those labeled "disabled" had the right to beg, they were often displaced by able-bodied poor who often mimicked disabilities to secure alms (see McCall 1979, 177–78).[11] Disability became synonymous with beggary, and beggary became synonymous with failure—failure to be wholly human because human worth was increasingly being associated with work.

The "disabled" poor were declared socially, economically, and politically "impotent." The overt distinction between the able-bodied and the impotent poor was constantly reinforced by a succession of poor laws under the Tudors and early Stuarts (see Beier 1985, 9). Human worth was defined in terms of one's commitment to work—a sign of grace, a sign of "potency" as a human being. In England, the poor laws of the sixteenth century were designed specifically for the "impotent poor," not for the "sturdy beggars." A 1626 handbook for justices of the peace explains:

> The person naturally disabled, either in wit or member, as an idiot, lunatic, blind, lame, etc., not being able to work . . . all these . . . are to be provided for by the overseers [of the poor] of necessary relief, and are to have allowances proportional and according to the continuation and measure of their maladies and needs. (quoted in MacDonald 1981, 6)

But the term *disabled* was still an adjective applied to a wide range of people who, for myriad reasons, were unable to work. They were diverse. They were in no sense a single category of humanity, "the disabled."

The Need for Uniform, Able-Bodied Labor Power and the Emergence of Ideologies of Individualism and Equality

The merchants in the towns and the new entrepreneurial landowners in the countryside shunned these complex and parochial obligations and simply employed laborers to perform specific tasks, paying them wages. They maintained no personal relationship. Here, beyond the old face-to-face communities, the profit-oriented and alienating environments of the early manufactories favored uniform labor. Communication idiosyncrasies also had no place. Uniformity of communication, like uniformity of physical competence, was demanded and required. Ways of communicating became more uniform and less flexible. No long-term obligations existed. People were forced to compete on the labor market for work and, in the process, were considered individually responsible for their own futures. The relationship was with the mill, the factory, or the farm, not with the owner, and life outside the workplace was the individual's own affair.

Emergent capitalism demanded a new view of labor and of the labor market, a view of the individual devoid of the kin-based and feudal responsibilities to share profits or to care for those who were not directly productive. The individual person with a self-contained identity was being born. Associated with this new individualism was to emerge a concept of equality. Individual rights and equality guaranteed before the law were assumed to exist. Whether the individual was envisaged as basically selfish and anarchic, as with Hobbes, or as rational, cooperative, and oriented toward the protection of individual interests, as with Locke, the "individual man [became] the axiom, and society the derivative" (Williams 1965, 94). Society and the community were freed of all obligations. Individuals could henceforth bask in the glory of individual achievement, denying that their privileged access to resources was by virtue of their membership in socially and culturally privileged groups, or they could suffer an asocial isolation and introverted guilt if they and others decreed that they had failed. The glory or the fault was assumed to lie with the individual.

The Transformation of the Family and the Increasing Isolation and Marginalization of People Deemed Disabled

Family life was changing, and these changes affected the ability and even willingness of parents to adjust to the needs and aspirations of those children who were in some sense physically, sensorially, or behaviorally different. The feudal family had been a unit of production, with all its members recognized as part of the productive process. It was an extended family of more than two generations, linked through complex ties of kinship, affinity, and community. The aged who were no longer productive remained integral to its identity, and the frail, the simple, the crippled, the deformed, and the different were, where poverty or disease did not threaten the family, cared for and made productive. But as trends changed, the concept of production began to involve the employment of labor power rather than people and denied any social responsibilities beyond the immediate and even nuclear family.[12]

At the same time, the family was being defined as a female realm, women being associated with all that was private, communal, caring, and moral, whereas men, being seen as individuated and rationally calculating, were identified with the public world. The large numbers of women who were forced to work in the public world were defined as temporary interlopers from the private realm and were paid less than men. Extra, "unproductive" members of the family increasingly now were seen as a burden. The only legitimate unproductive members were those who would be productive in the future—able-bodied children. In poor households where all worked—men, women, and children—any unproductive members could no longer be cared for. Because the site of work had changed and the conditions of work were regimented and individuated, unproductive family members could not accompany others to work, could not compete for work under the new laboring conditions, and had no one to care for them at home.

But developments at home did not solely affect the gradual cultural construction of the concept *the disabled.* Merchants and their sponsors sought riches wherever they were to be found, and many were to be found across the seas. As merchants voyaged out across the globe, they first sought riches, then markets, and finally, new production sites. Centuries of plundering the riches and indigenous industries of other countries eventually gave way to unequal competition with those industries. The amounts pillaged were staggering, with, for example, the amount plundered from India between 1750 and 1800 estimated at between £100,000,000 and £150,000,000 at a time when the British national income was only £125,000,000 (Mandel 1968, 443–44).[13] The subjugation of these vast populations to imperial domination required not only force of arms but also ideological legitimation. Imperialism, so vital an ingredient in the development of the new democratic economies, would affect heavily the views of humanity that were to construct and encompass the concept of the disabled. The harsh exploitative realities of the empire were, like those of capitalism at home, rationalized by means of ideologies that twisted the facts into new, palatable shapes for the emerging middle classes.

From Hierarchy to Democracy

Although the decentralized polities of feudalism were initially replaced with centralized monarchies, the economic and political turmoil that accompanied the breakdown of feudalism combined with the need of the new entrepreneurs to invest freely and individually threatened these hierarchical states. Revolutionary movements erupted constantly as feudalism crumbled. The divine monarchs lost their divinity—and many, their lives—and, at best, returned as figureheads of national identity, no longer the magnetic center of the nation. Democracy was being born.

In the emergent democracies, the legal system developed to guarantee individual rights and equality "before the law." First protected were the individual rights of those men with property, and the equality of these propertied males existed before the law. Gradually, the logic of egalitarianism was to incorporate more and more of democracy's potential citizens—women, racial minorities, and people who were disabled. But those moves were a long way off in the seventeenth century when the English Revolution gave people a taste of their potentially democratic future. Gradually, the law courts came to embody a legal order, rationally administered by legal experts in the interests of individual justice and social control. Eventually, political administration would also achieve the ultimate depersonalization of decision making through the development in the nineteenth century of government bureaucracies for the rational management of democracy's citizens, including people who were disabled.

The ideologies of egalitarianism and individualism that gradually dominated hierarchical views of the world not only eventually gave rise to universal suffrage but also generated the need for those in positions of power and privilege to justify extant inequalities in a new way. Gradually, these ideologies created a distinctive form of inequality, discrimination, a legitimization of prejudice, in an environment where socially and culturally sanctioned inequality had become inappropriate and unacceptable. People were discriminated against as being "equal but different." Inequalities were justified according to differences of gender, race, culture, and ability (see Dumont 1980, app.; 1986).

Now, a cosmology was needed that would allow an economy based on rampant inequality to coexist effectively with a polity that increasingly advocated individualism and equality not only before the law but also in the realization of a democratically chosen government. The new high priests of Western societies, the scientists, would play a vital role.

> The future beckoned urgently, and the promise it held out could only adequately be gauged by the chaos that might result if the forces of progress were not all combined in the task of bringing the new society into being. Of those forces the most important were science, the men of science, and all those who could see in the achievements of the scientific method . . . the key to the future direction and organization of society. (Kumar 1978, 26)

Notes

1. Feudalism emerged in Britain and Europe sometime during the ninth century and began to break down by the fifteenth century (see Anderson 1974). Feudal societies were decentralized societies, with each town, village, monastery, or fief being relatively autonomous economically and politically. They are characterized as feudal because the dominant economic and political unit was the fief in which a feudal lord ruled over a community bound by hereditary ties to serve him—to work his land, serve his household, and when required, provide military service. The feudal lord in turn owed knight service to higher lords and, ultimately, to a monarch. Villages of free peasants, the monasteries and nunneries, and the merchant-led towns were relatively independent of these feudal lords. See Merrington (1975) and Hilton (1973).

2. Childhood was much shorter than we define it today. Indeed, as a concept, it did not exist because infancy was followed by adulthood. Death in the early years was common, and by the time children reached the age of seven or eight years, they were expected to have taken on adult roles in production and adult responsibilities in family and community (see Ariès 1962, 128 ff., 329 ff.).

3. Shown in research by both Boswell (1990) and Shahar (1990).

4. The term *oblate* comes from the Latin *oblatio*, meaning offering. Oblates were children who lived in the monastery and were cared for by the monks. They became part of the monastic community, serving the monks and in some cases becoming monks themselves.

5. The Benedictine monastery of Cluny in France was recognized as the spiritual center of Western Christianity in the eleventh century.

6. See Banham (1991), Saint-Loup (1993), Lane (1984, 75) for the abbey of Saint-Jean in France, and see Plann (1997) for Spanish monastic connections.

7. See McCall (1979) and Mollat (1986).

8. See Mühlhäusler (1996).

9. See Groce's history of the deaf emigrants from the Weald in Kent who settled on Martha's Vineyard off the coast of Massachusetts in the seventeenth century (Groce 1985). Also see Branson, Miller, and Marsaja (1996, 1999).

10. Processes were also at work that would lead to widespread literacy and the associated standardization of languages. This trend would deal a heavy blow to the development and use of those community-based ways of communicating that catered to the specific needs of community members in all their difference, including the use of signing with people who were deaf.

11. The giving of alms bestowed religious merit on the giver.

12. The family in modern Western societies is often represented ideologically as a haven from the ruthless world of work—as a personalized, lifelong institution that contrasts with the task-oriented, skill-based, depersonalized, insecure, and temporary world of work. It is regarded as the realm of privacy in contrast to the public world of work; the female and nurturing family is in contrast to the male and ruthless labor market. In this way, the family is seen as disconnected from the production process and often is represented also as a feudal survivor. But the modern family is not a remnant from the past. It is integral to the effective operation of the economy. See Branson and Miller (1977), Kuhn and Wolpe (1978), and Barrett and McIntosh (1982).

13. Note that the Western imperial expansion that accompanied and succored the development of capitalism had nothing to do with the spread of civilization. It was not a case of contact between a progressive West and the stagnant East: "[T]he reason why Europe went to Asia, and not Asia to Europe, is that Asia was more self-sufficient, and had little need, and but scant desire, for the products of Europe" (Caldwell 1977, 62).

1

The Cosmological Tyranny of Science: From the New Philosophy to Eugenics

And new Philosophy calls all in doubt,
The element of fire is quite put out; . . .
'Tis all in peeces, all cohaerance gone

—John Donne, "The First Anniversary"

The Spectre, like a hoar-frost and a mildew, rose over Albion,
Saying: 'I am God, O Sons of Men! I am your Rational Power!
Am I not Bacon and Newton and Locke, who teach Humility to Man
Who teach Doubt and Experiment?

—William Blake, *Jerusalem*

For the people of Britain and western Europe in the fifteenth century, life and its vagaries were mysterious. If answers to its mysteries were to be found, they were to be found in the Scriptures, in the word of God interpreted by His priesthood, or in other religiosities with heritages lost in time. The world was God ordained. The community was a religious community. Doctors sought to work within the mysteries of an encompassing nature to promote healing; they were nature's servants, not her masters. And nature was fickle, sometimes kind, often cruel. Her creatures were diverse and unpredictable, the monstrous always on the margins of the known at the edge of the world, in the oceans, in lands unknown, beyond the grave, in the mysteries of health and illness, and in the mysteries of birth. Transformations of nature's God-given differences, oddities, were assumed possible only through miracles, as is evident in the case of Anne of Jesus (A Sister of Notre Dame de Namur 1932), a child, deaf and mute, who suddenly through a miracle at the age of seven in 1552 said "Ave Maria" and could speak and hear.

Religion and Science

Religion and science are fundamentally incompatible concepts today. Religion is seen as part of the private realm beyond the public worlds of work and politics, an individuated orientation to the metaphysical, based not in sensible proof but in faith. Science is conceptualized as part of the public world, secular, sensible, based in rational expertise, the source of a proven truth. But if we transcend these parochial concepts and examine the way they operate in society, the distinction becomes blurred, and the religious character of scientism is revealed.

Berger has defined religion as "the human enterprise by which a sacred cosmos is established," adding that "by sacred is meant . . . a quality of mysterious and awesome power" (Berger 1969, 25). This "mysterious and awesome power" may be seen to lie in people of power, whose peculiar qualities or training are believed to endow them with a power beyond the reach of those ordinary mortals. The religious side of science will be seen to emerge from the way it was viewed and acted on by its "congregation," the nonscientists who looked to the new science to fill the gap left by the disestablishment of the church as the source of knowledge. They developed a faith in the power of science and in the efficacy of the knowledge of it practitioners, ensuring that the scientists became the new high priests of the modern world, the effective ideologues of society.

Religion involves the handing down of the sacred, of knowledge, of an understanding, all of which is beyond the vagaries of everyday existence but relates to it, establishing a cosmic order. In an effort to establish their own order, medical scientists began to define the parameters of "normal" humanity; the biologists, the shape, contents, and future of the "natural" world. The logical processes and theories of science moved beyond the realm of scientific experimentation to become the epistemological and cosmological foundations of society. The epistemological processes and cosmological myths of science became so deeply ingrained in the collective consciousness, so deeply influential in the construction of subjectivities and the shaping of conventions and institutions, that they also shaped the progress of science itself. The development of science was determined by the epistemological and cosmological tyranny of the culture of science.

The transformation of Western ideology toward faith in science came about through radical religious changes, changes that turned the cosmos upside down as humanity took control and as God was relegated to the backseat in the shaping of humanity and its future. These changes were made possible by the breakdown of monastic authority and the emergence of radical clerics who paved the way for the Protestant Reformation, particularly Erasmus and his followers. They were inspired by intellectual developments within and beyond the church that highlighted the creative power of the human intellect and its ability to plan for the future through rationality, emphasizing "nature rather than grace, ethics rather than theology and action rather than contemplation" (Gilmore 1962, 204–5). Religion was being individuated and intellectualized.

With the intellectualization and individuation of religion, religion became "something personal, inner and transcendentally oriented" (Tambiah 1990, 4). In Calvinism in particular, the outward material and collective aspects of religious behavior were robbed of any primary religious significance. They became merely symbolic, evidence of an inner faith. The Protestant ethic (see Weber 1985) stressed personal religious worth expressed through individuated diligence in work rather than in the communal performance of religious rituals. The individual mind became the focus of religiosity, stressing the need of the faithful to think and work religiously rather than to show diligence in the performance of religiously charged actions. The church and its buildings, altars, paraphernalia, rituals, and prayers were robbed of their power and mystery as the focus shifted from group-based performance in which everyone in all their diverse abilities could effectively take part to a personal, intellectual commitment that demanded evidence of individual mental and occupational ability. "The Divine was relegated to some vague and impenetrable heaven, somewhere up in the skies. Man and man alone was the standard by which all things were measured. He was his own *raison d'être*" (Hazard 1973, 9).

As monarchs and republics rose and fell and rose again, those in power sought legitimacy for their power and their privilege. They engaged in the active promotion of those cosmologies that favored them. They looked to the wise men of their day to serve as ideologues, promoting some and rejecting others. We turn first to the work of these wise men.

The Battle of the Sciences and the Emergence of the New Philosophy

The roots of the epistemic violence that has been exercised to create and discriminate against "the disabled" lie in the radical transformation of Western cosmology from the fifteenth century, a cosmological and epistemological transformation associated with the triumph of a mechanistic science over its spiritualist opponents. A mode of thought and practice emerged to transform not only the world around us but also the consciousness of Western humanity.

In many accounts, the scientific and philosophical revolution is pictured as emanating directly and solely from scientists and philosophers. They are depicted as changing the view of the world, as establishing new epistemologies, cosmologies, ideologies: the Cartesian worldview, the Newtonian universe. But scientists and philosophers were, in fact, expressing in a particular way what others were expressing in different ways, some in words, others in actions. The poets, dramatists, novelists, and painters were not simply reflecting philosophical changes. They did not follow the philosophers' lead. The age was one of revolution, and the philosophers were only part of it, an important part insofar as their work was seized on by members of the establishment to rationalize their status and preserve their wealth and power. The fact that Copernicus was favored rather than Paracelsus and that Bacon was favored rather than Fludd expresses the way those in positions of power evaluated the effect that these philosophers would have on their authority. If anything, the academics were at the end of the chain of changes that shook Europe from at least the fifteenth century.

Many of these intellectuals were condemned as heretics, by no means the ideologues for their own time. They were to lay the ground for new legitimization of the establishment, for a new dominant cosmology, indeed, for a new common sense—in later times. Scientism, an ideological interpretation of the writings of the scientists, not just science, would become the new common sense that would reign hegemonic over people's minds and practices.

By the middle of the sixteenth century, Copernicus (1473–1543) had hypothesized that the earth was not the center of the universe "but merely one of many planets circling a minor star at the edge of the galaxy, [thus robbing] . . . man . . . of his proud position as the central figure of God's creation" (Capra 1983, 38). Sixty years later, Kepler (1571–1630) and Galileo (1564–1642) were proving Copernicus's thesis correct by means of new technology, the telescope, and the mysteries of mathematics. Kepler sought "the harmony of the spheres" whereas Galileo advocated the study of the cosmos by means of mathematical measurement, by studying those aspects of nature that could be measured and quantified. Galileo's cosmology was expressed through a new language, a sensible language, a language that dealt with only shapes, numbers, and observable movement. "Subjective mental projections" were excluded, those now being in the realm of metaphysics. And while Galileo experimented, Francis Bacon (1561–1625), passionately set forth the scientific, inductive method, portraying it as a means by which nature could be controlled, harnessed to the services of an explicitly patriarchal society to generate "progress."

This conviction that nature could be mastered, that humanity could be transformed through science, made the Royal Society the perfect base from which philosopher scientists were to begin a long engagement with people who were deaf and with sign languages. Their involvement catapulted deaf people into the philosophical limelight, forming and transforming their identities in the minds of the educated establishment as well as constructing a unitary category, "the deaf," about which to be theorized and on which to be experimented. But why did one sort of science triumph to condemn its rivals to the realms of art and the occult?

From the beginning of the battle between mechanistic science and the nonmechanistic sciences, the nonmechanistic sciences were the ones that were most radical, that rebelled against the establishment. The most impressive example of such radicalism was the Swiss physician Paracelsus (1493?–1541), a man well in advance of his contemporaries, particularly in his understanding of medicine and especially in the use of chemically based medicines. As far as many of his contemporaries were concerned, he worked miracles, but he never claimed to do more than help nature to work effectively. He rebelled against the academic conventions of his time, catering to no one, criticizing his contemporaries, constantly rocking the boat, and being denounced by the establishment. He supported the peasants in their struggles and asserted that science must be for the people and of the people: "Convinced that science must learn from the people and work for the people, he wrote in the vernacular" (Pachter 1951, 200). His cosmos was organic, a macrocosm to the microcosm of the individual.

But mechanistic science triumphed. The establishment of the science of Copernicus, Galileo, and Newton as the official scientific method was overtly political, the result of overt patronage by the establishment, in particular, the founding of the Royal Society of London after the restoration of the monarchy in 1660. Truth did not win out, the new did not supersede the old, nor did the modern replace the traditional. The power of the monarchy not only ensured the new scientific authority of the Royal Society but also protected it from what were seen as more radical and politically dangerous approaches to science such as those taken by "Paracelsian iatrochemists and hermeticists like Fludd" (Redner 1987, 45).

The new science thus banished its more radical opponents to the realms of poetry and the occult. Blake's Eden was a cosmos that was understood in terms of alternative sciences, the "nature" of Paracelsus. It was reflected later in the "scientific" writings of, for example, Goethe (1749–1832) and then Steiner (1861–1925), which saw the individual not as a unitary subject but as expressive of diverse qualities and rhythms in the natural world of sensitive chaos—of flux—qualities and rhythms that were not ordered and governed by laws but that were constantly forming and transforming in chaos and in harmony. The world of these banished scientists was a world in stark contrast to what Goethe called the "empirico-mechanico-dogmatic torture chamber" (Uberoi 1978) that was modern science.

Descartes (1596–1650) was the intellectual catalyst of his age. He pushed in one particular direction the contradictions inherent in the establishment view, in the dominant ideology. It was not the only direction that could be taken. Other radical points of view existed. But the human-centered, mathematically based theories of Descartes appealed to those excited by the prospect of humanity's control over its own destiny, a humanity dependent on neither God nor the church. Descartes's faith in disembodied human reason was accompanied by "an acute contempt for culture, which he called 'custom and example' and considered to be the source of all error. The human mind was so made as to ensure that, on its own, it would find the truth" (Gellner 1998, 43). He did not reject God but transformed the relationship between man and his God. More than anything else, the claims to rationality, to methods that removed the theories from the realm of subjectivity and from humanity itself, created an independence from God, the church, and the individual scientist. The scientific method replaced God as the ultimate source of all knowledge, as the source beyond humanity.

By the seventeenth century, science was firmly capturing the educated public's imagination. Familiarity with astronomy, mathematics, and the philosophy of language were the marks of the gentleman. The wealthy and educated, at least, could focus on a new religion and a new priesthood in their everyday lives. "Science was becoming an idol, an object of worship. It looked as if Science were going to . . . supersede Religion, and that it would supply the answer to all the longings of the human heart" (Hazard 1973, 363).

The Royal Society and the Legitimization of Rational Progress

The popularization of science and the enhancement of scientism moved on apace in Britain as John Wilkins (1613–1672), referred to by one of his juniors at Oxford University as "the greatest curioso of his time" (Wood 1813, xxxi), continued Bacon's mission, enlisting the King's patronage of science. Wilkins was the key player in the establishment of the Royal Society in 1663. While a chaplain in London in the 1640s, he along with John Wallis (1616–1703) and others had been active members of Robert Boyle's (1627–1691) "philosophical college," also called the "invisible college," the predecessor of the Royal Society.[1] Wilkins moved to Oxford as Warden of Wadham College in 1648, a year before Wallis. Meetings of the invisible college were held in his rooms at Wadham and included Christopher Wren, Robert Boyle, John Wallis, and later, a young John Locke (1632–1704).[2] Wilkins cultivated an environment—religious, political, and intellectual—that was conducive to the effective work of Newton (1642–1727) and those who followed.

To claim as Capra does that "the man who realized the Cartesian dream and completed the Scientific Revolution was Isaac Newton" (Capra 1983, 48) is something of an overstatement and certainly is not the product of a sociological imagination. The spread of science took some time, and the hegemonic saturation of the public consciousness by scientism a little longer. Also, great scientist that he was, Newton

Through Britain's Royal Society, philosopher scientists, like John Wallis and Robert Boyle, gained patronage and publicity for research on the nature of humanity, which catapulted deaf people into the philosophical limelight.

was also, albeit in secret, an astrologer—indeed, called by his latest biographer "the last sorcerer" (White 1997). His faith in the new science and the new philosophy was not nearly as complete as the faith of his followers. Nevertheless, Newton laid the ground for the realization of the fruits of science, provided for the translation of the new philosophy into the new technology, and provided for the widespread experience of the wonders of science, substantiating the faith in progress—scientific progress so essential to the emerging middle classes and their capitalist economy. Inspired by Descartes, Newton provided a blueprint for the industrial revolution. Inspired by Newton and by Hobbes (1588–1679), Locke was to lay the basis for a transformed academy as scientism reached into every pore of academic life.

With the founding of the Royal Society, the monarch became the patron of progress, not its victim, and, in the process, became of necessity not only the patron of the production of reason but also the patron of those institutions that sprang up to contain its opposite, unreason. As humanity's rational future became a possibility and the concomitant fear of chaos developed, madness, in particular, was seen as menacing, "a great disquiet, suddenly dawning on the horizon of European culture at the end of the Middle Ages" (Foucault 1973, 13). If reason was the source of all that was good, all that was creative, all that was progress, then its opposite had to be identified and emptied of its worth. Unreason became the great fear, the great danger.

After the restoration of the monarchy in 1660, Bethlehem Hospital, or Bedlam as it was and is more commonly known, the archetypal madhouse, became Bethlehem Royal Hospital. In 1675–1676, the hospital moved to a new building, designed by Robert Hooke in Moorfields, which challenged the Tuileries in Paris for beauty and grandeur. At the entrance were Cibber's famous statues of madness and melancholy. A forceful visual statement was being made to affect all who passed by. Here, indeed, was a metatext, a statement with far more effect than any written document, a text integral to the discursive construction of "the disabled." The king was protecting his subjects from the feared chaos of unreason.

The particular vision of chaos that science spawned eventually would create and thereby control "the disabled." It would do so by lumping together as one category of humanity all those physical, sensory, and behavioral qualities that had formerly been regarded and dealt with separately. Why?

From Flux to Chaos: The Creation of Disorder

Although the science of Paracelsus and of his followers through the ages saw nature as a sensitive chaos to be understood and worked with, mechanistic, unitary science interpreted the existing cosmological flux as disorder, "a disorderly and chaotic realm to be subdued and controlled" (Merchant 1980, 127). To quote Foucault, a "great threat . . . dawned on the horizon of the fifteenth century" (Foucault 1973, 35), the threat of unreason. Where once the mysteries of madness and healing had been accepted as part of nature's diversity, they now became a threat to be subdued. Society at large concentrated on the control of the witch: "Disorderly woman, like chaotic nature, needed to be controlled" (Merchant 1980, 127). But not just women—any adult or child who suffered from fits, from lack of comprehension or, indeed, whose behavior was seen as unusual was in danger of being assumed to be possessed by or in league with the devil and subject to trial and execution (Safford and Safford 1996, 20). Physical, mental, or behavioral disorders were condemned.

Bacon asserted the need to control nature through the new science. Hobbes and Locke rationalized the need to create a rational society, the need to control people. Humanity itself would be defined in terms of those whose physical and behavioral qualities were ordered. Therefore, those whose physical or behavioral qualities were diagnosed as disordered were seen to be in need not only of ordering, where possible, but also of containment, of control to protect the wider population. Control over disorder, human and natural, was to be achieved through human knowledge and technology.

> The fundamental social and intellectual problem for the seventeenth century was the problem of order. The perception of disorder, so important to the Baconian doctrine of dominion over nature, was also crucial to the rise of mechanism as a rational antidote to the disintegration of the organic cosmos. . . . Rational control over nature, society, and the self was achieved by redefining reality itself through the new machine metaphor. (Merchant 1980, 192–93)

So science penetrated everyday life not only as fashionable conversation among the establishment but also through the scientific experts as they became the "theologians" serving the interests of those in positions of economic and political power. Order and chaos were the dyad that set the parameters for academic debate about the natural world, about the world of conquered and different populations, about society at home, and about the self, the individual.

The Ordering of Nature and Humanity

The order of nature and humanity thus was threatened above all by those aspects seen as anomalous, the untidy aspects that did not conform to the emerging cosmology that defined the nature of the world, the nature of humanity, and the nature of humanity's place and purpose in that world. In the pursuit of order, the new scientists were classifying nature. Plants, animals, humans, and minerals were all being arranged in an ordered fashion. Each species of plant or animal was defined in terms of observed and documented characteristics, as were human beings. The senses of each species, their physical qualities, and eventually their behaviors were all classified to demonstrate the order of nature. Those that did not conform to these classificatory schemes were seen not as challenges to the reliability of the classificatory schemes of the new scientists but as anomalies that needed to be changed and, if not changed, then contained so their chaotic qualities would not spread.

At the same time, scientists were concerned with clarifying what they saw as a fundamental division between the human and nonhuman. Humanity alone was seen as possessing the intellectual power to understand and change the world. Therefore, this fundamental divide needed to be explained and thereby consolidated. Any threats to the distinctiveness of humanity were threats to progress.

> In early modern England the official concept of the animal was a negative one, helping to define, by contrast, what was supposedly distinctive and admirable about the human species. By embodying the antithesis of all that was valued and esteemed, the idea of the brute was as indispensable a prop to established human values as were the equally unrealistic notions held by contemporaries about witches or Papists. . . . The brute creation provided the most readily-available point of reference for the continuous process of human self-definition. Neither the same as humans, nor wholly dissimilar, the animals offered an almost inexhaustible fund of symbolic meaning. (Thomas 1983, 40)

The eventual marginalization of certain human differences by labeling them as pathological and, thus, as less than or other than human was directly tied to the marginalization of other nonhuman beings. As zoos developed, so too did the display of the human "others" in fairs, marketplaces, and hospitals for the insane such as Bedlam. As writers like Thomas (1983) and Berman (1990) have shown, the mechanization of the natural world involved a separation of humans from the animal world. Animals became the antithesis of humanity. In Descartes's terms, animals were mere "automata," devoid of feeling; their cries, mere noise, not responses to the feeling or emotions that humans experienced. The increasing marginalization of the animal world from the world of humans and the classification of animals as wild or tame was a fundamental aspect of the changing definitions of humanity that generated the concept of "the disabled" during the eighteenth and nineteenth centuries.

The concept of the "brute" that encompassed the animal world, divesting that world of feeling and of all that was valued as human also encompassed the part of the human species that did not live up to accepted measures of humanity. Animals could be oppressed and maltreated. The oppressed and maltreated of the human species were equated with animals to legitimate the acts of their oppressors: "Their dehumanization was a necessary precondition of their maltreatment" (Berman 1990). The colonized, the enslaved, manual workers, and women—even children—were all accorded degrees of animality and the "most beastlike of all were those on the margins of human society: the mad . . . and the vagrants" (Thomas 1983, 44). They were not just beastlike. They were feared because their differences—physical, behavioral, or both—were interpreted as violating the division between the categories of animal and human. They did not fit into the binary schemes that increasingly dominated Western cosmology. Like the monsters of myth, they were not only brutish but also monstrous, demanding not only inhuman treatment but also exorcism. Once the exorcism of the church had been denied, the new priests, the priests of science, were called on to provide both protection and treatment. Science drove the monsters away, claiming they were irrational, and industrial society created distinctly human territory as they banished the animals from town and home. Those humans deemed brutish, monstrous, or both were hidden from view—out of sight and out of mind. Those humans who did not conform to what was in science's classificatory schemes, to what would later be defined as "normal," were being lumped together as being pathological, as deviating from what classifiers of nature defined as normal and therefore acceptable—as deviating from humanity.

Particularly threatening and, at the same time, of prime scientific interest were those humans who were seen to bridge the gap between the human and animal worlds, the "wolf children," or children reared by animals. As we shall see in later chapters, the institutionalization and treatment of the "wild boy of Aveyron" consolidated the image of a person who was deaf and mute as being natural rather than cultural, as being closer to the animal than to the human.

Language as the Definiens of Humanity

The link between language and humanity played a vital part in the marginalization of people who were deaf because language above all was seen to separate the human from the animal (see chapter 3). Descartes's view of animals as "mere automata" stressed the uniqueness of the human mind. The Cartesian mind was anything but a mere brain. Animals, too, had brains. The mind was disembodied, metaphysical, and even mysterious. The mind expressed itself through the equally uniquely human facility of language.

Although debates would rage through the rest of the millennium about the nature of language, the dominant view was that language derived only from the faculty of speech.[3] Those without speech, thus, were labeled frequently as "mindless," as less than human. Those who were deaf were assumed to be incapable of learning language, incapable of human understanding.

The particular disabling effects of being identified as a "deaf mute" were influenced not only by Cartesian theories of the duality of mind and body that were linked to the binary opposition of the human and the animal but also by the sense-based philosophical traditions that emanated from Locke in the late-seventeenth century. Through Locke, the five senses came to dominate not only the conceptualization of human nature and human ability but also the conceptualization of society itself and of the place that those who were judged "sensible" or in some way "senseless" should occupy in society.

Human Nature; the Five Senses; and the Rational, "Sensible" Society

Humanity was being defined, or controlled, in scientific terms as was the wider society. Hobbes and Locke, in particular, developed scientific views of human nature and society that would exert a strong influence on the classification and treatment of human difference. For Locke, all individuals were born equal. As tabulae rasae, or clean slates, at birth, all human minds were equally lacking in subjectivity and destiny. Individual qualities were bestowed through the experience of the world by means of the five senses, through the agency of society operating according to "natural" laws. For Hobbes, the individual was inherently selfish and anarchic, in contrast to Locke's view of the inherently social, inherently cooperative individual. Hobbes stressed the importance of the establishment and maintenance of a law-governed order to avoid the chaos that might result if society were not subjected to social control. In Locke's view as in Hobbes's, all knowledge was gained through sensory perception in a sensible world that was empirically verifiable, thoroughly knowable, and dependent on rational, scientific research.

These images of an ordered, law-governed society, especially when coupled with the Hobbesian image of impending anarchy, reinforced the role of the democratic state as the representative guardian of rational control. Locke's theorizing reflected fundamental transformations in the view of the individual that were to become more and more widespread and basic to the emergent meritocratic democracies. The place of humanity in the cosmos and the view of the individual were thus being redefined.[4]

These definitions of modern man based in sensible views of the individual went some way toward providing a cosmos that was conducive to the progressive development of an individuated labor market and toward rationalizing differential wealth in terms of individual merit and individual ability. But these definitions could not rationalize the differences associated with the economy's prime source of capital, empire. An imperial consciousness demanded a different view of the individual, a view linked to biological and cultural difference. Evolutionism filled the gap, a vital ideological force not only abroad but also at home.

Evolutionism: Difference as Inferiority

The abiding fascination of the nineteenth century was with evolution, with the discovery of explanations for biological differences that were the consequence of natural laws rather than the work of God. Geology, archaeology, and biology combined to seek out the riddles of difference, the past increasingly populated by primitive, less progressive forms of animals and "humans." So involved was the middle-class popular imagination with these speculations that when Charles Darwin's *The Origin of the Species* was published in 1859, it was a best-seller. Here was not only a scientific work but also a scientific theory of biological progress, interpreted to rationalize the supremacy of humanity over other animals and the supremacy of contemporary humanity over past forms. The excitement was echoed over and over in popular fiction, the prime example being Jules Verne's *Journey to the Center of the Earth* (1864), which took the reader on a voyage through the living geology of evolution.

But the theories soon turned to explain the supremacy not only of contemporary humanity over past forms but also of certain contemporary humans over other contemporary humans. As far as the social scientists were concerned, they had discovered, in the new world, the "living stone age." Evolutionism became an explanation for the contemporary supremacy of particular human specimens over others—of the civilized over the uncivilized or primitive, the scientific over the superstitious, the industrious capitalist over the indolent peasant or lazy native. According the social scientists, not only was man evolving but also society was evolving, and some societies were more evolved than others.

Darwin wrote, "If the misery of our poor be caused not by the laws of nature, but by our institutions, great is our sin" (Gould 1984, title page). But Darwin's writing fed into an evolutionist environment and reinforced the existing ideological commitment of the middle classes to legitimize inequalities in terms of biological determinism. Their domination of those in the colonies, of the working classes, of women, and of "the disabled" were all legitimized by means of Social Darwinism.

Thus, the peoples who were contacted and were ruled in the colonies were classified and theorized about as well as formed and transformed by the discourses of Western science. They were classified into races, nations, tribes, clans, and lineages and were evaluated in scientific terms. Colonialism became the harbinger of progress, bringing rational civilization to the rest of the world. When the Western colonists entered those other worlds and sought to build effective political and ideological bases for the pursuit of the all-important economic activities that were the lifeblood of empire, they did so as rational administrators whose imperial right was seen to lie in their having entered the scientific age. Their cosmos was a cosmos devoid of any mysteries other than the wonders of science. Their lack of neutrality remained hidden beneath the facade of reason, of scientific rationality. Firmly held by the hegemony of scientific rationality, Western academics unwittingly engaged in epistemic violence. They became complicit in presenting to the world at large views of the colonized populations as being variations of the "other" against which the colonizers rationalized their imperialism.

Standards of humanity, of progress, and of desirability were all measured from the West. Fifteenth-, sixteenth-, and seventeenth-century reports of a "New World" populated by monsters akin to those of European myth and legend gave way to reports of a living stone age inhabited by genetically inferior beings living in less-developed, less-evolved, irrational sociocultural environments that were ruled by superstition. The less-than-human, the less-evolved, were out there, under the control of empire by means of rational administration to ensure the spread of scientific civilization and the destruction of irrational ways of life. The early images of monstrous humans with two heads or headless creatures with eyes in the middle of their stomachs or beings with beaks instead of mouths signaled the birth of racism as others were represented not only as different but also as pathological and, therefore, as inferior.

Thus, the West not only rationalized its colonial intervention but also provided itself with constant ideological justification for its own superiority by conducting scientific evaluations of these other races and other cultures. As Jahoda has so cogently and dramatically shown, the roots of modern prejudice lie in the overtly arrogant Western images of these colonized "savages" (Jahoda 1999).

Discourses about disease rather than the actual spread of the diseases supported the colonial process. During the Middle Ages, the label "leprosy" marginalized unwanted elements of society and drove them beyond the pale.[5] In a similar fashion, the colonized territories were represented as the sites of plague and pestilence, where diseases long since controlled in the West were rampant, particularly leprosy. The presence of these diseases reinforced the image of the colony as backward and the image of its population as physically or genetically inferior and prone to disease. We do not mean that the diseases did not exist or that Western medicine did not come to play an important part in their control and even their eradication, but their existence was exaggerated out of all proportion, and the image engulfed entire continents (see Watts 1997).

Ultimately, the oddities of the new world were paraded alongside the oddities at home. The sideshows that blossomed in Victorian society and on into the first half of the twentieth century were peopled with "freaks" from the West and the colonies. The Kalahari Bushman took his place alongside the dwarf, the giant, the limbless, and the Siamese twins. Their combination was a vital ideological practice in the imperialist construction of "the disabled" (see Bogdan 1988). Evolutionism provided the British upper and middle classes not only with a legitimacy for their own imperial domination of the colonial world but also with the rationale for seeking out and controlling people who threatened their evolutionary superiority at home. Those people who were classified as abnormal physically, mentally, behaviorally, or sensorially were evaluated in evolutionary terms. Head shapes, posture, skin color, and language use were noted and evaluated. Thus, the sign languages of deaf people were no longer evaluated as the basis for a potential "perfect universal language" but became identified with the sign languages of "savages" and with the early evolution of language.[6] The goal of therapists and educators at home became the same as that of the administrators and missionaries abroad: to promote the evolutionary advancement of the "savages" in their care. Racial identity had a particular effect on the degree to which the "savages" at home could be civilized through education. Thus, although deaf students were taught to speak as a civilizing process in an evolutionary era, many deaf African American students in racist America were not taught orally or even by a mixture of manualism and oralism (the combined method) but were taught through signs.[7]

Eugenics: Identifying and Condemning the Unfit

The age of empire was, therefore, also the age of eugenics, the study of the "improvement" of human stock by means of selectively breeding genetically desirable individuals and groups. The eugenics movement was one of the most overtly discriminatory movements in the history of Western civilization, a movement that sought not only to marginalize those deemed pathological but also, in its most extreme form, to eliminate them. It was created and developed by scientists.

The eugenics movement was an expression of the ideology of progress. It developed directly out of Darwinian theories of evolution, which were popularized as "the survival of the fittest," and Mendelian theories of heredity. The term *eugenics*, from the Greek *eugenes* meaning "good birth," was introduced in Britain in 1883 by Sir Francis Galton, Darwin's cousin. The eugenics movement focused from the start on the development of social control over human reproduction to engineer the physical and mental improvement of future generations. It focused in particular on racial qualities. Galton founded the Eugenics Society of Great Britain in 1908, but the German social Darwinist Alfred Ploetz had already founded a journal of racial and social biology in 1904 and a Society for Racial Hygiene in 1905, which added "eugenics" to its title in 1931. The American Eugenics Society was established in 1923, but an American Breeders Society with essentially the same goals had begun much earlier.[8]

The eugenics movement spread quickly to America and to British colonies such as Australia and South Africa. Throughout western Europe, it also had a strong effect, receiving its most dramatic and horrific expression in German Nazism. Intellectual, diagnostic, and pedagogical developments were not confined by the boundaries of the nation. Academics, medical specialists, educators, and scientists of all kinds read each others' books and journals, exchanged papers, and met at conferences. The history of the cultural construction of "the disabled" is the history of a process that spread throughout the Western world. The links among the English-speaking countries in the development of ideas and practices were particularly strong.

From the start, the eugenics movement linked physical beauty and hereditary fitness. Galton, in fact, "began his scientific career by compiling a 'beauty map' of Britain, for which he calculated the ratio of attractive to plain and ugly women he encountered at various locations" (Pernick 1997, 91). Eugenicists claimed that beauty, a beauty focusing on health and fitness, could be assessed objectively by the trained eye. As Pernick (1997) graphically shows, the eugenicists, through their propaganda, actively promoted a concept of beauty that was white and able-bodied while often portraying the undesirable "disabled" as non-whites.

Galton's theories and orientation toward humanity caught the public imagination as Darwin's work had already done and fed into the development of ideologies to support imperialism abroad as well as entrepreneurial capitalism and scientific progress at home. At home, pathological elements in the population threatened the assumed intellectual and genetic superiority of the middle classes. Intellectual pathologies were dealt with through confinement, brain surgery, drugs, and special education. Genetic pathologies, including hereditary deafness, demanded not only confinement but also more radical control. In its most extreme form, eugenics was a violent and inhumane movement that sought to eliminate these supposed pathologies through sterilization, the prohibition of marriage, and even murder. In its less violent forms, it involved psychological pressure on those deemed "disabled" to refrain from reproduction in the long-term interests of Western humanity.

Typical of the more aggressive eugenicist orientation was Stokes's *The Right to be Well Born or Horse Breeding in its Relation to Eugenics* (Stokes 1917). The author's photograph, facing the title page, speaks volumes. He stands proudly clad in tweed, his hair and thick moustache neatly trimmed and his prominent chin jutting forward. His eyes are sharp, or appear so, and are certainly not bespectacled. He appears the model of the well-born Anglo-American. Stokes writes:

> In breeding horses, we render impotent the unfit. We never try to render fit a sire by education. We have no sanatoriums for weak horses, to keep them alive at public expense, and then turn them loose to reproduce their unfitness, to refill more homes for defectives. The same rule should apply to humans. (Stokes 1917, 56)

Although we know that Alexander Graham Bell had a number of copies of Stokes's book in his library, Bell's orientation was somewhat different.[9] Bell's focus was on promoting the production of "well-born" people rather than the elimination of the "badly born." Bell wrote:

> Improvement depends upon *increasing the number and proportion of desirables born in successive generations of the population.* Hence, this should be the chief object of eugenics; and it is to be regretted that the efforts of eugenists have been mainly directed to the diminution of the undesirable class.
>
> So much has this been the case that the very word "eugenics" is suggestive to most minds of hereditary diseases and objectionable abnormalities; and of an attempt to interfere, by compulsory means, with the marriages of the defective and undesirable. This relates to cacogenics ("badly born") rather than to eugenics ("well born"). (Bell 1914, 6; Bell's italics)

Milder though Bell's position was, it still required the identification not only of the "well-born," the desirables, but also the concomitant identification of the undesirable class, those judged "defective." Eugenics was built on the diagnostic procedures that identified human "pathologies." It lumped together all those who in some sense had been diagnosed as pathological and labeled them "badly born," "defective" humans who, as Murphy (1995) has shown, were seen as "contaminators," threatening the population and the rational progress of Western humanity.

The otherness of the people diagnosed as pathological, especially when that pathology was present from birth, became akin to the otherness of another race or even another species. The progress of the Western powers was seen to lie not only in the rational organization of society but also in its genetic management, progress that not only would keep the chaotic forces of unreason in check but also would destroy them. Most people who were deaf at this time claimed and, indeed, most people who are deaf today claim to have become deaf as a result of illness or accident. The stigma of being born deaf was extreme.[10] (In later chapters, we will explore why people who were deaf were frequent targets for the eugenicists.)

Together, evolutionism and eugenics dominated developments in the social sciences, in the medical and psychological sciences, and in the pedagogical development of compulsory education. Anthropologists spent as much time measuring heads as they did studying culture (see Leach 1982), and psychology focused on the physical and intellectual measurement of mental pathology. Attention became increasingly intent on the effective promotion of particular physical types associated with intellectual and moral capacity. Goddard's screening of potential immigrants to the United States in the 1920s on the basis of physical characteristics and Hitler's identification of the true Aryan as well as his attempted extermination of what he saw as the racially inferior Jews were but extreme expressions of a general ideological trend (see Gilman 1991b). The German experience represents the most extreme example of an orientation toward the "other" that enveloped the Western world.[11]

Eugenics, Nazism, and the Elimination of Congenital Disabilities

The Law for the Prevention of Offspring with Hereditary Diseases took effect in Germany in January 1934, a law that "eventually led to the sterilization of approximately 375,000 German nationals" (Friedlander 1999, 5). The law began: "Any person suffering from a hereditary disease can be sterilized if medical knowledge indicates that his offspring will suffer from hereditary physical or mental damage" (quoted from Friedlander 1999, 5). Friedlander continues:

> The law defined a person "suffering from a hereditary disease," and thus a candidate for sterilization, as anyone afflicted with one of the following disabilities: congenital feeble-mindedness, schizophrenia, *folie circulaire* (manic-depressive psychosis), hereditary epilepsy, hereditary St. Vitus' dance (Huntington's chorea), hereditary blindness, hereditary deafness, severe hereditary physical deformity, and severe alcoholism, on a discretionary basis. (Friedlander 1999, 5)

Tens of thousands of people were sterilized against their will in the first year of the law, and by 1935, the law had been extended to provide for the forced abortion of potentially disabled babies. Marriages were prohibited where either party "suffered from a mental derangement or had a hereditary disease specified in the sterilization law" (Friedlander 1999, 6). By 1939, the German government began the mass murder of the "disabled," labeling the program "euthanasia" and "the destruction of life unworthy of life" (Friedlander 1999, 7). First, disabled infants and children were forcibly hospitalized and killed. At the same time, the hospitalization and killing of disabled adults began to be followed by the development of killing centers where adults were gassed. Popular opposition to the killings grew and Hitler ordered them stopped in August 1941, but the locus of the killing was simply shifted outside Germany to Poland and the Soviet Union.

Even inside Germany, where the murder of disabled children had not been stopped, the murder of disabled adults soon resumed. But henceforth, they were killed in selected state hospitals through starvation, overdoses of medication, or deadly injections.

> As the war continued, the decentralized killings became even more arbitrary and the killing hospitals came to resemble concentration camps. In the Pomeranian state hospital Meseritz-Obrawalde, one of the leading killing institutions of "wild" euthanasia, the staff not only killed those unable to work, but in addition also patients "who increased the workload of the nurses, were deafmute, sick, or disobedient." (Friedlander 1999, 11)

After the war, disabled people were not recognized as having been persecuted by the Nazis. Where a medical diagnosis of an hereditary "disabling" condition was found to have been "correct," the act of the Nazi regime was ruled by postwar courts to have followed "proper procedures." In 1964, a Jewish person who was deaf and who had been sterilized by the Nazis was recognized by the court as having been persecuted as a Jew, but the court ruled that "his sterilization as a deaf person did not constitute Nazi persecution" (Friedlander 1999, 11–12). The clinical gaze continued to cast those who were diagnosed "pathological," or beyond the pale of humanity, as not equal before the law.

The horror story of Nazi Germany was simply a logical step away from what was going on throughout the Western world between the wars. Moves toward the forced sterilization of "disabled" people and the prohibition of marriages between them were common in Britain, America, and Australia. The conditions under which severely disabled children were confined in institutions until relatively recently were just one step away from the killing hospitals described by Friedlander. The "euthanasia" of disabled infants was not confined to Nazi Germany. In America in the years 1910–1919, a Chicago surgeon, Harry Haiselden, publicized his active euthanasia of at least six infants he had diagnosed as "defectives." Publicizing his actions,

> he displayed the dying infants to journalists and wrote a book-length series about them for the Hearst newspapers. His campaign was front-page news for weeks at a time. He also wrote and starred in a feature motion picture, *The Black Stork*, a fictionalized account of his cases. (Pernick 1997, 89)

The public and professional support for Haiselden's actions in failing to care for defective babies and therefore letting them die was strong, though not for his publicizing his actions. Although "a series of legal investigations upheld Haiselden's refusal to treat impaired newborns, . . . he was expelled from the Chicago Medical Society for publicizing his actions" (Pernick 1997, 110 n. 52). As Pernick's research indicates (Pernick 1996, 1997), this form of euthanasia was entrusted to the doctors as objective scientists: "[P]opular support for giving doctors this . . . power [of life over death] depended on a broader progressive-era faith in the methods of science, a faith that was actively promoted by medical and eugenic leaders" (Pernick 1997, 110 n. 51). Today, the aborting of fetuses identified through ultrasound or blood tests as "disabled" is common. The clinical gaze continued and continues to define the contours of humanity.[12]

Notes

1. Boyle, natural philosopher and chemist, settled in Oxford from London in 1654. In 1668, he left Oxford for London where he stayed until his death. He was elected president of the Royal Society in 1680.

2. Wilkins resigned from Oxford in 1659 to become master of Trinity College, Cambridge. He lost the position after the restoration of the monarchy, having been on the side of parliament during the civil war, but he made peace with the royalists and soon moved through the ranks of the established church. Many of his belongings, his library, and some manuscripts were destroyed in the Great Fire of London in 1666. In 1668, he was made Bishop of Chester.

3. This philosophical heritage is still dominant today, evident in Umberto Eco's recent dismissal of any form of gesture as capable of constituting a language because gestures must, according to Eco, "depend (parasitically) on the semantic universe of the verbal language" (Eco 1995, 174). According to Eco, the gestures must be "anchored" through association with the words of a verbal language. In a similar vein, the philosopher Walter Ong wrote that "elaborated sign languages are substitutes for speech and dependent on oral speech systems, even when used by the congenitally deaf" (Ong 1982, 7).

4. Note that the French philosophers who inspired a revolution—Voltaire, Condillac, Diderot, Rousseau, and others—based their "sense realist" theories on the work of earlier British philosophers, particularly that of Locke.

5. To quote *Brewer's Dictionary of Phrase and Fable*, "The word is from Lat. *palum*, a stake; hence a fence, a territory with defined limits. Hence the phrases 'Within the pale' and 'Beyond the pale,' *pale* here meaning 'the bounds of civilization' or civilized behaviour.'" (Evans 1982, 824).

6. See chapter 7 and Baynton (1996, ch. 2).

7. See Baynton (1996, 45–46).

8. See Gould (1984).

9. We came across copies of Stokes's book in a collection of Bell's books on eugenics in the Volta Bureau in Washington, D.C.

10. Note that among those Deaf who have embraced the concept of Deaf Pride—pride in their distinctive languages, pride in being Deaf—being born deaf is now treasured.

11. For a more recent example of the use of IQ testing to claim the intellectual superiority of whites over blacks, see Jensen (1985).

12. We do not mean to imply by this observation that all doctors or even all eugenicists supported euthanasia by neglect. As we have pointed out in discussing Alexander Graham Bell's approach, many eugenicists overtly opposed the elimination of the "unfit," focusing instead on preventative measures such as influencing marriage patterns.

2

The Domestication of Difference: The Classification, Segregation, and Institutionalization of Unreason

> *It must be admitted that the normal man knows that he is so only in a world where every man is not normal. . . . In order for the normal man to believe himself so, and call himself so, he needs not the foretaste of disease but its projected shadow.*
>
> —Canguilhem 1988b, 286

By the eighteenth century, "reason" and science stood triumphant, and madness was marginalized and confined. People who were mad came to be seen as pitiful rather than dangerous and as in need of help. Madness was viewed as a form of chaos and degradation that must be contained. It was no longer the source of wisdom; rather, the antithesis of reason. When St. Luke's was opened in England in 1751, it was called an "asylum," not a madhouse, and casual sightseeing was banned from the outset (Porter 1987, 130). The orientation toward madness was shifting from confinement to treatment, treatment based on increasingly complex diagnosis. Central to the development of diagnostic procedures was the development of concepts of normality and pathology.

The Cultural Construction of Pathological Humanity: From Order versus Chaos to Normality versus Pathology

The father of scientific sociology, Auguste Comte (1798–1857), spearheaded the ideology of normality. The most important effect of this ideology on the construction of "the disabled" was the fact that he concentrated on normality as being equivalent to "the order of things," as a "normative order," and defined the pathology as "deficiency" or "excess." In Comte's positivism, the normative order was not simply a quality of social or natural phenomena to be discovered but a highly valued condition (see Canguilhem 1988b, 56–57).

The concept of normality entered not only the language of science but also the language of everyday life, especially that of the middle classes for whom the distinction between normality and pathology became a vital source of social control. Canguilhem wrote of the extension of "normal" into everyday life in France:

> Between 1759, when the word "normal" appeared, and 1834 when the word "normalized" appeared, a normative class had won the power to identify—a beautiful example of an ideological illusion—the function of social norms, whose content it determined, with the use that that class made of them. (Canguilhem 1988b, 246)

In England, the process occurred a little later, with the concepts being adopted from France. Thus, the term *normal* with its normative meaning of "not deviating or differing from a type or standard; regular, usual" is listed in the *Oxford English Dictionary* as having first appeared in 1828 and *normalize*, in 1868, both vital ideological components of the nineteenth-century worldview. The dialectic between scientific measurement and sociocultural evaluation was well under way as the etymology of "normality" moved toward the effective exclusion of the noncompliant as well as the effective marginalization and exclusion of the nonconformist, the different. "A norm draws its meaning, function and value from the fact of the existence, outside itself, of what does not meet the requirement it serves" (Canguilhem 1988b, 239). Marginalized, hidden, excluded, cast beyond the pale, damned to silence and to pseudo nonexistence, those diagnosed as the embodiment of the pathological were the essential foil to the arrogant "normality" of the definers and their fellow travelers. The concept of normality remained and remains at all times insecure, dependent on its opposite and in constant need of reaffirmation.

A view of a diverse humanity that was imbued with almost infinite difference gave way to a view of an essentially uniform humanity that was surrounded on its edges, on its margins, by the pathological foils to that uniformity or "normality." But no "pathological" population could exist until one was culturally constructed. And so, we turn to the processes of diagnosis, the ideological practice by which "the pathological" were separated from the former flux of humanity, the process by which normality was constructed and reconstructed through each diagnosis.

The Diagnosis of the Pathological

Diagnosis involves the interpretation and evaluation of characteristics and behaviors in terms of preconceived conceptualizations and classifications of the world. It is the taxonomic ordering of "reality." The medical classification, interpretation, and evaluation of human characteristics and behavior were developed through the transformation of concepts of health and illness that were based on the concepts of normality and pathology. How these diagnoses proceeded and how the body and human behavior were understood were rooted in the Cartesian dualism of mind and body.

The Cartesian dualism of mind and body, while elevating the products of the mind to the status of eternal, disembodied knowledge, also stressed the materiality of the body, which was to be understood like any other physical object—like a well-made clock, to use Descartes's own imagery. Accordingly, in the development of "scientific" medicine, the clinical gaze was directed to the physical body and to the taxonomies of pathologies that were built on knowledge gained from cadavers, from lifeless objects. Medical knowledge was to be based solely on sensory perception, on observation, on "a perpetual and objectively based correlation of the visible and the expressible" (Foucault 1975, 196).

The focus on death and on the dissection of cadavers resulted in a rush for bodies. The major but very limited official source of bodies in Britain was people sentenced to death as criminals. In France after the Revolution, the Reign of Terror in which people accused of being opposed to the Revolution were guillotined or slaughtered provided an unparalleled source of cadavers for dissection, but throughout Europe, the demand for bodies for medical schools was so great that an illegal trade in corpses flourished; people were paid to steal bodies from graves or even from houses where they lay awaiting their funerals. In 1829, Burke and Hare, two body snatchers in Edinburgh, were found guilty of murdering people to sell their bodies to anatomists. At the same time, Britain passed a law providing that bodies of poor people who died without relatives to pay for a funeral would be given to medical schools. In London, the famous surgeon Astley Cooper, who will feature in our discussion of the history of ear surgery in part 2, boasted that he could acquire in a few days the body of any person who had recently died in the United Kingdom through a wide network of body snatchers. The availability of severed heads in France provided for rapid advances in anatomical knowledge of the ear.

With the body reconstituted as a machine-like object, the clinical gaze focused on its order, on its "regularity," judged in terms of deviations from a physical "norm." Whereas medicine had, up to the end of the eighteenth century, focused on health rather than normality, nineteenth-century medicine was concerned more with normality than health (see Foucault 1975, 35). Its concern was with departures of the physical condition from what was understood as the normative standard. Both the clinical gaze and its objects of diagnosis were ruled by the five senses. The patient's health was judged not only in terms of the person's physical normality and pathology but also in terms of the effective functioning of the five senses. To lack one of the five senses was to become less than sensible or less than normal and, thus, to be incapable of sensibility or rationality.

So forceful was the sensible, empiricist focus promoted by Hobbes and Locke that the mind became nothing more than the product of sensory experience. Although Descartes's dualism survived to separate the psychological from the biological, his spiritual and even mystical view of mind disappeared from establishment medicine and psychology. The mind became nothing more than its observable products and, in the hands of psychiatry, little more than the physical brain, judged in terms of the normality of mentally induced behaviors and the normality of brain functioning. Disorderly behavior, if not the product of a disordered and therefore pathological body was assumed to be the product of a disordered and therefore pathological mind. Control, order, adherence to the norm, compliance with the norm, the expected, and the conventional were the marks of normality. Above all, as we pointed out in the previous chapter, the ongoing Cartesian separation of mind and body focused diagnostic procedures on language. The production of irrational language was seen as evidence of an irrational mind. The production of no language was frequently seen as evidence of mindlessness.

Thus, the experts who claimed control of the insane and the "disabled" at the end of the eighteenth century saw in their patients people who, because they could not reason in a way that measured up to their arbitrary normative standards, must have their lives controlled for them by others. Once confined and displayed during the seventeenth and eighteenth centuries, they became the objects of a new kind of display and of a new and more encompassing control in the nineteenth century. They were displayed to the clinical gaze and controlled not only physically but also to the very core of their being.

The Attempted Normalization of the Pathological: The Moral Therapy Movement

The focus on sensory development generated an inclination on the part of those who dealt with "the abnormal" to cure rather than simply to confine. The curative process was in turn seen as integrally linked to the sensory environment within which the treatment was to take place, thus giving rise to the concept of the asylum.

As with the diagnosis of physical pathology, the clinical gaze was, in the case of the diagnosis of mental disorders, on the body and its behavior. Although the use of drugs and a wide range of drastic mechanical therapies were used in the majority of cases, a new approach emerged, that was focused on the moral management of the patient, particularly through the influence of William Battie.[1] This individualistic and therapeutic approach to madness was referred to as "moral management" to indicate the need to deal also with the patient's mind and not just with the body.

The move to systemic, group-based moral therapy instead of individual moral management dates effectively from the founding of the York Retreat in 1796, founded in response to the death in 1793 of a young Quaker widow in the York Asylum who died under mysterious circumstances associated with the use of medical remedies and with general inhuman brutality. With missionary zeal, the practitioners in the York Retreat sought to return those who had gone insane to the rational world through moral regeneration. Normalization was the driving force. Through the thorough programming of their patients' lives, they hoped that order would triumph. For those recently rendered insane, the program would result in a return to normality; for the "fools" and "idiots," the "incurables," and those born to unreason, it would be a demonstration of the power of discipline, of order, of education, and above all, of morality. Many of those who collected the insane and "disabled" together in asylums were concerned as much with the saving of souls as with the transformation of behavior.

In 1792, four years before the establishment of the York Retreat, another establishment was founded: the Asylum for the Support and Education of the Deaf and Dumb Children of the Poor in the Grange Road in Bermondsey in London, for the "moral management" of deaf children. In these other asylums of the early nineteenth century, the asylums for the deaf and blind, the same missionary zeal prevailed (see chapter 5).

As mentioned above, moral management did not necessarily dispense with "medicines." The treatment of the body involved "medicine"; the treatment of the mind, "management." But medical treatments still were seen as useful in the context of wider therapeutics. In Paris at the National Institute for the Deaf, the surgeon Jean Marc Itard was exploring the mind of the wild boy of Aveyron and preparing to use a wide range of surgical and other medical procedures on the institute's pupils in an effort to make them hear. Although surgeons traveled throughout the Western world comparing techniques and training in new procedures, the role of surgery in the emerging schools for the people who were both poor and deaf varied from country to country.[2] Thus, while the Paris school in early nineteenth-century France became a virtual laboratory for Itard's horrendous experiments, the deaf asylum in Britain remained a place for the moral management of the mind, shunning the intrusion of "medicine."[3] In Napoleonic France, the state defined education as a public enterprise, a normalizing process in the interests of order and conformity (see Foucault 1979). However, in Britain, the state did not intrude into the educational sphere. Rather, a strong protestant ethic stressed the importance of charitable works through the establishment and private support of charitable institutions that were oriented toward moral uplift. But outside the schools, surgeons such as Cooper and Turnbull experimented on deaf adults.

The moralists and educators of the early nineteenth century wanted to normalize. But this predilection went against the grain of a society that demanded a clear boundary between the normal and the pathological, not only in theory but also in practice; against the grain of a polity and legal system that demanded rational electors and citizens; against the grain of an economy that demanded an individualized approach to work by able-bodied workers; and against the grain of privatized religions that stressed the vital importance of the work ethic and an individuated as well as rational relation to one's God.

"Moral management constitutes the individualistic, heroic phase of early psychiatry," writes Porter (1987, 222), but he adds, "this 'Herculean' phase proved short-lived. It was too personal to be permanent. Weberian bureaucratization set in, and the future was to lie with system rather than with charisma" (223). In this Age of Empire, the whole atmosphere and orientation of the asylum was transformed. The missionary zeal and the atmosphere of "family" were no longer appropriate. The "Darwinians" were particularly conscious of their social standing, of their professional status and superiority, of their honor in the community. They did not seek moral management and an identification with the humanity of their patients by means of a pseudo-kinship, as the moral managers had done. Rather, they sought to distance themselves from the pathological in the same way as the imperial power distanced itself from those it conquered through the assertion of racial and cultural superiority.

The Iron Cage of Bureaucracy[4]

By the end of the nineteenth century, the combined forces of industrialization and imperialism had created societies of enormous complexity. Economic and political relationships were rarely governed by community ties and responsibilities but were coordinated through "rational" administrative procedures. With the majority of the population living in relatively isolated families and alienated from their neighborhoods as well as at work, access to educational, medical, and leisure facilities depended increasingly on formalized, depersonalized, "rational" administrative structures and processes. The age of bureaucracy had dawned, and in the process, the whole character not only of psychology but also of childhood and education were transformed.

Compulsory schooling, dating in Britain from the Education Act of 1870, was generated by the logic of the ideology of equality and by a range of sometimes contradictory forces, including the demand for literate semiskilled and skilled workers and the demand of an increasingly bureaucratized administration for literate and numerate citizens. Whatever the causes, compulsory schooling demanded the effective coordination of teachers, schools, and curricula. Rational administration required an ordered educational environment. The idiosyncratic school, teacher, or pupil created administrative complexities. The formalization of teaching qualifications, the categorization of the teachers in terms of what and who they taught, the need for uniform curricula, and the need to categorize pupils into graded classes and vocationally oriented streams were all rationalized as administratively appropriate. Prospective pupils were tested to determine their appropriate places in the increasingly complex educational system. The tests themselves were "refined" and multiplied to meet these administrative demands.

As we proceed through the age of bureaucracy, the people who come to dominate the history of education are not innovative educators but professional administrators. We also enter an age of overt linguistic imperialism with respect to the education of linguistic minorities because the devaluation of minority languages and the imposition of the dominant language is not simply the decision of an individual school principal but also becomes government policy.

Professionalism and the Depersonalization of Disabilities

Professionalism was a vital ingredient in the consolidation of imperial superiority at home and abroad in the second half of the nineteenth century. The medical profession played a key role, not only in the assertion of professional authority and status but also in the biological legitimation of white, male, Anglo-Saxon, bourgeois superiority. This is the period when psychiatry consolidated its position and became a "profession" in which experts were dealing not only with the embodied impediments to rational progress but also with those "incipient lunatics" that threatened society (see Showalter 1987, chap. 4). It is also the period when, as we will see in detail in chapter 7, the professionalization of teaching drove teachers who were deaf from the schools and transformed education into therapy. Many histories of deaf education see the international commitment to oralism at the Milan Congress of Teachers of the Deaf in 1880 as causing the disenfranchisement of people who were deaf. History is much more complex than that. One can best understand specific influential moves such as the Milan Congress by exploring the interweaving of industrialization, imperialism, bureaucratization, and professionalization. A group of thoroughly socialized individuals who were middle class and who maintained an imperial orientation were reinterpreting the goals and purpose of deaf education. In doing so, they were, like so many around them, orienting themselves toward others in evolutionist terms that were soon to become distinctly eugenicist.

In this intensely professional, intensely imperialist, and thus, condescending environment, people who were diagnosed as being mad—especially the poor and females, rich as well as poor—fared badly. They were scorned and manipulated but, nonetheless, were the source of esteem for the doctors if they recovered. People who were disabled from birth fared even worse. They were condemned by the late-nineteenth century not only as racial degenerates but also as genetic incurables. To become deaf, blind, crippled, feebleminded, or mad, if not the result of a clear physical accident, was assumed to be the result of disease. Although the propensity to disease was sometimes seen as being associated with genetic weakness, disease might be dealt with, even cured. Those who suffered these "pathological" conditions from birth were, on the whole, simply cared for at best. In their case, pathology, was assumed to permeate the individual. They could not return to normality. At best, they could be studied scientifically—measured, observed, and even used for scientific experiments.

The intense scientific activity generated not only the technological advances that fed industrial capitalism but also the biological and psychological theories that gave rise to evolutionism and eugenics. These evolutionist and eugenicist theories provided an apparently rational legitimacy, on the one hand, for imperial domination abroad and, on the other hand, for domination based in class, race, ethnicity, gender, and able-bodiedness at home. Above all, they provided the rationale and the substance for the bureaucratic administration of citizens. Although bureaucracy took a number of forms in the West in the late-nineteenth and early twentieth centuries, all these forms relied on eugenicist processes in the categorization and administration of society. Through the first half of the twentieth century, variations of eugenics provided the ideological base for the development of administrative processes in a wide range of political settings. The rational administrative procedures of Britain and America depended as much on eugenicist views of humanity to provide the categories required for effective administration as the individuated charismatic dictatorship of Hitler did.

The complex intertwining of colonialism and Darwinian evolutionism produced a sense of hereditary superiority among the British upper and middle classes. This hereditary superiority was the rationale for their domination of colonial subjects and the working classes alike. Their superiority was now rationalized not only in terms of their dedication to work and their greater cultural refinement, their "distinction," to use

Bourdieu's term with its connotations of superior taste, but also in terms of their genetic superiority.[5] They saw themselves as biologically superior and could remain so only through the segregation of inferior stock at home and overseas.

The sources of madness and other pathologies were sought in biology, especially sources related to the genetic propensity for parents of particular quality to produce disabled, genetically inferior children. Parents were ostracized, and the "insane" were segregated simply to protect the rest of humanity. The white bourgeoisie asserted a superiority that was based not only in reason but also in nature. In this environment, those deemed physically "unnatural" (i.e., disabled), especially if they were racially different, fared particularly badly. They were the antithesis of what was desirable in a white, male, Anglo-Saxon, cultured, and rational human being.

To excel as a man meant to excel not only intellectually but also, at least as importantly, at sport. The Oxbridge blue; the Rhodes scholar; the cricket-playing, rugby-playing, polo-playing officer in colonial or military service: these were the pinnacles of able-bodiedness. The concepts of sport as the pursuit of competitive games, of the sportsman as one practicing and excelling in games, and of sportsmanship as derived from the effective and rational pursuit of sporting activities all emerge in the second half of the nineteenth century. Sport is no longer simply a dalliance, a casual pastime, but a serious business, the mark of bourgeois manliness, the hallmark of genetically advanced able-bodiedness. "A healthy body and a healthy mind" was more than a vague cliché or aphorism. It was the central article of faith of the Darwinian medical profession. Where mental disability occurred, this profession sought a physical sign—in head shape, spine, or general physique—and where physical "abnormality" occurred, they assumed mental problems would be found.

Prior to the First World War, the burgeoning psychiatric profession diagnosed the vast proportion of people who were not simply disabled in limb as "mentally retarded," "mentally defective," or "feebleminded."[6] This approach was consolidated by the development of intelligence quotient (IQ) tests in the early 1900s, allowing for the measurement of mental proficiency and the subsequent declaration of levels of intellectual pathology. Like the people in the colonies who were labeled "racially inferior," the people labeled "mentally retarded" were seen as evolutionary throwbacks, as evidence of "racial degeneration" as Down (1990) put it, labeling his patients who had Down's syndrome as "Mongols." Their treatment was as inhuman as the treatment meted out to native inhabitants of Australia or Africa who were seen to embody "the living stone age."

Formal Education as a Disabling Process

Toward the end of the nineteenth century, formal education emerges as possibly the most important agent of normalization in the West. The schools, shaped by the forces of professionalization and bureaucratization, with their cultural substance formed by the eugenics movement and developments in medicine and psychology, became the prime sites for the identification and treatment of disabilities.

The atmosphere that existed just before the First World War and before the introduction of IQ testing and in which children were deemed disabled by a clinical gaze is summed up in the following quotation from a report by the newly established medical inspectors in schools in the state of Victoria in Australia.[7] It became the basis for establishing the first "special school" in Victoria in 1912:

> [T]here is the first class—the hopeless idiot who will almost never be able to look after himself, but may be taught good manners and cleanly habits, and segregated in asylums so as not to be a nuisance both to himself and those about him. He further may be often rendered useful by teaching him some of the manual arts—farming, gardening, shoemaking, basket-weaving, etc. Into the asylum class tends to fall the epileptic. . . . The second main class is that of the child who is educable up to a certain point, and may, perhaps eventually be able to earn his living by manual labour. . . . These come to grief inevitably in the large classes of our primary school system. It is only by the organization of special classes where these children receive the personal attention of specially qualified teachers that the best results may be obtained. . . . The third class is made up of those who are merely dull, and whose attendance at a special school for a couple of years may bring them up to the age of standard again. These also will do little good in large classes where individual attention is practically out of the question. (quoted in Lewis 1983, 19)

The clinical gaze was diagnosing and classifying the children of Australia and, in the process, determining their futures and the roles they would play in the development of Australia's human potential. Children who were caught in the pathological net were doomed by being denied a normal education.

These "feebleminded" students were characterized as "so much grit in the hub of the educational machine" (Lewis, 1983, 21), and though special schools were advocated in part on humanitarian grounds, with a degree of concern for the orientation of at least the "dull" toward the public labor market, the prime orientation was segregationist. In 1930, the English Board of Control referred to these "feebleminded" students as "tainted stock." To people outside the special schools, the children inside were all of a kind—"subnormal," "disabled," "retarded."

The main tool used in the classification and marginalization of "disabled" children was the introduction of psychological tests, particularly Goddard's revision of the *Binet Scale*. These intelligence tests measured a child's IQ and were soon in use throughout the Western world, catering to a general perceived need for standardized tests that would allow for the effective streaming of children in an age of compulsory schooling.[8]

The testing of human intelligence dates essentially from the 1860s when the founder of the eugenics movement, Sir Francis Galton, attempted to develop intelligence tests to correlate intelligence with other aspects of an individual's behavior. By the late-nineteenth century, people were experimenting with a wide range of physical and intellectual tests, and in 1905, the French psychologists Alfred Binet and Théodore Simon produced tests to measure intellectual capacity (Binet and Simon 1905). Although Binet had developed his tests to identify "the retarded" to support the development of special schooling that would help those who, for whatever reason, performed poorly intellectually, his tests were soon oriented toward not only help but also segregation and oppression.

In America, Goddard, whose work had widespread influence throughout the English-speaking world, used the tests to overtly eugenic ends: to prevent the entry into America of migrants judged mentally defective on the basis of IQ tests. He biased testing culturally and linguistically and manipulated IQ scales to ensure that subjects were judged "moronic" and thus undesirable in an effort to support his conviction that certain ethnic groups were mentally inferior. Goddard was the one who divided the mentally defective into "idiots," "imbeciles," and "morons"; who ranged mental types along a unilinear scale that was overtly related to the linear evolutionary scales of races and social types of evolutionary anthropology; who linked mental performance to "moral fiber," assuming all criminals, prostitutes, and so forth to be "morons"; and who rationalized class differences as the result of hereditary difference in mental capacity, even doctoring photographs of mountain families to make them look sinister to support his views (see Gould 1984, 171).

In Goddard's hands, the clinical gaze reached new heights of fortune-telling brilliance as his assistants picked out the feebleminded on sight at the wharves. Although Goddard recanted to some degree in 1928, declaring that "feeble-mindedness (the moron) is *not incurable* . . . [, and] . . . the feeble-minded do not generally need to be segregated in institutions" (quoted in Gould 1984, 174; Goddard's italics), the damage had been done. The mania for testing was infectious; the need for the middle classes to rationalize and assert their superiority in an individualized competitive environment was uppermost ideologically. Mental capacity was assumed to be a measure of personal worth.

Language abilities were central to effective performance on tests. So, for example, "idiots" were characterized as those who "could not develop full speech" (Gould 1984, 158). Not surprisingly, the word "dumb" became synonymous with stupidity.[9] People who were deaf did not stand a chance. In many cases, deaf children and adults were not actually identified as deaf but were assumed to lack spoken language because they were "idiots." As idiots, they were assumed to be "ineducable" and were shut away in homes for the "mentally defective." Decades later, when these homes were closed down in an era of deinstitutionalization, adults emerged who were in no way "mentally defective" but only deaf. Amy (a pseudonym) now lives at a nursing home for the deaf in Melbourne, Australia. She is in her sixties. Until a few years ago, she lived at Kew Cottages, an asylum for the "mentally retarded." She had lived there virtually all her life because, as a child, she had been judged incapable of even doing an IQ test, diagnosed as "severely mentally retarded." She had never had her own bedroom. She had never communicated coherently with anyone. She had no language.

In Melbourne in the 1920s, Porteus enthusiastically embraced the use of the Goddard tests and then the equally biased *Stanford Revision of the Binet Scale* by Terman (see Gould 1984) before developing his own "now internationally famous Porteus Maze Test" (Lewis 1983, 34). The clinical gaze was now informed by and, even more, legitimized by rampant testing that was assumed to be objective and infallible, testing that was claimed to reveal stable, genetically based levels of intelligence. "The abnormal" were removed first and foremost because they hampered the education of "the normal" and to reduce, by means of training, their disturbing influence on society as adults.

But the segregation of "the abnormal" was not by any means motivated only by fear and by a concern with effective segregation. Humanitarian concerns were also important and, indeed, featured prominently in ideological justifications for segregated special education. The disabling effects of the process were rarely, if ever, expressed and understood. The tension between humanitarian and eugenicist motives was strong and explicit. The fear that "defectives" might proliferate as a result of their "humanitarian treatment" and associated rehabilitation remained strong.[10] The contradictions inherent in an egalitarian, individualistic, competitive, ruthless, and essentially unequal society remained as stark as ever.

During the interwar period, the concentration was on providing facilities for the effective segregation of "the feebleminded," a category encompassing a vast range of "conditions." At this stage, treatment, training, and therapy were given little attention as far as those judged "ineducable" were concerned. Eugenic anxieties were still uppermost, particularly among the middle classes.

The Postwar Era: Therapy, "Normalization," and Human Rights

In the period after the Second World War, theories and policies, though not necessarily practices, changed dramatically as the Age of Empire waned. Practices took some time to change, as is evident in Goffman's description of asylum life in the late 1950s in America where he describes the asylum as a place of confinement rather than of treatment (Goffman 1961) and in Rosemary Crossley and Annie MacDonald's description of conditions in "hospitals" for children who were severely disabled in Australia in the 1970s (Crossley and MacDonald 1979). But the excesses of Nazi Germany in the pursuit of eugenics had to be condemned outright rather than acknowledged as the extreme expression of a pervasive Western ideology.[11]

As the pendulum swung away from repressive segregation and back toward therapeutic treatment, toward more or less integration of "the disabled" into "normal" activities, and as it swung away from ineducability and toward training for living, the psychiatrists and medicos in general maintained their control over the lives of "the disabled." "Special education" blossomed. As the pendulum swung back to another era of therapy, the scientifically trained professionals became more than simply diagnosticians and prescribers of drugs, surgery, and segregation; they also became integral contributors to the growing bureaucracy concerned with special education (Tomlinson 1982, 53). The increasing role of diagnostic professionals from the 1940s to 1970s in Britain is shown in the makeup of the committee formed in 1973 under Mary Warnock to review educational provisions "for handicapped children and young people":

> The variety of professionals on this committee indicates the expansion of vested interests in the, by now, considerable field of special education. Administrators, doctors, psychologists, heads of special schools, social service directors, university professors, a retired NUT secretary, and a TUC secretary were represented on the committee. One parent of handicapped children was on the committee but she was also chairman of the education committee of the National Deaf Children's Society. One head of an ordinary school was a member. (Tomlinson 1982, 55)

With the move to compulsory secondary education by means of the 1944 Education Act in Britain, the testing of pupils for effective categorization and streaming into different compartments of the educational system intensified. With respect to "the disabled," the Act treated "'pupils who suffer from any disability of the mind or body' as a single group" (Kirp 1983, 79). Local education authorities were instructed "to ascertain who these children are, to determine their disability primarily through medical examination, and 'to provide for the education of a pupil with a serious disability in an appropriate special school, or any other suitable school where this was impractical or the disability was not serious'" (79). But those children diagnosed as "uneducable mental defectives" remained the responsibility of the Health Service until 1970 when they were placed under the responsibility of local education authorities and were integrated into special education.

The overt purpose of medical and psychological testing was to channel people toward different sections of the labor market according to their educational and vocational potential. That potential was established through IQ testing. This concern with educational and vocational potential is what gave rise to the increasing diversification of educational programs for deaf students. The educational and vocational potential of a child who was deaf was determined by the "level of hearing loss," in other words, by their potential to respond to an oral education. Children who were severely and profoundly deaf were sent to the old schools for the deaf and were assumed to be capable of only a very basic education because "education" was equated with language proficiency, and language proficiency was equated with proficiency in the dominant language, both spoken and written. The old deaf schools also increasingly took in children with multiple disabilities, a group that had formerly been denied access to the deaf schools and had been confined in noneducational asylums or simply kept at home. Their presence reinforced the image that all of the students who were deaf were essentially ineducable.

In Britain, America, and Australia, IQ testing in schools during the prewar period had been oriented toward the identification of "the feebleminded" to ensure their segregation for the protection of the normal population. Through the 1950s, IQ testing continued to yield a "subnormal" population "in need of" segregation of one sort or another, whether in special school or home. At the same time, testing was also yielding the students with high IQs who would be educated in selective high schools. Testing was increasingly legitimized as a practice that yielded not "the feebleminded" for segregation away from the mass of "normality" but, rather, two other groups: those in need of special, "remedial," or basic education and those highly intelligent students who would be trained as an intellectual elite to lead society toward the twenty-first century, into a golden age of innovative progress. The stress had shifted to the creative use of scientific testing as an aid to postwar progress, including the therapeutic training of "the subnormal" for participation in the workforce and, if necessary, participation through sheltered workshops. Bureaucratization that demanded even greater uniformity and the effective streaming of students toward different sections of the labor market encompassed the education system even more.

This concentration on the testing of individual aptitude and the development of specialized educational programs to cultivate these different aptitudes involved an ideological shift toward an even greater individualism. People who were diagnosed as in need of individuated therapeutic treatment now confronted a maze of therapists, specialists in the minutiae of "disabilities," including speech therapists, occupational therapists, physiotherapists, psychiatrists, child psychologists, and special education experts.

Deinstitutionalization and the Contemporary Construction of Disabling Practices

The stress on education rather than on care, on training for living rather than on long-term segregation, opened the door for a new wave of normalization, accompanied this time by deinstitutionalization. These policies and their attempted practice have confronted both people who are able-bodied and people who are labeled "disabled" with a range of problems. People who are labeled "disabled" face the very substantiated fear of "normalization" that results in the continuation of everyday discrimination accompanied by a convenient denial of special needs (see Barham 1992; Murphy 1991). For many people who are able-bodied, deinstitutionalization threatens not only their identity, especially when faced with the everyday presence of those formerly hidden away, but also the disciplined and ordered nature of their environment.

Deinstitutionalization is, on the whole, directly oriented toward the subversion of disabling practices, yet again, these efforts are themselves subverted by subtle, usually unrecognized processes. The general move toward deinstitutionalization that has affected "the disabled" in general will be discussed further in the concluding chapter. We deal here with the effect of deinstitutionalization in the context of schooling, with "mainstreaming," also referred to as "integration" or "inclusion."

Mainstreaming and the Retreat from Segregation

At the forefront of the battles of the 1960s and 1970s against established, rationalized, and intensely discriminatory bureaucratic processes were battles to transform education systems. People sought to break out of the cages of reason and pursue innovative educational processes. Innovative educators reemerged on the historical scene. Ivan Illich, Paulo Friere, A. S. Neale, and Neil Postman, among many, challenged systems that focused on normalization through standardized curricula and standardized classroom practice. They challenged the classificatory schemes that typecast pupils and streamed them into administratively tidy systems. In the process, they prompted the parents of children with disabilities to question the educational segregation and treatment of their children. The drive to desegregate children into the mainstream of everyday life presented schools and the community in general with a population that they rarely knew existed. It is a process that has been going on around the world (see Fulcher 1989; Barton 1989).

Pressure for the integration of the so-called "disabled" into the "normal" world, into the mainstream of everyday life, challenged society's most basic discourse: the nature of humanity. How effective was that challenge? We turn again to an Australian example because, in Australia, the adoption by the government of the state of Victoria of mainstreaming as an explicit and clearly articulated policy went far further in the establishment of mainstreaming as policy and, indeed, as practice than was the case in Britain. The Victorian program appeared to support Buckley and Birds's comment that while the education system in the United Kingdom had been extremely slow to address the link between the social and educational needs of people with disabilities, requiring "a paradigm shift in the way we think about people with disabilities in our society," this shift was "much further advanced in North America and Australia" (Buckley and Bird 1994, 15).[12] But was policy reflected in practice? The Australian case study highlights the links between mainstreaming and the ongoing cultural construction of "the disabled."

In 1984, the government of the state of Victoria stated its "commitment to provide necessary resources and . . . [its] concern with enrolling and supporting in regular schools children who were formerly segregated, or at risk of being segregated from them" (Office of the Director-General 1984, 8). That report of the ministerial review (a) explicitly opposed a view of disability that focused on professionals categorizing impairments by means of individually centered ascertainment, (b) explicitly recommended equalization of the relationship between parents and service providers, and (c) focused on the educational system or structure rather than on the child's named impairment. It asked that explanations for failure be sought not in the child but in "aspects of the education system" (9) and that these failures be rectified not by means of an orientation toward the "special educational needs" of the child because "this [approach] belongs to a deficit model" but, rather, by providing "additional educational requirements."

Research into the practice of mainstreaming showed that what resulted was a discriminatory practice far removed from the ideals outlined above. The formerly segregated "disabled" were expected to "assimilate," though only "as much as possible," to fit into the existing cultures and practices of the mainstream schools. Few teachers regarded total assimilation as possible but expected that specialist services would be required on a continuous basis to compensate for assumed deficiencies. "The disabled" remained marginalized, effectively segregated within the regular classroom as an "other," as "integration students."

Almost without exception, the program, especially at the secondary level, was understood as involving the use of special personnel (aides and therapists) and technology to cope with children with a pathology of body, behavior, or both in the regular classroom. The classroom, the curriculum, and the timetable remained as before and, ideally, the "normal" children proceeded as before, unhindered by the special needs of the "integration kids" who were looked after by specialist personnel and were integrated "where possible."[13]

As far as goals and guiding principles are concerned, the integration policy of the Victorian government, in its opposition to categorization and professionalism, appeared to go to the heart of discriminatory practice, seeking failure not in the child but in social structures and relationships. But the machinery devised to achieve its goals and the way that machinery was (and still is) interpreted and used by administrators and teachers often tended to work in the opposite direction. Research into mainstreaming in Britain revealed similar results, with teachers and administrators operating in terms of conventional categorizations of disability and assuming that special facilities would be provided for the integrated "disabled" to ensure that the "normal" pupils could proceed as before.[14] Indeed, many current mainstreaming practices overtly provide special educational facilities that are operated by special education teachers within mainstream schools, what is being referred to as "inclusion" rather than "integration." The children who were formerly segregated are now in the mainstream but are included as "disabled" students, their medically based categorizations intact.

Policies of normalization through deinstitutionalization have been widespread in Western societies over the last two decades.[15] The existing ideologies of normality have dominated the process of reform, the assumption being that people who were formerly segregated would adapt to the "normal" world, allowing the normal world to go about its business as before. This assumption is also infused with a feeling of benevolence at having allowed "the disabled" a pathway to assimilate into "normal" society. Studies of individual mainstreamed students have shown that some have benefited while others have not. Indeed, for many students, to be mainstreamed as "disabled" students is a marked improvement on being segregated, as Buckley and Bird (1994) have clearly established for Down's syndrome students in Britain. What we are concerned with showing here is the way the mainstreaming program, not simply as policy but as a cultural practice, serves to construct and maintain disabilities. The examination in later chapters of the mainstreaming of deaf students will build on the analysis presented here and will show how that mainstreaming resulted not in integration but in isolation.

Notes

1. Water shock therapies, electric shocks, and the revolving swing chair "capable of rotating a patient up to one hundred times a minute, which ultimately caused gushing of blood from ears and nose and unconsciousness" (Porter 1987, 221) were very much in vogue as the nineteenth century dawned. William Battie was a prestigious "mad-doctor" of the mid-eighteenth century who was instrumental in making the role of the mad-doctor respectable. He "rose to become President of the Royal College of Physicians" (Porter 1987, 167). An admirer of Locke, Battie advocated a "reasoned therapeutic optimism" in place of drugs, stressing the need for strict, humane management and declaring that "the Regimen in this is perhaps more important than any distemper" (quoted in Porter 1987, 207).

2. A clear example of the international approach to learning was the Quaker surgeon John Coakley Lettsom (1744–1815), who studied in London and on the Continent, graduated with a doctor of medicine from Leyden in 1769, and became a Fellow of the Royal Society in 1771.

3. See the section in chapter 5 entitled "Sign Language, the Clinical Gaze, and the Consolidation of L'Epée's Mission in France."

4. The phrase "the iron cage of bureaucracy" is taken from the work of the German sociologist Max Weber, in particular from the conclusion to his *The Protestant Ethic and the Spirit of Capitalism* (Weber 1985). Weber closely analyzed the various forms of rational administration associated with the rise of capitalism in the West and pointed to the difficulties in balancing the rational and creative aspects of leadership in the development of a just society. Anthony Giddens remains the most perceptive interpreter of Weber's sociology (see, in particular, Weber 1985, "Introduction"; Giddens 1971, 1972).

5. See Bourdieu (1984).

6. Worth noting here is the way the word "retard" is used colloquially today in day-to-day conversation and all too frequently in the media to refer to anyone perceived of as "disabled." A friend recalls being at a party while in a wheelchair after a car accident and overhearing someone inquiring, "Who's the retard?"

7. Note that although many people in Britain or America might look on Australia as a distant antipodean outpost of Britain, developments in Australia were influenced not only by developments in Britain but also by those in America and elsewhere in the Western world. Looking to Australian case studies is not intended to divert attention away from developments "in the West" but to provide pertinent examples of wider trends and developments. An imperial orientation is one that sees history as needing to focus on the center rather than on the periphery.

8. See, for example, Winzer (1993, 266–67) for the United States.

9. The etymology of the use of the word "dumb" to mean "stupid" is integrally linked to the use of language. It is in the nineteenth century that "dumb" is

used in relation to animals to stress the lack of language in "beasts" and their consequent stupidity—"a dumb ox" (*Oxford English Dictionary* 1969, vol. 4).

10. See, for example, the questions on the 1933 examination paper for the Special Teacher's Certificate of the Melbourne Teachers' College (Lewis 1983, 118) where these issues are explicitly raised for discussion.

11. As the work of Friedlander (1995, 1999) and Biesold (1999) has recently shown, although the Jewish holocaust is the most publicized aspect of Hitler's eugenically inspired policies, Hitler's programs of extermination and human experimentation also encompassed disabled people of all ethnic backgrounds.

12. It is important to note that although the development and implementation of mainstreaming policies in America and Australia was a bureaucratic matter involving government legislation, "special education" in Britain was left to the professionals, highlighting the distinctly British form of bureaucratization discussed above that involves an alliance between government and professionals in the pursuit of rational administration. As David Kirp notes, the Warnock Report of 1978 and the government white paper of 1980, *Special Needs in Education*, confirmed "the long-standing perception of British special education as almost exclusively the province of specialists, an institutionally marginal service isolated from ordinary schools and managed by a specialist group." (Kirp 1983, 78) For a discussion of the politics of mainstreaming in Britain, see Barton and Tomlinson (1984). For a discussion of the American mainstreaming programs and research into their implementation, see, for example, Kirp (1983) and Tanner, Linscott, and Galis (1996).

13. Note that the program was also perceived as a way of dealing more effectively with existing "problems" by employing aides to relieve classroom teachers. Whereas the ministerial review stressed that the prime concern of the Programme would be to increase the participation of "children with impairments, disabilities and problems in schooling in the education programmes and social life of regular schools" and with "maintaining the participation of all children" (Office of the Director General 1984, 8) in these processes, in practice, the orientation was toward an in-class or even "out of class but in-school" segregation not only of the formerly segregated but also of the formerly integrated "problem children." So the "problem children" became "disabled" and the "disabled" were identified as "problem children."

14. See, for example, Gregory and Bishop (1989) and Sellars and Palmer (1992).

15. See, for example, Murphy (1991).

PART TWO

The Cultural Construction of Deaf People as "Disabled": A Sociological History of Discrimination

Introduction

We now turn our attention to the processes by which deaf people became identified as a category of humanity, classified as "disabled" but distinguished from other forms of disability. Deaf people have been and continue to be the focus of intensive academic, educational, and medical attention and debate. All of the processes that we have examined so far in our historical overview of the cultural construction of "the disabled" have affected deaf people: the marginalization and institutionalization of unreason; surgical experimentation; the use of the clinical gaze to diagnose in terms of normality and pathology; normalization through specialized schooling; bureaucracy's "cages of reason"; the use of various forms of therapy; and finally, deinstitutionalization and mainstreaming.

All the processes associated with the disablement of people who are deaf are linked to their assumed inability to communicate. The central issue is language. We focus in particular on the use and abuse of sign languages in the history of deaf education. Discriminatory language policies will be shown to be particularly disabling within the context of the school, be it segregated or mainstreamed. Philosophers, educators, and medical professionals, often working together, have been the prime agents of these disabling processes as, through the centuries, they have praised, derided, transformed, and condemned the use of natural sign languages in the education of students who are deaf. The strategic use, misuse, manipulation, or rejection of sign languages has been central in determining the kind and amount of access that people who are deaf have had to the resources of their society and in determining to what degree and in what ways their identities as "deaf" and "disabled" have marginalized them and have resulted in discrimination.

As sociologists, we are concerned with delving below the threshold of consciousness. We intend to reveal the unconscious complicity of the upper and middle classes that occurred (a) through the agency of parents, teachers, academics, doctors, administrators, and therapists and (b) in the reproduction of the structured inequalities and associated discriminatory attitudes and practices that were based on the distinction between the able-bodied and the disabled and between the normal and the pathological. In understanding these subtle cultural processes, the concept of symbolic violence will be particularly important. Although we must not ignore the overt and far from invisible violence that people who are deaf and people labeled "disabled" have suffered and continue to suffer, much of the oppression that is experienced is the result of a violence exercised by people who are oriented toward the well-being—as they see it—of the people they diagnose and care for: "The gentle, invisible form of violence which is never recognized as such" (Bourdieu 1977b, 192). Teachers, parents, educational administrators, among others remain unaware of the consequences of their pursuit to educate people with disabilities through the dominant culture. They become unwitting agents of discriminatory structures and processes as they evaluate the world in terms of a view of humanity that is dominated by concepts of normality, sensibility, and linguistic competence that constantly reproduce "the disabled" and label people who are deaf as "disabled." Bourdieu (1991) has already demonstrated how vital an exploration of linguistic practices is in unearthing the parameters of symbolic violence and how integral the uses and abuses of linguistic differences are to the reproduction of cultural and social inequalities in the context of the reproduction of class-based inequalities. We now pursue those processes in the context of the cultural construction of people who are deaf as "disabled" by turning to the seventeenth century when deaf people cease to be part of a diverse population and when the concept of "the deaf" as a distinct group begins to appear.

As we consider the effect of the turbulent intellectual environment of seventeenth-century Britain on people who were deaf, we must clarify a number of issues relating to the use at that time of sign languages and manual alphabets by both deaf and hearing people. Although a range of manual systems have been developed over the centuries by hearing teachers of deaf students, the natural sign languages referred to throughout the book and on which many of these manual systems were based are as old and as ubiquitous as spoken languages. Throughout the world today—in the cities and rural areas of Western countries as well as in the towns, cities, and villages of Asia, Africa, the Pacific, and the rest of the non-Western world—we find sign languages being used for communication among people who are deaf and between people who are deaf and people who are hearing. The following statement by the philosopher of language Walter Ong is nonsense but is nonetheless a common misapprehension. He writes:

> Wherever human beings exist they have a language, and in every instance a language that exists basically as spoken and heard, in the world of sound. . . . Despite the richness of gesture, elaborated sign languages are substitutes for speech and dependent on oral speech systems, even when used by the congenitally deaf. (Ong 1982, 7)

Research in non-Western communities where sign languages are used among and with people who are deaf reveals full-fledged languages that are in no way dependent on oral speech systems. They are used as natural modes of communication.[1] Records of the use of sign languages among and with deaf people are scattered through the archives of European history, well into the Dark Ages and back into classical Greece and Rome. We have no reason to assume that these sign languages were not full-fledged languages, used in communities in the same way as they are in places like Indonesia today.

The historical record prior to the sixteenth century is scanty as far as the use of sign languages is concerned, but from the sixteenth century, we find clear evidence that, in Britain, sign languages were regularly used among people who were deaf and between deaf and hearing people. Sixteenth-century records show that marriages involving deaf people were performed using signs in Hereford and Leicester and that Edward Bone and John Kempe, two deaf people, used sign language in Cornwall in 1595.[2,3] In 1720, a deaf man, Benjamin Ferrers, was examined as a witness through "an Examination to be taken on the fingers upon the Report on Oath of one Mr. Ralph Ruffel, who swore he has been used to converse with him in that manner for seventeen years and upwards and that he understood his meaning perfectly by those signs" (Court of Common Pleas, London, 1720). In 1666, the diarist Samuel Pepys described a long signed conversation between a Captain Downing and a deaf boy about the progress of the great fire of London (Latham and Matthews 1982, 363). In the sixteenth and seventeenth centuries in Britain and Europe, people who were deaf lived in a linguistic environment in which signing in various forms was an accepted aspect of communication among hearing people, including communication through complex manual alphabets.

Work on monastic sign languages has shown that signed systems had been in use for a very long time. La Barre states that "the silent gestural language of European monks, designed to avoid interrupting the meditations of others, an allegedly international language of travelling medieval monks, [is] reliably dated from, at the latest, the fourth century A.D. onward" (La Barre 1964, 192–93) and quotes Rijnberk's *Le langage par signes chez les moines* (1954) as his source.[4] We know that, in the Middle Ages, unwanted children, especially those who were seen as having physical problems—people who were crippled or deaf, for example—were left on the doorsteps of monasteries to become part of the monastic community as oblates. The deaf children would have communicated through signing. Saint-Loup quotes St. Jerome from the fifth century, writing that "the Deaf can understand the Gospel with signs" (Saint-Loup 1993, 390), surely a reference to the formal education through sign language of people who were deaf. Banham mentions that the monastic sign systems were probably taught to the children in the monasteries around the tenth century in Britain (Banham 1991, 11). Some of the earliest educators of the deaf in the sixteenth century emerged from the Spanish monasteries.[5] What we do know for sure is that, in the seventeenth century, deaf children were being taught to read and write in at least one abbey in France, the abbey of Saint-Jean, and that they used sign language but did not speak (Lane 1984, 75). Very likely, this involvement of the abbeys in the education through sign language of children who were deaf was much more widespread.[6]

Although deaf people have developed and used manual alphabets at least since the days of the Roman Empire, for many centuries, manual alphabets were designed to serve the needs of the hearing community. Their use by secret societies and by religious orders is well documented. Only recently have manual alphabets become associated primarily and often exclusively with people who are deaf. Manual alphabets, now often called "deaf alphabets," are no longer seen as having any relevance for those hearing people who are not associated with the deaf community. Although most of the one-handed alphabets in use today derive from alphabets favored and adapted by hearing people either for teaching students who are deaf to speak (with the hand held next to the mouth) or for the development of initialized signs, the alphabets used as elements of natural sign languages appear to have been two-handed throughout Britain and Europe as well as in America (Branson et al. 1995).[7]

The first evidence we have of a manual alphabet being used in Britain for the education of deaf people is the one used by John Wallis in the 1650s, a two-handed alphabet, the same as the one used in Britain, Australia, and New Zealand today (see Defoe 1720). Wallis's records of his teaching techniques indicate quite clearly that he used the sign language and the two-handed alphabet that were used by deaf people. Arnold and Farrar go as far as to claim that the two-handed alphabet was an alphabet used by people who were deaf going back to Roman times (Farrar 1901).[8] The manual alphabet used among deaf people in France at the time the abbée de l'Epée began his school in Paris in the mid-1700s for students who were deaf and poor and the alphabet that was used in America prior to the introduction of formal education for deaf students were two-handed alphabets.

As we turn our attention to the early attempts by the new philosophers to educate deaf people in Britain, we must recognize that many of those who were deaf came to their education using a sign language and a manual alphabet. Throughout this part of the book, we will be examining how those who sought to educate and transform deaf people used, abused, and devalued their languages and signing conventions and, ultimately, "disabled" them. Some histories of deaf education credit l'Epée with having given language to people who were deaf through his system of methodological signs rather than with having taken language from them. Walter Ong went so far as to make the following claim:

> Until the pedagogical techniques for introducing deaf-mutes more thoroughly, if always indirectly, into the oral-aural world were perfected in the past few generations, deaf-mutes always grew up intellectually sub-normal. Left unattended, the congenitally deaf are more intellectually retarded than the congenitally blind. (Ong 1967, 142)

Before the development of formal education for deaf students, many people who were deaf were neither bereft of language nor "intellectually retarded." As we explore the role of language policies in the education and eventual disablement of deaf students, we must understand at all times that the natural sign languages referred to are languages as old as any spoken language.

The history that follows contains a cast of thousands. Dealing as it does with the rather neglected field of British deaf history, it involves people who, despite their national and often international importance in the history of deaf people and of deaf education, are unknown, even to most people familiar with the available literature. Therefore, we will provide brief footnoted portraits of the people who feature prominently as we proceed through the chapters in part 2.

Now we reenter the turbulent world of Britain in the seventeenth century. Feudalism has crumbled. A centralized state under an omnipotent monarch, greedy for wealth, has divested the church of its power, its authority, and its lands. Because of the black death and the growth of towns, many rural communities have become fragmented or have been destroyed. Poverty has engulfed or threatens to engulf many. The aristocracy and the merchant classes revel in increasingly elaborate luxury. And political revolutionaries, spurred on by their newfound freedom to rethink the shape of society, to construct the world in "rational" terms, threaten those in power. The British Enlightenment is in full swing.

Notes

1. See Johnson (1994) and Branson, Miller, and Marsaja (1996, 1999).

2. Parish book of St. Martin's, Leicester, for 1575.

3. Richard Carew's *Survey of Cornwall* (1602).

4. La Barre also lists a host of other documented and reported gestural and more generally kinesic communicative systems (La Barre 1964).

5. See Plann (1997).

6. Harlan Lane provides us with tantalizing evidence of the role of the monks in the education of deaf people and of the presence there of fluent sign language that was used in conjunction with fingerspelling. In 1745, M. d'Etavigny, a prosperous businessman of La Rochelle who had a sixteen-year-old deaf son, witnessed a demonstration of Jacob Pereire's success in teaching deaf pupils to speak. Harlan Lane writes of d'Etavigny's son, Azy:

> At the time he was sixteen and attending school in a Benedictine abbey in Normandy, where he had been for two or three years. Before that, he had spent eight years in the abbey of Saint-Jean at Amiens, and *had been taught with a half dozen other deaf children by a deaf old monk*.
>
> Thus it appears that the first recorded teacher of the deaf in France . . . was a deaf man himself. His name was Etienne De Fay, and he was born deaf of a noble family in 1670. *At the age of five he became a pupil at the abbey of Saint-Jean*. (Lane 1984, 75, italics added)

Pereire eventually visited the boy at the monastery two years later:

> Pereire . . . went to the abbey, where he found an intelligent eighteen-year-old who could read, write, *and sign*, but not speak. (76, italics added)

Pereire taught the boy to speak:

> . . . after eleven months, according to a written testimonial, he spoke 1,300 words that he understood, and many sentences. *His speech was, however, influenced by the grammar of his sign language*: he put all verbs in the infinitive and transposed word order. (76, italics added)

In the abbey, therefore, was not only, we presume, a system of monastic signs but also sign language.

7. See Stedt and Moores (1990) for a discussion of the development of initialized signs in France and America.

8. For further discussion of the evolution of the British manual alphabet and excellent illustrations, see Hay and Lee (1994).

3

The New Philosophy, Sign Language, and the Search for the Perfect Language in the Seventeenth Century

[O]ne must not forget that the relations of communication par excellence—linguistic exchanges—are also relations of symbolic power in which the power relations between speakers or their respective groups are actualized.

—Pierre Bourdieu, *Language and Symbolic Power*

We begin this history of the disablement of deaf people as most histories do, in ancient times. But the main focus is on the seventeenth century in Britain when, as outlined in chapter 2, in the battle of the sciences, the new philosophers triumphed over their more radical nonmechanistic fellows and the Royal Society provided legitimacy for rational progress. The seventeenth century was a time when philosophers engaged directly with deaf people in their search for an understanding of the contours of humanity and of the source and scope of human creativity. Mirzoeff has recently written that

> The constitution of deafness as a medicalized category of the body politic, and hence a social question, was the direct outcome of Enlightenment sensualist philosophy in general and the politics of the French Revolution in particular. (Mirzoeff 1995, 6)

Although this excerpt is a neat summary of general trends in France and even provides a guide as we trace the way that philosophical speculation on deaf people eventually gives way, at least in part, to medical experimentation, it glosses over the broader international trends that preceded and encompassed the essentially French Enlightenment of the eighteenth century. In particular, it ignores the effect on the general French and European intellectual scenes of British writers such as Bacon, Wilkins, Dalgarno, Wallis, Hobbes, and Locke. By the time of the French Enlightenment, the British Enlightenment was well in the past.[1]

Here, we will focus on those British philosophers of the seventeenth century, of the British Enlightenment, who engaged directly with people who were deaf and with their sign languages. All of these philosophers were key players in the development of the Western intellectual tradition. Some were foundation members of the Royal Society. Their writings were influential far beyond Britain's shores as they communicated freely with philosophers throughout Europe. Little has been written about these philosophers of language in relation to their engagement with deaf people and with sign languages. The small amount that has been written has often misrepresented the individuals and their work.[2]

Ancient and Medieval Attitudes toward Deaf People and Sign Language

For a thousand years from Roman times to the dynamic days of the Renaissance when British and European philosophers rediscovered the secular philosophy of the Greeks and Romans, intellectual life and education were conducted through the church. The philosophers of these times sought understanding in the word of God. Knowledge came through reading and writing. Wisdom was in the text. Their central educational goal was to teach their pupils to read and write.

These religious philosophers and teachers saw people who were deaf as part of God's complex world. They did not see it as right or proper that they should change deaf people. That kind of change would require a miracle, the intervention of God. The fact that those who were deaf did not speak or hear was not regarded as a problem. These clerical scholars did not regard all language as linked to sound, not even St. Augustine, despite the fact that many writers have claimed that he said deaf people could not be saved because they could not hear the priests. On the contrary, St. Augustine saw both signing and writing as viable avenues to knowledge and salvation (Zillman n.d.) because it was in the monasteries that many sign languages developed. These sign languages were not those used by deaf people but were sign languages developed by different orders of monks to cope with periods of silence when speaking was not allowed. Like the communities of feudal times and those of many non-Western countries today, monks' ways of communicating were flexible, adapting to the demands of their order and their members. The monasteries produced the first teachers of deaf people, teachers who taught through sign language. The venerable Bede, writing in the eighth century, describes how St. John of Beverley taught a boy who was deaf to speak, read, and write (Bede 1565, 115).[3] Although John of Beverley's ability to teach a pupil who was deaf to speak was seen as possible because he had been canonized, the teaching of reading and writing did not require sainthood but only that the medium of instruction be sign language, as it had been for John of Beverley.

In the fifteenth century, the first in a long line of educators who taught deaf students began to emerge with new aspirations for their pupils. They were intent not only on teaching their pupils to read and write but also to speak, performing what had formerly required miracles through the power of human knowledge. Some of these early educators were monks, but they were monks operating in a new environment. The educational goals of the intellectuals were changing, and the demands of people in society were also changing as they came to expect more control over themselves and their destinies. People no longer accepted the world as it was but sought to change it and began to look to learned people to transform what was formerly assumed to be God given. They now had new aspirations for their children who were deaf.

Teaching deaf people to speak became one of the new philosophy's great achievements and was seen as a measure of the philosopher's ability to change the course of human destiny. From the 1400s come the stories of Agricola of Heidelberg teaching a person who was deaf and mute to speak; of the Spaniards Ramírez de Carrión and Pedro de Castro teaching two members of the nobility who were deaf; of Pasch of Brandenburg teaching two children who were deaf to speak. The first person to systematize this new education process is usually said to have been the Spanish monk Pedro Ponce de León, who in the second half of the sixteenth century, educated three children who were deaf to read,

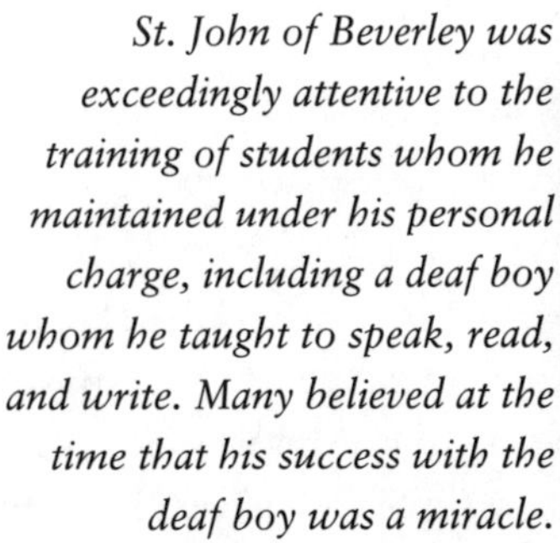

St. John of Beverley was exceedingly attentive to the training of students whom he maintained under his personal charge, including a deaf boy whom he taught to speak, read, and write. Many believed at the time that his success with the deaf boy was a miracle.

write, and speak to a degree. In these endeavors, Ponce de León was followed in Spain by Juan Pablo Bonet, who is well known for writing a book on the art of instructing the "deaf and dumb" to read (Bonet 1620, 1890). His book included drawings of a one-handed manual alphabet, which was to be used next to the face as an aid to teaching articulation.[4]

As men sought to perform the miracle of teaching deaf people to speak, reports of the methods used by some "teachers" in seventeenth-century Spain reflect the experimental nature of the educational process. Eriksson (1998, 32) attributes the following method to Manuel Ramirez de Carrión; however, Plann sees it as probably an account of a method used by the physician Pedro de Castro, an acquaintance of de Carrión:

> After the patient had been purged "according to his physical constitution, or temperament," the crown of the head was shaved, then slathered with an ointment concocted from spirits, saltpeter or purified niter, and oil of bitter almonds. The mixture was boiled until the spirits evaporated, after which one ounce of naphtha was mixed in well with a spatula. The salve was applied twice daily, and especially at night before the deaf person retired. In the morning, once his face was washed and his hair combed back with an ivory comb, the patient was spoken to at the bald spot, with the result that "the deaf-mute hears with clarity the voice that in no way could he hear through the ears." (Plann 1997, 51)

In Italy, Germany, Holland, and other parts of Europe, philosophers were also involved in achieving what had formerly required miracles.

Language and Rationality

"We make a country man dumb, whom we will not allow to speak but by the rules of grammar."

—Dryden, *Dufresnoy*
(quoted in Johnson 1755, s.v. "country")

Before the Renaissance, people lived in what has been called a "linguistic mosaic."[5] People switched from language to language and, possibly, from mode to mode, depending on the discursive processes involved. Spoken language was not dominated by written language.[6] Each form had its place and qualities. The written word often had magical qualities and was far removed from everyday discourse, which was about communicating, not about language. Illuminated manuscripts and signed conversations dominated many monks' lives. In the medieval world at large, signing appears to have been simply one possible discursive mode.

But from the fourteenth century, as rebellious clerics sought to question the authority of the church and its remoteness from the people, they turned away from the use of Latin and provided access to the word of God through the languages of everyday life. As intellectuals turned away from simply interpreting the word of God and sought knowledge and progress in and through the human mind, questioning all that had previously been taken for granted as God given, they made demands on their local languages that had never been made before. As they turned to question all around them and began to theorize all that previously had been simply accepted aspects of life, they also began to speculate about the vehicle for their theorizing, language itself.

Language was no longer a taken-for-granted aspect of a range of discursive processes but was the clue to the development of humanity in its own terms, through its own efforts. Language had to satisfy the demands of philosophy and science, not just the demands of day-to-day interaction. The question asked of any language and any mode was Is it an effective vehicle for creative intellectual activity? The change was marked in many countries by the development of academies to coordinate the use and development of the national language as the language of philosophy and science, which involved the systematization of grammar and spelling. This development occurred in Italy in 1582, in France in 1635, and in Spain in 1713. Moves to do the same in Britain were frequent from the seventeenth century on—by Dryden, Defoe, and

Jonathan Swift, for example—but were never successful (see Crystal 1987, 4). However, the linguistic self-consciousness of the British was no less intense, with dictionaries and grammars making their presence firmly felt.

As Europe entered the eighteenth century, this new consciousness of language involved three interrelated concerns: (1) the ability to develop and use language was seen as the fundamental dividing line between humans and animals; (2) clues to the origins and evolution of society were thought to lie within the origins of language; and (3) inquiries about the origin and diversification of language openly challenged the authority of the Bible (Harris 1995b, 272).

The search for a secular, demystified rationality dominated philosophical speculation. Descartes's visions of a new science were based on a view of knowledge that was dependent on individual human agency, intelligence, and innovation. Rational, creative thought was assumed possible, but what were to be its vehicles? How could that kind of thought be expressed? The answer, obviously, was by means of language. But what language? Did humanity need a special language of science, a language that transcended the mystifications and parochialism of the vernaculars? The intellectuals had a need to question the very nature of language itself, to explore the ancient theories, and to generate new ones.

Language became the key to the achievement of Descartes's ideals. The new philosophers sought the perfect language. The search for the perfect language gave birth, as side effects, to many linguistic theories "from taxonomy in the natural sciences to comparative linguistics, from formal languages to artificial intelligence and to the cognitive sciences" (Eco 1995, 19). The search for the perfect language played a vital part in the history of rationality and humanism and, in the process, not only laid the ground for the cultural construction of "the disabled" but also specifically focused on and thus helped to construct "the deaf" as a human category.

Two elements dominated the search for the perfect language: (1) the belief that a universal language had existed in the past, possibly before the fall of the Tower of Babel, and been lost; and (2) the possibility of constructing a new, perfect, and universal language through the development of linguistic theories. As we explore the way these philosophers grappled with the very nature of language, we confront for the first time the ambivalence of the hearing world's engagement with people who were deaf. Suddenly, the discursive processes engaged in by and with people who were deaf and mute became fascinating. The language of those who were mute suddenly had a philosophical status. Was it the original language? Did it hold the clue to the perfect language? If so, what was the status and role of deaf people in this possibility? Was sign language singular? Did all people who could not speak use the same natural language? Were all people who could not speak of a kind? Were deaf people and their language singular categories? These questions describe the issues that we begin to explore here.

Linguistics, Gesture, Deafness, and the Perfect Language

We return now to seventeenth-century Britain, to the birth of the Royal Society and the birth of linguistics. "Semiotics was defined by Locke in 1690, in Great Britain, and . . . in the same country was published in 1668 the *Essay towards a Real Character* by Bishop Wilkins, the first semiotic approach to an artificial language" (Eco 1995, 6). The search for the perfect language by Wilkins and his colleagues in the Invisible College, later The Royal Society, would focus the gaze of the educated public on people who were deaf and on their sign languages.

John Wilkins

Here, in our discussion of the rebirth of philosophical speculation on language and on sign languages in particular, we again turn to John Wilkins (1613–1672), the key player in the establishment of the Royal Society in 1663 who was particularly influential in the promotion of scientific activity and discussion at Oxford and then Cambridge. In 1640, Wilkins published a work called *A Discourse concerning A New World & Another Planet, In 2 Books, The First Book The Discovery of the New World: Or, a Discourse tending to prove, that 'tis probable there may be another Habitable World in the Moon. With a Discourse of the Possibility of a Passage thither. The Third impression. Corrected and enlarged. The second Book, now first published. A Discourse concerning a New Planet Tending to prove That 'tis probable our Earth is One of the Planets* (Wilkins 1640). The title shows how much this period was a time of great speculation, a time when philosophers experimented with new ideas and hoped for the achievement of wondrous results through the new philosophy, its mathematics, and its science.[7]

John Wilkins's interest in the nature of language led him and others to observe the sign language of deaf people. He eventually derived an alphabet of the hand.

Wilkins, like his fellow philosophers, was interested primarily in the nature of language. Language was the key to knowledge. The more perfect the language, the more perfect the knowledge, and knowledge was the key to the development of a new world, a world guided by human understanding. Thus, the philosophers questioned the foundations of language and knowledge. Was Aristotle correct in asserting that sound was basic to the production and understanding of language?[8] Was speech the direct expression of the mind and the source of all knowledge? What was the relationship among sound, the mind, and the soul, all of which were invisible and nonphysical? How perfect could language become as a vehicle of communication and as an expression of the wonders of the mind and the soul? What were the origins of language and was there, had there been, or could there be again a universal language? These kinds of questions prompted these British philosophers to become involved in the education of people who were deaf.

In 1641, Wilkins published *Mercury, or the secret and swift messenger: showing how a man may with privacy and speed communicate his thoughts to a friend at any distance* (Wilkins 1641), in which he acknowledged "dialogues of gestures."

> And 'tis a strange thing to behold, what Dialogues of gestures there will passe betwixt such as are borne both deafe and dumb; who are able by this meanes alone, to answer and reply unto one another as directly, as if they had the benefit of speech. 'tis a great part of the state and Majestie, belonging to the Turkish Emperor, that hee is attended by Mutes, with whom hee may discourse concerning any private businesse, which hee would not have others to understand. (Wilkins 1641, 112–13)[9]

Language was the source of understanding and communication, and through the language of gestures, understanding was assumed to be available to people who were deaf. Their humanity, their rationality, was realized through signing. Wilkins continues:

> It were a miserable thing, for a rationall soule, to be imprisoned in such a body, as had no way at all to expresse its cogitations: which would be so, in all that are borne deafe, if that which nature denied them, were not in this respect supplied, by a second nature, custome and use. (Wilkins 1641, 113)

Wilkins then goes on to speculate about the possibility of teaching people who are deaf to speak:

> But (by the way,) 'tis very observable which **Vallesius* [*Sacra Philos.* cap. 3] relates of *Pet. Pontius* a friend of us, who by an unheard of art taught the deafe to speak. . . . First learning them to write the name of any thing, hee should point to; and afterwards provoking them to such motions of the tongue as might answer the severall words. 'tis [sic] probable, that this invention, well followed, might be of singular use, for those that stand in need of such helps. (Wilkins 1641, 114)[10]

But the focus was not on the need to teach deaf people to speak. The issue of particular interest was the possibility of understanding without sound, the possibility that language was not dependent on "utterance":

> Though certainly that was far beyond it, (if true) which is related of an ancient Doctor, *gabriel Neale*, that he could understand any word by the meere motion of the lips, without any utterance. (Wilkins 1641, 114)

Wilkins also poses the possibility of gestural language being capable of infinite variety, of infinite "signification," a vehicle for creative expression like any language:

> The particular ways of discoursing by gestures, are not to be numbered, as being of almost infinite variety, according as the severall fancies of men shal impose significations, upon all such signes or actions, as are capable of sufficient difference. (Wilkins 1641, 115)

And in this exploration of the discursive potential of gestures, Wilkins turns his attention to antiquity, particularly to evidence of the use of fingerspelling and counting on the hands:

> But some there are of more especiall note for their use and antiquity. Such is that upon the joynts and fingers of the hand, commonly stiled *Arthrologia*, or *Dactylologia*, largely treated of by the venerable **Bede [*Lib. de loquelâ per gestum digitorum sive de indigitatione], *Pierius [*Hieroglyphic. lib. 37.c.I. & c Cælius Antiq. lect. l. 23.cap.12. Satyr 10.]*, and others. In whom you may see, how the Ancients were wont to expresse any number, by the severall postures of the hands and fingers; The numbers under a hundred, were denoted by the left hand, and those above, by the right hand. Hence *Iuvenal*, commending *Pylias* for his old age, says that hee reckoned his yeeres upon his right hand. (Wilkins 1641, 116)

Wilkins then goes on to derive an alphabet on the hand, which is expressed by pointing to different parts of the fingers and hand. The five vowels and the consonants T, Y, and Z correspond to the current two-handed alphabet used in Britain and Australia today, but the source of his alphabet is unknown.

The very nature of language, of how humanity could construct meaning and communicate understanding, was being questioned, and the speculations of influential philosophers like Wilkins were recognizing a role for people who were deaf in the new rational world that had been denied them by Aristotelian views of language that were integrally linked to sound.

Kenelm Digby

A few years later, another book appeared with an account of deaf people being taught to speak. In 1644, Sir Kenelm Digby published *Of Bodies, and of Man's Soul. To Discover the Immortality of Reasonable Souls. with two Discourses Of the Powder* [sic] *of Sympathy, and Of the Vegetation of Plants.—"Animae naturam, absque totius natura, Sifficienter cognosci posse existimas?" Plato in Phoedr* (Digby 1645). The book was published in London the next year and reprinted many times over the next twenty-five years. It contained a treatise on the nature of sound. Digby hypothesized that sound should be seen as motion. Again, sound and speech were stripped of their mystery:

> [I]t cannot be deny'd but that hearing is nothing else, but *the due perception of* motion: and that motion and sound are in themselvs one and the same thing, though express'd by different names, and comprised in our understanding under different notions. Which proposition seems to be yet

Physicist, naval commander, and philosopher, Sir Kenelm Digby published a book entitled Of Bodies, and of Man's Soul, *in which he suggested that reception of sound through the ear was not a prerequisite for the acquisition of language.*

> further convinced, by the ordinary experience of perceiving musick by mediation of a stick: for, how should a deaf man be capable of musick by holding a stick in his Teeth, whose other end lies upon the *Vial* or *Virginals*; were it not that the proportional shaking of the stick (working a like a dancing in the man's head) make a like motion in his brain, without passing through his ear; and consequently, without being otherwise sound, then as bear motion is sound. (Digby 1645, 307; Digby's italics)

In support of his treatise, Digby gives an account of a voyage to Spain in 1623 with the then Prince of Wales, where they saw the effects of education by a Spanish monk, assumed by Digby to be Bonet, who had taught a nobleman who was deaf (Luis de Velasco) to speak. The family had tried medical cures, but those cures had failed.[11] The fact that the reception of sound through the ear was not seen as a prerequisite for the acquisition of language was vital for the education of people who were deaf. What was vital for the philosophy of language was the linguistic potential that was seen to lie in the use of gestures and particularly in the development of manual alphabets that were not tied to sound.

John Bulwer

In the same year, 1644, John Bulwer published the first of two books dealing in part with the education of the deaf. The first book was *CHIROLOGIA OR THE NATURAL LANGUAGE of the Hand. Composed of the Speaking Motions, and Discoursing Gestures thereof.*

John Bulwer, an English physician, believed that the "language of the hand" was "the one language that was natural in all men especially for the deafened in the use of a manual alphabet."

whereunto is added Chironomis: or the Art of Manual Rhetoricke. Consisting of the Natual Expressions, digested by Art in the HAND, as the Chiefest Instrument of Eloquence, by HISTORICAL MANIFESTO's, exemplified Out of the Authentique Registers of Common Life, and civil Conversations: with types or CHYROGRAMS: along-with'd for illustrations of this Argument. The second book was *Philocophus: or the deafe and dumbe man's friend, exhibiting the philosophical verity of that subtle art, which may inable one with an observant Eie, to heare what any man speaks by the moving of his lips. UPON THE SAME Ground, wit the advantage of an Historical Exemplification, apparently proving, That a Man Borne Deafe and Dumbe, may be taught to Heare the sound of words with his Eie, and thence learn to speake with his tongue by J. B. named the Chirosopher.* The titles are very important because they reveal the complicated range of philosophical issues that led these philosophers to become involved with the education of people who were deaf. Deaf people provided an opportunity for these philosophers to put their theories to the test. In the society at large, their successes, or apparent successes, in teaching deaf people to speak were seen as evidence of the new philosophy and the new science's miraculous powers. Like the tales of travelers returned from voyages across the seas to newly discovered worlds, the tales of deaf people being taught to speak were received with excitement and awe.

But although teaching people who were deaf to speak generated particular excitement, popular attention was also focused on the wider speculation about the nature of language and on its relationship to speech. Communication through gesture and the skills in gestural language developed by deaf people also generated interest. People who were deaf became a talking point. An extract from Samuel Pepys's diary for 9 November 1666 describes a dancing party at a Mrs. Pierce's in London at the time of the great fire of London. During the evening, a youth appears who is deaf and who carries out a long signed conversation with a Captain Downing about the progress of the fire. Downing sends him off to get more information, and the youth reappears shortly with detailed explanations of the progress of the fire (Latham and Matthews 1982, 363). Pepys and others comment on the signing and are intrigued by it, specifically in relation to their philosophical speculation on the nature of language. Pepys's diaries also indicate the excitement of the time with general speculation on language. An entry for 11 January 1664 reads: "Thence to the coffee house, whither comes Sir W. Petty and Captain Grant, and we fell in talk . . . of Musique, the Universall Character—art of Memory." (12). In footnote 4, the editor adds the following note in relation to "Universall Character": "The attempt to produce a non-mathematical system of characters or symbols which could represent words in any language—a favourite project of the virtuoso of the time. The signs would represent not sounds (as in shorthand), but ideas." Pepys mentions a number of dinners with Wilkins and, later, would become close to Wallis.

On the 30 November 1667, Samuel Pepys sat next to Wilkins at a dinner and wrote how they were "talking of the universall speech, of which he hath a book coming out, did first inform me how man was certainly made for society. . . . And he says were it not for speech, man would be a very mean creature" (Latham and Matthews 1982, vol. 8, 554). In 1668, Wilkins published *An Essay towards a real character and a philosophical language*. He particularly acknowledged the work of two fellow members of the Royal Society, Wallis and William Holder.

Spurred on by the writings of Wilkins, Bulwer, Digby, and others, other philosophers became involved in debating the link between language acquisition and the education of deaf people as well as between language acquisition and the development of methods for teaching people who were deaf. Three other British philosophers of the seventeenth century were of particular importance in laying the ground for the segregation of "the deaf" as a category of humanity—Wallis, Holder, and Dalgarno.

At this time, education was not widespread. Most people were illiterate. Only the nobility and wealthy commoners received an education. So why educate deaf people? True, these philosophers mainly were involved with the education of the deaf children of the nobility or the wealthy. Those were the people who could afford to pay and who were eager for their deaf children to be educated like their other children. The teaching of deaf people to speak was also, as we have mentioned, a measure of the new learning's great achievements, of its ability to change the course of human destiny. But among these seventeenth-century British philosophers, not money nor philanthropy nor the performance of miracles made the education of the deaf so fascinating.

Sign Language and the Education of Deaf People

John Wallis and the British Tradition of Deaf Education

John Wallis's contributions are of particular importance. He laid the ground for the development of deaf education through the eighteenth and nineteenth centuries in Britain. Salvin Professor of Geometry at Oxford University, Wallis was one of the greatest mathematicians of his day. In 1653, he published *De Loquela, sive Sonorum Formatione, tractatus Grammatico-Pysicus* (Treatise of Speech) in which he speculated on the production of sound through speech, paying particular attention to the physical processes involved. He adopted a far from mystical approach to speech, seeing speech simply as a physical process through which language was expressed. Wallis tells us that the father of Daniel Whaley, a boy who was deaf, read the book and concluded that Wallis might be able to teach his son to speak, so he engaged Wallis as his son's tutor. The foundations for the pedagogical development of deaf education in Britain were being laid.

In 1662, in a letter to the philosopher Robert Boyle, Wallis mentions the problems involved in teaching a person who is deaf "when there is no other Language to express it in, but that of Dumb Signs" (quoted in Locke 1706, 29). Wallis was underestimating the scope of sign language, but this misjudgment was not surprising, and we also do not know how well Daniel could sign. Wallis saw this limitation, however, as a challenge:

> Considering . . . from how few and despicable Principles the whole body of Geometry, by continual consequence, is inforced; if so fair a Pile and curious Structure, may be rais'd, and stand fast upon so small a Bottom, I could not think it incredible, that we might attain some considerable Success in this Design, how little soever we had first to begin upon; and

Viewing speech simply as a physical process through which language was expressed, John Wallis became involved in teaching deaf students to read and write, and to express themselves either through signs or speech.

> from those litle [sic] Actions and Gestures, which have a kind of Natural Significancy in them, we might, if well managed, proceed gradualy to the Explication of a Compleat Language [through speech]. . . . (quoted in Locke 1706, 33)

So Wallis saw those "little actions and gestures," as he called them, as a basis for the development of a good education and began to shape its process:

> As to that of Speech, I must first, by the most significant Signs I can, make him to understand in what Posture and Motion I would have him apply his Tongue, Lips and other Organs of Speech. . . .
>
> As to that of Teaching him the Language, I must, (as Mathematicians do from a few Principles first granted) from that little Stock (that we have to begin upon) of such Actions and Gestures as have a kind of Natural Significancey, or some few Signs, which himself had before taken up to express his Thoughts as well as he could, Proceed to Teach him what I mean by somewhat else. . . .. (quoted in Locke 1706, 38–39)

Wallis was therefore stressing the need for education above all. He was saying quite clearly that there was no point in teaching articulation without teaching the pupil to read and write, without teaching him "our language." By "our language" in this context, he meant English, Latin, and other written languages. Later, when describing his teaching methods, he wrote:

> It will be convenient, all along, to have Pen, Ink and Paper ready at Hand, to write down in Words, what you signifie to him by Signs; and cause Him to write, (or shew him how to write) what He signifies by Signs. Which

way (of signifying their Mind by Signs) Deaf persons are often very good at. And we must endeavour to learn their Language, (if I may so call it) in order to teach them ours: By shewing them what Words answer to their Signs. (quoted in Locke 1706, 58)

Wallis also mentions the use of the manual alphabet:

> Twill next be very Convenient (because Pen and Ink is not always at Hand) that he be taught, How to design each Letter, by some certain Place, Position, or Motion of a Finger, Hand, or other part of the Body; (which may serve instead of Writing.) As for instance, The Five Vowels *a e i o u*; by pointing to the Top of the Five Fingers: And the other Letters *b c d*, & c. by such other Place or Posture of a Finger, or otherwise, as shall be agreed upon. (quoted in Locke 1706, 47)

We now know that the alphabet that Wallis used was, in fact, the alphabet used in Australia and Britain today. He certainly did not invent it.[12] Alphabets intrigued these philosophers of language. They were concerned with the relationship between the letters and sound, with the part they played in the generation of meaning, and with their potential in the search for the perfect, universal language—a set of characters, a classification system, and a grammar that would overcome the parochial, culture-bound qualities of the world's spoken and written languages.

Daniel Whaley was not Wallis's only pupil. In the early 1660s, Wallis also taught some speech to one other boy who was deaf, Alexander Popham. Popham had previously been taught to speak by William Holder but had lost his speech after having been away from Holder for two years. Wallis claimed to have taught Popham to speak and made no reference to Holder's previous work. A battle ensued through the pages of the Philosophical Transactions of the Royal Society (Holder 1678; Wallis 1678).[13] But whatever the rights or wrongs of the case, it was Wallis who was to have a lasting influence on the education of students who were deaf.

Wallis was not primarily involved with performing scientific miracles by making deaf people speak. He did not teach all his pupils to speak—only Whaley and Popham. In a letter to a Mr. Thomas Beverley in the 1690s, Wallis recalls that when teaching "Some other Deaf Persons, I have not attempted teaching them to Speak; but only so as (in good Measure) to understand a Language, and to express their Mind (tolerably well) in Writing" (quoted in Locke 1706, 45). We can assume from the previous quotations, that Wallis taught these pupils through fingerspelling and "their language" of signs.

William Holder felt that a thorough education in reading and writing was necessary in order for deaf people to become proficient in lipreading and speech.

William Holder

William Holder was also an influential member of the Royal Society and a close colleague of Wilkins. In 1669, Holder published *Elements of Speech: an Essay of Enquiry into The Natural Production of LETTERS: with an APPENDIX Concerning Persons Deaf and Dumb* (Holder 1669). Unlike Wallis, Holder was primarily concerned with teaching deaf people to speak. He looked to the design of an effective phonetic alphabet as a basis for teaching articulation. Holder writes that, in 1659, he had been given a deaf person, Alexander Popham, to teach. The pupil lived with Holder in his house (Holder 1694, 105–6), and in this context, Holder developed his method and experimented with alphabets. He tried to design a natural alphabet:

> [T]he chief design here intended by this account of the Natural alphabet, is, to prepare a more easie and expediate way to instruct such as are Deaf and Dumb onely by consequence of want of hearing (by shewing them the proper figures of the motions of the Organs, whereby Letters are formed) to be able to pronounce all Letters, Syllables, and words, and in good measure to discern them by eye, when pronounced by another. (Holder 1669, 15)

Holder was as concerned with teaching lipreading as well as with teaching speech and saw the effective use of lipreading as dependent on "a competent knowledge of the language" gained through a thorough education in reading and writing:

> In short, though it be impossible for a Deaf person, by his eye to distinguish letters singly spoken, (as it is likewise in words equivocal spoken, and

> letters whispered, to those that hear;) Yet in tract of speech, as a dubious word is easily known by the coherence of the rest; and a Dubious letter by the whole word; so may a deaf person, having obtained a competent knowledge of the language, and assisted by Sagacity, by some evident word discerned by his eye know the sense, and by the sense other words, and by the words the obscurer letters; and so notwithstanding this difficulty objected, make good use of this Institution, Language being defined, a Connecxion of the best signes for communication, and written language, visible signes of the signes audible; and the elements of each repectively letter spoken or written and the correspondence and mutual assistance of each to other, being such, as in the foregoing discourse is more fully shewn; you have a great help by shewing Letters and words written, to conduct a Deaf person on, in exercising him to expres the same by pronunciation; and what foever [sic] you gain upon him this way, will be retained and made use of in the other. (Holder 1669, 131)

Holder, unlike Wallis, was primarily concerned with teaching speech but regarded a knowledge of written language as a vital pathway to learning speech. He concentrated much of his attention on alphabets and gave instructions for the development of a manual alphabet for teaching articulation. For Holder, the alphabet was integrally linked to speech. He intended to transform the existing two-handed alphabet for teaching purposes and to develop special signs to enhance lipreading and articulation.

> [Y]ou need to shew him the connection between the written alphabet and the true alphabet of nature by rewriting the words and making signs to show the correct pronunciation, show him the position of the tongue, lips etc, by example. When he knows the alphabet then teach him the finger alphabet indicates vowels same as we use today, then come down a joint for b, c, d, f, g, use both sides of the hand in this way, he should then learn to converse on his fingers. Then move onto combination of letters and even signs for whole words so that it is easy to prompt him secretly. (Holder 1669, 131)

Determining what effect Holder had on developments in the education of children who were deaf is difficult, but clearly, Wallis's method and attitude dominated future developments, in particular, his use of fingerspelling and natural sign language as well as his separation of speech training from general education. Holder laid claim to being the first to educate a person who was deaf to speak and accused Wallis of making false claims in his letter to Boyle. The competition to be the first with respect to developing any part of a universal language and contributing to the related field of deaf education was very fierce. Holder was not the only person who accused Wallis of making false claims. George Dalgarno, a Scotsman who lived much of his life in Oxford and died there, felt particularly cheated not only by Wallis but also by Wilkins.

The Senses, People Who Are Deaf, and the Acquisition of Knowledge

George Dalgarno

George Dalgarno was a Scottish schoolmaster. He taught at a private school in Oxford but was in close contact with members of the University. His work focused on the development of a universal language, and he saw himself primarily as a grammarian.[14] In 1661, he published his book on a universal language titled *Ars Signorum, vulgo character universalis et lingua philosophica* (Dalgarno 1661). He felt that Wilkins had stolen many of his ideas, but little evidence exists to support this claim. Then in 1680, he published *Didascalocophus or The Deaf and Dumb mans Tutor, to which is added A Discourse of the Nature and number of Double Consonants: Both which Tracts being the first (for what the Author knows) that have been published upon either of the Subjects* (Dalgarno 1680). What is particularly interesting about this book is the attitude that Dalgarno takes toward the potential education of people who are deaf. Chapter 1, titled "A Deaf Man as capable of understanding an expressing a Language, as a Blind," begins in true Lockean fashion: "Tho the soul of man come into the world, *Tabula Rasa*; yet is it withal, *Tabula Cerata*; capable thro study and discipline, of having many fair, and goodly images, stampt upon it" (Dalgarno 1680, 1). In chapter 2, titled "A Deaf man capable of as Early Instruction in a language as a Blind," he states:

> Taking it for granted. That Deaf people are equal, in the faculties of Apprehension, and memory, not only to the Blind; but even to those that have all their senses: and having formerly shewn; that these faculties can as easily receive, and retain, the Images of things, by the conveiance of Figures, thro the Eye, as the Sounds thro the Ear: It will follow, That the Deaf man is, not only, as capable; but also, as soon capable of Instruction in Letters, as the blind man. And if we compare them, as to their intrinsick powers,

> has the advantage of him too; insomuch as he has a more distinct and perfect perception, of external Objects, then [sic] the other. . . . (Dalgarno 1680, 8)

Dalgarno constantly asserts the superiority of people who are deaf. However, he views the ability to take in information through the eye, including lipreading, as difficult and inadequate. Thus, lipreading is seen as less effective than fingerspelling. Dalgarno also asserts that people who are deaf face no real barrier in learning to speak. Dalgarno is somewhat skeptical of Kenelm Digby's claims about a Spanish boy who was deaf having been taught to recognize all letters by lipreading and to reproduce them. Dalgarno concerns himself with devising the most effective way to teach reading and writing to people who are deaf. He stresses the need to learn the alphabet above all things, seeing fingerspelling as being

> the readiest, so it may become the quickest way of intercourse and communication with dumb persons. . . . [A]nother piece of useful care will be, to keep him from any other way of Signing, than by Letters. . . . Add to this; that his familiars about him be officious in nothing, but the intercourse of letters, that is, either by Grammatology, or Dactylology. (Dalgarno 1680, 47)

Like other educators later in the history of the deaf education, Dalgarno wanted to use fingerspelling only to ensure that people who were deaf gained knowledge of English and of the written word. Unlike Wallis, he devalued signing. In chapter 8, "Of an Alphabet upon the Fingers" (Dalgarno 1680), Dalgarno designs his own manual alphabet, with all letters on the palm of one hand and with combinations of letters such as *th* indicated by touching part of the palm with the fingernail rather than with the flesh of the finger. This alphabet was never adopted.

But in Dalgarno's work in particular, we see an orientation toward people who are deaf that does not regard either their deafness or their muteness as being a barrier to education and the effective acquisition of knowledge. Although Dalgarno devalued the linguistic qualities of signing, he did not devalue deaf people themselves. His work showed that philosophy itself does not necessarily disable. The philosophical speculation of seventeenth-century Britain generated a range of interpretations of both deafness and sign language. Which interpretations came to dominate the wider ideological evaluation of deaf people and their languages was influenced by economic, political, medical, and pedagogical issues beyond the concerns of the new philosophers of language.

A Note on Sign Language and the Search for the Perfect Language in France

Nearly a century after Wallis and Holder had stirred the interests of the Royal Society with their achievements in educating deaf pupils, Jacob Rodriguez Pereire amazed the Royal Academy of Sciences in Paris with his achievements in educating his student Saboureux de Fontenay. At the same time, intrigued by the signing of his deaf pupils, the abbée de l'Epée was exploring the linguistic and educational potential of manual communication. We will focus on Pereire and, particularly, on l'Epée in more detail in the following chapter. Here, we simply draw the links between the work of the British philosophers of Britain's seventeenth-century "enlightenment" and the speculations of their French counterparts a century later.

L'Epée was spurred on in the development of his educational program for the people of Paris who were deaf and poor, not only by his priestly concern for their moral and spiritual well-being but also through his philosophical interest in the nature and scientific potential of language. Building on the work of his contemporaries—Diderot (1713–1784) and Condillac (1714–1780) in particular—l'Epée was convinced that, in the sign language of his pupils, he had discovered the basis for the development of a universal language, that "Holy Grail" that had obsessed the English in the previous century and that was the talk of the Salons in Paris in the mid-eighteenth century.[15] He considered natural sign language to be limited, unsuitable as an educational medium, and set out to develop his universal language, his system of methodological signs, through the application of the new linguistics, the emerging "rational," "scientific" knowledge of grammar.

"The Deaf" as a Category of Humanity

The competition among Wallis, Holder, and Dalgarno in seventeenth-century Britain and, indeed, between Pereire and l'Epée in eighteenth-century France was evidence of the integral role that the education of deaf people had come to play in the development of the philosophy of language. Although people who were deaf were in many ways pawns in an intellectual "game," pawns in the development of a new ideological approach to language and its potential, they were nonetheless being distinguished as a category of humanity with particular qualities and aptitudes, a categorization that involved them as deaf people. Their deafness and muteness was seen increasingly as the essence of their subjectivity. Deafness, once simply a puzzling aspect of God's order, had now become a condition that marked off an entire group of players in the chess game of life. "The deaf" had become a category of humanity, pawns to be moved around the board to suit the strategies of the philosophical players. Deafness had become a human condition, and "the deaf" were singular.

In later centuries, people who were deaf were to be reduced to being yet another group of "disabled" people, not deemed worthy of any special attention, rather, requiring therapy, along with burgeoning categories of "the disabled." But in seventeenth-century Britain, they were defined as a category as they also were to be in eighteenth-century France. They were constituted as a category because of the role they were seen to play in the development of an understanding of human rationality. That human knowledge, indeed, could overcome deafness and muteness and could teach deaf people to speak was a triumph for human reason. That people who were deaf could learn to speak or that they, indeed, could express themselves through signed language was also a measure of human reason and of the ingenuity of humanity.

But the battle lines were forming for the debates between manualists and oralists two hundred years later. For some philosophers, Aristotle's claims that language was tied to speech rendered signing secondary to speech, a poor imitation. Speech and sound were spiritual and creative. Gesture was simply a material, nonspiritual imitation of speech (compare Mirzoeff 1995, 19). For others such as Dalgarno, gesture was as meaningful a communicative medium as speech. In later chapters, we will consider the battles that ensued between the manualists and oralists as deafness ceased to be conceptualized as a viable and effective human state and was diagnosed as a pathology, a condition to be therapeutically transformed.

At the beginning of the eighteenth century in Britain, people who were deaf were therefore considered to be as capable of reason as anyone. If they were perfectly educable and capable of being considered reasonable beings, what forces were at work that would cast them beyond the pale and categorize them as "disabled"? The answer lies in the processes explored in chapters 1 and 2: People who were deaf, along with a host of others, were encompassed by the cosmological tyranny of a scientific discourse that distinguished between the "normal" and the "pathological."

Deafness became a condition not simply to be lived with but to be transformed. And the transformation of deaf people, like their education in the seventeenth century and most of the eighteenth century, became firmly identified with "progress." They were to be defined not simply as "other" but as "pathological" in a world that no longer reveled in difference but, rather, feared it. The transformation of the pathological was to become a measure of humanity's control over its own destiny, a measure of the power of the scientific method.

The ultimate responsibility for the diagnosis and treatment of those whose differences were interpreted as threatening the rational order fell to an increasingly specialized set of professionals. As the nineteenth century dawned, so too did the professional society, a society dominated ideologically by experts disciplined in professions, in the practical application of the fruits of science, in the ideological practice of scientism. In relation, especially, to the education and treatment of deaf people in Britain, the roots of that professionalism lie in the transformation of deaf education during the eighteenth century wherein deaf education ceased to be associated primarily with philosophical speculation and became a business.

Notes

1. With respect to the development of rational secular thought,

> [t]he English . . . were the first bearers of the torch. In that land with many Protestant sects the hand of the church was lighter, and political issues were attenuated by the Glorious Revolution of 1688. The oft raised question, "whether England had an Enlightenment" (meaning in the eighteenth century) is thus otiose. It was already a fact. (Crocker 1995, 3)

2. Harlan Lane's representation of Wallis is a case in point (Lane 1988, 103–6). The neglect or misinterpretation of this period in the education of deaf people has been rectified to some degree very recently by the publication of Jonathan Rée's *I See a Voice* (1999). Rée's philosophical analysis of these seventeenth-century British philosophers appeared when this section of our manuscript was complete. Our treatment of these philosophers and their engagement with people who were deaf is based on primary archival research, particularly in the Farrar Collection in the John Rylands Library in Deansgate in Manchester (see Branson and Miller 1998b). Our interpretation is also sociological rather than philosophical.

3. Bede (Bæda) (675–735) was a British Benedictine monk who was placed under the guardianship of Benedict Bishop, the Abbot of Wearmouth, when he was seven years old. A historian, biographer, and generally the most learned man

of his time, he was ordained by Bishop John of Beverley and spent most of his life at St. Paul's at Jarrow.

4. See Plann (1997) for an in-depth discussion of Bonet.

5. A concept introduced at a session of International Association of Applied Linguistics (AILA) 1996 in Finland by a discussant, Professor Yamuna Kachru of the department of linguistics at the University of Illinois, who pointed out that, in many non-Western situations, literate and nonliterate languages coexist perfectly naturally and effectively in a "linguistic mosaic" as people switch from language to language depending on the discursive processes involved. The Western model remains an essentially monolingual model insofar as people are assumed to have a "first language," even in a multilingual situation. One language is assumed to be primary.

6. Note here that the concept of a "linguistic mosaic" supports the argument that writing systems did not necessarily develop to represent speech (see Olson 1996, 65ff.). According to Olson, "[I]t may be argued . . . that writing systems were created not to represent speech, but to communicate information. The relation to speech is at best indirect" (Olson 1996, 68).

7. We have included the full titles of works by Wilkins and others in the main text. They not only explain, far more than the titles of today, the contents of the book but also teach us much about the intellectual culture of their time.

8. In the fourth century B.C., Aristotle said, "Men that are born deaf are in all cases also dumb; that is, they can make vocal sounds, but they cannot speak" (536b.3–4 [Thompson's numbering]). Regarding the nature of language, Aristotle observed:

> Voice and sound are different from one another; and language differs from voice and sound . . . language is the articulation of vocal sounds by the instrumentality of the tongue. Thus, the voice and larynx can emit vocal or vowel sounds; the tongue and the lips make non-vocal or consonantal sounds; and out of these vocal and non-vocal sounds language is composed. (535a.27–535b.line 4)

He therefore assumed that language is linked directly to the various physical abilities required to produce a range of particular sounds. As we shall see, nearly two thousand years later, the effect of Aristotle on the evaluation of people who were deaf and of their language was profound.

9. The attendants who were deaf and mute in the Turkish court are also mentioned in Sibscota (1670). The name George Sibscota appears to be a nom de plume. The author is unknown. The book *The Deaf and Dumb Man's Discourse*. . . . is, in fact, a translation of an essay in Latin included in a collection of select dissertations by Anthony Deusing, professor of medicine in Groningen, Holland, published in 1660.

10. See Vallesii (1608). Pet. Pontius is Ponce de León.

11. As Susan Plann points out, the description was full of inaccuracies: Manuel Ramírez de Carrión was who Digby met and who was teaching Luis de Velasco, and de Carrión was not a priest. (Plann 1997, 63–66).

12. The source of the alphabet is unknown. It was not, contrary to Lane's claim (Lane 1984, 105–6), the alphabet developed by Dalgarno.

13. For a succinct discussion of the controversy, see Scott (1938, 85–87).

14. For a discussion of Dalgarno's work on the development of a universal language, see Eco (1995, ch. 11) and Stewart (1854).

15. See Diderot (1751). L'Epée was particularly influenced by the philosophy of Condillac, who in turn, was the main interpreter of Locke to the mid-eighteenth-century French intellectual scene.

4

The Formalization of Deaf Education and the Cultural Construction of "the Deaf" and "Deafness" in the Eighteenth Century

As the education of people who were deaf became more formalized through the eighteenth century, the confrontation between "the universal tongue of knowledge and power" and the "vulgar," natural language of deaf people became more complex and more overt.

> [N]either Bernard nor the archers nor I myself could understand what she was saying in her peasant tongue. For all her shouting, she was as if mute. There are words that give power, others that make us all the more derelict, and to this latter category belong the vulgar words of the simple, to whom the Lord has not granted the boon of self-expression in the universal tongue of knowledge and power. (Eco 1984, 330)

The philosophical speculation of the seventeenth century that had found deaf people and signing so intriguing gradually gave way to less mystical, more pragmatic orientations toward people who were deaf and toward their education. The debates about the links between language and sound as well as between language and knowledge continued to involve speculation about the signing conversations of people who were deaf, but they were being encompassed by new views of humanity.

Deaf people were increasingly thought of as "other": other than human beings who had all five senses; as an other, a unitary category; and as other than rational, in need of rationalization.

But no singular process was at work. According to followers of Locke, who considered human beings as being tabulae rasae at birth on which knowledge gained through the senses would be inscribed, people who were deaf were capable of as much education as their senses would allow. Dalgarno maintained that no educational limitations were imposed by their sensibility. For some, sign language was an adequate and effective avenue to knowledge; for others, access to speech was essential. For some, people who were deaf were forever deprived of effective language and effective intellectual development; for others, their development was assured through sign language, through the effective acquisition of spoken and written language, or both. According to those who followed Leibnitz, people who were deaf retained more of their mystery because they were seen not as being tabulae rasae but as possessing all the innate ideas bestowed on human beings.[1] The goal was to unlock their innate ideas and give them the opportunity to effectively express and develop those ideas. Again, debate raged as to whether giving them this opportunity required teaching them speech and lipreading as well as whether instruction should be through speech or could be through sign. Nevertheless, as with madness, the orientation was toward their normalization through treatment, their rationalization through education. "The deaf" per se were being defined as the embodiment of elements of unreason and, therefore, in need of scientific intervention.

Here, we continue to concentrate on the development of deaf education in Britain. We explore the continuities between the earlier philosophical orientations that were documented in the last chapter and later developments through the eighteenth century and into the nineteenth century. We also, albeit briefly, compare these British processes with those in France. In eighteenth-century France, developments would take place that were to affect the education and wider conceptualization and treatment of deaf people throughout the world. These French developments have been well documented, and although our interpretation of those developments differs somewhat from the interpretations offered previously, we reflect on the French scene here primarily to place the British developments in a wider historical context. Above all, we intend to show how philosophical and pedagogical developments on both sides of the Channel reflected and contributed to the idea that people who were deaf were disabled.

But speculation on the educability of deaf people was not confined to the meetings and transactions of the Royal Society. Educators such as Wallis and Henry Baker were not alone in developing the images of deaf people and their intellectual potential. The literary representations of people who were deaf, mute, or both that fired the public imagination of the early eighteenth century in the popular works of Wallis's brother-in-law, also Henry Baker's father-in-law, Daniel Defoe, linked Wallis's philosophical "experiments" in the later-seventeenth century and Baker's therapeutic and educational achievements in the mid-eighteenth century.

Daniel Defoe, Duncan Campbell, and Dickory Cronke

Daniel Defoe (1661?–1731), a popular novelist, journalist as well as political and religious activist who was imprisoned and placed in the stocks for his radical views and for debt, was intrigued by deafness and muteness as well as by the linguistic and educational potential of signs.[2] Through his books, fictional and nonfictional, and his journal articles, Defoe popularized the philosophical issues that had filled the *Transactions of the Royal Society*.[3] Literate people throughout Britain and beyond waited eagerly for his next forthright contribution to the philosophical, political, and religious debates of his day, just as their descendents eagerly awaited the latest Dickens work, a century and more later. Two prominent men featured in his writing: the London "deaf and dumb soothsayer" Duncan Campbell (Defoe 1720) and the Cornish "dumb philosopher" Dickory Cronke who, by the age of three, was found to be mute but was able to hear and who learned to read and write but used signs (Defoe 1717).

Through these historical figures, Defoe drew attention to the educational potential of those who were deaf, mute, or both and, especially, drew attention to the educational potential of fingerspelling and signing. For example, we find the first pictorial representation of the manual alphabet used by Wallis in Defoe's account of Duncan Campbell (Defoe 1720, 37). Defoe was concerned, not with the process of teaching the person who was mute to speak, but with the questions around the educability of people who were deaf, mute, or both. In *The History of the Life and Adventures of Mr. Duncan Campbell* (Defoe 1720), Defoe discusses the achievements of a range of prominent people who were deaf. He mentions Wallis teaching Alexander Popham and lists others:

Duncan Campbell is thought to be the first deaf main character in Western literature.

> The Uncle of his present Sardinian Majesty, Sir John Gawdy, Sir Thomas Knotcliff, Sir———Gostwick, Sir Henry Lydall, and Mr Richard Lyns of Oxford, were all of this Number, and yet Men Eminent in their several Capacities, for understanding many Authors, and Expressing themselves in Writing with wonderful Facility. (Defoe 1720, 54)

He adds,

> In Hatton Garden, there now Lives a Miracle of Wit and good Nature, I mean the Daughter of Mr Loggin, who, tho' born Deaf and Dumb, (and she has a Brother who has the same Impediments) yet writes her Mind down upon any Subject with such Acuteness, as would Amaze Learned Men themselves. (Defoe 1720, 54)

Defoe's representations of people who were deaf, mute, or both convey a sense of mystery and of powers lost on people who could hear and speak. Duncan Campbell was a soothsayer sought out by the wealthy of London for his fortune-telling powers. Dickory Cronke was a prophetic philosopher who made "Prophetical Observations upon the Affairs of Europe, more particularly of Great Britain, from 1720, to 1729" (Defoe 1717, title). The miraculous is never far away as Cronke "comes to his speech" "some days before he died" (Defoe 1717, title). A person who is mute is also seen to have a special moral quality and, thus, becomes the perfect subject for a morality tale. In the Preface to *The Dumb philosopher or great Britain's Wonder* . . . (Defoe 1717), Defoe writes that the dumb philosopher is "introduced to a wicked and degenerate Generation, as a proper emblem of virtue and morality." He writes of the character Dick Cronke, son of a tin miner,

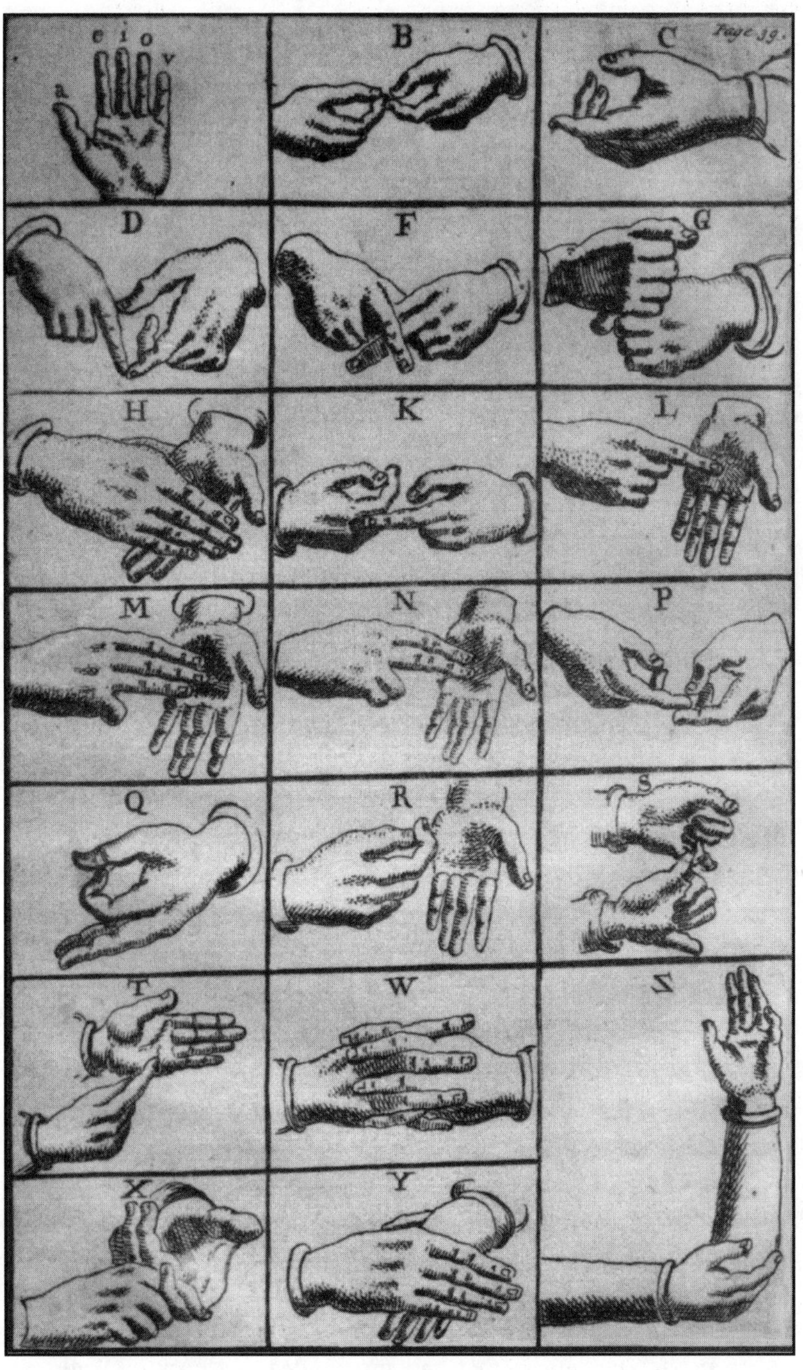

In The History of the Life and Adventures of Mr. Duncan Campbell, *Daniel Defoe illustrates the manual alphabet used by John Wallis.*

> He never gave the least sign of complaint or dissatisfaction with anything unless it was when he heard the tiners swear, or saw them drunk, and then too he would get out of their way, as soon as he had let them see by some significant signs how scandalous and ridiculous they made themselves, and against the next time he met them, would be sure to have a paper ready writ, wherein he would present the folly of their drunkenness . . . (Defoe 1717, 18)

Defoe's books on Duncan Campbell and Dickory Cronke were well into multiple editions and exciting the popular imagination by the time his future son-in-law, Henry Baker, decided to become a teacher of students who were deaf.

Eighteenth-Century Britain: Deaf Education as Private Enterprise

In mid-eighteenth-century Britain, the education of deaf people left the philosophical realm and became a private enterprise.[4] Techniques were developed to teach them through signing, the manual alphabet, and the acquisition of speech and lipreading. The techniques were kept secret. The teachers were assumed to possess exceptional skills, skills based in rational knowledge that was developed scientifically. The mystery of their methods was not the mystery of magic but the mystery of science. So Henry Baker (1698–1774), whose work we turn to next, was first and foremost a scientist in the eyes of those who sought his services. He was a scientist who had formalized the ideas and practices of his predecessor, Wallis, to develop the techniques required to gain "miraculous" results through the art of reason.

Henry Baker: Poet, Scientist, and Peripatetic School Teacher

Although Baker was himself a highly respected experimental scientist, a member of and for many years secretary to the Royal Society, his educational work with people who were deaf was regarded as a business, not as an aspect of his work as a scientist. This view was a radical departure from the atmosphere that had surrounded the work of Wallis and Holder, whose experiments and, indeed, debates were reported to and became the subject of much discussion in the Royal Society. Also note-

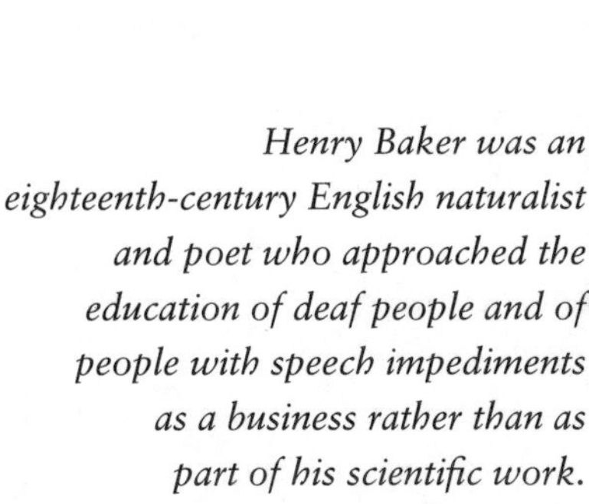

Henry Baker was an eighteenth-century English naturalist and poet who approached the education of deaf people and of people with speech impediments as a business rather than as part of his scientific work.

worthy is the fact that Baker made most of his money, not from educating people who were deaf, but from curing speech impediments, again, through secret processes assumed scientific. In February 1740, he was elected Fellow of the Society of Antiquaries and, in March, a fellow of the Royal Society for which he was secretary for many years. His work on polyps with Folkes was published in the *Transactions of the Royal Society* and, in 1743, as a separate treatise. In the same year, he wrote *The Microscope Made Easy*, a best-seller, and in 1744, was given the Copley medal for his work on salt crystals. He died in 1774 at his apartments in the Strand, in London.

After Baker's death, his grandson, the Reverend William Baker, who had been bequeathed Baker's personal papers, wrote a brief memoir of his grandfather based on Henry Baker's own notes and written as though Henry Baker were writing in the first person.[5] The following passage from the memoirs describes how Baker first became involved in the education of deaf people.

> April 26th, 1720 I took leave of Mr. Parker and went to Enfield, on an invitation from Mr. foster [sic] (added note: this visit was not to Mr. Sergeant foster [sic] but to Mr. john forster [sic] an attorney father of the Seargeant [sic]) who was my relation by marriage—my visit there was intended for amusement of about 1 month, . . . but providence so ordered that I stayed in the family until my marriage in 1729—for this gentlman [sic] having a daughter (Jane Forster a sister of the Seargent) born deaf and consequently dumb who was then about 8 years old. heaven [sic] put into my thoughts a method of instructing her to write, read, understand and speak the English language; which communicating to her father he entrusted me

> to make a trial and from that time would never part with me till I had perfected her in the language, and taught her not only to read, write and speak it readily, but likewise to understand the speech of others by sight, and be able to hold a regular conversation with them on any subject. (n.d. a, parenthetical elements are Baker's)

Baker carefully protected his "method" through legal agreements with his clients and stressed that he alone could perform these educational tasks through scientific techniques. He claimed that "heaven put into my thoughts" a method of instruction, but clearly, he read Wallis's work closely, following and building on his methods.[6]

Baker's routine is outlined in a letter he wrote in 1747 to the Reverend Doctor Doddridge of Northampton outlining his work with people who were deaf and speech impaired and its relationship to his scientific work:

> When I was about twenty years of age, having a relation (a girl) who was born deaf (and consequently dumb), it came into my thoughts, that such a person might be instructed to write, read, and speak. I immediately made the experiment; and my scholar, in about a year, could read in any book distinctly, speak very intelligibly most common words, and understand a great deal of language. This success brought people about me, who were under the same misfortune; and the handsome offers that were proposed, led me, contrary to my first intention, to give the same assistance to others; and new ones still applying from time to time, this has been my employment for twenty-five years; during which, I have brought several, under those unhappy circumstances, to speak the English language fluently, and converse easily, from understanding what others say, by only observing the motions of their organs of voice while speaking; to read and comprehend all common books, and to write their mind, either by letter or otherwise, in as sensible, and in a better and more correct style than people usually do. Along with this, I have also assisted great numbers to get rid of hesitation, stammering, lisping, and various other impediments of speech; and have constantly some sufferers of such nature under my direction, who come from different parts, and whom I spend all my mornings in attending where they are lodged; for no persuasions could ever induce me to take any home; the attention and fatigue of teaching them making it necessary that I should be quite undisturbed at all other times; so that after four or five o'clock my days' work is over: but then, what with visits of friends, attending the Royal Society, answering correspondents, preparing one thing or other for the press, and other necessary avocations, I can seldom command an hour. (Baker Letters)

The education of people who were deaf was becoming a technique to be applied, not an experiment to be learned from. Their "impediments" were dealt with scientifically. But this science still was being applied only to privileged individuals. The social construction of "deafness" and of "the deaf" was still some way off.

The workbooks of Baker's deaf pupils give some indication of the multifaceted nature of Baker's educational goals. One pupil, John Hodges, writes, "Mr Baker pays a great deal of money to my father to teach me to read write and speak." In 1731, William Gwillym writes: "Mr Baker will see me first then go to Master Forster. Mr Baker lodges at Mr Stephens, a booksellers. Mr Forster has 5 children. The eldest John is a parson, James is a lawyer, William is deaf, his two daughters Jane and Amy both deaf but can now speak." Mary Jeffreys writes: "I came to London a year ago I could read and write but not speak I was dumb." William writes: "I come from Hereford where I learned to write from Mr, [sic] Williams the writing master, . . . my brothers and sisters are at school in Oxford but I will not go because Mr Baker is the only one who can teach speech." John Gildart writes: "I must always open my mouth a great deal when I speak and I must throw out my breath. If I do not open my mouth I will speak like a baby." By 1760, Gildart wrote: "I now speak a great deal and I read and write my task very well. Mr. Baker went to kiss the King's hand."

Baker used to bring the Old Bailey sessions papers for the pupils to read. The focus was definitely on Baker's particular expertise on teaching speech, but the education was a rounded and worldly one. Baker did not have a school as such, but his pupils did meet at his house on occasions and were acquainted with each other's family situation and educational progress.

Baker used signing extensively, which is evident from the following legal agreement between Baker and a client:

> Whereas Henry Baker . . . hath invented and for many years practiced the art of teaching such as have the misfortune to be deaf and dumb to read, speak, and understand the English language, and amongst others he instructed in the said matters Lady Mary and Lady Anne O'Bryen two Daughters of the R^{t} Honble the Earl of Inchequin; and Whereas Morough O'Bryen Esqr of Mortimer Street, Cavendish Square is greatly desirous of learning the Signs made use of by the S^{d} Henry Baker in teaching the said Ladies, that he may be the better inabled to converse with Lady Mary O'Bryen for whom he has the highest regard: It is hereby mutually agreed

> between them this twenty ninth day of January in the year one thousand seven hundred and fifty three as follows . . .
>
> . . . Henry Baker promises to instruct him . . . and that he will to the utmst [sic] of his power make him acquainted with the Signs and means necessary for his understanding and being understood by the Ladies Mary and Anne O'Bryen . . .
>
> . . . Morough O'Bryen doth hereby promise . . . not at any time either in the whole or in the part divulge to anybody the signs or method which the s[d] [sic] Henry Baker shall teach him. . . . (Baker Papers)

Again, Baker was protecting his "business" by claiming to have invented from scratch not only his method but also the signing that was used as an integral part of instruction and as a mode of communication with hearing friends and relatives. The source and nature of the sign language that he used remains unknown, but links to Wallis and also to his father-in-law Daniel Defoe, who had written about the education of people who were deaf through Wallis's methods prior to Baker's involvement in teaching Jane Forster, indicate close links to signing conventions of his time.[7]

Thomas Braidwood: Full-Time Schoolmaster

Unlike Baker, Thomas Braidwood (1715–1806) had no links with the Royal Society or the world of scientific experimentation. He was a schoolmaster. After graduating from the University of Edinburgh, he became an assistant master at Hamilton Grammar School before establishing his own private school for teaching mathematics. At that stage, Braidwood appears to have had no contact with deaf people. He continued to teach mathematics until he was forty-five years old, when he was asked by a wealthy wine merchant, Alexander Sheriff, from the town of Leith near Edinburgh to admit his son, Charles, who was deaf.

Some accounts of the education of Charles claim that his father had read Wallis and that he specifically asked that Braidwood put these principles into practice with his son (Gallaudet 1875, 154). The year was 1760, the same time as Henry Baker was teaching his last pupils. Braidwood accepted the challenge and taught the boy not only mathematics and to read and write but also to speak and lipread. A few accounts of the education of Charles Sheriff mention that Braidwood did in fact embark on the new venture "using ideas in the Philosophical transactions."[8] Joseph Watson, Braidwood's nephew who was trained by Braidwood, states quite clearly that Braidwood's method was founded on the same principles as those of Dr. John Wallis as outlined in his letter to Robert

Boyle (Watson 1809, xxiii). Braidwood's success soon brought requests from other parents, and the number of pupils in his school who were deaf increased until the mathematics school was closed and Braidwood renamed his school "Mr Braidwood's Academy for the Deaf and Dumb."

Braidwood claimed, in an advertisement in the *Scots Magazine* in August 1767, to "undertake to teach anyone of a tolerable genius in the space of about three years to speak and to read distinctly" (quoted in Pritchard 1963, 215). Braidwood's reputation spread, and demand was heavy. In 1768, a poem by Charles Sheriff, "On Seeing Garrick Act," was published in several newspapers and magazines (quoted in Hay and Lee 1993/4, 2).[9] By 1769, Braidwood was writing to the *Scots Magazine* that thirty pupils had had to be turned away from the school. He claimed that only a few pupils could be taken at the same time and that the education was expensive. He urged financial assistance to those who could not afford the fees and offered to "communicate his skill to three or four ingenious young men" (Braidwood 1769, 342). No such funds or young men were forthcoming so Braidwood's school continued as a private school for the children of the wealthy. A nephew, John Braidwood (born 1756), became Thomas's assistant in 1775. Much later, John's sons, John and Thomas, were also to play their part in the history of deaf education, in both Britain and America. A second nephew, Joseph Watson (1765–1829), was also to be taken on as an assistant in 1784, but we will return to Joseph Watson shortly.

What then were Braidwood's methods and results? Like Baker, he kept his methods a secret to protect his livelihood, but unlike Baker, he trained others to teach through his own methods. Those assistants were not necessarily as secretive. Also, visitors to his academy left records of what they saw. Certainly, people of the time focused on his ability to teach deaf pupils to speak, but we must remember that the education of people who were deaf was seen as miraculous whether or not the pupils spoke. Therefore, Charles Sheriff's poem was evidence of educational success, not of the ability to speak. His command of the English language in print is what impressed people. When the American Francis Green commented in detail on the education of his son, Charles Green, under Braidwood, he stressed three things: first, Braidwood's conviction that learning to write was not adequate and that "it is almost impossible for *deaf* persons, without the use of *speech*, to be *perfect* in their ideas" (Green 1783, 167; Green's italics); second, the success of his son in learning to speak; and third, the high quality of his general education. Of his second visit to his son in 1782, Green writes:

> On my next visit, in September 1782, his improvements were very perceptible in speech, the construction of language, and in writing: He had made a good beginning in *arithmetic*, and *surprising* progress in the arts of drawing and *painting*. I found him capable of not only comparing ideas, and drawing inferences, but expressing his sentiments with judgement [sic]. On my desiring him to attempt something he thought himself unequal to, I set him the example by doing it myself: Upon which, he shook his head, and with a smile, replied (distinctly, viva voce), "*You are a man, Sir, I am a boy. . . .*" (Green 1783, 167ff.; Green's italics)

An earlier American pupil, Thomas Bolling, was described in a letter written in 1841 by Colonel William Bolling as having "the manners of the most polished gentleman. His articulation so perfect, that his family and friends and servants understood him in conversation" (Bolling Letters). The evidence of famous writers such as Samuel Johnson, Thomas Pennant, and Lord Monboddo who visited the academy also reported the high educational standards and admirable speaking abilities of at least those students selected by Braidwood to perform for the visitors.[10]

With respect to the academic content of the education received by Braidwood's pupils, we can gauge the high standards set and achieved not only by the education of eminent scientists such as John Goodricke, the famous astronomer, but also by the aspirations of Braidwood for Charles Green, which he outlined in a letter to Francis Green written on 20 July 1782:[11]

> As to the plan of his education (mentioned by you) we are of opinion, that he should continue in the study of the *English language, arithmetic, geography, geometry*, &c. until he is pretty much master of them. We think, if Charles is master of the English language, the *sciences*, the *French*, and as much *Latin* as may give him a competent knowledge of the derivation of words, it would be sufficient; and it would be a pity not to keep him employed as much as possible in *drawing*, that appearing to be his *forte*.—As to dancing, we refer the time to yourself, &c. (Green 1783, 154–55; Green's italics).

To what degree signing was used as part of the teaching process is not clear, but we do know that Braidwood's pupils signed and that they used fingerspelling. Hugo Arnot's *The History of Edinburgh from the Earliest Accounts to the Present Time* (Arnot 1788) includes a description of Braidwood's academy that specifically mentions the use of gestures and fingerspelling (Arnot 1788, 425–26). We know that his teacher trainee, Watson, used the two-handed alphabet as integral to the teaching

Thomas Bolling, an American, was sent to Scotland to be educated by Thomas Braidwood.

process. We have already quoted evidence that Braidwood's first pupil, Charles Sheriff, signed, and ample evidence shows that other pupils of Braidwood's also signed—the deaf parliamentarian Francis Humberstone McKenzie, for example. Some evidence also indicates that Thomas Bolling, one of Braidwood's four American pupils signed. An American deaf man who met Bolling stated that

> I had a pleasant conversation with him, and he told me that he was educated by Mr Braidwood at Edinburg [sic]. He was a nicely dressed gentleman, and passed for a speaking person. . . . I found his signs a little different from ours. I have not heard anything about him for a long time. (*The Deaf-Mutes Journal* 1876)[12]

Samuel Johnson's description of a girl to whom he presented an arithmetic problem is also interesting: "She looked upon it, and quivering her fingers in a manner which I thought very pretty, but of which I know not whether it was art or play, multiplied the sum regularly in two lines, observing the decimal place. . . ." (Johnson 1775, 382–83). The philosopher and champion of Dalgarno, Dugald Stewart, comments on the "natural language," or sign language, of Braidwood's pupils in Edinburgh (Stewart 1860, 16).

Braidwood taught all his pupils in one room. He moved about the classroom giving individual attention to each pupil, checking each one's work. He was concerned primarily with imparting a first-class education rather than with focusing on articulation, especially if the pupil showed no aptitude for speech. One of Braidwood's most eminent pupils, the astronomer John Goodricke, is reported never to have spoken, and other former pupils were reported to be incomprehensible.

Baker and Braidwood, therefore, transformed the scientific experiments of Wallis and Holder into teaching methods that they applied systematically in educating deaf children of the wealthy. Baker embodied the educated gentleman scientist, the skilled tutor with expertise based in his secular, scientific education and experience. He had no formal school as such but was a schoolmaster in the fashion of the day, a peripatetic schoolmaster. Braidwood took the education of people who were deaf one step further by establishing Britain's first school for deaf people, his "Academy for the Deaf and Dumb." Note that Braidwood's school was an academy, an institution of learning, not an asylum. The term "asylum" would not be used in relation to the education of people who were deaf until the turn of the century in Britain when education for people who were poor and deaf began and became a charity as well as a mission. However, in France, the institutionalization of the education of children who were poor and deaf first took place in the mid-eighteenth century.

The French Enlightenment, Linguistic Speculation, and Deaf Education

In France and Germany, the situation in the first half of the eighteenth century was similar to that in Britain, with individuals developing secret techniques for the education of people who were deaf, especially for teaching them speech and lipreading. But although, in Britain, the days for presenting before the Royal Society the results of teaching people who were deaf had passed and deaf education had become an accepted though secret scientific technique, in France, these presentations were just beginning. Again, at the philosophical level, Britain had been the torchbearer.[13]

Nearly a century after the practice of presenting students who were deaf to the Royal Society in Britain had passed, Jacob Rodriguez Pereire dominated the scene at the Royal Academy in mid-eighteenth-century France, especially through the remarkable achievements of his student Saboureux de Fontenay:

> In January of 1751, midway between his twelfth and thirteenth birthdays, Saboureux de Fontenay was presented to members of the Royal Academy of Sciences in Paris. The academicians had been convoked to examine the deaf boy's astonishing command of spoken French. Their report states that he pronounced "clearly and distinctly" all the French vowels and consonants, including the "complicated" nasal sounds. He also recited the Lord's Prayer

Jacob Rodriguez Pereire taught his deaf students to speak by touch and vibration through muscles.

> in Latin, and demonstrated that he understood a few French expressions conveyed to him by fingerspelling. This impressive achievement by the second talking deaf person to be observed at the academy was taken to confirm the pedagogical talents of their teacher, Jacob Rodriguez Pereire. As a consequence of this examination, and as a reward for bringing greater glory to the most enlightened nation on earth and to its language, King Louis XV granted Pereire an income for life, securing his reputation as the greatest "demutiser" of the deaf in Europe. (Lane 1984, 14)

The French Enlightenment was indeed far more self-conscious, elegant, and vibrant than anything Britain had seen in the preceding century. And in the process, people who were deaf in France were, for a time, to achieve and experience a prominence in French society unlike anything that would be seen for a very long time anywhere in the world. Ironically, in the process, "the deaf," like the mad, would eventually enter the asylum and become objects of sympathy and pity, their deafness firmly categorized and medicalized.

The story that relates the founding of the school for children who were deaf and poor in Paris has been told many times and has entered the realm of myth and legend.[14] In France, and especially in the United States, the period from the 1760s when the school was founded by l'Epée until the early 1800s is presented as a kind of Elysian golden age inhabited by deaf and hearing demigods. Their busts and portraits—l'Epée, Sicard, Massieu, Clerc, Berthier, Bébian, in particular—adorn the places where deaf history and culture are honored. Today, they are honored above all for the role they played in the development of the education of deaf people through sign language, in particular, for the heritage that flowered, not in France, but in the United States.

However, there is another side to these developments. Although the work of l'Epée and his successors did indeed establish for all to see that people who were deaf could be educated to participate creatively in the intellectual, vocational, and artistic realms of social life, these educators also laid the ground for the effective medicalization of deafness and for the entry of deaf people into the ranks of the "disabled." Just as the institutionalization of madness, or "great confinement," laid the ground for the classification, medicalization, secularization, and thus demystification of madness, transforming it into a condition that was pitied rather than feared or simply tolerated, so too would the institutionalization of children who were deaf and poor provide the basis by which these same processes would define and marginalize deaf people. Schools were developed as a way to discipline those aspects of society that were being seen as anomalous. Unreason and the abnormal not only were embodied but also herded together, disciplined, and controlled in precisely the way that Foucault has so eloquently described when documenting the increasing formalization and standardization of schools and prisons in the "normalization" of Western humanity (Foucault 1979).

More clearly than with any other individual, we see, in the transformations of l'Epée's philosophy and pedagogy, the radical changes that occurred in the education and conceptualization of people who were deaf during the eighteenth century. Through the following brief biographical sketch of l'Epée, we see the shift from a concern with the philosophy of language to the development of the asylum, a shift that was oriented toward the humanist transformation of people who were deaf through education, through the rational application of scientific techniques, and particularly, through the transformation of their language from its natural, "vulgar" form and content to an approximation of "the universal tongue of knowledge and power."

L'Epée: The Institutionalization and Rationalization of Deaf People

Charles Michel de l'Epée (1712–1789), a Jansenist priest and barrister, was an educated and devout man who, in his forties, became involved in educating two sisters who were deaf, which led to a lifelong dedication to the education of children who were deaf and poor in Paris.[15] L'Epée became intrigued by the possibilities that sign language provided as a medium for education. He was influenced in his subsequent educational and religious crusade for Paris's people who were poor and deaf by two distinctly eighteenth-century preoccupations: first, the philosophical engagement with language as the path to knowledge and, second, the charitable uplifting of poor people. As we pointed out in the previous chapter, l'Epée was convinced that, in sign language, he had discovered the basis for developing a universal language. He was also convinced that the rational development of sign language was the medium through which people who were deaf could be educated.[16] He regarded the natural sign language of his pupils as completely inadequate as a medium for education and set out to develop a system of methodological signs.

Through his rational, methodological signs, l'Epée was rationalizing the natural world, domesticating the beasts of the slums by providing them with a language forged by scientific principles, a cultured language of reason that transcended their "vulgar," natural language. For many, l'Epée at last had succeeded in developing a universal language adequate to the tasks of philosophy.[17] Bazot commented in the early 1800s, that, until l'Epée created the universal language of signs, there was only dactylology and added, "Il était réservé à l'abbé de l'Epée de créer le langage universel de l'intelligence avec lequel on peut s'entendre et communiquer dans tous les idiômes de l'univers" (Bazot 1819, 23). Bazot declared that the natural sign language of deaf people was a natural, simple, and even vulgar language, which became, in the hands of l'Epée and his successor Sicard, a universal language capable of metaphysical, scientific, and philosophical expression (Bazot 1819, 27n. 19).

Twice weekly, l'Epée opened his house to the public to view his success with his pupils. The success lay in their ability to reproduce sentences in a number of languages after they had been dictated in methodological sign and to answer signed questions in written French. This ability was seen as evidence of both the universality of his methodological sign language and of the educational success of his method.

L'Epée: The Myth

Popular representations of l'Epée's work were soon to picture him as the archetypal selfless benefactor, ministering to the poorest of the poor, who were bereft of not only adequate physical sustenance but also the sense of hearing and, therefore, access to spoken language. Four decades after he had established his school and a decade after his death, l'Epée became

Charles Michel de l'Epée's philosophy and pedagogy radically changed the education and conceptualization of people who were deaf during the eighteenth century.

a hero of the popular stage throughout Europe and Britain. The real abbé disappeared, and a new, mythic figure emerged, imbued with the emerging values of a new century.

On Saturday, 14 December 1799, a new play was performed at the Théâtre Français in Paris. The play was titled *L'Abbé de L'Épée, Comédie Historique en Cinq Actes et en Prose* by J. N. Bouilly (Bouilly 1800). On 24 February 1801, a play titled *Deaf and Dumb: or, The Orphan Protected: An Historical Drama in Five Acts* was performed at The Theatre Royal in Drury Lane in London. It was the first English translation of Bouilly's play. Others soon appeared.[18] The play was the story of l'Epée's most mysterious pupil, a nobleman cast out by relatives, the Count of Solar, and of the abbé's fight for his recognition and for the restoration of his title and inheritance. It drew large audiences year after year throughout Britain and Europe. In postrevolutionary France, Bouilly's play excited complex social and political reactions that were popular with the masses and therefore with Napoleon but that were scorned by the intelligentsia (see Mirzoeff 1995, 74ff.).

In Britain, Bouilly's play was treated as good entertainment, especially the silent signing performance of the actress playing Solar, called "Julio" in one version and "Theodore" in another. The lack of speech was equated with innocence. The prologue ends:

> Think not, we mean, in decency's neglect,
> To sport with frailty, and to mock defect;
> To bid mean souls with selfish triumph see
> Two wants, at least, from which themselves are free.

> The Sage yet lives whose toils immortal shew,
> What human powers without these aids can do.
> Taught by commanding genius to restrain
> Their causeless pride—who hear and speak in vain.
> To prove that pertness wisely had resign'd
> Her fluent utterance for a fluent mind;
> And chang'd for ears, with folly's jargon fraught,
> The keener sense of uncorrupted thought. (Bouilly 1801b)

People who were deaf, thus, were set apart as being uncorrupted by speech and hearing but possessing keen minds capable of effective education. The appeals to Christian charity not to "mock defect" signaled the presence of a new age of benevolence (compare Lane 1992). The triumph of the hearing educator over the barriers of deafness was embodied in the oft-quoted response in Bouilly's play of Theodore to the question Who is the greatest genius that France has ever produced? He writes the following reply: "Science would decide for D'Alembert, and Nature say, Buffon; Wit and Taste present Voltaire; and Sentiment pleads for Rousseau; but Genius and Humanity cry out for De l'Epée; and him I call the greatest of all human creatures" (Bouilly 1801b, 45).

But, lest all this French seriousness oppress the nonrevolutionary Britons, the English version ended with the actress who had played Solar coming forward with the following epilogue, an addition not in the original French play:

> Here's Dumby come to speak—'twas ten to one
> That I had talked before the play was done.
> Of all authors, he is far most cunning
> Who can ensure a woman's tongue from running.
> Speech is our nature—If I err convict me—
> What bachelor so rude to contradict me? (Bouilly 1801b, 82)

The English version ended with laughter as if to assure the audience that the play in no way threatened their "normality" or the status quo. But public consciousness about the education of people who were deaf and the viability of sign language as a medium of education and communication was raised. The public fascination with the education of deaf people that had been raised by Defoe early in the eighteenth century was rekindled at the beginning of the nineteenth century by Bouilly's play and would be stirred further by Dickens later in the century.

The Man and the Myth: The Influence of l'Epée on the Development of Deaf Education in Britain

L'Epée's work not only entertained London's theatergoers but also stirred the rising tide of charity and benevolence. Braidwood's appeals in *Scots Magazine* for financial support to enable parents to have their children educated had failed as had his appeal for "young men of genius" to come forward to be trained as teachers. Possibly, the time was not yet right to appeal to the growing charitable orientations of the wealthy, and possibly, Braidwood needed the overt support of the church. But Braidwood had been prepared to teach students who were poor and deaf as well as to train teachers. Aware of the work of l'Epée in Paris, Francis Green, Charles Green's father, agitated to get education for students who were poor and deaf established in England. In 1783, he wrote:

> It is much regretted, that since the time Messrs. Braidwood began to practice this ingenious method, these gentlemen have been under the mortifying and cruel necessity of refusing the charge and instruction, as I understand, of upwards of *an hundred* (chiefly *deaf* persons). Although they have with *humanity*, *benevolence*, and *generosity*, maintained and taught several children of indigent parents *gratis*, yet that violence have they been obliged to do to their inclinations, for the following good reasons: First, it would have been eventually deceiving themselves, as well as their pupils and friends; *labouring without thorough effect*, consequently bringing into contempt and disuse a method, which with no small labor and assiduity they have brought to a great degree of perfection, were they (*themselves*) to pretend to instruct more than a certain number at a time; their joint attention and tuition cannot (I think) be applied to many more than *twenty*, at once, with full effect.
>
> Secondly, a necessary and laudable regard to their own family forbade their undertaking what must be an insupportable burthen [sic] to any single family; for many of the parents of such objects were incapable even of reimbursing the necessary expenses of maintenance, &c. . . . (Green 1783; Green's italics)

In the spirit of charity, Green put forward a plan for a fund that would be administered by a governor and directors for the establishment of a school for students who were poor and deaf. L'Epée was aware of the plan and expressed anxiety about it because he understood the method used by the Braidwoods to be similar to that of the German oralist Heineke (he was wrong). The plan came to nothing. But the center of deaf education in Britain did shift from Edinburgh to London. In 1783, the King made £100 per annum available to Braidwood to establish his school in London, and so, in the same year, the school moved to Grove House in Hackney outside London. In the following year, another nephew of Thomas Braidwood, Joseph Watson, began to teach at the academy under the instruction of Thomas and John Braidwood.

The Development of Schooling for Students Who Were Poor and Deaf in Britain

In Britain, the teaching of students who were deaf was, like schooling in general, on the verge of entering a new phase as education spread beyond the privileged classes. In France beginning from 1771, l'Epée taught his pupils in his father's house, but by the end of the century, a separate public institution had been established. The same process was at work in London. Eight years after the Braidwoods moved to Hackney, the Reverend John Townsend, minister to the congregational church in Jamaica Row in Bermondsey in South London was approached by Mrs. Creasy, a member of his congregation:

> In his ministerial relation, Mr Townsend became acquainted with a lady, whose son was deaf and dumb, and who had been a pupil of Mr. Braidwood's almost ten years. The youth evinced an intellectual capacity which caused delight and surprise to the good pastor, who was astonished at the facility and accuracy, with which ideas were received and communicated. Mrs. C., the lady referred to, sympathising with those mothers whose circumstances precluded their incurring the expense of 1500£., (which was the sum paid by herself) pleaded the cause of those afflicted and destitute outcasts of society, until Mr. T. entered into her feelings of commiseration, and decided with her on the *necessity* and *practicability* of having a charitable Institution for the deaf and dumb children of the poor.
>
> On the Sabbath day, June 1st, 1792, were commenced the subscriptions, which were to receive additions little calculated on, by the small band who gave their first offering to induce their excellent pastor to begin this noble work of mercy. Three friends contributed one guinea each; Mr Townsend gave the fourth. (Townsend 1831, 36–37; Townsend's italics)

Townsend took the cause to heart and worked tirelessly to enlist support. Most vital was the support of the philanthropist Henry Thornton and of the Anglican Minister of Bermondsey, the Reverend Henry Cox Mason.

After meeting the deaf son of one of his congregants, the Reverend John Townsend worked tirelessly with the Reverend Henry Cox Mason to raise money for an institution for poverty-stricken deaf children.

At a time when religious differences were often bitterly felt, especially between the established church and dissenters, Townsend succeeded in securing the cooperation of both dissenter and churchman, clergy and laity, in the establishment of a school. Joseph Watson, Thomas Braidwood's nephew, read the leaflets circulated by the Reverends Townsend and Mason and offered his services as teacher at the proposed school. His offer was soon accepted.

On Thursday, 30 August 1792, at 6.30 P.M., a meeting was held in the Paul's Head Tavern in Bermondsey "for the Purpose of Establishing in Bermondsey an Asylum for the Support and Education of the Deaf and Dumb Children of the Poor." Braidwood's school for the wealthy remained an academy; however, the newly established school for students who were poor and deaf—a move toward mass education—was an asylum, oriented in large part toward the moral management of the "impotent poor."

As schools for the deaf rapidly emerged throughout Britain, Europe, America, and the British colonies in the nineteenth century, the relationship between developments in France and those in Britain was far from straightforward. Two distinct ideological orientations were at work: the missionary zeal of the British and the increasingly medical orientation of the French. In Britain, where imperial rather than revolutionary sentiments dominated the dawning of the nineteenth century, deaf education became, above all, a mission. Medicine would not dominate the British educational process for some time, in contrast to France, but it would do so eventually. In France, reason, above all, was reorganizing the cosmos. Humanity was being firmly diagnosed, classified, rationalized, demystified, and institutionalized. In this process, medicine was to play a major role as the clinical gaze absorbed not only those labeled insane but also, among others, those who were deaf. In 1800, as if to herald the dramatically disabling qualities of the century that was dawning, l'abbé Roch-Ambroise-Cucurron Sicard (1742–1822), l'Epée's successor as head of the Paris school, appointed a young surgeon, Jean-Marc Itard, as resident physician at the school (see Lane 1988, 126).

The Clinical Gaze on the Deaf Body

True to the contemporary development of "scientific" medicine, the clinical gaze on deafness was directed to the physical body, more specifically, to knowledge gained from cadavers (Foucault 1975, 196). The rush for bodies at the end of the eighteenth century and the ready availability of guillotined heads in France aided surgeons in identifying most features of the middle and inner ear by the end of the eighteenth century. The surgical treatment of the ear was developing, particularly in France, Germany, and Britain. Surgeons used the eustachian catheter in attempts to clear blockages that could affect hearing, and they carried out early mastoid operations. At the turn of the nineteenth century in Britain, Astley Cooper became well known for his operations in which he punctured the tympanic membrane and for the partial return of hearing in his patients that was claimed to result from the operation. He was awarded a medal in 1802 for his account of twenty such cases. However, this operation was only temporarily successful as the tympanic membrane would invariably grow back. The search for medical cures for deafness continued apace, focusing not on the total individual but on the manipulation of the person's anatomy, the "pathological" body. The experiments of surgeons such as Saunders, Cooper, and Curtis in Britain; Itard and Deleau in France; Hendrisksz and Guyot in Holland; and Himley in Germany paved the way for greater professionalization of aural surgery, which paralleled the moves to professionalism in other areas of medicine and beyond.[19]

The relationship between the educational and medical appropriation of people who were deaf and of deafness was complex. In Britain and in America, an overtly religious mission to save souls as well as to feed and clothe needy bodies dominated the education of children who were poor and deaf and kept in check the experimental surgeons, who had little concern for souls and a fervent need for bodies—alive or dead. For the surgeons seeking cures, the attitudes of these pious missionaries were frustrating because surgeons saw the educational process as an integral part of the broader medical process, the treatment of a pathological condition that was embodied in a pathological individual. Medical treatises on the ear almost invariably contained sections on deaf education.[20]

In France, where the spirit of the philosophers dominated educational processes (see Saisselin 1995, 395–97), the medical experimentation of the early nineteenth century was much more welcome as a valid and kindred aspect of the search for a philosophical-scientific understanding of humanity. The pedagogical gaze was at the same time a clinical gaze.

Sign Language, the Clinical Gaze, and the Consolidation of l'Epée's Mission in France

In Catholic, postrevolutionary France, although a clear priority was to provide people who were poor and deaf with access to the church, the focus of the education for poor people was more overtly intellectual than in Britain. Poor people were the heroes of the hour, and the potential creativity of all citizens was acknowledged. Intellectuals and artists who were deaf emerged, and soon, the schools were absorbing teachers who were deaf. Four decades earlier than in Britain, an educated deaf community emerged to add its voice to debates about the education and general treatment of deaf people.

But despite the public prominence of deaf intellectuals such as Berthier, Massieu, and Clerc as well as of an increasing band of deaf painters and sculptors (see Mirzoeff 1995), the Paris school for the deaf was, in the last decade of the eighteenth century and the first two decades of the nineteenth century, a place of intense contradictions. Although its brilliant deaf pupils were publicly hailed for their intellectual and artistic achievements, in general, people who were deaf constantly were linked conceptually with children in need of care, with the "savages" of the emerging colonies, and with the mad. In fact, "the deaf and the insane were dealt with by the same department of the Ministry of the Interior throughout the nineteenth century. The stigma of deafness was doubled by that of madness" (Mirzoeff 1995, 98).

The Paris school for the deaf walled in its students. Sometimes, pupils would try to escape, even by digging under the wall. On capture, one escapee in 1805 was sent to a lunatic asylum. The school was part of the confinement of unreason, and behind its walls, the medicalization of deafness dramatically developed. The philosophical concerns of the eighteenth century gave way to medical concerns as deafness became a pathological "sickness," with "sign language . . . less of a philosophical problem than a symptom" (64). "The asylum and the Institute sought to contain and control the margins of rationality, not to set them loose" (66).

Deafness was defined as a pathological condition, and for two decades, the Paris school physician, Itard, set out to find a cure. The school became his laboratory; the students, his "guinea pigs" in aural surgery. For the first decade, Itard's attentions were focused on the much publicized wild boy of Aveyron, but when his attempts to teach the boy to speak failed, he turned his attentions to the pupils.[21] He applied electric shocks to ears; placed leeches and white-hot metal on pupils' necks; pierced eardrums; fractured skulls; inserted probes in pupils' eustachian tubes; and applied blistering agents to necks, ears, and faces. Pain, infection, and even death resulted (Lane 1988, 132–36). Depressed by his failures, Itard turned to trying to teach the students to speak. He then turned to teaching the pupils to hear, never giving up on his conviction that, apart from with the congenitally deaf, cures could be found.

Alongside Itard's medical orientation to deafness was the evolutionist orientation of Joseph Marie, Baron De Gérando (1772–1842), director of the Paris Institute from 1820:

> Joseph Marie, Baron De Gérando, philosopher, administrator, historian, and philanthropist, conducted philanthropy the way generals wage war: it was organized, it was imposed by force, it was self-righteous. He conducted it in external affairs, where the "beneficiaries" called it imperialism, and he conducted it in internal affairs, where the "beneficiaries" called it paternalism. These are two sides of the same coin. (Lane 1988, 144)

De Gérando embodied the ideal of the imperial nineteenth-century scientist philosopher. His assumed intellectual and cultural superiority was constantly constructed through not only the creation of inferior others but also the creation of a dependence that these lesser beings had on himself and those of his own kind. Those who were poor, who were non-Western, or who were deaf were all pictured in his voluminous writings as being similar: childlike, uncultured, evolutionarily inferior, mentally inferior, and linguistically inferior. They all needed the superior philanthropist, the paternal guidance that only the cultured, educated segment of Western civilization could provide. He regarded sign language as primitive and universal; saw the system of methodological signs as having provided an initial path to learning; regarded the search for medical cures for deafness as being of prime importance; and promoted oralism as the path to learning beyond the limitations of signing. He looked to the philosophy of Locke to support his educational orientations but regarded people who were deaf as qualitatively distinct from "normal" human beings, claiming that they, as deaf people, did not have the potential to achieve "normal" intellectual or artistic creativity (see De Gérando 1827b, 594).

De Gérando is often represented as the destroyer of all that l'Epée and Sicard had achieved. This interpretation of history results essentially from the simplistic representation of the history of the education of deaf people as a battle between manualists and oralists. De Gérando certainly moved against the spirit of the majority of staff members and students in the institute to establish in Paris a predominantly oralist education for people who were deaf and to disenfranchise teachers who were deaf. But De Gérando, in fact, built on the benevolence and educational aspirations of his predecessors. L'Epée and Sicard had both taught articulation and had both regarded sign language, especially natural sign language, as being of limited value. De Gérando moved not against the tradition of his predecessors but against the aspirations and orientations of his deaf and hearing contemporaries such as Berthier and Bébian in the institute. What happened was that the traditions of the institute were reinterpreted through imperialist lenses worn, not by a priest, but by a former soldier, a "worldly" gentleman scholar of the nineteenth century.

Despite the emergence of myths to the contrary, l'Epée and Sicard, in fact, also regarded people who were deaf as being intrinsically incapable of the same achievements as hearing people and attributed all the achievements of their pupils to the pupils' access to the scientific methods of their teachers, including the sign language developed by l'Epée and built on by Sicard. Together, l'Epée and Sicard not only carried out the "great confinement" of people who were deaf but also constructed them as a unitary category, distinct from and other than ordinary, "normal" human beings, a category of humanity who, by 1833, was described as "suffering" from a pathological medical condition, *surdi-mutité*, or "deaf-mutism."

Itard had been appointed by Sicard and firmly supported by De Gérando. The pedagogical gaze that isolated and singularized "the deaf" was reinforced by the clinical gaze that defined them as clinically pathological. Coupled with the clinical gaze was the imperial gaze of De Gérando, defining deaf people not only as pathological but also as culturally inferior, removed from postrevolutionary France by countless generations of evolutionary development. In 1853, Itard's successor, Prosper Ménière wrote:

> The deaf believe that they are our equals in all respects. We should be generous and not destroy that illusion. But whatever they believe, deafness is an infirmity and we should repair it whether the person who has it is disturbed by it or not. (quoted Mirzoeff 1995, 98).

The Paris school for the deaf was an agency through which the unitary and pathological character of deaf people was culturally constructed. As Didier Séguillon has shown, the entire routine of the Paris school through the nineteenth and first half of the twentieth centuries was medically coordinated as the clinical gaze sought to identify and ameliorate physical and behavioral "pathologies." "Gymnastics plays a key role. . . . The body of the deaf pupil is put under daily medical watch. Hydrotherapy treatments are prescribed to all pupils" (Séguillon 1996, 261). From 1889, with the pure oral method prescribed as the only method to be used, sign language was forbidden. "Demutisation is described as an hygienic factor and relies on a special breathing education in order to improve the child's voice" (265). It is not until after 1968 that "the influence of medicine weakens" (271).

In Britain, similar processes were at work but were expressed in a distinctly British way. They were still linked to Wallis through Henry Baker and the Braidwoods, heirs to the British "enlightenment" of the seventeenth century, rather than to the French Enlightenment of the eighteenth century. These educators were vehemently Protestant rather than Catholic, and in their Protestantism, they were concerned, above all, with the moral management rather than the medical transformation of their pupils. Although l'Epée's work in France was known by those who were involved in the development of education for students in Britain who were poor and deaf, the pedagogies that developed by no means reflected developments in France.

Yet despite these differences, by the beginning of the nineteenth century, educational and medical developments throughout the Western world were all expressions of an essentially uniform orientation toward humanity, a view of humanity as essentially "normal," surrounded on the edges, on the margins, by the "pathological" foils to this normality.

Educational and medical developments were interweaving expressions of an ideological practice by which the pathological was being separated out from the former coalescence of humanity. Through its charitable and essentially imperial orientation toward those in need of salvation—be they Indians, Chinese, Africans, or deaf people, even the missionary zeal that encompassed educational developments in Britain and, to a slightly less degree, those in America served to construct the concept that people who were deaf were marginal, were different, were an "other."

Notes

1. Gottfried Wilhelm Leibnitz (1646–1716) was a German philosopher and mathematician. He provided a view of innate abilities and knowledge that was different from the view of his contemporary, Locke. Sensory impairment intrigued Leibnitz, especially the question How can comprehension occur if things are not experienced or sensed? Locke's ideas were closely linked to Aristotle's whereas those of Leibnitz were linked to Plato's. Leibnitz's philosophical work on innate ideas and the nature of language exerted an important influence on developments in deaf education.

2. Daniel Defoe is best known today as the author of the novels *Robinson Crusoe* and *Moll Flanders*.

3. In 1728, for example, Defoe and Henry Baker (Baker using the pseudonym Henry Stonecastle) founded the *Universal Spectator and Weekly Journal*.

4. This period is also when philosophers become "scientists," when "science" refers to specialized branches of study, and when "philosophy" becomes the generalization of those truths established by "science" (*Oxford English Dictionary* 1969, vol. 14, s.v. "entry").

5. The papers of Henry Baker later came into the possession of Thomas Arnold of Northampton, one of the most important influences on the development of oralism in Britain in the late 1900s (see chapter 7 of this volume). The papers are currently in the Farrar Collection of the John Rylands Library of the University of Manchester in Deansgate, Manchester, United Kingdom.

6. See correspondence (Baker Letters) for 1738 between Henry Baker and Thomas Walls.

7. The manual alphabet used by Wallis was reproduced by Defoe in his book of the deaf soothsayer Duncan Cambell (Defoe 1720), where Defoe also mentions the work of Wallis.

8. See, for example, *A Brief Historical Sketch* (1835).

9. A friendship between Charles Sheriff and Garrick appears to have ensued. Murphy Arthur (Arthur 1801, 180–86) describes the friendship between Mr. Sheriff, a pupil of Braidwood's who became a well-known painter, and Garrick. Arthur reports that Sheriff could read and write well, but his speech was incom-

prehensible. He adds that Sheriff could repeat Garrick's performance in signs. In about 1773, when asked how he could understand Garrick, he replied, "His face is his language" (Arthur 1801, 186).

10. See Johnson (1775); Johnson and Boswell (1924) in which Johnson comments on Braidwood's school on pages 147–49 and Boswell remarks on the same visit on page 430; Monboddo (1773) where, in book 1, chapter 14 "That Articulation is not Natural to Man" (p. 171ff.), he discusses the teaching of the deaf people to speak and, in particular, comments on his personal experiences at Braidwood's academy in Edinburgh; and Pennant (1774, 256–8) for a description of Braidwood Academy.

11. John Goodricke (1764–1786) received his first education at The Braidwood Academy in Edinburgh and was reported as having "by the assistance of Mr Braidwood, . . . made surprising proficiency, becoming a very tolerable classic, and an excellent mathematician" (quoted in Lang and Meath-Lang 1995, 150). He was elected a fellow of the Royal Society at the age of twenty-one and received the prestigious Copley Medal for his methodical observations of the changing qualities of key stars. He died two weeks after his election to the Royal Society. See Lang and Meath-Lang (1995).

12. The letter is somewhat confusing because the writer, a Thomas Jefferson, claims to have met Bolling in 1840. Thomas Bolling died in 1836. Either the writer's memory was vague about dates or he actually met William Bolling, the nephew of Thomas Bolling, who had been educated in America by John Braidwood, Thomas Braidwood's grandson. Jefferson may have been told by William that he had been educated by Mr. Braidwood *of* Edinburgh, not *at* Edinburgh.

13. On 21 May, 1662, Wallis had brought Daniel Whaley before the Royal Society. Wallis recalls,

> [Whaley] did in the presence of the society (to the great satisfaction of the Company) pronounce very distinctly enough such words as were by the Company proposed to him, and though not altogether in the usual Tone or Accent, yet so as easily to be understood. (Whaley to Oldenburg, July 11, 1670, quoted in Scott 1938, 85)

14. See Lane (1988) and, for an excellent discussion of the philosophical issues associated with l'Epée's work, see Mirzoeff (1995).

15. Although Lane (1988) remains a vital and valuable source for information on l'Epée, numerous additional sources are available, as our own cataloging of the Farrar Collection in the John Rylands Library in Deansgate, Manchester, United Kingdom, has shown. The interpretation in this text is derived from these primary sources.

16. As we have already indicated, l'Epée was particularly influenced by the philosophy of Condillac, the main interpreter of Locke in mid-eighteenth-century France. L'Epée therefore saw the deaf pupil as a tabula rasa whose intellect could be developed through the sense of sight, particularly, through the language of methodological signs, which provided access not only to language but also to philosophical language.

17. Ferdinand Berthier, the greatest deaf intellectual to come out of the Paris institution wrote: "Son génie, planant sur la sphère des possibilités, a déjà saisi ce qui échappe aux regards vulgaires, et le globe entier retenria bientôt des succès inouis obtenus par ce grand homme à l'aide de la mimique, cette langue universelle vainement cherchée par les philosophes et par les savants de tous les siècles et de tous les pays" (Berthier circa 1870, 5).

18. See Bouilly (1801a, 1801b, 1802, 1803). The 1803 edition, in fact, claims to be a translation by Benjamin Thompson from German of a play by Augustus von Kotzebue. No mention is made either of von Kotzebue's play being a translation of that by Bouilly or of the English translation of 1801.

19. For discussions of the early history of aural surgery, see Wilde (1853), Hartmann (1881), and Kerr Love (1896). For an example of claims to the curability of deafness by an influential surgeon in the first half of the nineteenth century, see Curtis (1829, 1836, 1846), and for a discussion of such claims, see Day (1835). For a balanced critique of Curtis's work and claims, see Wilde (1853, 36ff.). An illustration of the approach to aural surgery in the late-seventeenth and early eighteenth centuries can be found in Du Verney (1737).

20. See, for example, Wilde (1853) and Curtis (1829).

21. For discussion of this much publicized case, see Itard (1817, 1932) and Lane (1976).

5

The "Great Confinement" of Deaf People through Education in the Nineteenth Century

[W]e have the historical testimony of the British schools, forcibly summed up by Professor Baker, as follows, in correcting an error into which I had fallen:

"You are wrong," says he, "in considering the English system as being based on articulation. I will go further, and state that, as a system, it never was based on articulation . . .

". . . In the earliest days of the institution at Birmingham . . . articulation was the exception . . . at present in [the London institution] . . . articulation is by no means the exclusive vehicle of instruction. . . .

"At . . . Edinburgh, . . . articulation . . . early gave way to means more universally applicable. Of the other institutions in these isles, (about twenty,) not one has adopted articulation, except in the cases of those pupils who could hear a little, or who had become deaf after they had acquired speech."

—Edward Miner Gallaudet quoting Charles Baker (Gallaudet 1867, 49–50)

The nineteenth century was a time of radical educational change throughout the Western world and its colonies. The education of the masses and not of only the privileged few became an essential ideological practice as a democratic polity asserted its control over the coordination of newly industrialized economies. Here were the beginnings of those normalizing strategies that we discussed in part one. To quote Foucault, the school, like other disciplinary institutions

> . . . traces the limit that will define difference in relation to all other differences, the external frontier of the abnormal. . . .The perpetual penalty that traverses all points and supervises every instant in the disciplinary institutions compares, differentiates, hierarchizes, homogenizes, excludes. In short, it normalizes. (Foucault 1979, 183)

Through the nineteenth century, the practice to contain children who were poor and deaf in asylums for the purpose of their education was even more complex as an ideological practice because, although it was overtly oriented toward normalization, this containment was designed in ways that, like the special schools discussed in chapter 2, never allowed for complete normalization. Rather, through apparent normalizing strategies, it ensured the opposite—the ongoing cultural construction of deaf people as "the pathological," as "disabled."

The expansion or rapid development of schools for the deaf, which were usually referred to as "asylums" or "institutions," radically transformed the general orientation toward deaf people and toward their treatment. Unlike the children of wealthy parents, the children of poor parents were dependent and vulnerable. Their bodies and souls were free game. To varying degrees depending on the national, religious, and cultural context, missionaries and surgeons became as much a part of their education as the teachers themselves. In the process, their otherness was culturally constructed in tune with the dominant ideologies of the nineteenth century. Ideological commitment to reason; to scientism; to the imperial domination of those deemed less "civilized," less human, abnormal; and to the achievement of social honor through the performance of good works all influenced the lives of deaf people.

In this chapter, we examine the philosophical and pedagogical developments that took place in the education of people who were deaf through the nineteenth century. Initially, we will examine the way the large-scale, institutionalized education of deaf people developed in Britain and America. In the previous chapter, we have already commented on events in France. Although equally important developments occurred throughout the rest of Europe and beyond, the case studies described here lay the ground for understanding the way relatively idiosyncratic national developments in the first half of the nineteenth century gave way, by the end of the century, to relative uniformity throughout the Western world. These national developments were not independent of one another but, rather, were formed and transformed in response not only to national pressures but also to international pressures.

In the process, we will also question many of the interpretations of the history of deaf education that have become virtually sacred writ in the field of deaf studies: interpretations about manualism and oralism, the so-called English System, the Milan Congress, the combined system, and the varied use of signing. The French and American stories have been told many times, but the British story tends to have been caricatured because of scant research. Basing her conclusions on available secondary sources, Crickmore states that "by the mid-19th century, in Britain, the oral German method had been almost totally overcome by the use of the manual French Method for instructing the deaf students" (Crickmore 1995, 51). Britain certainly had not adopted the "German method" and, as we shall show, did not experience a change from oralism to some sort of manualism through the nineteenth century. British schools certainly did not adopt the "French method."[1] We have already established that Britain's so-called oralist heritage attributed to Wallis, Henry Baker, and Thomas Braidwood was, in fact, far from oralist in method or orientation. What we will show is that developments through the nineteenth century were distinctly British, that they can be understood in terms of the teaching traditions outlined in the previous two chapters, and that if Britain imported any methods from continental Europe, it did not occur until the late-nineteenth century when British oralists claimed to be using "the German method." Of equal significance in the late-nineteenth century was the introduction of "the combined method" from America. But through the first three-quarters of the nineteenth century, developments were distinctly British.

Language, Literacy, and the Education of the Masses

The education of the masses rather than just the privileged was associated above all with the spread of literacy, while at the same time aiding the saving of souls by providing access to the word of God through the Bible. Literacy levels became the hallmarks of progress at home and of the spread of Western "civilization" abroad. But literacy did not mean merely knowledge of a language's written form; it meant literacy in particular languages, in the languages of rational administration and rational intellectual endeavor. Literacy meant literacy in a Western language, and throughout vast areas of the globe, that language was English.

For example, although subjects of the British Empire in India spoke and wrote languages that had been vehicles for the transmission of knowledge for millennia, the British Empire imposed English as the language of education, often with the active support of Indian intellectuals such as Ramohan Roy.[2] British educators were convinced that English was the perfect vehicle for the transmission and development of scientific thought. English was assumed to be conceptually and structurally superior, at least by the British, to all other languages but, particularly, to the languages of minorities at home and abroad. Whether the devaluation was of Hindi, of Bengali, of Welsh, of Gaelic, or of natural sign languages, all these linguistic minorities at home and abroad suffered the same linguistic imperialism. But in the case of deaf people, the linguistic imperialism was compounded by discrimination against "the disabled."

Rounding Up the Deaf: Deaf Education in Britain in the First Half of the Nineteenth Century

In the atmosphere of evangelical fervor and missionary zeal that gripped Protestant Britain in the nineteenth century, people who were poor and deaf provided wealthy people who were in the pursuit of social honor and devout people who were seeking religious worth the opportunity to exercise charity. When the Asylum for the Support and Education of the Deaf and Dumb Children of the Poor was founded in Bermondsey in London on 14 November 1792 and the first election took place, four children were admitted along with two more in the course of the year.[3] As would happen so often in the future, many deaf children and their parents went away disappointed. At each half-yearly election, a committee examined candidates and determined who should be admitted. Only a small number of those seeking admission were accepted mainly because the school could not afford to admit more:

> so melancholy were the lists of candidates at the half yearly admissions, that the public began to see the extent of a malady till then almost unknown. In some families the whole number of children were deaf and dumb, in others *half* were thus afflicted; cases were numerous of five out of six, and it was

> ascertained that in twenty families, containing one hundred and fifty-five children, there were no fewer than seventy-eight deaf and dumb. (Townsend 1831, 39; Townsend's italics)

Financial support for the school increased but so did the applications. Townsend and Mason worked tirelessly to raise more support, and although the Reverend Mason died in February 1804, three years later, on 11 July 1807, the Duke of Gloucester laid the first stone of a new building in the Old Kent Road. On that stone was the following inscription:

> A SOCIETY TO PROVIDE EDUCATION FOR THE DEAF AND DUMB CHILDREN OF INDIGENT PARENTS, WAS FIRST PROJECTED AND ESTABLISHED IN LONDON, A.D. 1792, BY THE REV. JOHN TOWNSEND AND THE REV. HENRY COX MASON. AND THIS FIRST STONE OF A NEW ASYLUM, BUILT BY VOLUNTARY CONTRIBUTIONS, WAS LAID ON THE 11TH OF JULY, IN THE YEAR OF OUR LORD 1807, AND THE 47TH OF THE REIGN OF KING GEORGE III, BY HIS MAJESTY'S NEPHEW, HIS ROYAL HIGHNESS PRINCE WILLIAM, DUKE OF GLOUCESTER. (see Townsend 1831, 40)

By 1809, the building was complete and seventy pupils moved in. Originally designed for 150 pupils, it was enlarged to receive 180 and again to receive 200. Townsend tirelessly toured the country preaching to raise money, appealing to people's humanity and sense of charity.

This time was an era during which charity became an honorable activity, a sign of one's nobility of spirit as well as of one's honor and success. Deaf people were seen as objects of pity, in need of charity. But what made contributing to the school particularly satisfying to these benefactors was the fact that the school achieved results that helped to improve the quality of life and to achieve what had formerly been thought impossible. So demonstrations of the achievements of the pupils to existing and prospective benefactors were a vital aspect of raising funds. The demonstrations were no longer for the Royal Society; the focus, no longer philosophical. Rather, the demonstrations were for the upper and middle classes, those with money to give to a worthy cause. At these demonstrations, selected scholars not only demonstrated their scholastic achievements but also performed for the gatherings by speaking. Teaching deaf people to speak remained a vital drawing card. The public still wanted miracles:

> Several of the scholars were introduced to the company, after dinner, to whom they showed their writing, ciphering, and exercise books, and answered such questions as were put to them, both by writing and speaking.

Townsend and Mason's fund-raising efforts led to the establishment of the Old Kent Road school in London.

> Afterwards three of them recited verses to the company, who seemed much pleased, and to understand them perfectly, for I observed that they applauded very much when the last speaker concluded. (Letter to Dr. Watson by a former pupil, quoted in Townsend 1831, 47)

The belief that deaf people could be educated was no longer an issue, though the methods used to achieve those ends were to excite continual controversy.

The teaching of the catechism was central to the educational goals of all the schools that sprang up throughout Britain. Among the wealthy, literacy was a mark of their cultivated lifestyle, but when it was provided for the poor, it was justified as providing access to the New Testament, the path to salvation. Education was justified ideologically by means of the ideology of equality. However, the potential contradiction wherein the poor working class, who, by definition, were "uncultured," were achieving culture through literacy was deflected by a focus on the education of poor people as a mission to save souls, like the education of the "savages" of the New World with whom "the deaf" were often equated.

The education of wealthy people who were deaf remained something of a private enterprise in which heads of schools were provided with the opportunity to take private pupils. At the meeting in the Paul's Head Tavern on Thursday, 30 August 1792, Joseph Watson's appointment as teacher was confirmed, and the group decided that Watson should be allowed £21/10/- per annum for each child, in return for which he would be responsible for their education; for finding them lodging and sustenance; and for pens, ink, paper, and all necessary books.[4] The group also determined that he be allowed no more than eight private pupils at any one time. These pupils were known as "parlor pupils."

Although the education of the wealthy parlor pupils often involved concentration on the teaching of speech, the education of the pupils who were poor involved little if any speech training but proceeded through sign language and fingerspelling, usually taught by deaf teachers. As outlined above, wealthy people were equated with culture; poor people, with nature, particularly, people who were deaf and poor, whose natural sign language was a mark of their uncultured, uncivilized natural qualities.

The fact that wealthy students were taught to speak, however, did not mean that these parlor pupils were not educated also through the medium of natural sign language.[5] Natural sign language was used as a medium of communication throughout the schools, as it had been at least since Wallis. The deaf teacher and evangelist Mathew Burns had been a parlor pupil under Joseph Watson in the early days of the Old Kent Road school, and although he could speak, he was a fluent signer and used natural sign language as the medium of instruction in his own schools in Edinburgh, Aberdeen, and Bristol as well as later as in his role as an influential missioner to adult deaf people. Francis Maginn, who would play a vital role in the development of the British Deaf and Dumb Association in the late-nineteenth century and who fought hard to establish the combined system in Britain as well as to train and employ deaf teachers, had also been a parlor pupil at the Old Kent Road school under Watson.[6]

The training of teachers and the spread of schools for deaf students was made all the more practicable with the publication of Watson's book, *Instruction of the Deaf and Dumb; or a Theoretical and Practical View of the Means by Which They are Taught to Speak and Understand a Language; Containing Hints for the Correction of Impediments in Speech: together with a Vocabulary Illustrated by Numerous*

Joseph Watson, who had been trained by Thomas Braidwood and who taught at Braidwood's school, was the first teacher and principal at the Old Kent Road school.

Copperplates, representing the most common Objects necessary to be named by Beginners (Watson 1809). In this vital set of books, Watson not only outlined the philosophical principles on which his teaching was based and the practical way in which teaching should proceed but also provided a large illustrated vocabulary for use both in school and by parents prior to formal schooling. He advocated that parents teach elementary reading and writing by way of the picture vocabulary:

> The plates of our vocabulary . . . present a field sufficiently amusing and instructive for the employment of such young learners, under maternal guidance, even if they do nothing more than learn to distinguish the objects they represent, by pointing them out. But I recommend the earliest possible use of the pen, or rather, the slate and pencil, by which, and by the manual alphabet, the names of these objects may be learnt to be correctly spelt. (Watson 1809, 133)

Watson recognized the vital importance of visual experience in the education of deaf children and, thus, provided a rich visual experience as a foundation on which the teacher could teach a vocabulary both tangible and abstract. Those vibrant pictures became the basis for unlimited stories and for discussions about verbs, adverbs, and adjectives—movements and qualities that are often difficult to convey unless they are tangibly linked to visual experience.

Watson taught in the same manner as that described for Henry Baker and the Braidwoods in which the students built a vocabulary and grammatical correctness in a grammatical knowledge of English by copying

Watson's book on deaf education also included a large set of illustrations, which facilitated language development.

questions and replies and then were engaged by masters in conversation on these matters. The subject matter was designed to provide knowledge of a range of subjects—religion, geography, general knowledge, science, and so on (Watson 1809, 1820). When the reply needed to be in English, the students used writing or fingerspelling, unless they were parlor pupils, who might use articulation.

In the first half of the nineteenth century, the education of deaf students began to expand and diversify as schools were established throughout Britain and Ireland, employing many of the teachers trained by the Braidwoods or Watson. Despite the fact that some schools rejected articulation whereas others focused increasingly on articulation, the British approach to signing was fairly consistent. Educators did not attempt to formalize natural signing into a language that complied with hearing notions of grammatical language as the French were doing. The use of fingerspelling was very heavy, but all except the Birmingham school under Hopper and the schools in Belfast and Dublin in Ireland used the two-handed system rather than the one-handed system that was favored for the teaching of speech.[7] Signs were often equated with words and were used individually as frozen signs. As we shall explain in more detail in the next chapter, the conviction that education must be in and through written English and that the use of signing in any form was simply a necessary avenue to this goal, which was a dominant conviction in British schools, resulted in British Sign Language remaining closer to a natural language system than sign languages in France and the United States where sign languages were artificial, having been "developed" lexically and syntactically.

Education and the Cultural Construction of Deafness: The Clinical Gaze on Deaf People in Britain

> [A]lthough I admit that speech is a good and natural exercise for the lungs and voice, I have never discovered that it is requisite for health; nor that the pupils of an institution in which articulation is not taught have worse health than those of one where it is an object of attainment. I must therefore decide against giving up the time now bestowed on the acquisition of language and useful knowledge by my pupils, to devote it to the specious acquirement of articulation. (Charles Baker, quoted in Gallaudet 1867, 13)

In virtually all the English schools, the missionary orientation prevailed, with teachers taking an active role in the spiritual lives of local deaf communities. The influence of medical researchers on the schools was more muted than in France. In 1800, the year that Sicard appointed Itard at the Paris school, the committee of the newly established London school in Bermondsey (before its move to the Old Kent Road) resolved

> . . . that this Institution is established only for the purpose of instruction. It is the opinion of the Committee that they cannot permit the pupils received by them for education to be subjected to any medical treatment whatsoever in regard to their deafness while in the Asylum. (quoted in Beaver 1992, 46)

Prominent teachers such as Charles Baker (Doncaster) and Robert Kinniburgh (Edinburgh) exposed the futility of attempts to cure congenital deafness and opposed experimentation by surgeons such as Turnbull, who claimed to have cured pupils who had attended their schools (Wilde 1853, 55ff.).

Some surgeons did seek to reproduce the direct alliance between education and surgical experimentation that Itard's much publicized work embodied. Early in the century, John Harrison Curtis, the self-acclaimed "Aurist To Their Royal Highnesses The Duchess Of Kent [deaf] And The Duchess of Gloucester, And Director And Surgeon To The Institution" (Curtis 1846) railed against the orientation toward deaf education practiced by l'Epée and Sicard:[8]

> Their object was to provide a substitute for speech; they set out with the assumption, about which they appear never to have had the smallest doubt, that the deaf and dumb were without the remotest chance of possessing the faculties of hearing and speech . . . . (Curtis 1846, 37)

Curtis was mistaken about their attitude toward teaching speech but claimed that most deafness occurring after birth is curable and quoted Itard in support of his position. He was more cautious about criticizing his contemporaries at the London school, but he did criticize the process by which pupils were selected for admission, claiming in a letter to the London school in 1817 that an aurist be appointed to inspect all infants prior to admission and that admission be on medical grounds (43). In his favor, and in contrast to contemporaries such as Cooper and Itard, Curtis counseled caution in experimentation and opposed surgical treatment unless absolutely necessary. Curtis was, in fact, more in the tradition of the preceding century. He did not enter into the full spirit of the new age of medicine with its focus on anatomy and the development of technologies for the surgical manipulation of the physical body.[9]

So although able-bodied poor people who did not work were condemned, "disabled" poor people were ideal objects for missionary work. Deaf people were subjected, like those deemed insane, to contradictory treatment. Missioners and educators, often one and the same, reflected the moral therapy movement in their concern for uplifting deaf people spiritually and morally so they could take their places alongside the "normal" members of society.[10] Their confinement was a confinement oriented toward moral regeneration, which included the normalizing process of education. Normalization through discipline was the driving force. Like those who gathered the insane and "disabled" together in asylums, the teachers of deaf students in the asylums for poor and deaf people in Britain were concerned as much with the saving of souls as with education. Their cures came through the power of literacy, a literacy allowing access to the word of God.

But as we shall see in the next chapter, just as the moral therapy movement in the treatment of the insane gave way to more depersonalized, individuated, and overtly medical orientations toward the professional treatment of unreason, so too was the overt, religiously inspired benevolence of the early nineteenth century educators to give way to individuated, therapeutic treatment by professional teachers.

Unlike the situation in France, the surgeons did not use the schools as research hospitals but conducted their experiments elsewhere. Nonetheless, they constantly saw their experimentation as integral to the educational process. The complex interweaving of benevolence, education, and medical research at the beginning of the nineteenth century was embodied in the writing and work of the Quaker physician John Coakley Lettsom (1744–1815), the author of a popular three-volume publication titled *Hints Designed to Promote Beneficence, Temperance, and Medical Science* (Lettsom 1801). Section six dealt with "Hints Respecting the Support and Education of the Deaf and Dumb Children of the Poor" (95–115). Lettsom, who studied in London and on the continent, graduating with an M.D. from Leyden in 1769, became a Fellow of the Royal Society in 1771. He was a wealthy benefactor and philanthropist and was involved in the development of facilities for poor people and in the reform of prisons. He worked continuously as a medical practitioner until his death. In the same philanthropical spirit, the great surgeon William Wilde (1815–1876) who had studied aural and ophthalmic surgery in London, Vienna, and Berlin, founded St Mark's Ophthalmic Hospital in Dublin.[11] He provided free services to poor people with diseases of the eye or ear and became the medical officer for the school for the deaf in Dublin. His book *Practical Observations on Aural Surgery and the Nature and Treatment of Diseases of the Ear, with Illustrations* (Wilde 1853) contained not only a comprehensive history of the medical treatment of deafness up to the mid-nineteenth century but also a history of the education of the deaf. The extensive section on "Deaf-Dumbness" was later printed separately. These surgeons were not only overtly involved in the education of the deaf but also cast their clinical gaze through lenses of benevolence.

Deaf Education in Nineteenth-Century America

Developments in eighteenth- and early nineteenth-century Britain and France were the backdrop against which the education of deaf people was to develop in America. Again, a strong missionary focus took hold in the orientation toward the education of the deaf, a complex mix of British and French dispositions toward language and humanity:

> The pervasiveness of religion, whether manifested in varieties of orthodox or liberal Protestantism or, in a few notable instances, reformulated by deists, determined the reception of European ideas in America. (Kloppenberg 1995, 371)[12]

In early nineteenth-century America, religious piety, practical philosophy, and the exercise of democratic power, which were embodied in leaders like John Adams and Thomas Jefferson, combined in an atmosphere of overt egalitarianism. As discussed in chapter 2, this overtly religious atmosphere that was coupled with a moral commitment to the ideology of equality generated a discriminatory practice grounded in the assertion that people were indeed equal but that they were also different, which became the basis for ongoing inequalities determined by race, class, gender, and "ability." Baynton writes about the teachers of people who were deaf in mid-nineteenth-century America:

> They were apt to speak of their work as an adventure among a people so different from the hearing that to live among them was to explore a rich and profoundly mysterious world. Teaching deaf students was akin to "*missionary* work among unenlightened nations." It was, in short, a "high and momentous undertaking." (Baynton 1996, 71; Baynton's italics)

The cultural construction and disablement of "the deaf" in the United States followed a pattern not dissimilar from the basic trends outlined previously for Britain and France—the confinement, the stereotyping of deaf people, the paternalism—but interpreted through the distinct culture of postrevolutionary America.

In 1815, when schools for people who were poor and deaf were established in London, Birmingham, and Edinburgh, the Reverend Thomas Gallaudet arrived in Britain as a familiar expression of the new age. Religious, pious, and full of benevolence toward those less fortunate than himself, he condemned those who did not uphold the values that he and, by no means he alone, so righteously proclaimed. Like people in all ages and all places, he saw the values of his age and his culture as not only right but also self-evident. He was also in a hurry.

Gallaudet was on a mission on behalf of a group of benefactors that included the eminent surgeon Mason Cogswell of Hartford, Connectcut, to learn the latest techniques for educating deaf children so a school for deaf children could be established in America. His meetings with Watson in London, Braidwood in Birmingham, and Kinniburgh in Edinburgh did not yield the results he had hoped for. He claimed that they refused to reveal their teaching methods, but in reality, he was not prepared for a long apprenticeship as a teacher in one of the schools. At that time, teacher training involved learning through active participation in the teaching process over many years.

Teachers, including deaf teachers, were being trained in all institutions. As for revealing methods, Joseph Watson, six years earlier in 1809, had published his *Instruction of the Deaf and Dumb; or a Theoretical and Practical View of the Means by Which They are Taught to Speak and Understand a Language; Containing Hints for the Correction of Impediments in Speech: together with a Vocabulary Illustrated by Numerous Copperplates, representing the most common Objects necessary to be named by Beginners*. At the same time, John Braidwood was teaching deaf students in the United States in Virginia and would soon, in 1817, very successfully train the Reverend John Kirkpatrick to carry on the Braidwood family's method of educating deaf students. On 14 October 1815, John Braidwood's mother (Thomas Braidwood's daughter Isabella) wrote to him from London as follows:

> We were very much surprised and rather alarmed lately by the application of a Gallaydett [sic] from Connecticut, he informed your brother that he had been sent over by some gentlemen who wished to form an Institution for Deaf and Dumb and he wished to receive instruction in our art. Having flattered ourselves that you were long ere this established, we have felt much at a loss to acct [account] for this event, and trusting that you are in life and in the practice of your profession we have judged it proper to have no concern with him, but we have recommended his making application to you. (Braidwood Papers)

The Braidwoods were therefore concerned as to why Gallaudet had not sought John's services in America. Gallaudet wrote to Cogswell:

> The mother of Mr Braidwood who is in America, will be much obliged by any information you can give me respecting him. Do take some pains to do this. I wish to oblige her, and write all you know of him, be it good, bad or indifferent. (Braidwood Papers)

The Braidwoods agreed to reveal their methods to Gallaudet, providing he remained in Britain to train at one of the schools and serve a three-year apprenticeship as others had done. Gallaudet was advised to return to America and seek the services of John Braidwood. Gallaudet wrote to Cogswell outlining his knowledge of John's departure from Edinburgh, assuming him to have left in disgrace and to be a dissipated character of little consequence (Bell 1900a, 397–98).

While in London, Gallaudet met the abbé Sicard, who was in London lecturing and exhibiting his star pupils Massieu and Clerc. Impressed by their achievements, Gallaudet asked to visit the Paris Institute. He was welcomed and, so, abandoned his mission in Britain to seek greater satisfaction with Sicard in Paris.

Whether or not Watson and others extended Gallaudet the courtesy he deserved or felt he deserved is one thing, but the historical reality is rather different from the myth. Watson was, in fact, out of town when Gallaudet first sought to visit the Old Kent Road school and was later not able to provide Gallaudet with the attention he desired at short notice. Despite the mystification about the method perpetrated by Thomas and Isabella Braidwood, the method was not "a secret" but had been both published and passed on to a range of teachers beyond "the Braidwood family" by the time Gallaudet arrived in Britain. Neither the teachers involved nor the Braidwoods themselves were using the method exclusively or even primarily "for their own pecuniary benefit."

The method in question was being used in schools for children who were poor and deaf, and only a small minority were being taught as private pupils. William Hunter, the first deaf teacher trained in Britain to teach deaf students and a teacher at the Old Kent Road school, was in fact trained by a deaf man, John Creasy, between 1802 and 1804, more than a decade before Gallaudet arrived in London. Creasy himself was not a teacher but learned the art as a pupil at Braidwood's academies in Edinburgh and London (Lee 1997, 7). Creasy's mother was instrumental in the establishment of the school for people who were poor and deaf in London. The training of teachers was taken seriously, and a long apprenticeship was assumed to be required. It is important to note that although Gallaudet might have been welcomed more cordially by Sicard than by Sicard's friend Joseph Watson, he gained no more than a cursory knowledge of the French method but, rather, took an expert, Laurent Clerc, with him to America to provide the expertise and to train others.

During his time in Europe, the Reverend Thomas Gallaudet only gained a cursory knowledge of the French method in instructing deaf students and brought an expert, Laurent Clerc, back to America.

Gallaudet had been informed that John Braidwood was already in the United States and could provide the expertise that Laurent Clerc eventually provided.

John Braidwood and the First School for the Deaf in America

Whether or not John Braidwood was "the drunkard" as he has been labeled by educational experts in the United States today—and there seems little doubt that he was prone to wandering off on binges without warning—he was an effective, skilled, and popular teacher, as William Albert Bolling's notebooks bear witness. He also proved himself to be a good teacher trainer. In 1817, when Braidwood returned penniless from one of his wanderings, the school for the deaf was moved from Cobbs, Virginia, to Manchester, Virginia, in association with the "classical school for young ladies" run by the Reverend John Kirkpatrick in the Masonic Building in Manchester. An advertisement in local newspapers in July 1817 included the following statement:

> His [Braidwood's] stay in Virginia it is expected will be but temporary, yet of such continuance as will afford him an opportunity of rendering important service to such Pupils as may be immediately placed under his tuition and also of communicating to Mr Kirkpatrick that knowledge of his profes-

> sion, as will efficiently qualify him to manage and complete the Education of such children, after Mr Braidwood's departure from the State. (quoted in Bell 1900a, 493)

Apparently at that stage, Braidwood had expected to become involved with the New York School; the directors there were looking for a person acquainted with the Braidwood system to take charge. The New York School was planned at that time but did not open until 1818.

Whatever Braidwood's personal problems, he trained Kirkpatrick successfully. By March 1818, when Braidwood again became "unreliable," Kirkpatrick carried on the school on his own. By September, he was advertising the school as his and was offering a classically Braidwood-style education. Kirkpatrick set up his school and taught with success in Manchester until mid-1819 when, soon after being ordained, he moved to Cumberland County, Virginia. He appears to have continued with the education of deaf students, but the illness and then early death of his wife ended his work as a teacher of deaf people.[13]

Gallaudet stayed in Paris for a few months, and although he learned little of the techniques of instruction, he secured the services of Laurent Clerc who, after signing a contract with Gallaudet, set off with Gallaudet to America to establish the school in Hartford, Connecticut. Ironically, Clerc signed a contract including

> a prohibition for three years against activities that might jeopardize the success of the Hartford school; that is Clerc was not to assist potential competitors, sell his services to "any other establishment," or give any "instruction or public lectures . . . except under the direction of Mr Gallaudet." (Van Cleve and Crouch 1989, 39)

Although Gallaudet had branded the Braidwoods' protection of their methods unreasonable, he imposed the same restrictions on his own teacher, and "[i]n January of 1817, with the American School [in Connecticut] nearly ready to open, Gallaudet and Clerc journeyed to New York to attempt to block the establishment there of a potential rival" (Van Cleve and Crouch 1989, 43).

The Development of Methodological Signs in America

Despite Gallaudet and Clerc's efforts, rival schools were successfully established:

> By 1843, six states had followed Connecticut's example and provided for state-supported or state-operated residential schools for deaf children: New York in 1818, Pennsylvania in 1820, Kentucky in 1823, Ohio in 1827, Virginia in 1838, and Indiana in 1843. Persons trained in the American School in Connecticut were instrumental in the early success of every one of these institutions. Like the school in Hartford, each of these was staunchly manual in its approach. . . . (Van Cleve and Crouch 1989, 47)

Staunchly manual they were, but the manualism used in the schools was formed and transformed by the demands of reason, as the "natural" deaf were "cultured" through the acquisition of the English language. The signing that was first used in the American schools was modeled on the methodological signs used in the Paris school. The students were neither using nor learning natural sign languages as media of instruction. The system of fingerspelling was changed from the two-handed system brought by immigrants to the one-handed system favored originally by teachers of articulation.[14] The use of fingerspelling to spell out English was extremely widespread, and any signing that developed in the context of schooling was geared to the needs and form of English.

Edwin Mann's discussion of developments in the Hartford and New York schools in the 1830s (Mann 1836) indicates how the schools were involved, through the influence of Vaysee (sic) from the institution of Paris and of Peet from Hartford, in the decreasing use of the complex system of methodological signs and the development of "a single sign dialect in the schools for the deaf and dumb on this continent" (Mann 1836, 178). Peet himself indicated later that the move away from a sign-for-a-word system of methodological signs toward greater use of fingerspelling and the development of initialized signs owed much to De Gérando (Peet 1868, 49).

The problems associated with these language policies will be discussed in the following chapter. Much of the current literature on the history of the use of sign languages in deaf education reads like a spaghetti western, a history populated by goodies and baddies, by manualists and oralists. In fact, the situation was far more complex. But in all these varied educational environments within and beyond national boundaries, the use and abuse of natural sign language continued to reflect the forming and transforming relations of symbolic power.

In addition, deaf people in America, like those in Britain, France, and elsewhere, were being confined and categorized as a unitary and pathological presence. For many of those deaf people, the schools provided them with access to one another and to the wider world, opening up unthought-of horizons, thus, demonstrating the contradictory nature of the educational process. At the same time, people who were deaf were being culturally constructed as equal but different, all sharing a unitary difference, a difference that was soon to be identified as "disabled." Although most had experienced the hardships of individual discrimination before, they were now to experience a shared discrimination, being discriminated against as a category of humanity, as "deaf" and "disabled."

The Cultural Construction of Rational Order: The Role of Deaf Teachers in the Early Mass Education of the Deaf

During the early nineteenth century in Britain, France, and America, and later in Australia, the use of signing in its various forms as the mode of communication between teachers and pupils promoted the employment of deaf teachers. In some cases, the deaf teachers were employed as assistants; in other cases, they were full-fledged teachers in their own right; and in other situations, they were principals of schools and sometimes their founders. The use of deaf teachers was, in part, born of necessity; in part, a recognition of the intelligence and skill of the educated deaf person; and in part, a measure of the level and orientation of the education that was seen as appropriate for students who were poor and deaf as opposed to wealthy people who were deaf. The anonymous author of Townsend's "Memoirs" wrote: "It is now . . . proved that those afflicted objects of our sympathy, are not only capable of being taught but of conveying instruction to others" (Townsend 1831, 47). Watson himself wrote,

> I have found, by experience, that one deaf person may be employed to teach another with the happiest effect. So much so, that when I happen to be, for the moment, at a loss to make one of slow apprehension understand a lesson, I turn him over to one of his schoolfellows, who has learnt it; and never without advantage to both. (Watson 1809, xxxvii)

In 1804, Watson employed one of his own former pupils, William Hunter, who was one of the original class of six of 1792 and the first of many deaf teachers. For the next eighty years, deaf teachers were to work in schools throughout Britain, usually as low-paid assistants, but as in France, they were important role models for their pupils and the leaders of an emerging community. A few deaf teachers were to establish and head their own schools for deaf students.

In the history of British schools for the deaf, three deaf principals emerge. In each case, they administrated small schools, either on their own or with support from a family member (wife or sister). In 1832, a deaf Scot, Matthew Burns, originally educated at the Old Kent Road school in London, advertised the opening of a day school for "Teaching the DEAF and DUMB who have no other means of Instruction, in Edinburgh and its vicinity." His assistant was a deaf man by the name of Drysdale. Drysdale had been educated at the Edinburgh school and had trained as a pupil-teacher under Kinniburgh where he met the future Mrs. Drysdale, also an assistant to Kinniburgh. In 1834, Burns was approached to become headmaster of the Aberdeen school where he stayed until 1841. From there, he moved with his hearing sister to become the foundation principal of the Bristol school. He stayed in Bristol only eighteen months before giving up teaching to become a full-time missionary to deaf people in London.

Drysdale meanwhile continued successfully to run the day school in Edinburgh. On his marriage in 1846, he and his wife moved to Dundee where the need for a school had been felt. There, using their own funds, they established a school in Meadow Street Dundee, which was opened on 9 March 1846, and also established a regular Sunday service for deaf adults of Dundee. After four years, Drysdale built new premises at Dudhope Bank and moved in with his deaf pupils. One year after the establishment of the school, a group of philanthropic men established the Dundee Association for the Education of the Deaf and Dumb. This organization found funds to cover fees and board for children who were deaf and poor and also paid rent on the house. The funds were therefore controlled separately by the association, the meetings of which Drysdale did not usually attend. He and his wife were left to develop the curriculum and teach the children.

The case of the Dundee school is revealing. The board of benefactors showed no inclination to interfere in the schooling of the deaf pupils. Their concern was with being benefactors, with the pursuit of charitable works. They were concerned with providing facilities for the education of the "other," not with transforming the students into hearing people. Drysdale remained as principal of the school and as missioner to the deaf people of Dundee until his death in 1880, a period of thirty-five years. After his death, his wife continued the school for a short period on her own before asking the Board of the Dundee Association for the Education of the Deaf and Dumb to appoint James Barland (also deaf) as the

Matthew Burns was one of three deaf headmasters in the history of British schools for deaf children.

new principal. Barland, Drysdale's nephew, had trained with him as a pupil-teacher, having also been educated at the school. He gave up his teaching position at Swansea and returned to Dundee. The school later came under the aegis of the British School Board, discussed in the following chapter; its teachers were hearing and its orientation was oral.

Many other qualified deaf teachers also had trained under the pupil-teacher system. The Edinburgh school under Kinniburgh used a pupil-teacher method of training. Alexander Atkinson recounts in his memoirs how Joseph Turner was employed as an assistant from approximately 1816 (Atkinson 1865, 97ff.). Drysdale also trained in this way as did Thomas Pattison who later founded the school for the deaf in Sydney, Australia. In addition, the Old Kent Road school supported many of its early teaching needs using the pupil-teacher scheme. During the first fifty years, the majority of its teachers were deaf as "old scholars turned into young teachers, taken out of one class to be put in charge of another" (Elliott 1911). The first female deaf teacher was appointed in 1837, and a second, Mary Ann Cattermole, was appointed one year later (Brown 1994, 11).

The use of deaf teachers was seen as desirable in the interests of effective educational achievements. Where deaf teachers were employed, signing was usually the medium of instruction, and the object was to achieve a good basic education in literacy and numeracy. Students were thereby provided with access to the word of God and were also provided with the possibility of active employment. The deaf teachers were in no way anomalous because no attempt was made to transform the pupils into anything other than deaf people. The students were at school to become educated deaf people, and deaf teachers were often the most effective instructors.

However, despite the skills of these teachers, they did not receive promotion. Why? Those governing the schools assumed that these teachers

The Edinburgh Institute for the Deaf and Dumb where Kinniburgh trained many deaf students.

needed the supervision of hearing superiors and that they were relevant only in the teaching of a basic education. The British system used natural sign language as a mode of communication but regarded written and spoken English as the language of education. Thus, deaf teachers were not seen as possessing the complete range of language skills required of a full-fledged, autonomous teacher. A few exceptions occurred, but on the whole, the deaf teachers remained as assistants, were lowly paid, and were assumed incapable of the range of competencies possessed by competent hearing teachers.

In 1841–1842, nine deaf teachers and only three hearing teachers taught at the Old Kent Road school. By 1851, the situation had been reversed, with the number of deaf teachers down to four and the number of hearing teachers up to eight. Although the drop in the number of deaf teachers was mainly caused by their deaths, the school made few attempts to replace them or to train others. By 1873, only Banton remained as a deaf teacher at the school. This situation caused concern because of problems involved with supervising the students, particularly after hours; therefore, the Committee of the Asylum decided to appoint another pupil-teacher to be trained by Banton.

The situation in Britain in the 1870s contrasted markedly with what was happening in America where the establishment in 1864 of the National Deaf Mute College, now Gallaudet University, in Washington, D.C., consolidated the higher education of deaf people, or rather, white deaf men (see Winzer 1993, 234ff.), educating them for potential entry to teaching posts. These men filled positions in the manual schools whereas mainly women taught in the oral schools.[15] But even in America, deaf teachers, despite their large numbers and the high standard of their education, were paid less than hearing teachers and were denied the same levels of authority and autonomy. "It was said that even a well-educated deaf person had inherent limitations . . ." (Winzer 1993, 245).

The 1860s in Australia provide an interesting additional case study. Very much an offshoot of British traditions, formal education for deaf people began in Australia in 1860 with the establishment of schools in Sydney and Melbourne. Both were founded by educated deaf men, the Sydney school by Thomas Pattison, who had trained as a teaching assistant in Edinburgh under Kinniburgh, and the Melbourne school by Frederick John Rose, a former pupil of the school in the Old Kent Road. The Sydney school was taken over very swiftly by a hearing principal, Samuel Watson, who soon introduced articulation classes. In Melbourne, Rose remained in firm control of the school until the 1880s when hearing administrators and teachers began to override his authority and insist on the introduction of oralism into the school, at least, for selected pupils. Schools in Australia's other state capitals were established by the end of the century, most being founded by former pupils and teachers from the Melbourne school. Samuel Johnson arrived in Melbourne from England in the late 1870s with ideas of establishing oral classes; however, he failed because of Rose's opposition and left Melbourne for Adelaide where he established a school using a version of the combined method. All schools had oral classes by the late 1880s, but they did not reject the use of signs until after the Second World War.

Until the late-nineteenth century in Australia, as in Britain and America, the focus of the educational process for deaf students was on the education of deaf people qua deaf people and on their spiritual well-being. Educators did not attempt to transform them into hearing people. The use of signing and of deaf teachers was considered appropriate to their sensibilities and identities.

Beyond the Schools: Deaf Teachers, Deaf Missioners, and the Development of Deaf Communities

In the previous chapter, in commenting on the disabling aspects of l'Epée's legacy in France, we pointed out that in Catholic, postrevolutionary

In 1860, an educated deaf man, Frederick John Rose, established one of the first Australian schools for the deaf in Melbourne.

France, where poor people were the heroes of the hour, the potential creativity of all citizens was acknowledged, and deaf intellectuals and artists emerged. As a result, decades earlier than in Britain, an educated deaf community emerged that focused on the needs of deaf people and on the development of institutions catering to the needs of adult deaf people.

Eventually in Britain and America, deaf teachers along with deaf missioners also became the important leaders in the development of deaf communities, playing instrumental roles to set up services for adult deaf people.[16] In London, the early leaders were the teachers and former pupils of the Old Kent Road school, who met in London in 1840 to establish social and religious services for adult deaf people and who soon were to be under the fervently evangelical leadership of the former founder-principal of the Bristol school for the deaf, Matthew Burns. In Paris, teachers like Massieu, Clerc, and Berthier actively fought for the rights of deaf pupils and adults. Berthier, in particular, was instrumental not only in establishing the Comité des Sourds-Muets, which established the famous annual Banquets in memory of l'Epée (the first held in 1834), but also in advocating a "deaf-mute nation" (Mirzoeff 1995, 119).[17] In America, deaf teachers like the Tillinghasts together with former pupils of schools founded formal and informal deaf associations throughout the country (see Van Cleve and Crouch 1989). In addition, Joseph A. Tillinghast, one of the sons of the deaf teacher David Tillinghast, went to northern Ireland at Maginn's request to develop Irish deaf education through the combined method.[18] In Australia, from 1860 and continuing for sixty years, former Old Kent Road pupil Frederick John Rose, the founder-principal of the school for the deaf in Melbourne, was, within his school and then beyond in the wider community, the driving force behind the development of services for deaf people of all ages (see Branson and Miller 1996a).

These developments beyond the schools also demonstrated the general nineteenth-century ideological willingness to recognize deaf people as having a deaf identity. Churches for the Deaf and Associations for the Deaf focused on the needs of deaf people qua deaf people. Hearing people generally remained in control of these institutions, and all institutions had a disabling effect insofar as they continued to define deaf people in terms of suffering a lack or needing charity. But deaf people were allowed to be deaf. The only attempt to transform them involved, like the native inhabitants of the Empire, saving their souls and civilizing their minds while ensuring that they remained "other." They were still an accepted aspect of humanity, part of the social and cultural fabric, albeit defined as defective and disabled.

But toward the end of the nineteenth century, the cultural construction of deaf people as "disabled" was to undergo radical transformations. The focus was to shift from the education of deaf people as deaf people to the transformation of deaf people into "disabled" hearing individuals. Medical and pedagogical forces oriented toward pure oralism and speech therapy would begin to influence points of view. Their triumph was some way off, but as Western societies generally moved toward professionalism and bureaucratic administration, they provided the means whereby the pedagogical aspirations of a minority of educators would triumph over the majority.

To understand these complex and interweaving processes, we turn first to consider how evolutionism and eugenics influenced and transformed attitudes toward deaf people. We then trace the ideological triumph, though never the complete practical triumph, of pure oralism in Britain. We consider this triumph in the context of new forms of linguistic imperialism as the widespread use and abuse of natural sign languages in deaf education was replaced with an increasing ban on the use of any form of signing.

Notes

1. The effect of French methods was restricted to the Cabra schools in Dublin, Ireland.

2. As we shall see, the same was true of deaf education, with deaf people such as Abraham Farrar, who actively supported pure oralism (see chapter 6), and Francis Maginn, who was a driving force in the promotion of the combined method (see chapter 7).

3. For further discussion of the founding of the school in Bermondsey, see Lee and Hay (n.d.) and Beaver (1992).

4. Paul's Head Tavern was a coffeehouse opposite the Guildhall in London. Seventeenth-century philosophers had met in the London coffeehouses to discuss language and education. Pepys had met in these coffeehouses with Wallis and others. The foundation of the London school continued in this tradition.

5. For a description of the education of a parlor pupil, see Raymond Lee's discussion of the education of the deaf barrister John William Lowe (Lee 1999).

6. Maginn was to study for four years at the Columbia Institution (now Gallaudet University) where he established strong links with Edward Miner Gallaudet. He will feature prominently in later chapters.

7. Hopper introduced the one-handed alphabet into the classroom after visits to continental schools that convinced him of its greater efficiency for use in the classroom. In Dublin, the Catholic school established in 1846 by the Society for Founding and Maintaining the Catholic Institution for the Deaf and Dumb used a one-handed alphabet based on the French manual alphabet used by l'Epée (see E. M. Gallaudet's report on methods used in Britain and Ireland in the *Tenth Annual Report of the Columbia Institution* for 1867 [Gallaudet 1867, 14]). On his 1867 tour of institutions in Britain and Europe, Gallaudet visited schools in Britain, Ireland, France, Germany, Belgium, Switzerland, and Italy. In reporting on his visit, he classified the schools in terms of their methods of instruction: (1) "the natural method," using the natural sign language of the pupils and no articulation; (2) the "artificial method" or oralism; and (3) "the combined method" using elements of manualism and oralism. He visited only nine schools using "the natural method." Five of these were in Britain and three in Ireland. Only one was to be found in Europe, in Switzerland (Gallaudet 1867).

8. Curtis established the first hospital devoted to diseases of the ear in Soho in London in 1816. The hospital later became the Royal Ear Hospital (see Porter 1997, 385).

9. Extremely critical of Curtis, who he saw as incompetent and who he considered to be a plagiarist, Wilde describes Curtis's methods through "the writings of a [unidentified] foreigner":

> "Curtis," says the writer, "treats every discharge from the ear exclusively, and in a summary way, by means of astringents; obstructions of the Eustachian tube, with emetics and perforation of the membrana tympan; whilst, in spite of all the entreaties of Saissy, he has never once practised catheterism of the Eustacian tube on the living subject. He makes tinnitus the chief symptom of nervous deafness, which he treats with purgatives, especially calomel, as long as the strength of the patient holds out." "In all doubtful cases the chief attention is directed merely to ascertain whether the liquor Cotunnii be partially or totally deficient!! or whether hardened wax exist in the meatus." "In the otitis of children he sticks opium into the affected ear, &c., so that throughout all his writings nothing but the most crude empiricism is to be met with; and yet among his compatriots, as well as abroad, Curtis generally possesses the reputation of being a distinguished aurist." (Wilde 1853, 36)

10. The term "missioner" was used widely in the United Kingdom and Australia throughout the nineteenth century. It referred to those in charge of a mission, an institution, and not just to a vocation. Retired teachers often turned to missionary work—for example, Matthew Burns, William Stainer, and David Buxton—see chapter 6.

11. William Wilde was the father of the celebrated novelist, playwright, and poet Oscar Wilde, who was later to rail against the dependence of many services in Britain on charity (Wilde 1966, 1079).

12. For discussion of the missions to the deaf in America, see Berg (1984).

13. As indicated in a letter to Alexander Graham Bell from Kirkpatrick's daughter, the original being in the Volta Bureau, Washington, D.C.

14. See Thornton (1793) for a description of the use of the two-handed alphabet by deaf people in America in the late-eighteenth century, and see Stedt and Moores (1990) for discussion of the development of signing in educational contexts.

15. By 1901, eight deaf teachers were teaching in Britain—one in each of the following institutions: Belfast, Dundee, Edinburgh, Donaldson's Hospital (Edinburgh), Glasgow School Board evening class, Leeds school board, Liverpool, and Swansea. At the same time, 243 deaf teachers and principals were working in America (*Newsletter of the British Deaf and Dumb Association* 1901, 10).

16. For an account of the work of deaf missioners in the United States, such as H. W. Syle and A. W. Mann, as well as of the work of Reverend Dr. Thomas Gallaudet, brother of Edward Miner Gallaudet, see Berg (1984).

17. For a description of the 1835 banquet, see Berthier (1852).

18. Letters between Joseph Tillinghast and Francis Maginn in the Gallaudet University Archives.

6

The Alienation and Individuation of Deaf People: Eugenics and Pure Oralism in the Late-Nineteenth Century

In chapter 2, we discussed how professionalism and the depersonalization of disabilities generally affected the way that people regarded and treated those who were deemed to be disabled. The medical definitions that defined deafness and deaf people themselves as pathological and in need of treatment were transforming the educational goals and orientations maintained by hearing teachers, parents, and benefactors. The moral therapy movement with its personal even familial approach to the treatment of those deemed "insane" was replaced by diagnoses and treatments that divorced the individual from society and dealt with symptoms rather than with the whole person. Similarly, the mission-oriented approach that characterized the education of deaf students throughout most of the of the nineteenth century would be replaced with an approach that sought to transform pupils by overcoming their symptoms—deafness and muteness—through lipreading, technological developments in hearing aides, and speech training. Again, the main agency of this process was professionalism. Professionalizing "teachers of the deaf" was a process that not only reoriented the teaching process but also drove the deaf teachers from the classrooms and challenged the authority of deaf people in other walks of life, including that of deaf missioners.

Forces of professionalism would encompass the teaching of deaf students in the same way they encompassed the treatment of other forms of unreason. The new scientific professionals who emerged through the later half of the nineteenth century would distance themselves from individual suffering by conceptually separating the patient from his or her "condition." In the same way, through this professional approach by teachers of the deaf, deafness became a pathological syndrome to be measured and dealt with therapeutically, with the teaching process itself becoming part of that therapy. Hence, we turn to the years through the second half of the nineteenth century and the first half of the twentieth century to document the rise and consolidation of professions that were formed to deal specifically with the culturally constructed field of "disabilities," including "the deaf," and with the accompanying "technopoly" as Postman (1993) calls it—the subordination of people to technology, a process that consolidates and accentuates the alienation of the "disabling" condition from the individual.

Margret Winzer writes:

> When Laurent Clerc (1785–1869) first stepped onto American shores, no public special institutions existed in the young nation except for a small hospital for the insane in Virginia. By the time of Clerc's death a flourishing complex of institutions reached across North America. To Clerc, the term *special education* would not have been familiar; it would not emerge until 1884. But Clerc was intimately associated with efforts to assist exceptional students with settings and programs designed to cater to their unique needs. (Winzer 1993, 83; Winzer's italics)

Clerc certainly would not have seen deaf people as one with the insane, as "disabled" people in need of special education, nor would he have agreed with euphemistic references to the "disabled" as "exceptional students." That unitary and benevolent orientation toward "handicapped people" was a result of the next hundred years of cultural "development," developments that lumped a host of what would have been for Clerc or Gallaudet or Watson strange bedfellows indeed—the insane, the deaf, the blind, "feeble-minded youth," "idiotic and feeble-minded children," and "mentally retarded children"—as "handicapped people" in need of "special education." The lumping of these people together was directly linked to the evolutionist and eugenicist consciousness that pervaded Western societies.

Darwinism, Evolutionism, and the Devaluation of Signing

As we outlined in chapter 1, Darwin's theories of biological evolution generated a range of theories about social and cultural evolution. These theories not only sought to understand the stages through which societies had passed in "evolving" toward their present state but also sought to classify existing races and cultures in terms of the stages they had reached in the overall evolution of humanity. Western industrial societies were assumed to be most evolved and hunter-gatherer societies such as those of Australian aboriginal people to be least evolved.

By the end of the nineteenth century, the evolution of language was of particular interest to "evolutionist" anthropologists such as Edward Tylor. Theorizing about the origins of language, Tylor claimed that gesture was the earliest form of language and that speech developed at a later date. Gestural systems of communication, thus, were seen as "primitive," as lower on the evolutionary scale than spoken languages. Although evaluations of sign languages as "savage" and "basic" were not new—they were evident in the earlier writing of Joseph Watson in Britain and those of l'Epée, Sicard, and De Gérando in France—the evolutionists reinforced the existing linguistic imperialism in a new way. Signing, whether natural or methodological, was evaluated as primitive and savage, as having no value in a civilized, advanced society.[1] This appraisal was a starkly different evaluation of signing from that of seventeenth-century Britain or eighteenth-century France.

The excitement that Wilkins, Dalgarno, and then l'Epée felt on discovering the "sign languages of deaf people, seeing in them a pathway to the development of the 'perfect language,'" gave way to imperial disdain. The "perfect language" was no longer possibly a gestural system but was assumed to be a Western spoken and written language of science and learning. Gestural systems were used by "savages" and "deaf mutes." The use of signing was thus seen as a retrograde step. The move to pure oralism throughout the Western world could therefore be interpreted as an evolutionary step up, a step away from "savagery." Thus, the arch-oralist Susanna Hull could write in 1877:

> Spoken language is the product of ages—the workmanship of many minds; one of the cornerstones of civilization and the crown of history. Indeed, without it, history, such as we have it, could never have been.

> When, therefore, we give our deaf children a sign-language, we give them an instrument for expressing their thoughts, but a very poor and feeble one. We push them back in the world's history to the infancy of our race. They may, as French-system teachers love to boast, be understood, to some extent, by American Indians and other savage tribes! But shall sons and daughters of this nineteenth century be content with this? (Hull 1877, 236)

However, we cannot begin to consider how and why pure oralism triumphed over various manual systems through the twentieth century until we look more deeply at the effect that evolutionism had not only on the language of deaf education but also on the evaluation and treatment of deaf people in general. For the Darwinists and the evolutionists, the laws of nature needed to be harnessed to ensure effective human development. Evolutionist control over the natural development of humans received explicit expression in eugenics. Thus, we must now consider the eugenics movement in relation to the cultural construction of deaf people as disabled. The eugenics movement was a prime ideological force in the construction of deafness as an individual pathology, a medical condition rendering the individual "unfit." In a particularly forceful way, it expressed an aspect of the definition of deafness that is often ignored—that of deafness as a medical pathology to be dealt with individually and therapeutically. Forces were at work to alienate deaf people from their difference, from their own sensibility.

Evolutionism, Eugenics, and Deaf People

> Dr. E. A. Fay has made a study of the records gathered by the Volta Bureau. He finds that there have been 4,471 marriages between deaf persons. 14.1% of these deaf matings report no children. There are 6,782 children reported from parents, both of whom are deaf, 24.7% of children from these deaf parents are themselves deaf. Are not such marriages criminal and should not the State interfere? (Stokes 1917, 63)

An ardent eugenicist reached these conclusions from Fay's work. Fay's own position, however, was more restrained.

> For those who have deaf relatives, the question of advice is delicate and difficult; and I do not think it necessary to offer any. I have told you of the liability of such persons to have deaf offspring. I leave it to yourself to judge

> whether it is right and proper for you to marry. President Gallaudet has said that he would rank high in his esteem a deaf person who remained unmarried, because there was a danger of deaf offspring; that he would honor him for his unselfishness. I think all persons of good judgment and a high sense of honor would agree with him. But one piece of advice I do not hesitate to give you all; under no circumstances whatever marry a person who is related to you in any degree of consanguinity. (Fay 1898, 78)

Fay's words concluded a lecture delivered to students at Gallaudet College, Washington D.C., on February 23, 1900. They echoed a talk given three years earlier at Gallaudet by Alexander Graham Bell, a talk interpreted into sign language by Fay.[2] Bell, too, counseled against marriage between deaf people and, particularly, between people related through consanguinity. The basis for their counsel was clear: deafness was a pathology that threatened the normal majority.

Interest in the effect of deaf marriages on the incidence of deafness was by no means new. In 1857, Buxton had published an article "On the Marriage and Intermarriage of the Deaf and Dumb" (Buxton 1857). Buxton's conclusions were based on all available relevant statistics for Britain, Ireland, and America:

> Enough has probably now been said—and for the opinions advanced ample evidence has, I think, been adduced—to establish the proposition which I undertook to maintain, namely, that there is no sufficient reason for prohibiting the marriages of deaf persons with the hearing; but that it is, at the same time highly inexpedient that the deaf and dumb should marry with each other. (Buxton 1857, 16)

Like many theories to follow, including those of Bell, Fay, and Gallaudet, the conclusions were flawed statistically and genetically, but they reinforced, with apparent scientific support, a conviction that deaf people should not develop any sense of community based in shared deafness but that they should interact with the hearing world as individuals. In the 1870s, Elliott introduced coeducational classes at the Old Kent Road school in London but stressed the need to keep the girls and boys separate in the playground lest they form personal attachments that might lead to relationships, which might result in deaf offspring.

Bell went so far as to express fears that segregating the education of deaf people in residential schools coupled with using sign language rather than the speech of the wider (normal) society would lead to a distinct deaf variety of the human race (Bell 1884b). Bell attracted close media attention wherever he went, and although his statements were often quoted out of context, his anxieties about consanguineous marriages, his fervent belief that deaf people should be integrated as individuals into the wider society, and his conviction that they should not form any sort of community served both the oralist cause and that of more extreme eugenicists. As a highly respected scientist who had been responsible for some of the most dramatic technological developments of his time, Bell's statements were also accorded a legitimacy that had little to do with the validity of his assumptions about heredity. Both his statistics and his genetic theory were, in fact, faulty.

Quite clearly, the concept of a deaf community posed a distinct threat to the Western establishment just as the concept of the "idiot family" posed a threat. The concept of community was itself a threat to the individualism that dominated Western middle-class ideology. Just as black power and women's movements later threatened the white, male establishment by asserting and practicing communal unity—communal unity that transformed these people's individuated isolation in separate households and gave them a strength that the individuated white male did not possess—the implicit and occasionally explicit assertion of deaf communal identity threatened the "normal," individuated hearing world.

In chapter 1, we traced the horrors of sterilization and extermination programs in Germany as the Nazi government sought to eliminate the hereditary forms of "disability" from the population altogether. As we stressed in that chapter, the actions of the Nazi regime were only one step removed from those of eugenicists throughout the Western world in the interwar period. Biesold's devastating study has now shown (Biesold 1999) that deaf people in Germany during the 1930s were encompassed by laws that progressed from forcing them to be sterilized and prohibiting them from marrying to so-called "euthanasia" laws, which allowed, first, deaf children and then also deaf adults to be killed.

The prime foci for locating the hereditary deaf were the schools for the deaf and the adult deaf associations. The German government's main agents in the identification of the hereditary deaf population were teachers of the deaf (see Biesold 1999). Thousands of deaf people were murdered. In the postwar period, although Jews were recognized as having been persecuted by the Nazi regime, those whose medical diagnoses confirmed that they "suffered" from an hereditary disability were seen by the postwar courts as having been dealt with through proper procedures, as not having suffered persecution at the hands of the Nazis. When supported by medical diagnoses, the eugenicist policies remained legitimate in the eyes of the postwar, anti-Nazi regimes (see Friedlander 1999).

Nazi eugenics pushed the logic for the elimination of genetically deaf people to the most horrific scenario of all: sterilization and, eventually, murder in hospitals and gas chambers. But throughout the Western world at the end of the nineteenth century, in education and in the wider community, the orientation moved away from benevolent tolerance and acceptance toward the elimination of deaf people's identity by means of linguistic genocide, therapy, and technology. By removing teachers who were deaf and teachers who could sign from the classroom and even the playground, the educational process would seek to destroy those aspects of deaf people's identity associated with their recognition as an acceptable albeit devalued part of nature's diversity.

The Use, Abuse, and Prohibition of Natural Sign Language in Deaf Education

In all histories of deaf education, 1880 is seen as the year in which the decisive triumph of oralism occurred by means of the International Congress of Teachers of the Deaf in Milan. At the Milan Congress, the Italian oralist, the abbé Tarra, proposed resolutions calling for the worldwide adoption of pure oralism and the rejection of sign languages in schools for the deaf, resolutions that were passed by large majorities, including the majority of the British delegation. The effect of the Milan Congress is overstated. Signing continued to be used in schools for some time, not only in America but also in Britain and Australia. What Milan did mark very clearly was a change in the overall conceptualization of the educational process as it applied to deaf people. The purpose of that education was changing. The disablement of people who were deaf had, as outlined at the end of the last chapter, reached a new phase.

The change was, as always, a subtle one because the agents who were involved in the disabling processes—teachers, parents, doctors and therapists, clerics, welfare workers, and administrators—remained, on the whole, oriented toward the welfare of deaf people. But their social and cultural environment was generating dispositions that promoted a new type of discriminatory behavior. Darwinism, eugenics, and advances in medicine and technology focused the benevolence of teachers, parents, and others associated with deaf people on the individual deaf person rather than on "the deaf" as a section of society. They sought to develop pedagogical and therapeutic processes that would transform the individual to fit the wider "normal," "civilized" society. By removing signing and deaf teachers from the classroom and even the playground, they sought to normalize the deaf individual. They sought to destroy deaf people's difference, to destroy the cultural aspects of their deafness. In the process, they would destroy those aspects of deaf people's identity associated with the recognition that deaf people were an acceptable albeit devalued part of nature's diversity. The symbolic violence of this linguistic imperialism was particularly destructive.

The Use and Abuse of Natural Sign Language in Britain, France, and America

The move to mass education of deaf people had been associated with a move to the use of sign language as a medium of education. As David Buxton wrote in an outline of the history of deaf education in 1876,

> [W]hen it became common to congregate considerable numbers of children in the public Institutions, their inmates resorted naturally to the language which was natural to them. It is indeed as natural for the deaf to "sign," as for ducks to swim. We know that ducks have wings and can fly; so the deaf have tongues and can speak; but the readiness and grace with which they sign, in contrast with the speech of the born deaf, can only be paralleled by the contrast between the graceful floating and the awkward flying of the ordinary water fowl. (1876, 98–99)

Mirzoeff writes "It was no coincidence that in turning from educating deaf aristocrats, who had often been taught orally, to the deaf poor, l'Epée used sign language as proper to the 'natural' mass of the poor" (Mirzoeff 1995, 34). Why was it "no coincidence"? Essentially because, although the wealthy were equated with culture, the poor were equated with nature and the deaf poor, particularly so.[3] Natural sign language was evaluated by most educators as a natural, universal language, a "savage" language that could not meet the demands of an education based on the cultured, civilized Western world. It was, therefore, not a viable medium of education and was, at best, a bridge to the acquisition of the languages of culture—written, spoken, and even signed. L'Epée's methodological signs embodied the transformation of natural language into a language of culture and reason.

What part did sign language play in Watson's educational system? The simple answer is that he used sign language and the manual alphabet constantly in both theory and practice. Like his predecessors, Wallis and the Braidwoods, Watson advocated the careful learning and use of natural sign language:

> [E]veryone, who would undertake the arduous task of successfully teaching the deaf and dumb, should closely turn his attention to the study of that language termed *natural*, where it consists of gesture and feature, in order to enable him to comprehend, as far as possible, the signs of his scholars. . . .
>
> Of how much importance it is to a teacher of the deaf and dumb to understand their signs, will be readily apprehended, if any one will attempt, either to teach or to learn a language, without having another, common to master and scholar. (Watson 1809, 81–82; Watson's italics)

Signing was an essential part of the British system, which was by no means "oral." Watson was also perfectly aware of the fact that, within a community of deaf people, sign language was made up of not only natural gestures but also arbitrary signs, as are all true languages (Watson 1809, 78).

But Watson, like l'Epée and Sicard (Bazot 1819), did not see natural sign language as a language equivalent to English or as an equivalent to other literate languages such as French, German, or Latin. Sign language was seen as equivalent to the "rude and imperfect language," the "barbarous speech" of a "south-Sea Islander" (83–84), an overtly imperialist interpretation to be echoed later in the century by De Gérando in France. Watson saw sign language as a means to an end, the means by which a teacher could teach the literate languages of the West that he described as "regular, copious, and polished" (83). Linguistic imperialism was a driving force in the education of deaf people in France, Britain, and later in America, but it took varying forms.

The British system, the system that came in a direct line from Wallis to Baker and Thomas Braidwood, on to John Braidwood and Joseph Watson, and then on to Robert Kinniburgh and Charles Baker and those they trained, differed from the system in France. The difference was by no means a matter of oralism versus manualism. British deaf education for most of the nineteenth century was, as we have stressed, not oralist. It differed from France's and later from America's approaches in the way it made use of sign language. As we look briefly at the different forms of linguistic imperialism, we note an important point: Watson and a stream of later educators such as Charles Baker were well acquainted with educational writing and activities in France and the rest of Europe. Watson read French and Latin fluently and read widely. Sicard respected and admired Watson's work, an admiration that was mutual.

Watson explicitly opposed the "artificial language of methodized signs" (Bazot 1819, 84) that had been devised by l'Epée, and he saw no point in substituting sign language, methodized or natural, for English as the language of learning. This issue was where he differed from Sicard. The essential difference was not the acceptance or rejection of articulation as an aspect of education but the role of sign language. Both Watson and Sicard taught articulation and proudly displayed their successful pupils, indeed, displaying them together in June 1815 (see Brown 1994, 11). But although Sicard continued to teach articulation, he accepted sign language or, rather, the system of methodological signs as an effective intellectual medium and did not see the learning of speech as a necessary element of deaf education.[4] Watson, in the British tradition, saw sign language as a natural language, essential as an educational medium but, primarily, as the mode through which access to English, the perfect medium of education as far as the British were concerned, was obtained. Education in the British tradition should then proceed through written English, relying heavily on the use of the manual alphabet to represent the written word manually (see Watson 1809, 121–22).

The British approach was about to expand and diversify as schools were established throughout Britain and Ireland. A basic consistency of approaches to teaching remained, however, because many of the teachers were trained by the Braidwoods or by Watson. Despite the fact that some schools rejected articulation while others focused increasingly on articulation, the British approach to signing was fairly consistent. No attempts were made to formalize natural signing into a language that complied with hearing people's notions of grammatical language as the French were doing. As mentioned above, the use of fingerspelling was very heavy, and signs were often equated with words. The British opposition to systems of methodological signs, in fact, resulted in British Sign Language remaining far more natural than was the case in France and the United States where sign languages were artificially "developed" grammatically and through the addition of new vocabulary. In 1867, Gallaudet noted the much greater use of books and printed materials in Britain than in America (Gallaudet 1867, 12). And virtually all those schools in Gallaudet's survey using what he called "the natural method," "based on a free use of the natural language of the deaf mute and of pantomimic gestures," were British or Irish (10–11).

Some of the early British teachers of the deaf, in fact, saw their system as very similar to the version of the French system favored by Bébian, Sicard's successor in Paris (Kinniburgh 1847).[5] Bébian, fluent in the sign language of deaf people, was completely opposed to l'Epée's methodological signs (Bébian 1817). He saw natural sign language as a complex, rich, and effective vehicle for education (Bébian 1817, 1825, 1827). This link with Bébian is clearly outlined by W. R. Scott in his book *The Deaf and Dumb: Their Education and Social Position* (Scott 1870), which provides the most complete view of the use of sign language in the education of deaf people in Britain during the nineteenth century. Scott was trained by Charles Baker at the Doncaster Institution and became principal of the West England Institution for the Education of the Deaf and Dumb at Exeter from 1841 until his death in 1877. He was described as "an excellent and graphic signer" (*The British Deaf Monthly* 1897, 179). Scott favored the extensive use of the manual alphabet in teaching. He recognized sign language as a language of arbitrary signs with a distinct grammar and a vocabulary that could not be equated with the "words" of speech and writing. Scott has been virtually ignored by historians and linguists of sign languages but, in fact, provided what appears to be the earliest comprehensive linguistic analysis of British Sign Language. He was highly critical of the use of methodological signs, namely, the development of a sign for a word:

> We have heard of teachers who would sign through a lesson, giving sign for word in regular succession, in the belief that each sign they made was of equal importance and would necessarily give the idea. We could hardly suppose that there could have been teachers with such "madness" in their methods. (Scott 1870, 130–31)[6]

Like Watson, Scott stated clearly that there was no need to teach sign language to deaf people; it was their language. Therefore, he made no attempt to develop sign language proficiency among the pupils. They did not study sign language in the same way as their hearing peers studied English. Sign language was a given, a language of communication but not of learning. The teacher made use of it to teach the curriculum, to promote literacy in English. The pupils, too, valued the British system and fought hard at times to retain it, as is evidenced by the rebellion of students at the Birmingham school at Edgbaston in 1826 when the new Swiss principal, Louis Du Puget, attempted to change the system introduced by Thomas Braidwood (Lee 1998, 7). It took the arrival of Charles Baker in the same year to restore order (Baker 1875).

In France, the use of methodological signs gave way to increasing oralism much earlier than in Britain, especially through the influence of Itard and De Gérando. Moves by Berthier and Bébian to establish the use of natural sign language as a viable medium of instruction were soon laid to rest, and the firm dominance of the cultured language of French, in written and oral forms, continued to triumph over the natural sign language. In the tradition established by l'Epée, the opposition of nature to culture continued to devalue natural sign language and to deny it the status of an educational medium. For l'Epée, natural language needed to be thoroughly transformed through the development of signed French, his system of methodological signs. For De Gérando, natural sign language had to pave the way for the direct acquisition of written and spoken French. Through both l'Epée's and De Gérando's approaches, deaf people were themselves devalued.

In America, the system of methodological signs was introduced by Laurent Clerc through the establishment of the school at Hartford, Connecticut.[7] His predecessors in the education of deaf people in America, John Braidwood and the Reverend John Kirkpatrick, used natural sign language as a path to the acquisition of what they regarded as the language of education—written and spoken English. Although natural sign language was praised in the Hartford school as a medium of communication, it was viewed as a (natural) basis on which more specialized (cultured) educational media—signed English and written English—could be established and used (see Van Cleve and Crouch 1989). The opposition of nature and culture remained, stressing the vital role of introduced languages in the education of deaf people.

Although educators in America, as in France, supported the use of signing as a mode of instruction in the first half of the nineteenth century, the signing used for instruction in literacy was not natural sign language but, rather, a mixture of natural signs, methodological signs, initialized signs, and fingerspelling. Isaac Lewis Peet, who succeeded his father Harvey Peet as principal of the New York Institution, wrote in 1868 that "the colloquial language of signs . . . is deficient in general terms" (Peet 1869, 99) and stated with respect to the development of initialized signs that

> [t]he writer thinks that whatever the merits or demerits of this system may be, it is allowable to him to claim, in a modified sense, the authorship of most of the signs he has indicated, as well as of many others of the like composition. For some years, as teacher of intelligent classes of deaf-mutes, he has laboured to extend and improve the language of signs and has been enthusiastically aided by his pupils. (Peet 1869, 101–2)

Natural sign language was not seen as a viable medium for education.

We find, therefore, far closer links among the British systems and those used in France and America than is often admitted by those historians who tend to see the history of deaf education as a simplistic division between manualists and oralists. Those histories ignore the nature of those "manualisms" and the degree to which they involved the exercise of symbolic power by hearing educators over the natural signing of their deaf pupils. We can achieve a far more revealing understanding of the complex history surrounding the use of signing in deaf education by considering attitudes toward the use of natural sign languages than we can by turning to a category like "manualism." After all, natural sign language was seen to be the defining aspect of deaf humanity.

Linguistic imperialism was as vital a factor in the disabling of deaf people in France and America as it was in Britain. In all three situations, the natural language of deaf people, so integral to their identity and sense of self-respect, was thoroughly devalued. While natural sign language was defined as inadequate to the task of education, deaf people themselves were being defined as incapable in their "natural" state of achieving cultural development. Deaf people were being devalued as uncultured, "natural," even "primitive," and thus in need of intervention by the cultured hearing world. In Britain, natural sign language supplemented by copious fingerspelling in English was seen as an avenue to effective education. In France, the natural language of the pupils was thoroughly transformed and, in fact, disabled to represent written French. In America, France's methodological signs and the one-handed alphabet were adapted to the grammatical and pedagogical demands of the dominant language of English, replacing the American forms of natural sign languages and the two-handed alphabet that had been used by the deaf students of Paris. Even Clerc's legitimacy lay in his education by Sicard and Massieu in the use of methodological signs. Not his deafness but his cultured acquisition of hearing languages—methodological signs, French, and English—is what defined his pedagogical authority.

The devaluation of deaf people's natural sign language signaled and promoted the cultural construction of deaf people as "other." Their newly constructed otherness was akin to that of other "natural," "uncivilized" peoples. Deaf people themselves were in turn devalued, but they were allowed to possess a "deaf" identity. Through the first three-quarters of the nineteenth century in all three countries discussed above, manual communication in various guises was used in most schools. All these schools acknowledged the need for communication systems that were "deaf" rather than "hearing."

The complexity of the linguistic environment within deaf schools in Britain during the nineteenth century is well illustrated in various survey results that document the methods used in British schools for the deaf.[8] In one of the most comprehensive surveys, which was published in 1881, Edward Fay wrote the following:

> By the "manual" method is meant the course of instruction which employs the sign language, the manual alphabet, and writing as the chief means in the education of the deaf, and has facility in the comprehension and use of written language as its principal object. . . .
>
> By the "oral" method is meant that in which signs are used as little as possible; the manual alphabet is discarded altogether, and articulation and lip-reading, together with writing, are made the chief means as well as the end of instruction. . . .
>
> The "combined" method is not so easy to define, as the term is employed indiscriminately with reference to several distinct methods, such as (1) the free use of both signs and articulation, with the same pupils and the same teachers throughout their course of instruction; (2) the general instruction of all pupils is by means of the manual method, with the special training of a part of them in articulation and lip-reading as an accomplishment; (3) the instruction of some pupils by the manual method and others by the oral method in the same institution; (4)—though this is rather a combined *system*—the employment of the manual method and the oral method in separate schools under the same general management, pupils being sent to one establishment or the other as seems best with regard to each individual case. (Fay 1881)

The results of Fay's survey are particularly interesting because they reveal an overwhelming preference for the manual method, with articulation simply seen as an accomplishment available to those with an aptitude for speech. Pure oralism, Fay's "oralism" category, is confined to private schools and those controlled by the Association for Oral Instruction. As we shall see, the teachers and benefactors from these private schools plus Stainer from the London School Board and Elliott from Margate "represented" Britain at the Congress of Teachers of the Deaf in Milan in 1880. The pure oralists were, as documented below, aggressive and evangelical in the promotion of their method and had significant financial support from private benefactors such as the Baroness Mayer de Rothschild and B. St. John Ackers, barrister and member of parliament. But the bulk of the teachers of deaf students were comfortable with the British manual tradition.[9]

Using the results of Fay's survey, if we look at, as one category, the number of schools teaching solely or primarily by the manual method, where, if articulation is taught at all, it is taught as an additional skill to those with the necessary aptitude, and, as another category, the number of schools teaching by means of pure oralism and the combination of oralism and manualism, then 66 percent of British schools for the deaf were manual, 14 percent were combined, and 21 percent were pure oral schools. This analysis is based on the number of schools, not the number of pupils. Were the number of pupils to be taken into account, the manual slice would be much more dominant. Apart from the London School Board schools where Stainer was a very recent and reluctant convert to oralism, the oral schools were all small private schools catering, not to the needs of poor people, but to the demands of wealthy, "cultured" parents.[10]

The Emergence of Pure Oralism in Britain

Although we are concerned above all with revealing and interpreting the social and cultural consequences of philosophical and pedagogical ideas as well as their realization in practice, we must return to the realm of pedagogical theory and practice to understand the way that pure oralism emerged and eventually triumphed on the British scene. The appeals for legitimacy that were made by pure oralism's advocates and practitioners to a mixture of religious, humanitarian, and scientific ideologies and the appeals to science that were so necessary and powerful in late nineteenth century Britain demanded the presence of intellectual leaders. For some time, Joseph Watson remained the lone theorist and comprehensive writer on the education of deaf students in Britain, but three other great theorists emerged through the century: Charles Baker

(1803–1874); W. R. Scott (1811–1877), trained by Charles Baker; and finally, Thomas Arnold (1816–1897), who also initially worked under Baker at Doncaster.

Baker (1837, 1842) laid great stress on writing and on the use of the manual alphabet.[11] Although he was a competent signer, he did not favor the use of natural sign language as the main medium of instruction throughout all the years of schooling. Baker was an intellectual whose pedagogical writings extended well beyond the education of deaf children. In 1831, he wrote:

> Although the deaf and dumb have been gathered together in various institutions for forty years, no attempt has yet been made to supply such a course of practical lessons as they required, both as school exercises and as aids to the acquisition of language when not under the instruction of their teacher. (quoted Thomas Baker 1875, 206)

Baker's *Education of the Senses* (Baker 1837) was his first step to supply this "course of practical lessons." It was followed by a number of articles for the *Penny Encyclopœdia* and for the *Journal of Education.* His book *The Circle of Knowledge*, a graded reading book for children of all ages, was used throughout the world, was adopted by the British and French royal families for the education of their children, and was translated into French and Chinese. For Baker, the education of deaf children was simply an expression of wider educational processes; language was at the center of all education. He was critical of l'Epée's system of signs, claiming that sign language is a natural language that is limited in scope and that to attempt to develop an artificial language is doomed to failure. He claimed that a developed language could never be a true language conveying ideas but that it simply conveyed another language that must, in turn, be understood. He said of fingerspelling, or dactylology,

> Dactylology is nothing more than a substitute for our artificial alphabet; it conveys no ideas but is merely a vehicle of language,—a convenient one, because ready at all times, and in situations and circumstances when writing materials are inaccessible. (Baker 1837, 94)

His former assistant teacher, W. R. Scott, was, as we have indicated, more sympathetic to the use of sign language, stressing its educational importance and taking time to study it thoroughly (Scott [1849] 1870).

But the pedagogical influence of Baker and Scott was limited by changing times. Baker died in 1874 and Scott in 1877, just as pure oralism

Charles Baker, teacher and educational theorist, criticized l'Epée's system of signs, believing that sign languages were limited in scope and couldn't convey complex ideas.

came up over the pedagogical horizon, an expression of the individuating, alienating social processes discussed above. Thomas Arnold, minister of the Doddridge Chapel in Northampton, was, in collaboration with his star deaf pupil Abraham Farrar, to become Britain's intellectual champion of pure oralism. Through the integration of their biographies and our knowledge of the history and society of their times, we turn to explore the complex triumph of pure oralism and its dramatic consequences in the disablement of deaf people.

The Exception and the Rule: Thomas Arnold, Abraham Farrar, and the Ideological Triumph of Pure Oralism in Britain

Arnold taught only private pupils and then very few, but his manual for teaching deaf people speech and lipreading as well as for educating deaf people in general became the central texts in Britain for pure oralists and, above all, for the professional training of pure oralist teachers (Arnold 1881, 1888, 1891).[12] Arnold, however, did not believe that deaf children should be prevented from using sign language among themselves. His central concern was that speech should become the medium of instruction as early as possible and that students learn to think in English words. His learning and his influential contacts were vital to the disproportionate publicity given to the oralists and to the generation of support for the oralist cause from wealthy benefactors, parliamentarians, and even royalty. In fact, Arnold, through his most famous pupil, Abraham Farrar, was to be a catalyst in the development of oralism in Britain.

Thomas Arnold developed a manual for instructing deaf people how to speak and lipread that became one of the core texts for oralists.

Farrar's story is important because it demonstrates the intense power of the ideology of individualism and the vital link between oralism and the individuation of deaf people.[13]

Farrar was the only son of an extremely wealthy Yorkshire landowner. When Farrar was three years old, he caught scarlet fever and lost his hearing completely. Choosing not to send him to any of the public institutions, Farrar's father sought the services of the Reverend Thomas Arnold who had had experience with the teaching of deaf students earlier in his career. On 23 January 1868, his seventh birthday, Farrar began his education with Arnold.

For the next six years, Farrar was the only child in the household. In addition to speech and lipreading, he was also given a good classical education. Farrar had Arnold's undivided attention in "class," and he was ideal raw material, being extremely intelligent with a thirst for knowledge and having had no contact with sign language. Farrar, therefore, was, in every sense, the pure oral student. For Arnold, Farrar was the perfect test case of his method.

> . . . I was greatly favoured in having the son of Mr. and Mrs. Farrar as my pupil. From the first day until the last of his education they confided in my sincerity and ability, patiently waited till the work was achieved that made him the first of deaf students in the Empire, rejoiced with me in my success, sympathised with me in struggling with difficulties, and gave not a few proofs of their liberality. The crucial test I had devised had all the time, liberty, and encouragement it required to make it perfect. . . .
>
> . . . I was happy to have him as my crucial test. He ended the contention. (Arnold 1895, 69)

Farrar's success, in fact, proved little because it bore virtually no relationship to the environment of the school classroom. James Howard, who succeeded Charles Baker as head of the Yorkshire Institution for the Deaf and Dumb in Doncaster and who introduced the oralist system in the Doncaster school under the influence of the Italian oralist the abbé Ballestra, emphasized this point when he wrote in response to an article by Farrar (1883),

> Mr. Farrar doubtless enjoyed exceptional privileges, inasmuch as expense was no object in his education. He was taught at reputedly the best private school for the deaf in the kingdom, and was permitted to remain under instruction several years;
>
> . . . the very system advocated by Mr Farrar has been in operation in the Yorkshire County Institution at Doncaster for the last eight years. . . .
>
> . . . We labour, however, here under great disadvantages. Our pupils are for the greater part children of poor parents, who only allow them to remain at school an average of four years; and for lack of funds our teaching staff is not so numerous as it should be, the classes consisting of from 12 to 20 pupils, instead of the maximum number under one teacher being limited to ten—a *sine qua non* to success under the Oral system. . . . (Howard 1883)

Howard still had great hopes for the success of the oral system in schools, hopes that were rarely fulfilled over the next hundred years. However, Arnold's "crucial test" did produce what leaders needed above all else in their campaign to establish a national, pure-oralist educational system—a live success to be paraded before the wealthy and the powerful in their pursuit of this oral educational system for deaf students.

On 12 September 1874, Arnold took Farrar with him to one of his lectures for the first time. Farrar then demonstrated his ability to copy sounds made by Arnold and answered a series of simple questions. Farrar concluded his demonstration by reading from the first chapter of the Gospel of St. John in Latin and then repeating verses from a poem. The newspaper reported that he "articulated with considerable accuracy" but that "a want of flexibility was noticeable" in his voice (Howard 1883).

The following year at a public lecture, Farrar made his usual presentation of following a dictation by Arnold and won the admiration of the audience:

> With astonishing readiness and accuracy, and by an evident exercise of his reasoning faculties, not from memory, demonstrated a proposition from the

> second book of Euclid: gave the extraction of the square root from a number and the exposition of that extraction with algebraic proof. The pupil, in English analysis and Latin translation, as well as in mathematics, showed himself equal in intelligence and acquirement's to most boys of his age if not superior. . . .[14]

One effect of this demonstration was to gain the support of the local member of Parliament, a Mr. Phipps, to lobby the government to provide, in practice and not just in theory, education for all deaf children. The Elementary Education Act of 1870 had made education compulsory for all, including deaf children, but the means was not provided, and the educational needs of thousands of children who were poor and deaf remained neglected. Farrar's success provided added support to extend the School Board classes for deaf students that had begun in September 1874 under William Stainer. The example of Farrar and the evangelical fervor of Arnold for the oral method were soon to result in the School Board classes following the oral method.

In 1876, Farrar entered and passed the local examination of Cambridge University just prior to his sixteenth birthday. Farrar's success brought Arnold a great deal of publicity. He was personally congratulated by both King Edward and the Prince of Wales. Farrar's success was reported in many of the papers of the day, including the *Leeds Mercury* in his hometown of Leeds.

In 1877, Arnold engaged a local science master and an Oxford scholar to prepare Farrar for the London University matriculation examinations. In 1880, Farrar was awarded the Queen's Prize in chemistry and geology at the South Kensington Science and Art Examinations. In 1881, he matriculated from London University after sitting for exams that included Latin, Greek, French, geometry, algebra, natural philosophy, chemistry, English language, history, and grammar with dictation. Again, Farrar's success was reported widely in newspapers throughout the country.[15] By now, Farrar had become the living proof of the pure oral method and was called on to give public exhibitions. His effect on popular attitudes and on those with power and wealth was enormous.

Farrar's effect was enhanced by his also being the embodiment of the cultured gentleman—landed, cultured, classically educated—a stark contrast to the pupils of the crowded public schools for the deaf. Oralism, thus, was seen to be the agent of culture whereas signing remained associated with the uncultured, "natural" world. Deaf from natural causes, Farrar was presented as having become a virtual hearing person through the agency of a pure oralist education. In his 1899 article, "The Limitations of the Pure Oral Method," Ernest Abraham wrote:

> Mr. Farrar had every advantage that the average victim of Pure Oralism has not. He had intelligence, means, individual instruction for a practically unlimited period, and a prince of teachers; yet he admits that *he* cannot take in an average sermon or lecture by lip-reading, and that his speech is adequate only to the ordinary transactions of life. . . .
>
> Mr. Farrar is the brilliant exception that proves the rule that the Pure Oral method is quite unsuitable for general application. (Abraham 1899, 261)

But the hegemony of individualism triumphed. The exception set the course for the education of generations of deaf students. To understand further the historical process of disablement, we turn back to the Milan Congress of 1880.

The International Congress of Teachers of the Deaf, Milan 1880

The passing of the abbé Tarra's resolution for the universal adoption of pure oralism in the education of the deaf was reported enthusiastically in the London *Times*.[16] The *Times* report, strongly influenced by some prominent oralist delegates from Britain, claimed virtual universal support among teachers of the deaf for pure oralism—"The result is a virtual unanimity of preference for oral teaching which might seem to overbear all possibility of opposition"—and marveled at the performances during the Congress by Italian oral students.[17] After nearly a century of educating poor and deaf students through sign language, the popular imagination was again being stirred by the idea of teaching deaf mutes to speak. But subtle changes from the reactions of earlier centuries were apparent. The focus was less on education and more on the physical production of speech, on the "vocal utterance," as a passport to the hearing world. The oralists were concerned with emancipating deaf people from their deafness and, thus, from their pathological condition as well with providing deaf individuals the means to deny their deaf identity through therapeutic education. Education was becoming a cure for lack of speech. For the first time, the education of deaf students in England had a different goal from the education of hearing students. Speech and not knowledge was beginning to dominate the deaf child's education.

This description is not intended to paint all pure oralists with the same brush. Some, like Arnold, focused on what they assumed to be the educational value of pure oralism. Arnold saw the mastering of speech as the avenue to the mastery of those ideas expressed in the spoken language, in his case, English. But his public demonstrations focused heavily on the ability to speak, and the ability of deaf people to speak was what sparked the public imagination. The demonstration of even a mild reflection of oral competence was seen as a grand scientific achievement.

So fervent a crusade had oralism become that many pure oralists ignored the criticisms of other scientific experts. The very people who were to lay the basis for wholesale IQ testing with its disastrous results, the French psychologists Binet and Simon, were completely ignored when they concluded the following after a "scientific" evaluation of the achievements of Paris graduates from oralist institutions:

> People are mistaken about the practical result of the oral method. It seems to us a sort of luxury education, which boosts morale rather than yielding useful and tangible results. It does not enable deaf-mutes to get jobs; it does not permit them to exchange ideas with strangers; it does not allow them even a consecutive conversation with intimates; and deaf-mutes who have not learned to speak earn their living just as easily as those who have acquired this semblance of speech. (quoted in Lane 1988, 400)

Fired up by Arnold's eloquence and Farrar's example, by results that gelled with their goals for deaf individuals, the oralists ignored information, scientific or otherwise, that did not support their views. In their eyes, oralism meant progress, civilization in opposition to savagery, German rationality in opposition to French romanticism.

The pure oralists were fervent, self-righteous, politically effective, and well-connected. They pursued their cause with a missionary zeal, none more so than the oralists' chief spokesperson, Susanna Hull. Susanna Hull was one of Britain's earliest and most fervent pure oralists. In her school in 1868, Alexander Graham Bell had first applied his father's methods of "visible speech," and she remained a dedicated follower of Bell's methods. Her evolutionist views on the use of sign language were clearly stated.[18] In 1881, she wrote to the *American Annals of the Deaf* in response to Edward Miner Gallaudet's report of the Milan Congress, a report that had claimed the vote in favor of oralism was entirely unrepresentative of teachers of deaf students throughout the world, especially in Britain. Her response was full of evangelical fervor, not for the religious salvation of deaf people, though religious fervor was also there, but for the salvation of deaf people from deafness and dumbness, for their emancipation from the slavery to silence that she saw "manualism" as imposing on them:

> What did America do when the sons of another soil were enslaved upon her shores, debarred from the privileges her citizens enjoyed? Did not the North confront the South, the hands of brothers become dyed with brothers' blood, rather than that such a crime should continue? And shall this same America sit down and say of her own children, "Our deaf shall remain dumb, because our hearts are too selfish, our tongues too idle to plead for those whom our education has deprived of the power of vocal utterance?" Ten thousand times, No! The time for deliverance has come. Other nations have risen; who shall forbid America to be amongst the foremost? Surely not Dr. Gallaudet.
>
> By the memory of his "sainted mother," his honoured father, we call upon him to revise his verdict, to lend his power, his influence, his knowledge, his great ability, to forward that which he acknowledges as superior, and America's deaf shall yet rise up and bless him with their so long-withheld God-given *voices*. (Hull 1881, 97–98; Hull's italics)

Thus, by means of oralist education, taught as we shall see by an increasingly professionalized body of hearing teachers, deafness and a deaf identity were being defined as pathological conditions to be denied and overcome. Deafness was a symptom to be treated, ameliorated, and denied, though never quite cured.

Although throughout most of the nineteenth century the vast majority of teachers of deaf students, whether deaf or hearing, had been male, the triumph of pure oralism would involve a radical feminization of the role of teacher of deaf students. This feminization occurred when the teaching of deaf students was redefined as a caring profession akin to nursing, a profession that, given the medical focus on therapy, required mothering and nursing rather than intellectual stimulation. This new definition of the profession linked deaf people to the ideologically defined private world of women rather than to what was seen as the public, "able-bodied" world of men. The feminization of teaching reinforced the oral method, giving added meaning to the use of the "mother method" of language acquisition developed by the German oralists, especially Hill.

But the transition to pure oralism did not occur overnight. As Gallaudet himself made clear, of the eight English delegates to the Congress, only six had any experience of teaching deaf students: "six were ardent articulationists, and only two [Stainer and Elliott] at all favourable to any other method—a proportion which entirely misrepresents the present sentiment of English teachers of the deaf" (Gallaudet 1881, 3). Note that the Americans were not the lone votes against the abbé Tarra's pure oralism resolution at Milan. Richard Elliott, the principal of the Margate school voted with Gallaudet—"the . . . resolutions were adopted, the only negative voices being those of the American delegates and one English delegate, Mr. Richard Elliott, headmaster of the old London Institution" (Gallaudet 1881, 5; see also Van Cleve and Crouch 1989, 110). In addition, an Italian teacher rose to his feet during the debate on Tarra's motions, begging delegates not to kill the sign languages and to consult with deaf people themselves before voting.[19] Apart from one American deaf delegate, James Denison, deaf people at the Congress had not been admitted as voting delegates.

After Gallaudet's report of the Milan Congress, the English delegates plus their interpreter at the Congress, but minus Elliott, wrote to the *American Annals of the Deaf* objecting to the "charges of unfairness in the constitution and management of the Congress made by Dr. E. M. Gallaudet in the last number of the *Annals*" (Arnold et al. 1881, 138–39). As they themselves indicated, two of their number had small private schools; two had no teaching experience but were "well known . . . for their benevolent interest in the education of the deaf" (138); two were principal and secretary respectively of "the Training College for Teachers" (in fact, the Society for Training Teachers of the Deaf and Diffusion of the "German" System in the United Kingdom); and the remaining voting delegate, William Stainer, was in charge of the schools of the London School Board. They also stated that "Mr. Elliott, who voted with the minority in the Convention, was requested to sign the protest, but declined to do so" (138).

The English report of the Congress (Society for Training Teachers of the Deaf and for the Diffusion of the German System 1880) was prepared from notes made by Kinsey and did not mention Elliott's vote against the pure oralist resolution. Buxton and Stainer, two giants in the British education of deaf students, had both spent the early years of their teaching careers at the Old Kent Road school where they used

At the Milan Congress, Richard Elliott, the principal of the school for the deaf in Margate, England, voted with Edward Miner Gallaudet, to oppose pure oralist instruction.

the manual method. However, Buxton had become an increasingly ardent oralist until, by Milan, he was, as the Reverend F. W. G. Gilby put it, an "extra pure-oralist" ("Memoirs," 149).[20] Stainer was a later and reluctant convert. A closer examination of these two giants reveals important clues about the changes taking place.

Both Stainer and Buxton had embodied the teacher as missionary. Both had served their apprenticeships at the Old Kent Road school. Both were fluent signers. Both had gone on to take charge of other schools. Both were religious men taking an active role in providing religious services for adult deaf people. In 1870, along with Charles Baker and the heads of the New York and Hartford schools, Buxton was one of the group of four who were first awarded an honorary doctorate by Gallaudet's Columbia Institute. His involvement in the teaching of articulation and lipreading grew gradually. In 1876, at the Twentieth Annual Congress of the National Association for the Promotion of Social Science, Buxton stated:

> I am not going to deny that, in some cases, oral teaching may be practiced with very great success. I have done it myself many a time; but until the advocates of the system can train up a sufficiently numerous class of "experts" to supply the whole teaching power of every institution—which I most ardently wish they would do—we must go on with the best means attainable, and in the best way we can. . . . (1874)

The wealthy philanthropist, barrister, and member of parliament St. John Ackers was to provide the means to train experts, and by 1878, Buxton was secretary of the newly founded Society for Training Teachers of the Deaf and Diffusion of the "German" System in the United Kingdom, and an ardent pure oralist. At Milan, he spoke in favor of the abbé Tarra's resolutions:

> When I began my work as a teacher of the deaf, every Eastern voyager went to India round the Cape. Waghorn had not tracked the overland route; de Lesseps had not cut through the Isthmus, and joined the Western to the Eastern seas. A parallel change has taken place in the work we are considering, so far as my own and other countries are concerned. I began to teach on the "sign" system. I "went round the Cape." There was no Suez Canal then. There is now. And by that superior route I mean to go, as I most strenuously and earnestly urge its adoption upon you. It goes straight to its destined port. Other systems stop short of it. (Buxton 1880)

What Buxton failed to understand was that the destination had changed. In his early years, he had focused on the saving of souls and the education of deaf people. He was now turning to focus on the transformation of deaf people into pseudohearing people. "The readiness and grace with which they sign" (quoted in *The Deaf and Dumb Herald and Public Intelligencer* 1876, 99), was now seen as little consequence in their education.

Pure Oralism, Sign Language, and the Rationalization of the Education of the Deaf

But pure oralists like Buxton and Stainer did not advocate banning the use of sign language altogether, only in education. The use of sign language was being relegated to the irrational, emotional, nonscientific realm of religion. Oralism was being identified with rationality. When not educating deaf pupils, when involved in religion rather than in education, Buxton used sign language. In 1889 in London, Buxton and Edward Miner Gallaudet together interpreted a lecture by the Dean of Westminster Abbey (Draper 1889, 33). Gilby's picture of Buxton and Stainer in their later years is both amusing and revealing. Writing in his unpublished autobiography of the period 1895–1898, and specifically of the battles between the oralists and the exponents of the "silent method," Gilby wrote:

Though the teachers of the deaf, Reverend David Buxton, left, and the Reverend William Stainer, right, were fluent signers, they both came to believe that oralism was superior. Their conversion to oralism and its inherent contradictions with their ready use of signing in church services, is documented by the prominent CODA minister, the Reverend F. W. G. Gilby, bottom.

> I remember that Dr. Buxton was living, an extra pure-oralist though he was in theory, he ended up his days by acting as a missionary to the deaf, and was acting as such in 1895 when I got there [to St. Saviours in Oxford Street London]. A foremost champion of pure oralism, he was polite enough to come and lunch with me and to honour me with his company. He was a master of pure English but "how are the mighty fallen," and he was now "preaching to the deaf on his fingers!" Sunday after Sunday in his old age he came to be using the method he had for a number of years been cursing up hill and down dale. Of course the same might be said, and was said, of Dr. William Stainer. He too preached and signed with the most evident happiness and gusto; moreover, he was good at it, and master of it, and it provided a portion of his means of livelihood. But he had gone with the tide reviling the silent method, and where was the consistency in all of this? ("Memoirs" 149)

The consistency lay in the conceptual contrast between the transformational role of education and the natural role of religion. Education was fast becoming a branch of medicine as it focused on "the disabled." Its treatment of its pupils increasingly hinged on the diagnosis of degrees of deafness. Deaf students were subjected to testing to determine appropriate individual treatment, boosted, in particular, by the work of scientists such as Alexander Graham Bell as they developed technologies to test levels of hearing or deafness. Deafness was, in fact, virtually denied as it became divided into levels of "hearing loss."

The language used by Gilby to describe the activities of the pure oralists is revealing. They "reviled" the silent method, "cursing [it] up hill and down dale." He mentions also that the pure oralists "in the person of Mr. St. John Ackers, said the very bitterest things about the manualists" ("Memoirs," 148). As far as the pure oralists were concerned, they had right on their side; they had found the way and must destroy all in their path. They saw the "silent method" as standing in the way of progress, of progress through reason, through science and technology. Their claims to rationality and efficiency through the pure oralist method signaled an alliance between followers of oralism and members of government to bureaucratize deaf education. The "cage of reason" was an oralist cage, but not just a pure oralist one. The opponents of pure oralism were not pure manualists; they were supporters of "the combined method" for whom natural sign language was also inappropriate for education. Natural sign language, so much part of the British scene for three centuries, was now relegated to the realm of religion.

Notes

1. For an excellent discussion of these evolutionist views of sign language, see Baynton (1996, chap. 2).

2. After graduating from the University of Michigan in 1862, Edward Fay (1843–1923) went to teach at the New York Institution for the Deaf where his father had also taught. Three years later in 1866, Edward Miner Gallaudet invited him to join the staff of the recently established National Deaf-Mute College (now Gallaudet University). In 1885, he became vice president, a position he held until his retirement in 1920. A well-educated man, he taught Latin, French, and German, but he also knew Greek, Spanish, and Italian. In 1870, he became editor of the *American Annals of the Deaf*, a position he held until his retirement. He was a frequent contributor to the journal, and each year he published extensive statistics on aspects of deaf education (see Van Cleve 1987).

3. Worth noting is the parallel here with feminist discussions of the devaluation of women through their association with nature. The male is to the female as culture is to nature. For a discussion of these debates, see Moore (1988, 13 ff.).

4. See Sicard (1808a, 1808b, 1814).

5. Roch-Ambroise-Auguste Bébian (1789–1839) began teaching at the Paris Institute under Sicard in 1808. He criticized the use of methodological signs in 1817 in his *Essai sur les Sourds-Muets et sur le langage naturel*, advocating the use of natural sign language (Bébian 1817). He joined the deaf students and teachers in criticizing the policies of De Gérando, especially with respect to the introduction of oralism and the ongoing use of methodological signs. He was dismissed from the school in 1820. Bébian refused offers of appointment as head of schools for the deaf in St. Petersburg and in New York and founded a school for the deaf in the rue Montparnasse in Paris in 1826. He became director of the school for the deaf in Rouen in 1832, but after conflicting with the administrators of the school, he left in 1834. He wrote texts for the instruction of deaf students and on the practical administration of schools for the deaf. His most enduring legacy is his linguistic work on natural sign language.

6. As we will indicate later in chapter 9, this description could well describe the currently popular method of "Total Communication."

7. Clerc was committed to the use of methodological signs and rejected Bébian's call for the use of natural sign language. See Karacostas (1993, 135).

8. See Ringland and Gelston (1856) and Gallaudet (1867).

9. Baroness Mayer de Rothschild was the founder of the Jewish Deaf school in London in 1863 and of a private college for training oral teachers of deaf students in Fitzroy Square, London, in 1878. B. St. John Ackers was the founder in 1878 of the Training College for Teachers of the Deaf at Ealing in London.

10. Letters held in the archives of Gallaudet University reveal that Stainer had been reluctant to adopt pure oralism in the School Board schools but had felt obliged to do so because of pressure from his superiors. His greatest pleasure in later life was, as Gilby's memoirs also reveal (Gilby "Memoirs," 149), was

preaching in natural sign language, what became known later as British Sign Language (BSL).

11. Charles Baker (1803–1874) was born 31 July 1803, the second son of Thomas Baker of Birmingham. From 1826 to 1829, he was assistant at the Deaf and Dumb Institution at Edgbaston. In 1829, he was invited to assist the Reverend William Fenton in the establishment of a Deaf and Dumb Institution at Doncaster in Yorkshire. He was head of the Doncaster institution until his death in 1874. Baker's large library of books on the education of deaf students was sold by his wife to Gallaudet University within six months of his death, much to the displeasure of the school's board and other British teachers of the deaf.

12. The two volumes of Arnold's manual (1888, 1891) were edited and revised by Abraham Farrar into a one-volume work (Farrar 1901). Arnold wrote at length on the history of oralism and claimed his method as his own. Interestingly, Henry Baker wrote to the Reverend Dr. Doddridge of Northampton in 1747 about his teaching, as quoted in chapter 7. Arnold had ready access to the Doddridge papers and also to those of Henry Baker. These possible links between Baker's methods and those of Arnold are currently being explored.

13. For a more detailed biography of Farrar, see Branson and Miller (1998b).

14. *Northampton Mercury*, 16 October, 1875.

15. These included the *Times, Standard, Daily News, Daily Telegraph*, and a wide range of specialist and regional papers such as the *Sunday School Chronicle, Hand and Heart, Northampton Mercury, Deaf and Dumb Magazine, Sheffield and Rotherham Independent, The Leeds Mercury, The Northampton Herald*, and *The Lancet*.

16. *Times*, 28 September, 1880.

17. Ibid.

18. See Hull (1877, 236).

19. Gallaudet papers, Gallaudet University Archives.

20. Gilby was an extremely prominent figure on the British deaf scene and was the son of deaf parents. His father had been one of Britain's leading deaf missioners, and Gilby was an ordained Anglican minister based at the London church for the deaf, St. Saviours in Oxford Street. He was a fluent signer and extremely popular with the deaf community. His unpublished memoirs provide invaluable portraits of prominent figures and events through the nineteenth and early twentieth centuries.

7

Cages of Reason—Bureaucratization and the Education of Deaf People in the Twentieth Century: Teacher Training, Therapy, and Technology

In chapter 2, we outlined how professionalism, bureaucratization, and eugenics affected the cultural construction of "the disabled" through the late-nineteenth century and into the twentieth. Here, we explore those processes in relation to the education of deaf students. We continue to focus on developments in Britain but turn also to related developments in America and Australia. The histories of these three countries were not self-contained but interrelated. Australia was a colonial outpost of Britain, borrowing constantly from Britain for pedagogical ideas, recruiting staff members direct from Britain and Ireland, and eventually sending teachers to Britain for certification. American and British developments constantly affected each other as leading educators in both countries exchanged ideas, attended conferences, and looked to one another for expertise. Through the late-nineteenth century and the first half of the twentieth, the forces of professionalization and bureaucratization along with the ideological dominance of eugenicism encompassed the transformation of deaf education and the associated transformation of processes that labeled a person as "disabled."

The particular form that bureaucratization took in Britain radically transformed the environment within which the education of deaf students took place as well as the character and orientation of teachers. During this period, individual schools lost financial and administrative autonomy. Formal certification of teachers dominated teacher training from 1909. Pressures mounted with the initiation of compulsory primary education in 1870 and, later, of compulsory secondary education in 1944. These changes produced dramatic consequences for deaf students, particularly profoundly and congenitally deaf students. The character of our history changes in this period as heads of schools cease to be kings of little empires in which they are pedagogically idiosyncratic and creative and become part of a large, faceless bureaucracy. In this bureaucratic age, individuals disappear from the historical record. We no longer look to creative and dedicated individuals like Braidwood, l'Epée, Fay, Gallaudet, Charles Baker, or Thomas Arnold as the sources of education development. Rather, the history of education becomes the history of education acts and the work of education departments and government agencies. The influential people, if individuals emerge at all, are those who influence the shape and content of public policy. Thus, although the presence of St. John Ackers, barrister and member of parliament, at the Milan Congress of 1880 might have seemed anomalous at the time, his presence announced the arrival of new figures on the historical stage, those linked directly to government and to the institutionalized training of experts.

A significantly wide range of factors influenced the development of deaf education in Britain in the late-nineteenth century: the peculiarities and timing of British bureaucratization; Britain's involvement in major wars at the turn of the century and through the first half of the twentieth century; the effect of the British Empire on the character of the British class system and on class consciousness; and an intensely imperial orientation toward the English language. If we were to conclude, as so many have done, that the contrasts between the development of deaf education in Britain and America were somehow caused by divergent responses to and participation in the Milan Congress, responses that were linked to differences between a supposedly "oralist" Braidwood heritage in Britain and a "manualist" Gallaudet heritage in America—as is so often assumed—we would miss the point entirely. Britain's heritage was far from "oralist," as we have shown. The driving force of history by the end of the nineteenth century was the state and its need for the effective rationalization of educational processes.

The administrative rationalization of educational structures and processes toward the end of the nineteenth century was also associated with a more general rationalization of teaching methods. Included in this trend was a reorientation of teaching toward practicality. The high educational ideals of the earlier decades in the nineteenth century gave way to more vocationally oriented schooling. In an atmosphere dominated by rationality and pragmatism, educators and administrators labeled natural sign language as completely impractical and nonrational, and they responded to extreme ideological pressure to rationalize the form and content of any other varieties of manualism they used. However, to understand what influenced these linguistic processes, we need to understand the driving force behind the widespread rationalization of schooling—bureaucratization. In Britain, the beginning of the bureaucracy in deaf education dates essentially from 1885 as the Royal Commission on the Conditions and Education of the Deaf and Blind began.

The Royal Commission on the Conditions and Education of the Deaf and Blind

As we have already shown, Britain was not in any sense mainly oralist before the Milan Congress or as a result of that conference. The same was true in Australia, as we shall see. Of greater effect on the use of oralism was the Royal Commission on the Conditions and Education of the Deaf and Blind conducted from 1885 to 1889. The report mentioned the oral system in favorable terms and also referred to the two Cabra schools in Dublin as "two of the older-fashioned institutions" (United Kingdom 1890, 72) where signs were used. The sympathies of the chairman of the commission were clearly with the oralists. Just after the commission had begun, he opened a new wing of the Manchester school for the deaf and declared, "if only the education of the deaf were begun at an early age, 99 out of 100 of the deaf and dumb could be taught to speak by the oral system" (quoted in Green 1997, 30). In truly eugenic style, the report speculated on the causes of congenital deafness and mentioned that, in Germany, Switzerland, and Italy "where the oral system prevails" (United Kingdom 1890, 68), deaf people were less likely to marry other deaf people than in countries where signing was used. The report also mentioned that the religious activities of deaf people were conducted in sign and that, among older deaf people, one could find opposition to oralism. The report concluded that, although the oral system would ultimately prevail, they "do not, however, recommend such a sudden change of system as was carried out in France after, and in consequence of the Milan Conference" (Royal Commission 1890, 76). They concluded that all deaf children should be taught for one year at least on the oral system and pointed to the need for state aid for the training of teachers.

The Royal Commission heard a vast number of submissions and sought opinions from experts from overseas as well as from within Britain. In the wake of the Milan Congress, the oralists saw the commission as an opportunity to press for widespread conversion to pure oralism in Britain and were particularly diligent in the preparation of submissions. Through their lobbying, Alexander Graham Bell was invited to appear before the commission to represent "pure oralism." Aware of the political importance of the commission and of the fact that deaf people were not being consulted by the commission, the deaf missioner and parliamentary lobbyist Francis Maginn lobbied successfully for the commission to invite Edward Miner Gallaudet to represent "the combined method" and not the forms of manualism predominant in the British schools.[1] Although the report did favor a move to as much "oralism" as feasible, its recommendations were oriented more toward funding and coordinating the administrative processes required to realize compulsory elementary education for deaf students than toward dictating what method should be used. The commission's underlying assumption held that deafness was an essentially medical condition that should be alleviated in the best way possible to allow deaf people to be assimilated into hearing society, which played into the hands of the pure oralists as they interpreted the findings of the commission for the wider public.

Many teachers of deaf students and many deaf people themselves were opposed to the recommendations of the commission, to the way those recommendations were reached, and to the way the recommendations were reported in the press. A group of eminent British teachers of deaf students wrote to *The School Master*, objecting to their reporting of the Royal Commission, objecting to the bias of reporting in favor of pure oralism, and clearly stating that the majority of British teachers of the deaf were not in favor of pure oralism. They concluded nine years after Milan,

> We fear that too much attention has been paid to the exaggerated statements of those who advocate the pure oral method, while the views of the deaf and dumb themselves, who are the persons most directly interested, are taken little account of, or else contemptuously pooh-poohed. In many cases

> the pupils taught on the pure oral method find their so-called speech is of very little real service to them, how hopeless it is for them to attempt to read the lips of strangers with any degree of comfort or certainty, and, further, how little lip-reading can be depended upon for holding anything approaching connected conversation. There is no doubt that the orally-taught are often compelled to fall back upon the ordinary means of intercourse used by deaf mutes—viz., the manual alphabet and signs. Both in America and in England the "combined method" is the one most generally followed, and while we hope that one of the results of the prolonged and laborious work of the Commission will be liberal State aid for the education of the deaf, we do most sincerely trust (and here we speak in [sic] behalf of many hundreds of this afflicted class) that the pure oral method will not become the general system of instruction throughout the United Kingdom. (Sleight et al. 1889)

These British teachers' fears that the pure oral method was to become the general system of instruction throughout Britain were eventually realized by the mid-twentieth century, but the "combined method" in its varied forms was predominant throughout much of Britain well into the twentieth century. In the final decades of the nineteenth century, the "combined method," especially as conceptualized in America by Gallaudet and his colleagues, was to affect strongly the use of articulation and the forms of signing used in deaf education. The effect would continue right to the present because this "combined method" of the late-nineteenth century was to provide the base for the reintroduction of signing into deaf education beginning in the 1960s. Through Maginn, Elliott, and others on whom he bestowed academic honors, Gallaudet's championing of "the combined method" in which articulation was prominent hastened the breakdown of British manualism in which natural sign language and fingerspelling were predominant.

The Rationalization of Signing through the Combined Method

Edward Miner Gallaudet is quite rightfully seen as fighting for the use of signing in deaf education at a time when "pure oralism" was about to engulf the education of deaf students throughout the world, and he was not alone, as our coverage of British reactions to Milan has shown. Ironically, his form of the "combined method" in fact promoted the teaching and use of articulation in deaf education.

Edward Miner Gallaudet's "combined method" promoted the teaching and use of articulation in deaf education.

By the time of the Milan Congress the concept of a "combined method" was widely used. As Fay's survey showed, the concept referred to a range of different methods that combined articulation and signing. To understand the history of deaf education through the last decades of the nineteenth century and the early decades of the twentieth, one must understand how the concept of a combined method came to dominate debates about method and to understand the unconscious "symbolic violence" that was involved in supporting and using this approach. The combined method and not some sort of pure manualism is what deaf and hearing people who opposed pure oralism increasingly sought to retain. Thus, as Moores has clearly established, E. M. Gallaudet was not the champion of the manual-only method in deaf education. In fact, "E. M. Gallaudet played the key role in establishing oral education in schools for deaf children in the United States and was instrumental in gaining acceptance of a combined oral-manual philosophy" (Moores 1978, 59). It was Gallaudet who constantly encouraged the teaching of articulation—speech and lipreading—in all schools for the deaf.

> [T]he man who in 1871 argued that sign language was used to excess . . . felt constrained to defend the value of sign language in 1887 . . . and, clearly on the defensive, before the end of the century wrote an article entitled "Must the Sign Language Go?" . . . It has been pointed out . . . that Gallaudet's position was consistent over the years. In 1868 he was in opposition to the prevalent manual-only system, and in 1899 he was speaking out just as strongly against the dominant wave of the oral-only method. (Moores 1978, 60)

At the Columbia Institution, signing was essentially devalued as a medium of instruction in educational matters.

On 27 February 1891, a letter appeared in *Science* from Edward Fay, the vice president of the Columbia Institution for the Deaf (Gallaudet College). In a previous issue, Alexander Graham Bell had stated that "in the Columbia Institution a foreign language (the sign language) is used as the medium of instruction, whereas the rival methods employ the English language alone for this purpose" (quoted in Fay 1891). Fay replied:

> In the Columbia Institution the sign language is not used as THE medium of instruction. In some classes it is used as a medium of instruction, being employed to communicate with deaf children at the beginning course, when they have no other means of communication whatever, and to promote their mental development. . . . It is also used but very sparingly, in the earlier part of the course of instruction in connection with the English language, to explain and illustrate the meaning of words where otherwise the explanation could not be given at all; and it is used throughout the whole course for public lectures and devotional exercises, no means of using the English language having yet been discovered which will satisfactorily take its place for this purpose. . . . There are classes in both the Kendall School and the National College—the two departments of the Columbia Institution—in which English is the only medium of instruction. (Fay 1891)

The description of the use made of signing could be a description of language use in schools throughout Britain for most of the nineteenth century, the main difference being the nature of the sign language in use. In Britain, the sign language used was natural sign language and fingerspelling. In Gallaudet's college, it was a language of French and American heritage that was constructed for education, formed and transformed by teachers of deaf students from l'Epée to Edward Miner Gallaudet.[2] Gallaudet personally gave sign language lessons to his students to teach them the signs required for their education. A former student of the college, Olaf Hanson, is quoted in *The Silent World* as saying,

> Hearing people have sometimes asked me if I "graduated in signs at the college." One can hardly help smiling at such questions, but I replied that we do not, as a rule, use signs at the college.
>
> This is the truth. In the recitation room the students use finger spelling almost exclusively, and in general conversation the majority prefer this

mode of communication; though it must be admitted that a few whose proficiency in language is not all that could be desired, use signs to a greater extent than is good for them. (Hanson 1891–1909)

Described in this quote was "the combined system" that Francis Maginn, who had been a former student at the Old Kent Road school and at Gallaudet's college, sought Gallaudet's help to establish in opposition to pure oralism in Britain and that Samuel Johnson sought, again through Gallaudet, to retain in Adelaide, in opposition to the development of pure oralism in Australia. Although the concept of the combined method was applied to virtually any situation where elements of signing and oralism were found together, the approach that was designed for education and that combined the use of articulation, fingerspelling, and specialized, often initialized (Peet 1869), signs was the one that dominated the fight against pure oralism in both America and Britain.[3] In 1890, at the first British National Deaf Conference that was held in the lecture hall of St. Saviour's church for the deaf in London, Maginn said,

> Before I went to America I was rather one-sided, and opposed the teaching of speech too much. But after entering the celebrated College in Washington, I saw that not only could speech be taught with much success, but that those educated on the combined system spoke better than those educated on the so-called pure oral method. (quoted in Grant 1993, 103)

The following resolution, proposed by Maginn, was carried by a large majority: "That this conference is of the opinion that the combined system, as advocated by Dr. E. M. Gallaudet before the Royal Commission, is calculated to confer the greatest benefit upon the greatest number of the deaf and dumb" (Grant 1993, 103). When Maginn succeeded in attracting Joseph Tillinghast from America to head the school in Belfast, he wrote to Gallaudet, "We have BEATEN the English."[4] Grant notes that "support for the combined system was to become one of the fundamental policies of the BDDA. Universal adoption of its modern development—Total Communication—remains to this day one of the BDA's chief objectives" (103).[5] The symbolic violence of Total Communication will be discussed in the following chapter, but of importance here is that the American view of the combined method hastened the devaluation of natural sign language in Britain.

Even among so-called manualists, signing became thoroughly subordinate to and, most importantly, transformed by the prime focus on the acquisition of English, both spoken and written. The idea of using natural sign language as a language of instruction, indeed, the idea of sign languages as languages in their own right, distinct from any spoken language, was fast disappearing. Signing was becoming, in the eyes of educators, little more than a mode, a visual way of supporting the acquisition of the dominant spoken language. At the same time, schools using the combined system, whatever its makeup, did at least recognize the sensibilities of their pupils and, above all, understood the need for deaf people to communicate with one another through manual means. By 1925 in England and Wales, only 25 percent of deaf pupils were receiving some instruction through fingerspelling or some form of manual communication (Brill 1984, 80), and no deaf instructors were teaching; all manual communication of any kind was being used by hearing teachers (Brill 1984, 94). The English missions, in contrast to those in America, were all run by hearing people (Brill 1984, 99).

The alienation and individuation of groups who were judged "pathological" increasingly encompassed deaf people, and pure oralism was the main agent in the alienation process. In their battles with those who sought to retain elements of signing as an integral part of deaf education, the pure oralists had at least two trump cards up their sleeves: their alliance with medicine and bureaucracy in the classification of deafness and deaf students and their control over the training of teachers of deaf students.

The early twentieth century was an era of extreme imperial arrogance and industrial development. In Britain, although the depression of the 1890s had shouted to the world a warning of the vagaries within the developing world economic system, those in positions of power and influence could see nothing but progress through the rational, scientific appropriation of the world's natural resources—human as well as vegetable and mineral. The exploitation of labor power at home and abroad was severe and ruthless, and the domination of the whole system by white middle- and upper-class males was extreme. Nonetheless, the whole edifice relied more than ever on ideological commitment to individualism and equality, generating stark contradictions among the faceless workers and privatized women for whom ideals of individuality and equality produced the opposite results. The era, therefore, also gave rise to movements designed to achieve the human rights embodied in written and unwritten "constitutions"—for universal suffrage, for women's rights, and for the rights of individuals who were equal before the law.

As people sought to realize these central ideals, education emerged as a vital ideological practice—a process to which all should have equal access as individuals, where each could achieve her or his individual potential in the acquisition of skills for eventual sale on the labor market. At the same time, the schooling process also continued to serve as a normalizing process, as it serves today. As deaf children entered the schools for the deaf at the dawning of the twentieth century, the majority did so defined as pathological individuals with what was interpreted as a medical condition, deafness, in need of therapeutic treatment that included education to alleviate their symptoms of deafness as much as possible and, thereby, at least to some degree, to make them seem normal.

We must stress, of course, that the agents in these processes of disablement—academics, scientists, teachers, benefactors, parents, and deaf people themselves—were rarely conscious of the disabling effects stemming from their ideas and actions. Although a sociological imagination reveals the discriminatory and oppressive social and cultural consequences of pure oralism, many of the oralists firmly believed that they were doing the best for their deaf pupils and that they were, indeed, the true "friends of the deaf." At this point, we continue to delve below the threshold of consciousness to explore the unknown, the ignored, and the usually unintended social and cultural consequences of everyday behavior. We turn first to explore the effect of the bureaucratization of schooling on deaf education in Britain. The effect was, as we shall show, dramatic to say the least.

Bureaucracy and the Cultural Construction through Education of Deaf People as "Disabled" in Britain

> In the twentieth century there were children whose lives were no more than a shuttling to and fro between Poor Law Institution and Deaf Institution, and only the book-keeping aspect of the tragedy seemed to matter. (Hodgson 1953, 295)

As the education of deaf students ceased to be a charity supported by benefactors and became a responsibility of the state, the disabling consequences of the schooling process increased. In Britain and Europe, these processes were also radically influenced by the social, economic, and political effect of war, in particular, the Boer War in South Africa (1899–1902), the First World War (1914–1918), and the Second World

War (1939–1945). Until 1907, the "one-third clause" required schools to continue to find one-third of their income from charity, but charity was no longer as forthcoming as before. War and the depression of 1890 had had an effect, but more than that, the expectations of society at large were changing. Although the expectation in France and America that the state would take prime or sole responsibility for education had been in place for some time, education in Britain had remained dependent on private enterprise and the Protestant ethic of charitable works until late in the nineteenth century. But by the 1880s, the British were embracing the bureaucratic ethos with enthusiasm, looking to the state to coordinate the Empire, the army, and education.

Of interest here is that attempts by Charles Baker to establish regular conferences of principals of schools for the deaf in the early 1850s resulted in two conferences but that the conferences ceased to operate by 1852 (Principals of the Institutions for the Deaf and Dumb 1852). The conferences were revived in 1878 by Richard Elliott and David Buxton as the Conference of Headmasters of Institutions and of Other Workers for the Education of the Deaf and Dumb, which became an influential force in the establishment of oralist education for deaf students in Britain. By 1878, the focus had shifted from the purely educational concerns of principals like Baker to the combined educational, medical, and welfare orientation of "workers for the education of the deaf and dumb." These professionals were integral to the bureaucratization process and by 1890 were a vital force to increase professionalism, stressing in their proceedings the need for inspections of schools and the training of teachers in special institutions (*Proceedings of the Conference of Headmasters. . . .* 1890).

From the 1880s, the responsibility for providing deaf children with schooling was shared by the British Treasury and local educational authorities. Although many of the old schools continued as before, some with substantial endowments from wealthy benefactors, the payment of fees was now a government responsibility. As far as most local educational authorities were concerned, the education of deaf students was an administrative problem and a low priority. Although the 1889 report of the Royal Commission had recommended substantial expenditure on the education of deaf people and had at least focused reasonable attention on methodological and pedagogical issues, bureaucracy and financial shortages reduced the education of deaf children to an administrative process requiring rational classificatory procedures and the cheapest solutions.

The 1902 Education Act focused on the need to extend compulsory education into the secondary sphere but paid no attention to deaf education. Most deaf education continued only at the primary level with no nursery or secondary provisions until well after the First World War. Local education authorities sought the cheapest educational solutions for the children in their localities, "moving children from school to school to save a few pounds" (Hodgson 1953, 291) and, in many cases, not sending deaf children to deaf schools at all but, rather, leaving them to cope at home or in schools without any relevant staff or facilities. Although interest groups such as teachers of deaf students, deaf associations such as the British Deaf Association, missioners to the deaf community, and their supporters in and out of parliament lobbied for increased expenditure on deaf education, they had little effect through the first three decades of the twentieth century.

Administrative concerns increasingly dominated the course of deaf education. Recruitment for the Boer War had revealed high levels of unfitness among recruits, generating increased anxiety among eugenicists and prompting increasing medical surveillance of and control over the population. The 1907 Education Act made providing school medical services compulsory. Inspections of school children throughout Britain by the medical branch of the board of education, which was headed by Dr. Eicholz, revealed larger numbers of deaf children than previously thought. The bureaucratic state, with its administrative classification of deafness as a medical condition and its associated treatment of the deaf child as a pathological individual, was becoming the main agent in the cultural construction of the deaf as "disabled." The pure oralists were in the wings, but for more than half a century after the Milan Congress, the iron cage of bureaucracy is what defined the cultural parameters of deafness. Although the board of education recommended in the first decade of the twentieth century that "the English language be taught by the oral method where possible" (Hodgson 1953, 292), administrative concern with what went on in the schools was minimal. The bureaucrats expected the medicos to define deafness, and the medicos expected the oralist teachers to provide the treatment required to cure or at least ameliorate the medical "condition." Local education authorities evaded their legal responsibilities toward deaf children where possible, discriminating by neglect:

> The State was really indifferent to the deaf. The attitude was still that of the 1889 Report [of the Royal Commission], which classified the deaf and

> the blind with the idiots and imbeciles. By this administrative cruelty the State committed to one pitiful residuum all the children who would never fire a gun. . . . The deaf did not matter. (Hodgson 1953, 292)

By 1913, twenty local education authorities were spending nothing on deaf education.

The dual effect of bureaucracy and science on the defining of deaf people was significant with the passing of the Mental Deficiency Bill in 1913, arousing, as Hodgson recalls, "the obvious fear that doctors ignorant of the effects of deafness on behaviour would certify as defective deaf children who were merely neglected" (Hodgson 1953, 293–94). He adds, "The worst thought was that such wrongful certification would save a local authority the expense of educating the child" (294). The institutionalization of deaf children as "mental defectives" was far from uncommon.

In 1914, war came again, which affected economically and, this time, demographically the education of the deaf. Men left the teaching profession to join the armed forces. Schools that were already underfunded and now understaffed were forced to take in refugee deaf children from Belgium. Deaf children were admitted to schools at a later age than other children to defer costs. In the 1920s, as Britain suffered a postwar economic slump, the cost of educating a deaf pupil at a residential deaf school was stated to be £75 a year and was considered by the president of the board of education, the Rt. Hon. H. A. L. Fisher, to be "unduly expensive" (Hodgson 1953, 295). In comparison, according to Hodgson's study, "At that time the average American expenditure on a deaf child was 500 dollars a year, and 800 dollars in the most progressive States" (295). By the 1920s, educational standards were still slipping lower, and deaf education was governed almost solely by administrative considerations. The cage of reason was as restrictive as ever.

Although parents with private means could still find specialized schooling for their deaf children at schools like Arnold's old school, the Spring Hill School in Northampton, the vast majority of deaf children received little but neglect between the wars. Government inquiries in 1932 and 1938 by the first and second Eicholz committees respectively, revealed the tragic state of affairs in the education of deaf children. The focus of the recommendations was on providing adequate educational facilities for children with some hearing, "a sad instance of the bias of official interest in favour of the speaking and partially hearing deaf children" (Hodgson 1953, 296). But just as the 1938 report had begun to focus attention on the needs of at least some deaf people, Britain was again at war.

The immediate postwar period saw the passing of the 1944 Education Act, designed to ensure compulsory secondary education for all. But deaf students saw little improvement apart from the establishment of secondary education for the very privileged few at the newly established Mary Hare Grammar School in 1946, complemented in 1955 by the Burwood Park School, a secondary technical school, opened and supported by private subscription.[6] By 1950, hundreds of deaf children of school age were not able to find places in schools for the deaf.

The failure to provide adequate funding to schools for the deaf had two basic consequences: many schools were forced to close whereas others, no longer able to cover the costs associated with residential pupils, became day schools. The lack of places in deaf schools for many deaf children and the shift to day schools for many of those who could find a place were associated with a general redefinition in British society of the very nature of childhood itself and of the role of the family in the moral development of the child. These general changes were to have particularly disabling consequences for deaf children.

The Day School and the Redefinition and Individuation of Childhood

The early nineteenth century had seen the development of the private boarding school, or "public schools" as they were and are known in Britain. The boarding school became a place apart in which childhood was managed "to mould children on the pattern of an ideal human being" (Ariès 1962, 284). This goal directly linked to the evolutionist and proto-eugenicist intent of the white upper and middle classes. Boarding schools were, as were the asylums for deaf people as well as for those who were blind or mad, also controlled moral environments where the rational society took command. But the development of compulsory education at the end of the nineteenth century gave the nature and management of childhood a new twist. Ariès writes:

> The change which occurred in the school population at the end of the nineteenth century in favour of the day-boys did not interrupt this tendency to set children apart, but it turned it in the direction of family life. The

> family was substituted for the school as the predominant moral setting. . . . The central concern of the individual family was its own children. (Ariès 1962, 285)

The state not only was asserting control over educational processes but also was, albeit unconsciously, undermining the development of communal educational environments and reasserting the ideology of individualism. As the old residential schools for the deaf became less and less viable financially, day schools increased, and the vast majority of deaf children became "pathological" individuals within hearing families instead of members of a deaf educational community where language and identity could be shared.

The move in Britain away from residential schools for deaf students toward day schools was essentially governed by financial considerations, but it was part of the general trend discussed by Ariès and also was promoted explicitly by the pure oralists. Bell campaigned for day schools for deaf students to ensure that these children remained integrated within their hearing families rather than allowed to form close communal bonds with their deaf peers. Of the remaining schools for deaf students in Britain in 1925, twelve were independent residential schools, eight were residential schools run by local authorities, and the remaining twenty-nine were day schools run by local authorities (McLoughlin 1987, 77). From 1947 on, this trend toward the individuation of the child was to be promoted further by moving away from special schools for those judged "partially hearing" and moving toward "partially hearing units" in mainstream schools. These moves paved the way for deaf students to be included in the integration or mainstreaming movement of the late 1980s.

In 1950, the Advisory Council on Education in Scotland published a report drawing attention to the language problems faced by deaf students under the oral system, the "oral failures." By this stage, all deaf education in Britain was essentially oralist though not necessarily purely oralist. In fact, oralism never became a formal educational policy in Britain at either the professional or the governmental levels. The intensely disabling effect of the age of bureaucracy had promoted the cause of pure oralism, often, by default because, as the machinery of government sought to classify and administer, it looked not only to the medicos to diagnose but also to the teachers to provide the pedagogical environment required to assimilate the deaf child into the hearing world as much as possible. Thus, we return to the other side of the coin of bureaucratization, professionalism, and its links to pure oralism.

Teacher Training in Schools for Deaf Children in Nineteenth-Century Britain

Writing at a time when formal teacher training for teachers of the deaf had been established and when pure oralism was dominant, the Reverend F. W. G. Gilby reflected on earlier times when teachers were trained on the job and the use of signing was accepted.

> I am inclined to think that the old uncertified and sometimes rather illiterate teacher who was a volunteer, and worked from sheer love of the deaf, was at times able to produce results in the lives of his pupils in the way of forming character aright which are not met with so often now. Some teachers who are now paid decent salaries have not the fire of those old pioneers who evolved their own methods, building upon those of [Henry] Baker and [Thomas] Braidwood. We have certainly got rid of the old atmosphere, the fear of change, and of fresh air. But religious principles are less and less being inculcated. The old order has broken up as I see it, in order that God might fulfil himself in other ways, and some of these better ways have not yet arrived. The way for them has however been cleared. Too much has been expected from the oral method and too much has been promised by two or three outstanding boastful spirits . . . articulation, lipreading and silent methods, will all go forward and have their just places, in the education of the deaf child. A teacher who has learned but one method of teaching is surely only partially equipped for his task. ("Mem^irs," 144–45)

Jacoby notes that, in Britain, "the arrested growth of administrative centralization permitted the aristocratic rule of the eighteenth century and the autonomy of local institutions with amateur and unpaid officers who often failed to perform their duties" (Jacoby 1973, 165). Although many teachers of deaf children in the nineteenth century did not "fail to perform their duties," the education of deaf students was characterized by the autonomy of the individual schools and an in-house mode of training. Jacoby's general comments are filled out by Silberman as he analyzes how expertise in administration became formalized and standardized in Britain and America during the later-nineteenth century. By the end of the nineteenth century, "experts" of many kinds attempted "to create uniform definitions of expert training" (Silberman 1993, 417). Professionals sought certification through formal educational institutions, thereby committing "themselves to a body of norms governing the use of expertise as a condition of certification" (Silberman 1993, 418). These were precisely the processes that transformed the schooling of deaf students.

The Apprenticeship System

For most of the nineteenth century, school teachers in general had been trained through an apprenticeship system in the schools; the same was true for teachers of deaf children. No teacher training institutions had been established. The Braidwood legacy spread only through the pupil-teacher system. The process of learning on the job, whether through Braidwood or within the parish schools, was slow. Thomas Braidwood, for example, trained assistant teachers at the school over a seven-year period. His assistants were mainly family members: his daughter Isabella, nephew and son-in-law John, grandsons John and Thomas, and nephew Joseph Watson. This system of training teachers in the schools had become the practical way to supply teachers for the burgeoning number of deaf schools that had been established as charity institutions for children of poor families.[7]

With the rapid expansion of the first London school for children who were poor and deaf, Joseph Watson had used the apprenticeship method to train teachers, a method of training continued both by Thomas Watson, Joseph's son, and then by Thomas's son, the Reverend James Watson. The Old Kent Road school thus provided many of the headmasters and teachers for the other schools as they were established in quick succession. Many of the most prominent teachers in the 1800s started their careers in this way. Entry into the school was usually by way of a recommendation from a family friend or relative. Thus, David Buxton joined the staff of the Old Kent Road school in 1841 when he was nineteen years old, on the recommendation of the Reverend Alexander Watson of St. Andrews Ancoats, a relative of Dr. Watson whom he had met through a mutual interest in literature. Buxton lived at the school for ten years, first as a junior before rising to the position of assistant head teacher. He left in 1851 to become headmaster of the Liverpool Institution, replacing the Reverend Rhind who had also trained at the Old Kent Road school under Joseph Watson.

William Stainer, who was to become one of the leaders among educators of deaf people, also joined the school as a trainee teacher when he was fourteen years old. He had previously taught students at St. Thomas's endowed school, where his father was master, and had been a student at the National Society's Training School at Westminster. Ordained in 1872, he took responsibility for the establishment of the London Metropolitan School Board classes in 1874, the first to be established under a local authority after the passing of the 1870 Education Act.

Another contemporary of Stainer and Buxton at the Old Kent Road school, E. J. Chidely, attended the school as a youth and taught there from 1838 until 1856 when he took over the headmasters position of Claremont Institution, Dublin. Two other contemporaries of Stainer and Buxton, McDiarmid and Large, also became principals at Donaldson's Hospital, Edinburgh after being trained at the Old Kent Road school.[8]

A few prominent pioneers started life as schoolmasters in schools for hearing children and then moved into the field of deaf education. Andrew Patterson, who was a teacher of deaf children for almost fifty years, started work as a schoolmaster in Devonshire. While there, he became friendly with a Mr. H. B. Bingham, the then headmaster of the Exeter Deaf and Dumb School. Not long afterwards, Bingham became headmaster of the Manchester School and soon asked Andrew Patterson to join him as assistant master. After five years, Patterson left to establish the Newcastle Deaf, Dumb and Blind Schools before returning to Manchester as headmaster upon Bingham's retirement in 1842, a position he held until 1883. Richard Elliott, who had had a village school in the Weald, Kent before becoming second master at Latymer Endowed School Hammersmith, joined the Old Kent Road school in 1857. His knowledge of deaf education was also learned on the job. This tradition of apprenticeships explains why the methods used and the curricula taught in Britain were so consistent.

The Braidwood influence was not confined to London. In Edinburgh, Robert Kinniburgh was trained by John Braidwood and took over from him after his departure for America. Kinniburgh also received additional training from Watson in London. Thomas Braidwood, a grandson of the first Braidwood, was headmaster of the Birmingham Institution at Edgbaston, close to where Charles Baker lived as a child. After viewing a public examination of the students at that school, Baker became interested in their education. By the age of fourteen, he was already a popular

Sunday school teacher and well known to the leading men of the city. When Braidwood had to leave Birmingham for a few weeks in 1818, Baker was the obvious choice to take over, which he did successfully. Braidwood refused to consider him for a permanent position in the school, and so at the age of seventeen, Baker took charge of a small school at Wednesbury. He returned to Birmingham in 1826. By then, Braidwood had died, and Du Puget, a pupil of Petsalozzi, was headmaster. He employed Baker who stayed for three years. In 1829, after three years' teaching experience, he was appointed as headmaster of the newly established Yorkshire Institution at Doncaster. Before long, Baker's chief assistant, Sleight, whom he had trained, took over as headmaster of the newly founded Brighton Institution. Sleight was, in fact, second choice; the governing board had already offered the position to Thomas Arnold who had declined the position on religious grounds.

In addition, the church, the missions, and the schools were known to interchange personnel. In 1854, Samuel Smith, a young teacher who had trained under Charles Baker at Doncaster, was employed as a missionary by the Association in Aid of the Deaf, a post he held until his death in 1883. Similarly, Charles Rhind began his training as a teacher at the Old Kent Road school under Dr. Watson when he was sixteen and, after being principal at Ulster, Aberystwith, Swansea, and Edinburgh, joined Smith as a missioner in 1860. He was ordained in 1878 and then in 1883 succeeded Smith as missioner to the Association in Aid of the Deaf until his death in 1888. In other cases, qualified ministers or missionaries who often had been connected with the provision of Sunday schools later became principals of schools. The Reverend John Kingham is a good example, having first been involved with Sunday schools that included "the deaf and dumb" before being elected as principal of the Ulster Institution in 1853.

The Certification of Teachers of the Deaf

The oralists were the prime movers in the establishment of formal training for teachers of the deaf in Britain. In 1872, The Association for the Oral Instruction of the Deaf and Dumb and Training College for Teachers was established through the ongoing patronage of the Baroness Mayer de Rothschild with William Van Praagh of the Jews' Deaf and Dumb Home as director. The college was established as an extension of the Jewish oral school, the Jews' Deaf and Dumb Home, which had been founded by the Baroness de Rothschild in 1863. The new school's purpose was twofold: to educate non-Jewish children through the pure oral method and to train teachers in the method.

Six years later, in 1878, the Training College for Teachers of the Deaf was established by B. St. John Ackers at Ealing in London with Arthur Kinsey as principal and David Buxton as secretary. The full name of the college was the Society for Training Teachers of the Deaf and Diffusion of the "German" System in the United Kingdom. Its first "graduate" was a Miss Isabel Jennings in 1879. As in America, the trainees for teaching through the oral method were virtually all women. At the Ealing College, out of nearly one hundred trainees during its first ten years, only two were men, and they were paid a salary to attend whereas all women paid fees.

At a conference held by the Economic Science Section of the British Association in August 1879, Farrar demonstrated the success of the oral method after papers advocating its adoption in schools for the deaf and dumb were presented by David Buxton and Susannah Hull. In response, the British Association established a committee to report on the education of deaf students and, in 1880, recommended state support for deaf education through the "German" system and state aid to training institutions (*Report of the Fiftieth Meeting of the British Association for the Advancement of Science* 1880).

Both the Milan Congress and the Royal Commission further stimulated these moves for the formal training of teachers of deaf people. The Governing Bodies of Institutions for the Deaf in Great Britain met to consider the Milan Congress on 17 March 1881. Susanna Hull, from the oral group who had been in Milan, suggested the following motion:

> [I]n the teaching of the deaf as of hearing children, the conference earnestly recommends to the governing bodies of institutions of the deaf that a certificate from a training college be required of every applicant for the position of teacher. (Gallaudet 1881, 269)

At the conference of Headmasters of Institutions and of other workers for the education of the Deaf and Dumb, held at the Statistical Societies rooms, Kings College London from 22–24 June 1881, discussion again focused on the need to train teachers, particularly in the oral method, rather than a plan to continue the traditional pupil-teacher system (*Proceedings of the Conference of Headmasters. . . .* 1881). During the Conference of English Headmasters (London, 1–3 July 1885), "at the suggestion of Mr. Elliott, of Margate, and Mr. Stainer, of London, the head-masters of English institutions decided to organize an Examining

Board for teachers of the deaf" (Fay 1885, 173–74). Those at the conference decided that knowledge of articulation and knowledge of signs and fingerspelling "will probably be optional on the part of candidates, but the certificate will specify the subjects in which they have passed" (1885, 174).

Thus, in 1885, the College of Teachers of the Deaf was founded with Sir John Ackers as president and Richard Elliott and William Stainer as vice presidents. The college was incorporated on 21 May 1887. At the conference of Headmasters of Institutions and of other workers for the education of the Deaf and Dumb, held at Royal Association in aid of Deaf and Dumb, St. Saviours, Oxford St., London, 8–10 January 1890, talk focused strongly on the need for increasing professionalism, the need for inspections of schools, and the need for the training of teachers in special institutions (*Proceedings of the Conference of Headmasters. . . .* 1890). The first number of the journal *The Teacher of the Deaf*, published in January 1903, raised the topic of the registration of teachers of deaf students as a vital issue and indicated clearly how this issue was integrally linked to the certification of teachers, a certification process dependent on examination processes run by existing training colleges. This article signaled an ongoing obsession with the professionalization of teachers of deaf students that continued to dominate editorials in the journal, especially under the editorship of Susanna Hull.

On 1 September 1909, the board of education brought into effect regulations requiring all new teachers of deaf students to have special training and certification that was recognized by the board in addition to any training that was required for elementary school teachers. In 1912, the Ealing and Fitzroy Square colleges were amalgamated as the National Association for the Oral Instruction of the Deaf. The Ealing and Fitzroy Square colleges were closed in 1918 and 1919, respectively. In 1919, Sir James Jones, a wealthy industrialist who had a deaf son, provided funds to establish the National Training College for Teachers of the Deaf in the University of Manchester. The centralization and professionalization of teacher training for teachers of the deaf had been achieved.

The Education of Deaf People Becomes a Caring Profession: The Feminization of Teaching

The formalizing and centralizing of teacher training for the education of deaf people was part of a wider process of professionalization that was accompanied by the feminization of the profession, especially at the primary level. These processes signaled not only a new role for the state in the administration of education but also changing attitudes toward childhood, changes that were to accentuate the individuation of the deaf child. The education of deaf people was thenceforth virtually, though not entirely, oral. It was completely dominated by hearing people. Deaf people were now deprived of any control over their own education, indeed, over their own deafness. They were objects to be dealt with by teachers, doctors, and welfare workers. Their alienation was extreme.

In America, the disenfranchisement of deaf teachers also accompanied the institutionalization of teacher training and the associated increasing concentration on the teaching of articulation. In 1891, Gallaudet applied to Congress for funds to establish a teacher-training school at Gallaudet College. Gallaudet assured Bell that deaf students would not be admitted (see Mackay 1997, 246–47). Bell's wishes were fulfilled: "The new teacher-training school established in 1891 at Gallaudet College, a liberal arts college primarily for deaf students, itself refused, as a matter of policy, to train deaf teachers" (Baynton 1996, 25). Similarly, women increasingly predominated in the profession

> as the image of both deaf people and the occupation of teaching deaf people was domesticated—in both senses of the word. The virtues of the intrepid [male] explorer and rescuer of lost souls gave way to the homely and passive [female] virtues of patience and fidelity. (Baynton 1996, 71)[9]

As Winzer notes,

> Nearly all women choosing deaf education as an occupation during the final three decades of the nineteenth century took positions in oral schools. Here, despite their exclusion from specific universities and their denial of status in the manual institutions, they could receive training and achieve certified expertise. In fact, in many schools it became an unwritten policy to hire only women. (Winzer 1993, 241)

The predominance of women in the profession starkly signaled the radical transformation of orientations toward the education of deaf students and of wider social dispositions toward deafness and deaf people. Deaf people were no longer conceptualized as an interesting "people" akin to a tribe of "savages." They were no longer culturally different objects of intellectual and missionary speculation, no longer the province of the gentleman explorer and amateur anthropologist. Their difference was thoroughly individuated, an individual and pathological expression of the "normal" individual, the difference defined as a lack, a "hearing loss," to be remedied through pedagogical and technological means. Now, "disabled" individuals were in need of care and cure. The education of deaf students had become a caring profession, like nursing—the province of women.

Education as Therapy: The Alliance of Bureaucracy, Oralism, and Technology

The ultimate disabling of "the deaf" as a cultural and linguistic group through the individuation of their deafness, which defined deafness as a lack, as a loss, was expressed not only in the move to pure oralism and in the feminization of the teaching profession but also in the renewed focus on making deaf people hear through technological aids. Although ear trumpets and other aids had been made and used for centuries, the use of aids in education did not begin until the end of the nineteenth century, in tandem with the spread of pure oralism. In the late 1880s, the Royal School for the Deaf at Margate experimented with the use of the audiphone, an American invention designed to allow deaf people to hear through their teeth. The audiphone was a large, curved, comb-like object held against the teeth to pick up the vibrations of a person's voice. The device proved to be a failure, giving rise to the comment: "The only use of the audiphone is to those who sell it" (quoted in Beaver 1992, 146).

In 1895, the medical officer at Margate "invented and patented a tele-transmitter and earphone powered by three dry-cell batteries which enabled speech reading to take place and which several children could use if the number of earphones was increased. This was the start of teaching with hearing aids at Margate" (Beaver 1992, 146). This period was a time of scientific invention, with the wireless and telephone making a particular effect. The development of hearing aids was a spin-off that was advanced by the involvement of Alexander Graham Bell in the lives and education of deaf people.

The development of hearing aids to counteract "hearing loss" continued apace and with great ingenuity, as the pages of *The Albion Magazine* clearly illustrate. *The Albion Magazine*, begun in 1908, was specifically oriented to providing deaf people with information about the latest developments in hearing aids while alerting them to the dangers of consulting "quacks" claiming to cure deafness. Lists of "Quacks the Deaf should avoid" appeared in each number of the magazine. The magazine included articles on the development of the audiphone for class use, which involved linking students by tubes to a central transmitter, and articles on the wonders to be found at "The Paradise for the Deaf," a shop in the Strand, London, established in the early 1800s, which stocked a vast range of hearing aids, including acoustic chairs and invisible aids secured beneath the hair (Yellon 1908). Science and technology were assumed to be triumphing over quackery.

Alexander Graham Bell's genius in the development of acoustic equipment, not least of which, of course, was the telephone, stimulated widespread research into the development of acoustic equipment both to test and to promote hearing. Various attempts were made to develop this equipment such as individual and group hearing aids, but not until the late 1920s did inventors develop audiometers that were considered to be capable of effectively testing hearing. Wearable hearing aids did not emerge until the 1930s, and only much later, in the 1950s, were small, lightweight hearing aids developed.

By the 1930s, audiometers for testing hearing and hearing aids were becoming standard equipment in schools for the deaf. The students were wired up, plugged in, and turned on to the hearing world—supposedly. Technological progress, it was assumed or at least hoped, was overcoming the frailties of nature. Science was triumphant. But deaf people remained a pathological presence. Developments in the production of hearing aids proceeded apace with the development of transistors and then of microchip and digital technology. For those for whom the amplification of sound is successful, the technology has provided clearer and more effective access to the hearing world. Of that fact there is no doubt, but for deaf people for whom sign language is the only language they can access in any comprehensive way, these technological developments are of little beneficial consequence as far as access to sound-based languages is concerned. Their actual consequence is that the hearing authorities continue to assume that science can overcome the supposed pathology of deafness and that oral education is both viable and desirable.

As the cages of reason encompassed the education of the deaf, oralism triumphed, even where the combined method was used; signing was rationalized and thus transformed to meet the needs of teaching spoken English. But the triumph of oralism was essentially hollow for two reasons. First, as the government and its agencies assumed control of education, they failed. In an era of wars and economic depression, they did not deliver the necessary financial support to provide the resources needed by deaf students and their teachers. Second, pure oralism as a method failed to generate educated, speaking graduates, except in the most exceptional and privileged cases. In an atmosphere of increasing prosperity after the Second World War, oralist teachers looked to technology and therapy to provide the key to success.

Notes

1. For a discussion of Fay's 1881 survey of the methods used in British schools, see chapter 6 and the appendix to this volume.

2. For a discussion of the battles over the use of various forms of signing in deaf education in nineteenth-century America, including methodological signs, natural signs, and initialized signs, see Stedt and Moores (1990).

3. Initialized signs are signs that use at least the first letter of the English word as the basis for the development of the sign.

4. Gallaudet correspondence, Gallaudet University Archives.

5. British Deaf and Dumb Association (BDDA), which became the British Deaf Association (BDA).

6. For information on the Mary Hare school and Mary Hare herself, see Boyce and Lavery (1997, 1999). The current prospectus of the Mary Hare school, including a history of the school, is also available on the World Wide Web at http://www.bme.jhu.edu/~tratnana/mhgs.html.

7. This tradition of teacher training explains why Thomas Gallaudet could not be given details about teaching techniques in a short time. To learn about teaching techniques, he had to serve an apprenticeship.

8. For a history of Donaldson's College, Edinburgh, formerly Donaldson's Hospital, see Montgomery (1997).

9. See Baynton (1996, 71ff.) and Winzer (1993, 234ff.) for discussions of the increasing role of women in the education of deaf students beginning in the later-nineteenth century.

8

The Denial of Deafness in the Late-Twentieth Century: The Surgical Violence of Medicine and the Symbolic Violence of Mainstreaming

The years after the Second World War saw the firm consolidation of oralism throughout the Western world and of the technologies associated with the treatment of hearing loss. In Britain, Farrar's example continued to promote high hopes among parents and teachers of deaf students, but higher education for deaf people remained very limited. The Spring Hill School, the direct descendent of Arnold's school, closed during the Second World War to be effectively replaced in 1946 by the newly established Mary Hare Grammar School, the first secondary school for deaf students in Britain (see Boyce and Lavery 1997). In 1955, the Burwood Park School, a secondary technical school, was opened and was supported by private subscription. The education at both establishments was firmly oral and residential, with entry through competitive examinations.

The overall education of deaf children was governed by the view of deaf people as suffering a hearing loss and as being hearing impaired rather than deaf. Testing ensured that they were divided in terms of relative hearing impairment. As a result of government inquiries, special schools for the "partially deaf" were opened in Britain. By 1959, the term "partially deaf" had been replaced by the concept "partially hearing":

> This change in terminology reflected the developments in audiology and electronic hearing aids which made it easier to ascertain and exploit residual hearing. In consequence, the numbers of "deaf" children declined while the incidence of "partial hearing" rose. There was also greater emphasis on "integration" and the education of hearing-impaired children in ordinary rather than special schools. (Lysons 1987, 302)

Society had faith in the audiologist to measure the impairment and faith in the hearing aid technology to compensate for the loss. The hearing specialists and teachers assumed much about what the pupils could "hear" and achieve. Although academic excellence was a feature of the Mary Hare school and, to a lesser extent, the Burwood Park school, places were few, and competitive entrance ensured that those with cultural advantages of family background and, above all, who responded well to oralism, went on to higher education.

Through an alliance with medicine whereby deafness became a medical pathology to be therapeutically treated, oralists deprived deaf people of their linguistic unity and thereby fostered their individuated dependence on the wider hearing society. Deaf students remained firmly institutionalized in special schools or in special units within mainstream schools, but they were divided and ruled by an increasingly complex bevy of professionals—teachers, therapists, doctors, and acoustic engineers.

The increasing sophistication of audiometry in the 1930s and the assumed expertise of audiologists in determining levels of hearing ensured that deafness could be treated as an individual pathology. Professionals now assumed that no two deaf children were really equivalent in their deafness but, rather, that the individual levels of hearing loss or partial hearing could be rationally divided into groups according to educational potential. "Educational potential" meant potential to acquire spoken language through the use of "residual hearing," enhanced by means of hearing aids. The educability of a child varied according to the degree to which the technology was assumed able to compensate for the hearing loss. In 1938, the Eicholz committee had decided that all children with a hearing loss of more than 40 decibels on the Gramophone Audiometer were outside the terms of reference of its investigation into

"Children with Hearing Defects" and were essentially viewed as ineducable. By the late 1940s, the London School Board classified children having a hearing loss in the range of 37 to 79 decibels as "able to be educated using natural language" (Crickmore 1995, 114). "Natural language" was, of course, assumed to be spoken English.

The School as Clinic

Teacher training for teachers of deaf students not only ensured that all teachers were hearing but also, in the period after the Second World War, increasingly focused on speech therapy and the use of acoustic equipment. In schools, a vast amount of time was spent fixing and adjusting hearing aids and ear molds with most of the rest of the time spent on speech therapy. Education often lagged far behind. The children with "partial hearing" remained classified as "handicapped" and, thus, as "disabled," but they no longer had a deaf identity and did not have access to sign language. Even in the late 1980s during visits to leading oral schools in Britain to discuss educational programs, one was led straight to the clinic and workshop to be shown the facilities for testing hearing, making ear molds for hearing aids, and adjusting hearing aids. The central focus of the school was on its ability through science and technology to produce hearing, speaking students. Academic matters were secondary. The pedagogical gaze had become a clinical gaze.

The link between the clinical gaze and the schools was embodied in the leading teacher trainers and educational ambassadors in and for Britain through the 1940s and 1950s, Dr. Irene Ewing (1883–1959) and Professor Alexander Ewing (1896–1980) from the University of Manchester. In 1919, Dr. Irene Ewing, formerly Irene Goldsack, became the foundation lecturer and director of the National Training College for Teachers of the Deaf in the University of Manchester. In 1922, she married Dr. Alexander Ewing, who ran a private clinic for deaf people in Manchester from 1922 until 1944. The Ewings were ardent pure oralists and stressed the clinical aspects of the diagnosis and treatment of deafness. They toured the British Commonwealth spreading the "gospel" of pure oralism. Even beyond Britain and its Commonwealth, their effect was considerable, especially through the International Congress on Education of the Deaf held at Manchester in 1958.[1] At the opening of the Congress, "Sir A. W. G. Ewing spoke about deaf children in a new age and emphasized collaboration among otolaryngologists, pediatricians, medical officers, general practitioners, audiologists, teachers of the deaf, and parents as a regular working arrangement" (Brill 1984, 142).

In 1944, Dr. Alexander Ewing became Professor of Education of the Deaf in the University of Manchester and Director of the Education of the Deaf, a position he held until 1964. His orientation was overtly medical. At this stage, the deaf schools and units became virtual clinics. Deaf education became little more than audiometry and speech therapy. Professor Ewing received the Norman Gamble prize of the Royal Society of Medicine in 1943 and was knighted for his services to deaf education in 1959, the year of his wife's death.

Success in the Ewing-style school was directly equated with the ability to speak. Not to be able to speak was failure. Sign language was not simply scorned, it was forbidden. The goal, above all, was to transform the deaf child into a hearing adult. One senior British teacher of the deaf who had trained in the 1950s and who remained an ardent pure oralist in the Ewing tradition told the authors, "Oralism produces educated people. Education through signing produces educated deaf people." The goal was to transcend deafness, not to accept it. And, of course, only a minority of students could do so. Educational potential was identified with the level of hearing determined through clinical examination.

The reaction of one deaf student from the schools of the 1960s, the Deaf British activist and researcher Paddy Ladd, is telling.

> Oh Ewing, Oh Van Uden, what a marvelous choice you gave us deaf children![2] To see ourselves as stupid rather than to be able to see ourselves as deaf and accept it, and to work from there. I hope it gave you a sense of *real* achievement! (Ladd 1991, 93)

The wide effect of the Ewings can be seen from developments in Australia after their visit in 1950. In 1953 at the Fifth Triennial Conference of the Australian Association of Teachers of the Deaf at Darlington in Sydney, participants formally resolved that, henceforth, all education of deaf students in Australia would be oral, that sign language was not to be used as a medium of instruction, and that "finger spelling and gestures" were "outmoded." Professional teacher training for teachers of deaf students did not begin in Australia until 1954, after a psychologist went to Manchester in England to work with the Ewings and acquire the skills required to set up specialized training courses in Australia. Responding directly to developments in Britain in the 1950s, a pure oral government school, Glendonald, was established in Melbourne,

Australia. Students at the old Victorian School for Deaf Children in Melbourne (VSDC) were tested constantly and moved to the oral school if they showed potential to benefit from speech therapy. Students were made to feel that they were failures if they remained at VSDC. Jennifer Toms and Brian Bernal recall their days as profoundly deaf pupils at VSDC in the early 1950s:

> A separate school for oral deaf was built. It was the start of the division of the Deaf community. Those whose teachers felt were "clever" enough to learn to speak were removed and sent to the new oral only school where no teachers could sign. . . .
>
> But at the old deaf school excitement was happening for those of us left behind. Rumours ran rife. They built a new storey on the old school. Special children were to be chosen to go into a special class. Who would they pick??
>
> At last we knew. Jenny was one of the special ones. Full of hope and excitement we went to our new class. But we couldn't understand what the teachers said—they spoke.
>
> School sports—again we were tricked. We now had other schools to compete against. The great day arrived and the Glendonald (oral) school arrived. We couldn't communicate. They knew no signs and thought we were "dummies." We were too stupid to go to the oral school. (Bernal and Toms 1996, 58–59)

Those who were judged incapable of benefiting from oralism were essentially treated as outcasts and as capable of only basic education. They were segregated so they would not pollute those working in the oral tradition, and eventually, they were taught together with students with "multiple handicaps" (Bernal and Toms 1996, 59).

In the 1950s in Melbourne, a pure oral kindergarten was established not only to channel students into pure oral primary and secondary schooling but also to provide for the segregation of children at kindergarten level on the basis of their family background.[3] Children of Deaf parents who came from signing households were all sent to the VSDC, kept apart from the children of hearing and deaf parents who came from nonsigning households and who were sent to the oral Princess Elizabeth kindergarten. Professionals feared that the signers would teach the other children to sign and retard their educational potential, which was assumed to be entirely oral. Teachers not only counseled parents not to let their children sign but also sent letters home advising parents not to let their children socialize with other deaf people in the Adult Deaf Society, which was still a strong signing environment.

The Exception Determines the Rule

Through the twentieth century, publicists for oralism continued to look to the success of selected pupils, Farrar in particular, to support their faith in oralism.[4] Individual deaf people apart from Farrar continued to succeed through oralist systems, showing exceptional abilities to cope with voicing and lipreading and to achieve high standards of literacy in the dominant language.[5] But they were exceptions to the rule. Educational policies were based on the abilities and achievements of a very small minority. Ideological assertions of the existence of equality frequently claim legitimacy on the basis of the exceptional. Those who deny the existence of class-based, gender-based, racially based, or ethnically based barriers to success within the middle-class market often support their claims by giving publicity to the working-class boy who made it, the woman in a high position of responsibility, or to the "black" lawyer or "migrant" businessman. These denials, which revel in the cult of the individual, ignore the copious sociological research demonstrating time and again that these cases of upward mobility are exceptional and that, for the vast majority of the population, the cultural, economic, and political forces restricting access to society's resources operate to reproduce structured inequalities. Paddy Ladd poignantly places his own experience and "success" in this very context, writing of himself as Nigel:

> He was paraded in front of parents at the clinic: "Now Nigel, show the parents how well you speak. Thank you. Now, if you work hard, your children will be able to speak like Nigel." (Implied, if your child doesn't, then you are to blame for not working hard enough.) This was grossly deceitful for two reasons. One, that many of the parents had profoundly deaf children, who had little hope of being able to speak like Nigel. And it was also calculated to make Nigel feel better than those other deaf children, so that he would make the springboard into the hearing world, and leave those nasty traces of deafness behind. Thus Nigel began life with a carefully instilled pattern of self-deceit. The parallels between this approach and the capitalist Great Lie are remarkable—both say "You can make it to the top if you work hard. Anyone can." In reality, of course, only those with the resources can do it, apart from a determined few who trample everybody before them. For the majority of people who have neither resources nor killer instinct, there is nothing but the branding mark of failure. The fact that this is not the only approach to life or to deafness is kept well hidden. (Ladd 1991, 89)

The hegemony of individualism triumphed, and the exception, be he or she a Farrar or a Nigel, set the course for the education of generations of deaf students, creating educational and linguistic chaos. As Sir Richard Paget wrote,[6]

> It is curious that the vexed question of oralism . . . versus silent methods . . . has never been put to the test. . . . [T]here has apparently been no attempt to organize scientifically controlled experiments with comparable groups of deaf children, so as to discover the respective merits and ultimate results of the rival methods. Still less have any systematic attempts been made, except in America, to combine the two methods. (Hodgson 1953, x)

So strong did faith in oralism become that even the profoundly deaf spent virtually all their time at school learning to make sounds and read lips. Whole classes would sit in a ring waiting for their turn to say a word, waiting while the teacher spent time with each individual until satisfied with his or her pronunciation. As they waited, they were forced to sit on their hands so they could not sign and were even forbidden from signing in the playground. They went behind the toilet block to talk. Today, these pupils—from Britain, Australia, Canada, America, and throughout Europe—joke constantly about the bizarre absurdity of their "education" as they mimic their school experiences, sitting on their hands at international conferences and mouthing at one another or covering their mouths with a book while holding an object behind them and expecting their deaf friends to "listen" to what the teacher was saying. At school, those joked-about actions had been frustrating pantomimes that constantly asserted their incompetence, their "dumbness," as Bernal and Toms recall, recollections that gel with those of their British contemporaries who were interviewed by Jennifer Harris (Harris 1995).

The Use of Signed English

But there were teachers, parents, academics, and of course, deaf people themselves who were aware of the problems generated by the pure oral system, especially for those diagnosed as "severely" or "profoundly" deaf. As we indicated in chapter 2, the 1960s was a time when the ideological focus of virtually all Western countries shifted to "human rights," to the rights of minorities, including the emergence of movements that were opposed to existing mainstream educational conventions.[7] These alternative educational theories and associated alternative schools stimulated widespread questioning of existing educational practices in the mainstream and in "special education." In the 1960s, we saw an overt resurgence of "the combined method" and, in particular, the resurgence of debate about the use of signed versions of the dominant spoken languages. Although these moves away from pure oralism and toward the acknowledgement of deaf people's sensory and linguistic needs marked the beginning of a new era of education, at least for some deaf people, "the deaf" were still being defined and controlled by hearing experts.

The use of manual signs to accompany the teaching of articulation was by no means new in Britain or elsewhere, nor had signing disappeared from all classrooms of deaf students. Although oralism was recommended by the Ministry of Education and strongly supported beginning in the late-nineteenth century by the Association of Teachers of the Deaf, actual practice was left up to the individual school. Through the first half of the century, the British journal *The Teacher of the Deaf*, despite its often fervently pure oralist editorial stance, was filled with arguments for and against oralism. In 1949, E. L. Mundin, the headmaster of the recently established oral secondary school for the deaf, Mary Hare Grammar, summarized the then recent debates and concluded that one could not necessarily assume pure oralism to be the best method for all deaf pupils, stating "I have . . . borne constantly in mind the significant provision in the 1944 Education Act that every child shall receive an education suited to its age, ability and aptitude" (Mundin 1949, 7).

In 1958 under the chairmanship of A. W. Kettlewell, a multidisciplinary committee to review problems associated with the education of deaf children considered the place of manual communication in the education of the deaf students and concluded in 1960 that "members are agreed that there is no one answer to the problem of teaching language to all pupils" ("In the Interests of Deaf Children" 1961, 23). The Report of the Ministry of Education for 1960 indicated that the ministry "does not interfere with the discretion of teachers to use whatever methods they consider to be most helpful to a child's development" (Wilkinson 1961, 231). Referring to this document, the editor of *The Teacher of the Deaf* wrote,

> If by imposing a certain method on even a small minority of our deaf we are creating backwardness, surely we must reform their education to help them make the most of their natural gifts. . . . [W]e should not postpone any longer some definite plan of action based on these conclusions. (231)

By 1966, in response to pressure from deaf associations, teachers, parents associations such as the National Deaf Children's Society, and missioners to the deaf community, the government formed a committee under Professor M. M. Lewis to consider "the place, if any, of finger-spelling and signing in the education of the deaf" (Lewis 1968). The findings of the inquiry indicated a widespread mix of methods throughout Britain and indicated areas of controversy as well as the need for research but did not recommend one system over another. Nevertheless, the committee heralded the start of intense debate over the role of signing in many forms in the education of deaf students. On the whole, signing was still seen as necessary in the education of only profoundly deaf and multiply handicapped children, but the possible widespread use of the "combined method" in various forms was now high on the agenda and remained the preferred option of the British Deaf Association. As far as the educational administrators were concerned, however, the important concern was that all deaf children were efficiently organized in schools. What happened after they were placed in schools was of secondary concern.

Of particular interest was a resurgence of attention to the development by hearing experts of signing systems that could accompany the use and teaching of speech. In his preface to Hodgson's *The Deaf and Their Problems* (Hodgson 1953), Sir Richard Paget wrote,

> I am not an authority on the anatomy of the ear, and am not a teacher of the deaf. All I do claim is some knowledge of the nature and probable origin of human speech, and of its relation to the natural Sign language—subjects which up to the present time have been largely ignored, both by the authorities on speech and by specialists on the education of the totally deaf. (ix)

Paget's work on the origins of human speech focused on the links between the "essentially pantomimic gestures of our jaws, lips and tongue, etc." and what he regarded as the more primitive "pantomimic hand gestures" in the origins and development of language. The gestures and not the "noises of speech" were what he considered essential. He concluded with respect to the education of deaf students,

> To the now growing band of believers in the Gesture Theory of Human Speech it is a matter of indifference whether we teach the deaf to express words and names by gestures of their jaws, lips, tongue, etc., or by gestures of their hands—provided always that the hand-gestures shall have exactly the same meaning as the mouth-gestures. (Hodgson 1953, xii)

Paget referred to a number of educationalists in Britain through the 1930s and 1940s involved in the development of sign languages to accompany speech and, among them, the headmaster of the Doncaster School, E. S. Greenaway, who advocated simultaneous signing and speaking. In response, Paget, along with a number of teachers of deaf students and missioners to the deaf community, developed his "New Sign Language," or what was to become known in a revised form in the 1960s as the Paget-Gorman system. Paget's earlier system was adopted in a few schools but was fervently opposed by the pure oralists, so much so, that in 1948, "an experiment approved by the Ministry of Education had to be abandoned owing to the opposition from the leading centre of the pure oral advocates" (Hodgson 1953, xv).

Although British schools had tended to reject the use of methodological sign systems in favor of using fingerspelling combined with natural sign language, St. Mary's School for the Deaf in Dublin, Ireland, pursued until 1946 a "pure manual" method, using a system of Signed English developed in the mid-nineteenth century.[8] The Irish system of signed English had been developed by Father John Burke, adapted from the French methodological sign systems of Jamet in Caen, which had been used in the Paris school. The Irish system of signed English combined fingerspelling, signs from Irish Sign Language, initialized "methodic signs," and grammatical signs used as "linguistic markers." Although it disappeared from the schools in 1946, it was almost identical in design and purpose to the signed form of English referred to as Seeing Essential English (SEE), which was developed in America twenty years later.

However, the 1960s provided a very different environment than had existed twenty years earlier for experiments such as those of Paget and for the revival of forms of signed English in general. Discussions of alternatives were also stimulated by reports from British delegates who had attended international conferences, for example, the Gallaudet Conference of 1963. The keynote speaker at the 1963 conference declared: "The contribution of manual forms of communication to academic and social efficiency, the unique structural features of the language of signs and the association of the manual alphabet with the teaching of speech are of increasing interest" (Brill 1984, 164–65).

Schools began to experiment with the Paget-Gorman system, the Rochester Method that used one-handed fingerspelling and articulation, and the system of manually "Cued Speech" developed by R. Orin Cornett of Gallaudet College.[9] More widespread interest was shown in the development of forms of signed English to be used in conjunction with the teaching of spoken and written English. In 1973, the head of the Yorkshire School for the Deaf, F. Hockenhull, was quoted as saying, "It cannot be stressed too much that those arts which deaf children develop so easily are of limited use educationally unless they are refined by reason and systematically taught" (Woodford 1973, 198). The statement could have been made by 1'Epée two hundred years earlier. Research into the relative performance of oral and signing deaf children by Conrad (1979) reinforced the growing interest in the use of signing and also placed on the agenda, for the first time, the possible importance of the use of British Sign Language, as distinct from signed representations of English, in the education of deaf people.[10]

In the early 1960s, an American teacher, David Anthony, developed a manual system to represent written English grammatically so his deaf students could learn English more easily (Seeing Essential English [SEE 1]). This system encouraged other teachers to develop codes for the manual representation of English, resulting in variations of manually coded English developing out of SEE 1.[11] Three systems in particular were developed in this period: Anthony's Seeing Essential English (Anthony 1973), known as SEE 1; Wampler's Linguistics of Visual English (Wampler 1973), known as LOVE; and Gustason and her colleagues' Signing Exact English (Gustason 1973), known as SEE 2 and used quite widely in deaf education. These systems involved the development of many new signs. "In general they invent new signs, modify existing signs, and create signs for affixes, word endings, plurality and articles" (Evans 1982, 75). These signing systems had a big influence on the way signing was used in all institutions for the education of deaf people, including Gallaudet University, where a form using mainly American Sign Language signs but in English word order was developed for educating deaf children and was known simply as Signed English or SE (see Bornstein 1973).

Throughout the world, similar systems were developed, for example, early in Europe—Signed Swedish, Signed Danish, Signed German—and later in countries throughout Asia—Signed Indonesian (SIBI) (see Branson and Miller 1998a) and Signed Thai (see Santitrakool 1979). In Britain, these international moves stimulated the development of various signed English forms, with the Royal National Institute for the Deaf deciding in 1982 to concentrate their resources on the development of Signed English.

Signed English as Symbolic Violence

> [W]ith the formal introduction of signed English in 1973 (despite opposition from the Deaf community), the control of language moved to the hearing teachers in the classroom. The older Deaf were not there to correct the signing of the young and as the teachers didn't really know the new language either, communication broke down. (Bernal and Toms 1996, 60)

The development of signed forms of English reinforced the control of deaf people by means of linguistic and cultural deprivation. The "symbolic violence" of signed English, and indeed of signed forms of any dominant spoken language, were based on two familiar assumptions: first, the assumed superiority of English as a language for the transmission of knowledge and, second, the assumption that deaf people needed to be assimilated as much as possible into the hearing world by the use of the majority language. The development of signed forms of English not only devalued native sign languages but also sought to assimilate deaf people into the majority language and majority culture as overtly deficient participants. The process is precisely what Bourdieu described when he wrote that the educational system conceals, "by an apparently neutral attitude, the fact that it fills this function" (Bourdieu 1977a, 488), namely, the transmission of power and privilege.

The development of signed English served to reinforce the linguistic deprivation of deaf people and to represent their sensory difference as linguistic lack. Both oralism and signed forms of English give only partial access to language. Their use denies access to the richness and complexities of language that are essential for effective cultural expression and participation and, of course, for even moderate educational success.[12] In addition, hearing educators, the experts in signed English, had to act as mediators between the deaf and hearing worlds, thus, increasing the hearing educators' control.

The Resurgence of the Combined Method as Total Communication

Associated with the development of signed forms of English was the resurgence of forms of the combined method. Like signed English forms, Total Communication emerged or, rather, reemerged in America in the late 1960s as a philosophical approach to teaching deaf children that took many varied forms in practice. It was a philosophy open to myriad strategic interpretations by teachers. Woodward wrote in 1973,

> One "recent" development in deaf education is total communication, but there are almost as many definitions of total communication as there are proponents. . . . Whatever the definition of total communication, one aspect of total communication that is stressed by most proponents is the creation and use of a visual language system that closely parallels English, generally as closely as possible. (Woodward 1973, 1)

As a philosophy, Total Communication referred to "an approach that attempts to ensure the right of the deaf child to have access to any and all needed communication modalities" (Hicks, quoted in Evans and Hicks 1988, 567). In this spirit, the British Deaf Association supported the use of Total Communication in schools after the Education Act of 1981, just as they had supported the combined method in 1890 at the urging of Francis Maginn (see chapter 7). Although the efforts in some situations to realize the philosophy of Total Communication involved the development of bilingual situations using various expressions of English and natural sign language, these efforts usually involved and, indeed, still involve the use of manually supported English, with teachers signing at the same time they speak, which results in very confusing visual messages.[13]

Today, forms of Total Communication dominate the education of the deaf in Britain. Wendy Lynas (1994) cites research indicating that, in 1993, just over half the services offered in the 108 Local Education Authorities of England offered an oral-aural plus Total Communication approach and a further 30 percent offered an oral-aural plus Total Communication plus bilingual approach. A survey of British schools and units by I. King Jordan in 1980–1981 (Jordan 1982) revealed a ratio of oral programs to Total Communication programs in primary education of 60 percent to 40 percent and, in secondary education, of 65 percent to 35 percent. A repeat study by Dennis Child (Child 1991) in all forty schools for the deaf in the United Kingdom in 1989, though not including mainstream units, revealed ratios of oral programs to Total Communication programs of 30 percent to 70 percent at the primary level and of 45 percent to 65 percent at the secondary level. A survey of secondary units by Powers (Powers 1990) revealed that one-third were using some manual communication whereas nearly two-thirds of them used sign-supported English. These programs represent potentially extremely confusing linguistic environments.

Although the teachers of the late 1960s and of the 1970s and 1980s saw themselves as great innovators in the education of deaf people, they were, in fact, reinventing the wheel. As we have seen from the discussion in the previous chapter about teaching methods in British schools during the nineteenth century, both the philosophy and practice of Total Communication had been around for a long time even then. In the light of the far more recent strategic interpretation of Total Communication to mean the simultaneous use of speech and signed English, Scott's comments, made a century earlier, about the madness in such a method bear quoting again:

> We have heard of teachers who would sign through a lesson, giving sign for word in regular succession, in the belief that each sign they made was of equal importance and would necessarily give the idea. We could hardly suppose that there could have been teachers with such "madness" in their methods. (Scott 1870, 130–31)

The madness was indeed back, but in a new ideological environment. This new environment was intensely professionalized, one in which the student was thoroughly individuated and in which segregation was giving way to integration. Although the newly forged Total Communication approach recognized Deaf communities and their sign languages, at least in theory, the predominant purpose was the integration of deaf individuals into the hearing society as individuals.

The revolutionary educational movements of the 1960s and 1970s were overtly individualistic, stressing the rights and creativity of the individual in opposition to the faceless rationality of the bureaucratically regulated system. This individualistic orientation to education affected the education of deaf students through moves to deinstitutionalize special education. In Britain, this individuation reached its ultimate expression at the beginning of the 1980s:

> The Report of the Committee of Enquiry into the Education of Handicapped Children and Young People, issued in 1978, resulted in the enactment of the Education Act of 1981. This legislation replaced the existing categories of handicapped individuals, including those who are deaf and partially hearing, with the concept of special education provision based on the special educational needs of each child. (Lysons 1987, 302–3)

These moves toward individuation of "the disabled" found particular expression in the apparently antidiscriminatory practice of what is called, in its various cultural contexts, "integration," "inclusion," or "mainstreaming."

Mainstreaming and the Education of Deaf Students

In chapter 2, we examined how policies of "normalization" through deinstitutionalization, using mainstreaming as a potent and prominent example, have been pursued in a thoroughly hegemonic way. In other words, the existing ideologies of "normality" have dominated the process of reform, the assumption being that the formerly segregated would adapt to the normal world, allowing the normal world to go about its business as before but now infused with a feeling of benevolence at having allowed "the disabled" a pathway to assimilate into the normal society. Mainstreaming was seen to be, on the whole, a discriminatory practice. Its orientation toward normalizing formerly segregated students demanded their assimilation into the educational and cultural environment and demanded of them as much as of the other students: "that they have what it does not give . . . linguistic and cultural competence" (Bourdieu 1977a, 494).

The education of deaf students in mainstream schools is not new.[14] From the 1870s in Britain, in response to the 1870 Education Act, special classes for deaf children were established under the coordination of William Stainer in public elementary schools, especially in London day schools. Day schools for deaf children were also established throughout the country in preference to the traditional residential schools. But by the end of the nineteenth century, special classes in "mainstream" schools were virtually abandoned in favor of day schools. As the clinical approach asserted itself in the period after the Second World War and the concept of "partial hearing" replaced the concept of "deafness," the deaf school was seen as inappropriate for the "partially hearing." Thus in 1947, the first "partially hearing units" were opened in four London primary schools. By 1987, approximately four hundred "partially hearing units" had been established in England (Lysons 1987, 302). To serve these units, a system was organized wherein peripatetic teachers toured the schools, attending to the special needs of deaf students. But, as indicated above, the reclassification of some deaf people as "partially hearing" served two related ideological purposes: (1) it classified as "partially normal," as not being "disabled," those who could respond to sound and thus make use of new technologies, which therefore, placed them at least partially in the mainstream; and (2) at the same time, it reinforced the "disabled" status of those who were not "partially normal," the profoundly deaf. Profoundly deaf students remained institutionalized and were regarded as virtually uneducable. The ideology of institutionalization was not challenged.

But by the 1980s, the general move toward deinstitutionalization and the formal development of mainstreaming programs was resulting in the mainstreaming not only of "partially hearing" students in units but also of a wider range of deaf students. It was also resulting in the subsequent closure of many segregated schools for the deaf.[15] These moves involved a fundamental ideological shift, at least at the level of policy. As indicated in chapter 2, mainstreaming was challenging the very categorization of people as "disabled," demanding the acknowledgement and even celebration of human diversity as well as asking that this diversity be nourished, not through discriminatory institutionalization, but by providing facilities to accommodate individually based and not syndrome-based difference. In Britain, the 1985 Education Act established a national curriculum for all, challenging the whole basis of "special education."[16] In line with the radical educational movements of the 1960s and 1970s, the civil rights movements, and the international battles for human rights, mainstreaming brought to the fore the need to recognize the basic ideologies of equality and the rights of the individual. The individuation of deafness was, in fact, being reinforced in a new way.

Research into the integration of deaf students into mainstream classrooms through the 1980s indicated how counterproductive and isolating the integration of the deaf child could be.[17] "It was obvious that sitting in a normal classroom could be the reverse of integration while separate educational provision had always aimed at eventual full participation in the hearing world" (McLoughlin 1987, 85). The mainstreaming programs were assimilationist in orientation, expecting the individual deaf child to adjust linguistically and even in sensory terms to the environment of the mainstream school. Rather than achieving assimilation, mainstreaming for the deaf student often resulted in isolation. Research by Gregory and Bishop (1989) revealed that mainstream teachers did not know how to deal with deaf students and that teachers and hearing students tended not to regard the deaf students as part of the "normal" class or as "normal" members of the student body. Many teachers see the National Curriculum, imposed through the Education Reform Act of 1989, as compounding these problems rather than as opening up the curriculum to all students.[18]

The overt pursuit of mainstreaming as public policy occurred at the same time as consciousness of the special linguistic needs of deaf students was being raised and as these linguistic needs were being associated with the need for segregated educational environments. The overt move to deinstitutionalize education generated, particularly among deaf people themselves, a demand to return to segregated signing schools. The integration of deaf students was interpreted as the latest assault on the languages and potential sense of community of Deaf people and as the ultimate strategy to divide and rule:

> My experience of mainstreaming in England . . . leads me to believe that it is the most dangerous move yet against the early development of a deaf person's character, self-confidence and basic sense of identity. Forceful clumsy attempts to mainstream not only deny the facts about being deaf but destroy much that deaf people and their friends have worked so hard to create, and may in the last resort be seen as genocidal. (Ladd 1991, 88)

The failure of mainstreaming for deaf people is seen to stem basically from the fact that they are mainstreamed in terms of a medical model of deafness. Despite the overt opposition to the use of clinically based assessments and, thus, to the use of medical models of "disability," even the most radical integrationists continue to define deafness as a pathology, as a lack rather than as a cultural difference based in a linguistic difference. Given the overriding ideals of the mainstreaming movement, the mainstreaming of deaf students is a blatant contradiction.

Mainstreaming involves the attempted assimilation of minority groups into the linguistic and cultural environment of the mainstream educational system. Mainstreaming assumes either implicitly or explicitly that language immersion in the dominant language will generate linguistic competence. These assumptions fly in the face of research findings that consistently demonstrate, as indicated above, that, for those whose first language is a minority language, developing linguistic competence in the dominant language demands a bilingual environment (see Luetke-Stahlman 1986; Cummins 1984). In the case of deaf people, for whom access to the dominant language can never be as complete as for other students who use a minority language, the inappropriateness of mainstreaming is particularly marked.

The inappropriateness of mainstreaming is acknowledged both by oralists and by supporters of bilingual approaches using natural sign language and the dominant spoken language. The prospectus of the Mary Hare Grammar School pursues as pure oralist a program as one will find anywhere in Britain but, at the same time, stresses the need for a segregated educational environment.

Bilingualism in Deaf Education

Since Conrad published *The Deaf School Child* (Conrad 1979), research into the effect of different linguistic environments on the education of deaf students has continued to show that the acquisition of sign language as a first language by deaf children, whether they come from Deaf or hearing families, is basic to the effective acquisition of a second language and to educational success.[19] Also particularly important in stimulating interest to develop bilingual programs was the 1989 publication, *Unlocking the Curriculum* (Johnson, Liddell, and Erting 1989). *Unlocking the Curriculum* laid blame for poor achievement among deaf students, not at the door of oralism, but at the door of Total Communication, claiming that students needed as the language of instruction, not Signed English used in conjunction with speech, but American Sign Language.

In 1996, the British Deaf Association (BDA) stated in its education policy that "Deaf people have the right to a quality education throughout their lives, which accepts their linguistic cultural and social identity, which builds positive self esteem and which sets no limits to their learning." The organization added, "the BDA believes that bilingualism represents the most appropriate form of education for the majority of Deaf students." The bilingual mode of education requires at least partial segregation. The segregation involved is radically different from the "remedial" and "special educational" practices still associated with the segregation of deaf students. The use of native sign language as a medium of instruction for deaf people around the world is slowly developing and is based on a substantial amount of theoretical and empirical evidence. On the basis of this research and theory, bilingual programs are being established, unlike the move into oralism that could never claim theoretical and empirical support (Ewoldt 1979) but, instead, rested on an ideology that speech and hearing were normal and deafness was pathological. This research on sign language is also supported by many Deaf people as they reflect on their own linguistic progress and by hearing parents of deaf children (Fletcher 1991; Robinson 1991).[20] These people seek alternatives to mainstreaming, alternatives that attempt to move beyond the forces of assimilation and normalization to provide educational environments for deaf students that celebrate their difference rather than devalue it as a lack.

What then of the current and potential shape of Deaf education? Many Deaf people argue for a segregated education through sign language, a bilingual, segregated system.[21] For example, while the British Deaf Association campaigned with disability rights groups in the early 1990s, contributing to the Disability Discrimination Act of 1995, the National Union of the Deaf campaigned strongly against the integrationist policies of the Department of Education and Science. The educational potential of the segregated school for deaf students lies in its potential to provide, assuming it uses a comprehensive primary and secondary curriculum, the sort of education for deaf students that all-girls schools provide for girls.[22] Deaf people seek an environment in which they are not subjected to the symbolic violence of a hearing culture, in which they are not "disabled," and where they are not driven to struggle to be like hearing people. Above all, they seek an environment where they can relax into their deafness; can communicate effectively by means of a medium through which they understand everything, not snippets plucked from a distorted electronic stream of sound; and can be free to explore additional communicative strategies on their terms. Their focus on the potential of bilingualism parallels and responds to drives by other linguistic minorities to secure the right to be educated through the medium of their first languages.

Because access through the family to the appropriate native sign language as a first language is available only to a minority of deaf people, a truly bilingual education for deaf students requires that natural sign language be made available as a first language for all deaf children from birth. This condition is the case, for example, in Sweden and Denmark where professional instruction in Swedish and Danish Sign Language respectively is provided for all parents of deaf children as soon as deafness has been diagnosed, so a coherent linguistic environment is available to the child from the start of her or his linguistic development.

Many Deaf communities throughout the world seek the sort of social justice and educational innovation found, at least in terms of formal policy, in countries such as Sweden, where regulations were passed by parliament in 1981 guaranteeing the right of all Deaf people to be educated with the national sign language as their first language and as the medium for the acquisition of the national spoken and written language, Swedish. Thus, Ahlgren wrote in 1990,

> In Swedish schools for the deaf, Swedish Sign Language is officially the language of instruction in all subjects *including Swedish*. According to the official curriculum Swedish Sign Language is regarded the first language for the deaf pupils and written Swedish is their secondary language. . . . (Ahlgren 1990, 91, italics added)

But she added,

> The real picture of teaching in the deaf-schools is, however, not as bright as in the curriculum. We are in fact in the middle of a process where *the majority* of the teachers has come to accept Swedish Sign Language as a true language and therefore beneficial to the students but where this same majority still has a long way to go before they know sign language well enough to be sufficiently good teachers. (91, emphasis added)

The gap between policy and practice remains, and even if it is narrowing after more than a decade under progressive legislation, the struggle for the recognition of the native sign language—even among the teachers of deaf students—is still far from won.

The same is true of bilingual programs in Britain. The School for the Deaf in Derby, England, is committed to the development of a bilingual school with British Sign Language (BSL) as the language of instruction. The local Deaf community is involved with the pupils in the teaching process and in extracurricular activities. As in the Swedish case, the need for a truly bilingual education is recognized, but the acquisition by hearing teachers and administrators of the fluent linguistic skills that are required takes time. Robert C. Johnson has recently reported that in America,

> The percentage of deaf students reportedly taught through "Signs Without Voice" (a term used by Gallaudet researchers to indicate ASL), has risen during the last decade from less than half of one percent (1989–1990) to 4 percent (1996–1997), the latter percentage representing a small but significant number of students (roughly 1,870). Insufficient data are available to determine whether these students are truly being taught in ASL-English bilingual programs. . . . (Johnson 1999, 4)

An air of threatening symbolic violence still permeates the relationships between hearing and Deaf people as even those teachers who recognize the need for instruction through signing debate to what extent it should be used and what form of signing is appropriate. Signed forms of dominant written languages are often still taught to trainee teachers, and systems labeled "bilingual" often consist of a haphazard mixture of English, BSL, Signed English, and sign-supported English.[23]

Opposition to bilingual education from oralists, or aural-oralists as they now call themselves in an age of cochlear implants, often focuses on research claiming to show that children taught through aural-oral approaches achieve higher results than those taught through bilingual methods or Total Communication. A recent comprehensive review of the research literature (Powers, Gregory, and Thoutenhoofd 1999) has shown that "despite a significant amount of research there has been no major study in the UK since that of Conrad (1979)" and that "there is no substantive evidence to demonstrate any overall improvement in the education of deaf pupils since Conrad's study" (1). Powers, Gregory, and Thoutenhoofd show that "the measurement of language skills has focused almost exclusively on spoken language ability, sometimes assessed in the written form" and that there is "almost no information on the sign competence of deaf children" (3). Powers et al. also point to the dependence of studies on unrepresentative samples and their failure to account for the relevant variables involved.

Aural-oralist opposition to bilingualism continues to focus on the needs of the individual and to see the Deaf community's focus on the use of natural sign language in education as a threat to individual achievement and eventual assimilation into the hearing world. Lynas's extremely selective review of research on communication options in deaf education is a case in point (Lynas 1994). She concludes, without reference to any research, that "if deaf children are offered the prospect of talking, they are not thereby precluded from acquiring sign language at a later stage, but if signing is chosen for them they are unlikely ever to be able to talk" (Lynas 1994, 150). Research and experience in at least Sweden and Denmark show quite the opposite, with students using the national sign language as their first language and as the language of instruction and effectively accessing spoken languages as a second language through speech therapy and lipreading.

The problem with most research into the various communicative options in the education of deaf students is that these "options" are regarded simply as teaching methods. The issue of language is ignored or misunderstood. Bilingualism in deaf education focuses on the linguistic development of deaf children in their first and second—even third and fourth—languages. The central claim, supported by ample research, is simply that the effective acquisition and educational use of a first language promotes not only the acquisition of knowledge but also the acquisition of other languages, even spoken languages.

What we have been concerned with showing here is that the barriers—cultural, educational, and political—placed in the way of deaf people are often subtle, placed there subconsciously as hearing people operate in terms that are assumed to be governed by rationality or common sense, not by prejudice. These hearing people do not see the symbolic violence that their evaluations of language, behavior, and appearance perpetrate on those who are judged to be marginal. They do not realize that they—those who conform to the desired behavioral, physical, and cultural standards of the society—are the agents who marginalize and disable through their disposition toward others. Those who promote the integration of the so-called "disabled," including deaf people, into mainstream education and who see the segregated environment as restricting access to educational resources appeal to a common sense that is governed by an ideological commitment to egalitarianism, individualism, liberty, and social justice as well as to dispositions toward "normality." Thus, hearing parents seize on integration and oralism as the way to attain acceptability for their deaf child and for themselves. Both integration and oralism have received particular ideological support from the latest of science's technological and surgical "miracles." The assumptions that science can "overcome" the assumed pathology of deafness and that oral education is both viable and desirable have intensified since the development of the cochlear implant, which claims to provide hearing for those who do not find hearing aids useful. The cochlear implant claims to cure deafness in the profoundly deaf, to make deaf people hear. It is the "bionic ear."

The Cochlear Implant: The Latest of Science's Miracles

Harlan Lane writes,

> The connections among measurement practices, special education, and ear surgery are not only intellectual and abstract, they are also administrative and operational . . . one more reflection of the intimate relations in audism between measurement, education and medicine. . . .
>
> The cochlear implant teams . . . authorized to conduct surgery generally consist of a surgeon, several audiologists and speech/language pathologists, and special educators. (Lane 1992, 204)

> Cochlear implantation is a surgical procedure, lasting about three and a half hours under general anaesthesia, and it requires hospitalization for two to four days. A broad crescent-shaped incision is made behind the operated ear, and the skin flap is elevated. A piece of temporalis muscle is removed. A depression is drilled in the skull and reamed to make a seat for the internal electrical coil of the cochlear implant. A section of the mastoid bone is removed to expose the middle ear cavity. Further drilling exposes the membrane of the round window on the inner ear. Observing the procedure under a microscope, the surgeon pierces the membrane. A wire about 25 millimeters long is pushed through the opening. Sometimes the way is blocked by abnormal bone growth in the inner ear; the surgeon will generally drill through this but may have to settle in the end for only partial insertion of the wire. The wire seeks its own path as it moves around and up the coiled inner ear, shaped like a snail and called the cochlea, from the Latin for "snail." The exquisitely detailed microstructure of the inner ear is often ripped apart as the electrode weaves its way, crushing cells and perforating membranes; if there was any residual hearing in the ear, it is almost certainly destroyed. The auditory nerve itself is unlikely to be damaged, however, and the implant stimulates the auditory nerve directly. The internal coil is then sutured into place. Finally the skin is sewn back over the coil. (Lane 1992, 3–4)

Lane's description is meant to draw attention to the invasive and dangerous nature of the implant. Although the cochlear implant is simply the latest in a long line of technological innovations that are designed to make deaf people hear, its surgical nature links it as much to the surgical experiments of Itard and Cooper nearly two hundred years ago as to the work of Bell a century later. The apparent successes prove little. The children paraded across our television screens and at conferences of teachers in deaf education have been given intense individual therapy that has already been shown to yield results even without hearing aids let alone the implant. Farrar was the case in point.

In 1991, on the basis of a review of 229 publications on cochlear implants, the Scottish educator George Montgomery concluded that the claims made by publicists for cochlear implants are at best dubious and that the effect of the implant was limited, pointing out that regular hearing aids might well have produced the same results. He also points to the intense instruction given to implanted children in contrast to the attention received by "ordinary" deaf children (Montgomery 1991). A review of the debates about cochlear implants in the United States by Agnes Tellings in 1996 reached similar conclusions (Tellings 1996).

Reviewing the arguments for and against the implantation of children, Tellings points to the limited success of the implant related to hearing and producing speech but claims that no educational or medical grounds for rejecting the use of implants exist as long as implanted children are given the opportunity to learn both through oral instruction and through manual instruction (Tellings, 27). She dismisses "ethical" objections to the implant associated with a child's membership in the Deaf community "unless one adheres to a strict 'cultural-linguistic' model in which being deaf is completely comparable to being Turkish or being English" (29). The linguistic issues are misunderstood and misrepresented by Tellings. As we will show in the next chapter, the need for a fully accessible first language as the language of instruction in the early years of schooling has been clearly established. The fact that a natural sign language is the only language to which a deaf child, with or without an implant, has unproblematic access means that the use of a natural sign language as the language of instruction, particularly in early schooling, is desirable for all deaf children, just as children with Turkish as a first language should be educated during their early years in Turkish.

The cochlear implant has captured the imagination of the public, the attention of the media, and the copious finances of governments and private enterprise as the scientific miracle of the 1980s and 1990s. As Harlan Lane's research into the results of implants has shown (Lane 1992, 203 ff.; Lane, Hoffmeister, and Bahan 1996, 386 ff.), the surgery can be dangerous, and the results are far from miraculous. Serious adverse results, including damage to facial nerves causing disfigurement, have been reported for as many as one child in six in America (Lane 1992, 217). For children, further surgery is almost inevitable and will almost certainly be more dangerous than the original operation. Implant supporters are distributing massive propaganda associated with the implant, which is isolating and alienating the burgeoning Deaf community from the wider community, and these supporters are working as fervently as Bell and others ever did to destroy the concept and the reality of a Deaf community.

But the response of parents is overwhelming. General practitioners and audiologists are referring children for implants as though the miracle was guaranteed and uncomplicated. As one walks through the Royal Throat, Nose and Ear Hospital on Gray's Inn Road, London, to the stairs leading to the library of the Royal National Institute for Deaf People in the Institute of Laryngology and Otology, a department of University College, London, handwritten signs with arrows proclaim "cochlear implants this way."

Scientism remains the dominant ideology, the handmaiden of the economy and the polity, despite its need to counteract moves toward developing any sense of community that threatens the central ideology of individualism and, thus, the relationship of production and consumption. Deafness is firmly categorized as both a disabling condition and a condition in need of medical treatment, even despite successful moves by the Deaf community to gain recognition of themselves as a subcultural and linguistic community. The incongruity reveals the contradictory nature of the democratic capitalist society. Thus, in Australia in 1991, the government's language policy recognized Auslan (Australian Sign Language) as the language of the Deaf community and yet, at the same time, poured copious funding into the development of the Australian Nucleus-22 implant, which has been used worldwide and has given particular publicity to implants in children.

But whatever the technology involved, and the cochlear implant is but the latest in a long line, the issue is access to language, the effect of pedagogies and technologies on the development of linguistic competence. Support for the implant is based on the assumption that a little hearing is better than none at all, which itself is based on another set of assumptions that hearing and speech are the only natural form of communication and, therefore, that oralism is the only viable mode of communication for the society as a whole, the mode to which all members of society should and must adjust.

In a 1997 *Fox News* program dealing with the debate over cochlear implants, Mario Svirsky of Indiana University is quoted as saying, "We find that after implantation, they [children who are implanted early] start acquiring language at a faster rate." In this instance, "language" is identified solely with spoken language. The speed at which deaf children acquire sign language is not considered.

With respect to the first assumption that a little hearing is better than none at all, studies show that the transition from education in sign to oral education of deaf students was accompanied by deterioration in the performance of deaf students.[24] Oralism created an educational lack to accompany the assumed physical lack. The faith of the hearing world in technology leads to the assumption that once some hearing has been stimulated, the deaf person can be expected to participate effectively in the hearing world.

The Cochlear Implant and the New Oralism

As governments have begun to recognize the linguistic identities and needs of Deaf communities throughout the world and have begun to support programs for bilingual education of Deaf people, a resurgence of pure oralism has occurred, which is linked to the cochlear implant. Special programs have been developed to receive and train newly implanted children and to train parents to provide therapy regularly in the home.

> There is no evidence that these oralist practices at home, at school, and in the clinic are effective, any more than there was evidence of their effectiveness in the era before they were abandoned in favour of total communication. They are not undertaken because they are of proven value. They are sought by the implant teams because childhood implantation and oral education are expressions of the same underlying system of values. (Lane 1992, 205)

The medicalization of the deaf person continues to individualize and alienate, cutting the deaf child off from potential contact with the Deaf community and with access to the world through sign languages. At no time in our history has there been more overt stress on the miraculous abilities of science to cure deafness. The new performers at conferences of teachers of deaf students are like the performers of past centuries, deaf people who speak for the entertainment of the audience, but now, the miracle involves not only speaking but also hearing. Indeed, the focus now is on hearing. The miracle word is not *ephphatha*, "be opened," (Mark 7:34 Authorized [King James] Version) but, rather, "cochlear implant," a surgical not mystical opening of the ear. The miracle worker is not the Son of God but the scientist. Television programs feature prominent sportsmen and others whose children have received the miraculous "bionic ear," and interviewers pit members of the Deaf community in debate against university professors, manipulating the process to misrepresent Deaf points of view as reactionary, irrational, and based in ignorance of the scientific facts. Demonstrating classic prejudice in assuming deafness to be an individuated condition requiring individual treatment, interviewers repeatedly fail even to try to understand the nature of the Deaf community and imply that deaf people want to take deaf children away from their hearing families. The fact that many of the most fervent Deaf activists state quite clearly that speech therapy, lipreading instruction, and hearing aids should be available to Deaf people who want to access these services is ignored. Little has changed since the turn of the century when teachers began to advise parents not to let their children have any contact with the Deaf community for fear that this contact would hamper the normalization process. As we pointed out in previous chapters, the success stories of implanted children's hearing and speaking are not different or more miraculous than was Abraham Farrar's story 120 years ago because they, like Farrar, receive individualized and extremely intensive therapy.

Through the last five chapters, we have explored the history of the cultural construction of deaf people as "disabled" in the British context. Although particular individuals have emerged at times to exert a strong influence on the shape of deaf education and the social lives of deaf people, we have been concerned with demonstrating that these individuals have not been the prime movers of history. Biography, as C. Wright Mills stressed, is not enough. It must be combined with an historical understanding of the social environments within which those individuals lived. The individuals who have been featured here, from Wallis and Defoe through to the Ewings and Paddy Ladd, interpreted the educational process and strategically oriented themselves toward their tasks as teachers, missioners, therapists, pupils, parents, or administrators through lenses that were shaped by the cultural environments in which they lived. Therefore, to understand the history of the cultural construction of deaf people as "disabled" in Britain, we have had to place the events of that history in their wider ideological and cultural contexts, from the new philosophy of the seventeenth century through to the widespread deinstitutionalization that began in the 1980s.

As we begin to consider the current environment, in which the ideological forces of multiculturalism and ethnicity dominate the contemporary construction of identity in the West, we must move onto the international stage. Today, a heightened consciousness of ethnic identity both challenges and transforms identities that are based in nationalism. Deaf communities in the West and, to some extent, beyond the West are claiming a Deaf ethnicity that is based in the assertion of their linguistic human rights as linguistic minorities with minority subcultures.[25] In reviewing these achievements, particularly the victories associated with the achievement of linguistic human rights, we reveal how easily victories, at the same time, can be the basis for further oppression as those who can now celebrate their difference become the unwitting agents in the oppression of others.

Notes

1. See Lowe (1991) for the effect of the Ewings and the 1958 Congress on the education of deaf people in Germany.

2. Dutch educationalist who promoted oralism. For his views on language and education, see Van Uden (1986). For a response to Van Uden's argument, see Stokoe (1991).

3. The Princess Elizabeth Junior School (PEJS) was set up with money donated by the public after radio and newsreel advertisements about the value of an oral education. The high point of the advertisements was a deaf child saying the word "mummy" for the first time.

4. A Farrar School for the Deaf was established in Sydney in recognition of his example.

5. For example, the Australian Pierre Gorman, who gained a doctorate from Cambridge University, was for a time the librarian at the Royal National Institute for the Deaf in London and developed a signing system with Sir Richard Paget for teaching English—the Paget-Gorman System.

6. Sir Richard Arthur Surtees Paget (1869–1955), a barrister who was educated at Eton and Magdalen College, Oxford, came from wealthy landed gentry and was called to the bar in 1895. A distinguished lawyer, he was secretary to many legal commissions including the Court of Arbitration, under the Metropolitan Water Act and the Patent Law Committee. A lover of music and art, he published several songs. His academic work focused on linguistics and human speech. He published papers in the *Proceedings of the Royal Society*, the British Association, and the *Encyclopaedia Britannica* on the nature and artificial production of speech. His book *Human Speech* was published in 1932. He was interested in the production of artificial signing systems for the teaching of deaf students and, to this end, developed his New Sign Language with the Australian Pierre Gorman, known as the Paget-Gorman system. In 1953, he was president of the British Deaf and Dumb Association.

7. In the 1960s, the deaf teacher of deaf students, Boyce Williams, presented a list of ancillary rights for deaf people to be considered in relation to the Universal Declaration of Human Rights (Williams 1985).

8. See Griffey (1997) and Green (1997, 70–71), and for descriptions of the Dublin schools in the mid-nineteenth century, see the appendix to Wilde (1853) and "An Old Friend of the Deaf and Dumb" (1885).

9. The Aberdeen School for the Deaf in Scotland was still using the Paget-Gorman system in 1998 when it closed (*British Deaf News*, June 1998). The Rochester Method developed in the late-nineteenth century, when a teacher at the Rochester School for the Deaf in New York, Zenos Westervelt, "proposed the use of fi ngerspelling, but only in conjunction with speech and in the correct grammatical word order of English" (Evans 1982, 8). This kind of "simultaneous communication" became known as the "Rochester Method." Paul and Jack-

son note that, in the United States, "the Rochester Method was a commonly used system in the 1950s and 1960s" (Paul and Jackson 1993, 42).

10. Conrad's study was comprehensive and methodologically sound and, therefore, could not be dismissed by sheer rhetoric. Above all, it demonstrated that deaf children educated through the oral system achieved extremely low educational levels.

11. For example, in Australia, a committee set up in Victoria developed its own version of Signed English in the 1970s, accumulating a vocabulary from a range of sources, including Auslan, SEE 2, other native sign languages from different countries, and those signs developed by the committee—a conglomeration indeed. The majority of deaf people who had been asked to participate in the construction of the Australian version of Signed English, in fact, walked out of the committee. But the process continued regardless of the boycott by the Deaf community, indicative of the conviction held by the teachers of deaf students of their authority not only over education but also over signing as a mode. Certainly, their actions indicated clearly that Signed English belonged to the teachers of deaf students and not to Deaf people themselves.

12. Available studies of academic performance by profoundly deaf and "severely hearing impaired" students show that those students who have access to sign language as a full-fledged first language have higher literacy skills than those who have had no access to sign language but for whom the language of the hearing community is being promoted as a first language—that is, those using Signed English or oralist approaches. Thus, although Signed English may give some understanding of the English language, that understanding will always be limited and partial. Signed English, too, is not a language of communication but is confined to contrived situations like the classroom. It is not used within Deaf communities and, thus, has none of the natural dynamics of a natural language, being designed and imposed from outside. Its use reinforces the identification of Deaf people as being "disabled" by ensuring their linguistic dependence on their teachers who become the experts not only in spoken and written language but also in the legitimate form of signed language. Note that Signed English is based on the grammar of written English, not spoken English, which creates particular confusion when combined with lipreading.

13. Research from America and Denmark has shown that, in some cases, the signed portion of the so-called "Total Communication" process is unintelligible. See, for example, Johnson and Erting (1990), Strong and Chaarlson (1987), and Hansen (1989).

14. For a discussion of early mainstreaming in America, see Van Cleve (1993).

15. As occurred also in Australia, America, and other parts of the Western world. For discussions of the mainstreaming of deaf students in America, see Baynton (1996, 149 ff.), Karchmer and Allen (1999), and Allen and Schoem (1997).

16. The act also challenged the need for specialized teaching qualification for teachers of deaf students. The British Association for Teachers of the Deaf lobbied against the challenge and won (see Bannister 1992).

17. For a collection of responses to mainstreaming in Britain in its early days, see Montgomery (1981).

18. For discussion of the National Curriculum and its effect on the education of the deaf, see Gray (1993) and Webster (1990).

19. We have discussed this research in detail elsewhere (Branson and Miller 1991). For discussion of the fundamental link between the educational use of minority languages and human rights see *The Hague Recommendations Regarding the Educational Rights of National Minorities* (Foundation on Inter-Ethnic Relations 1996).

20. See, for example, Mason (1991) and Ladd (1991) as well as other articles in Taylor and Bishop (1991).

21. See, for example, Ladd (1991).

22. Research here and elsewhere has shown clearly that girls educated in single-sex environments perform better on the whole than those in coeducational settings (see Branson and Miller 1979; Yates 1987a, 1987b). The all-girls' school, transformed from a discriminatory curriculum based on preconceived notions of the "normal" girl to a comprehensive curriculum, has been shown to be an environment in which girls can achieve without being put down by the male society, without being constantly confronted by a male competitive presence, without being "disabled" by male values.

23. See Baker and Child (1993) and Powers, Gregory, and Thoutenhoofd (1999).

24. See, in particular, Conrad (1979), Lane (1988), Johnson, Liddell, and Erting (1989), and BBC (1988).

25. For discussions of the interweaving of ethnicity and nationalism in the current era, see Tambiah (1996), Comaroff (1995), and Castells (1997).

9

Ethno-Nationalism and Linguistic Imperialism: The State and the Limits of Change in the Battles for Human Rights for Deaf People

On 27 June 1999, four thousand people marched through London in support of British Sign Language (BSL), demanding its recognition as the language of the British Deaf community and asserting the right of deaf children to be educated in a bilingual environment with BSL as the language of instruction. They demanded "equal citizenship rights for Deaf people," and the formal recognition of their language was of central importance. Organized by the Federation of Deaf People, the march united all sides of the British Deaf community.[1] The march epitomized the atmosphere of victory and achievement of battles won as well as a confidence with respect to new battles still to be fought that now permeates gatherings of deaf people throughout the Western world.

Deaf pride and a sense of Deaf identity are strong and overt in Deaf clubs; at conferences on Deaf History, Deaf Studies, and sign language; at national and international meetings of Deaf societies and federations; in Deaf schools; at colleges and universities where centers and institutes for Deaf Studies and sign language research can be found; and of course, in those rarer universities and institutes for deaf people.[2] Everywhere this confidence and sense of pride is explicitly linked to the achievement of linguistic human rights, to the increasing recognition of sign languages as legitimate and primary languages for deaf people in education and in everyday life.

Although the transformation of practice as distinct from policy is a slow process, the qualitative transformation of Deaf identity from the damnation to the celebration of difference gels well with current cultural environments in the West in which a sense of ethnic identity is primary. We move beyond the nation-state because the orientations and achievements of Deaf communities throughout the world are increasingly dominated by international institutions. The international bureaucracies such as the United Nations, UNESCO, and the World Federation of the Deaf as well as the European Union of the Deaf tend to guide developments at national and subnational levels.

Although the nation remains the political structure within which programs are carried out, identity increasingly derives not from a sense of national pride but from membership in an ethnic group and from an assertion of cultural difference. Ethnicity, language, and new concepts of community dominate the fight against an increasingly international, individuated, and alienating world. In this final chapter of our investigation into the cultural construction of deaf people as "disabled," we also consider these international movements as Western Deaf leaders assert a Deaf identity that focuses on cultural difference, especially on linguistic difference, but that at the same time asserts the existence of both national Deaf communities and an international Deaf community.[3]

After briefly reviewing the current achievements and aspirations associated with the battle for deaf people's linguistic human rights in and through education in the West, we turn to examine a new symbolic violence associated not with the damnation of difference but with the denial of difference. Western Deaf and hearing champions of linguistic human rights for Deaf people are spreading the message of Deaf pride within and beyond the West. They assert with confidence that a Deaf identity is primary for all deaf people throughout the world, and that all deaf people are members of an international Deaf community.

Beyond the violence that has characterized the relationship between hearing and deaf people for centuries is a new symbolic violence, certainly a "gentle, invisible form of violence which is never recognized as such" (Bourdieu 1977b, 192). This new development is a symbolic violence of a classic imperialist kind because, as these aid workers spread the Deaf gospel throughout the world, they unwittingly are becoming agents in the creation and oppression of Deaf minorities.

Linguistic Human Rights and the International Deaf Community

Despite the problems experienced in even the most advanced countries with respect to the education of deaf people, Deaf communities throughout the world over the last two decades have begun, at last, to achieve recognition by national and international authorities that they are cultural minorities with distinct languages.[4] Even so, many government authorities and even some deaf people themselves still regard Deaf communities as "disabled" cultural minorities. At an international level, the World Federation of the Deaf has coordinated the fight to get worldwide recognition of sign languages as bona fide languages and to use these languages as media of instruction in the education of the deaf students. At the closing ceremony of the Tenth World Congress of the World Federation of the Deaf in Helsinki on 28 July 1987, a formal resolution was adopted on "sign language recognition." It began:

> **Whereas:** Recent research both in linguistics and in neurobiology has firmly established the spatial languages of deaf people as fully expressive languages which not only exhibit complex organizational properties, but also display grammatical devices not derived from spoken languages. Distinct sign languages are now seen as fully developed languages with complex rules of grammar, with a rich variety of inflectional processes and an extensive variety of derivational processes, built from both a vast vocabulary base and sophisticated grammatical devices for lexical expansion. These are also autonomous languages comfortably capable of intellectual wit, conversation, evocative disputation, and poetry.
>
> **Be it adopted:** The distinct national sign languages of indigenous deaf populations should be officially recognized as their natural language of right for direct communication.
>
> Deaf people who are advanced native speakers of their national sign language should also be recognized as the legitimate arbiters in the correct usage of the indigenous sign language, and should hold significant positions in research efforts to develop graphic educational materials in the sign language.

Embodied in this resolution is the long and complex linguistic history that we have explored here, a history of interaction between deaf people and the hearing authorities and experts on whom they have relied for access to the resources of their respective societies, especially education. It embodies, too, the battle for the recognition and use of natural sign languages rather than of systems that are based on spoken languages and designed by hearing experts.

In demanding the recognition and use of "the distinct national sign languages of indigenous deaf populations," the resolution also points to the framework within which these battles have been fought and within which solutions are assumed to exist: the nation-state. So far, in our exploration of the cultural construction of deaf people as "disabled," we have used the nation as a framework, focusing to varying degrees on Britain, America, France, and Australia. Although many of the processes at work have cut across national boundaries, the nation has been the political structure within which policy has been framed and practice coordinated. However, as we turn to consider the battles by Deaf communities to achieve linguistic human rights, we must look with a critic's eye at the very concept of "nation." We must "read against the grain" of nationalism.

The Modern Nation-State and the Emergence of National Languages

To use Ben Anderson's term, the nation is an "imagined community." It assumes the status of a community, encompassing and transforming traditional communities, claiming the loyalties and orientations that were formerly afforded the village, the lineage, the clan, the tribe, and the neighborhood. The modern concept of the nation is of a world defined by boundaries that contain a tangible and finite population. It is a world of maps and territories—a world of private and, by extension, national real estate. "In the older imagining, . . . states were defined by centres, borders were porous and indistinct, and sovereignties faded imperceptibly into one another" (Anderson 1991, 19)

The concept of nation with its tangible, bounded territory—a space to be occupied by individuals—supports the modern democratic state in which people are, of economic necessity, equal and individuated before the law; in which the community is an epiphenomenon; and in which territory is a resource to be traded. Identity is likewise individuated. It is divorced in all public purpose from community and bestowed not through communal membership but through the driver's license, the credit card, and the passport.

In this environment, language is likewise an individuated competence, an arbitrary bundle of arbitrary signs, separate from the world it seeks to describe and understand. It is a tool for the acquisition of financial, material, and cultural capital. The sign no longer is linked integrally to that which it describes, and language no longer is an integral part of one's identity that anchors a person to communal roots. Language is also defined by boundaries, not by its users. The national language is the language of the nation-state, not necessarily of its citizens—probably, the first language of most of those who wield power and authority in that public realm. Certainly, it is the basis for the linguistic competence required for success in the public realm, and it is the formal language of that realm's law, economics, politics, and education.

The orientation toward languages as national languages, as official languages, or as both also involves the standardization of language, or the development of codified, acceptable language in grammars and dictionaries. The communal and idiosyncratic aspects of language use give way to depersonalized, decentered language that is dominated by the written form. The national language that dominates within the borders of the state and throughout its spheres of influence beyond creates minority status for other languages within the nation-state. These minority languages are not used necessarily by a statistical minority but are culturally devalued and, frequently, operate as community languages. Their use signals community membership, in contrast to the individuated identity created by the national language.

The circumstances in which minority languages operate vary enormously throughout the world, and we make no attempt here to generalize further. The international atmosphere is well established by Phillipson, Rannut, and Skutnabb-Kangas: "It is only a few hundred of the world's 6–7,000 languages that have any kind of official status, and it is only speakers of official languages who enjoy all linguistic human rights" (Phillipson, Rannut, and Skutnabb-Kangas 1994, 2). Official languages are usually national languages, though not always so, as Bamgbose (1991) points out, giving the example of Kenya, where the national language is Swahili and the official language is English. An increasing number of comparable examples exist.

Nationalism and the Deaf Struggle for Linguistic Rights

For many people throughout the world, therefore, the nation and things national are central to their identities, taken-for-granted aspects of themselves and their surroundings. Although minority groups within a nation-state might feel alienated from the nation's culture, its official language, and its political or economic agenda, they frequently attempt to realize their rights and goals through the formation of national associations. Thus, for many Deaf people throughout the world, their minority culture and their minority rights are expressed nationally. National Deaf associations send national delegates to the Congresses of the World Federation of the Deaf, compete in national teams at the World Deaf Games, and so on. Throughout the world, the strategies pursued by Deaf communities in achieving recognition of the linguistic rights of deaf people involve the development and recognition of national sign languages. How are these languages constructed? By whom? How do situations vary among nations?

The promotion of national sign languages presents us with a dilemma associated with the hegemony of nationalism. As Deaf communities and policymakers attempt to realize the linguistic rights of deaf people, they have tended to promote national sign languages. This nationalism is manifested in the drive for the publication of national sign language dictionaries. As the World Federation of the Deaf report on the status of sign languages reveals, no country has a dictionary for more than one sign language. Of the forty-three countries surveyed, only six did not have sign language dictionaries, but all the rest had only one, a national sign language dictionary (World Federation of the Deaf, Scientific Commission on Sign Language 1993, 38).[5]

For an example of the process, we consider the publication of the *British Sign Language Dictionary* in 1992 (Brien 1992), which represented the much-awaited achievement of linguistic and cultural identity for the British Deaf community. Prepared for the Deaf community's own national association, the British Deaf Association, it also represented the Deaf community's assertion of control over sign language as opposed to control by the hearing-dominated CACDP, the Council for the Advancement of Communication with Deaf People, which coordinates the teaching and, thus, the representation of BSL as well as the certification of sign language interpreters and which, at that stage, was still identified with the use of Signed English.

But what does the concept of a national sign language involve in social, cultural, and linguistic terms? The dictionaries themselves embody not only the symbolic representation of a language and, thus, its recognition but also the standardization of language, the move toward linguistic purity that is a feature of literate languages.[6] The achievement of linguistic rights for the signing Deaf community, therefore, involves the following conundrum:

1. The recognition of sign languages is basic to the achievement of human rights for deaf people.
2. Education through sign languages is basic for the achievement of human rights and for the personal and educational development of all deaf people.[7]
3. The recognition of sign languages involves the assertion by national deaf associations of the existence of national sign languages, the drive for formal recognition of these languages as national sign languages, and for education through these respective languages for all deaf people nationally.
4. But the assertion and recognition of national sign languages can lead to the failure to recognize the existence of minority sign languages in precisely the same way as the assertion and promotion of national spoken and written languages leads to the oppression and suppression of minority spoken and written languages.
5. And yet the recognition of the sign language of the majority is an enormous and vital, even revolutionary, step forward for Deaf communities throughout the world. At one level, it is the recognition of a minority language, but at another, it is the suppression of other minority languages.

Particularly in the case of hereditarily deaf people, the forces of "modernization," of individualism and the breakdown of community and communities, have, as we have shown, been compounded by the medical model of deafness that describes deafness as individuated and pathological, a quality of the individual and not of the community. Hereditarily deaf people did not disappear, but the old forms of community of which deaf people were often accepted and integrated members did disappear. These people and their children, deaf and hearing, remained and remain the bearers and reproducers of the languages that had developed in their communities. Distinct Deaf communities emerged that were not face-to-face communities of deaf and hearing people but were school communities and the gatherings of deaf people in adult Deaf associations. The Deaf community in the West is now a network of Deaf people—from both Deaf and hearing families—that come together in family gatherings; at restaurants; on sporting occasions; at churches; at homes for elderly Deaf people; at clubs, especially, Deaf clubs and societies; and, of course, at school. They are bound together by their deafness, their subculture, and above all, their sign language with its immediate and total accessibility.

Most important, these Deaf communities have been conceptualized as national communities—the British Deaf Community, the Australian Deaf Community, the Swedish Deaf Community, and so on. Their unity has been expressed politically by asserting that the community uses a national sign language and that this language must be the vehicle through which the Deaf community accesses the resources of the wider society by means of interpreters and hearing people who are associated with the Deaf community and who learn the language. In particular, this language must be the vehicle to access education by means of signing teachers. To highlight the complexities of the linguistic politics involved, we turn to examine the short but dramatic history of the development and political recognition of Australia's national sign language, Auslan. Australia makes a revealing case study when we consider the relatively recent arrival of nonaboriginal settlers to its shores, its small population, its intensely multicultural character, and its explicit policies with respect to the status and use of minority languages. Australia could also be seen as a British outpost until American influences on deaf education and on the Deaf community began to make themselves felt beginning in the 1970s.

Auslan—A National Sign Language

The Australian case illustrates the effect, particularly through formal education, of linguistic imperialism on a language as it emerged from British and Irish roots. Australia's non-aboriginal deaf population was made up of individual settlers who came together to build a community. They came together primarily through the establishment of schools, particularly in the mid- to late-1800s. From this base, deaf adult associations and clubs were formed. The role of formal education and voluntary associations in the development of community characterizes the Australian situation as one not only linked to the circumstances of a settler colony but also historically specific to a Western complex society where formal associations link individuals together in the absence of traditional, community-based institutions. As Deaf communities developed in the capital cities, so, too, did the language in all its diversity. Although teachers, interpreters, and others who worked with deaf people gradually began to assert the existence of a national language, Deaf people themselves were, within their various communities, conscious of the development of regional differences.[8]

From the early days of its development, Auslan was subjected to nationalist forces as deaf and hearing champions of signing sought to standardize the language. The pressures for standardization came particularly from those involved in the early development of sign language interpreting, but it came also from leaders of Deaf communities in Australia's capital cities, who traveled a great deal to maintain contact and who stressed the need for national cooperation. In 1938, the hearing leaders of the welfare societies for the deaf, societies originally set up by deaf people but, by then, under the control of hearing professionals, met to coordinate the development of interpreter training for hearing people. These leaders decided that the sign language conventions to be used throughout Australia were to be those of the sign language of London. The responsibility for carrying out this process of standardization was bestowed not on a deaf signer but on a hearing missioner, a true bilingual who had signed from childhood but who was hearing nonetheless.

As is the case with language development in general, sign language use in Australia varied according to the circumstances and personnel involved. Before the introduction of pure oralism, the teachers, deaf and hearing, used large amounts of fingerspelling and were influenced in their syntax by English, particularly, once deaf teachers disappeared from the classroom. The language used by interpreters varied markedly depending on whether they were teachers acting as interpreters or were missioners to deaf people. But in the homes of the congenitally deaf, where signing was a true first language, is where natural sign language was nurtured and where distinctly Australian conventions emerged.

However, the public use of signing remained in the control of hearing teachers, interpreters, and missioners. Examination of films of public gatherings of deaf societies in the 1950s, when pure oralism was at its height in the schools, reveals interpreters signing in a way that is thoroughly dominated by English syntax and by a tendency to speak while signing, a practice common in other countries at the time. However, films of deaf people signing at gatherings of the Deaf community reveal the use of natural sign language, or what was to become known as Auslan. Yet, in the public arena, deaf people would not begin to control their language until the early 1990s.

The last few decades have seen a cultural and linguistic transformation of Australia that has included transformations of official language policy. The development of Auslan as the national language of the Australian Deaf community is linked to these multicultural, multilingual developments. The influx of a wide range of immigrants from Asia and the Middle East has created a multicultural and multilingual society, and multinationalism has been paraded since the 1970s as a positive feature of Australian society by a significant section of the establishment. At the same time, Australia has recognized the rights of Aborigines with respect to culture and language. The 1980s saw attempts to grapple with the linguistic complexities of this multicultural population through the development of formal language policies that were designed to provide guidelines for the use of Australia's languages in public life, including education.

Today, Auslan is recognized as a distinct language. In 1988, a dictionary of Auslan was published. In 1991, after submissions to the government from the Australian Sign Language Advisory Board (AUSLAB), a committee of the Australian Association of the Deaf, which is a Deaf-controlled national organization, the federal government stated the following in its national languages policy:

> It is now increasingly recognised that signing deaf people constitute a group like any other non-English-speaking language group in Australia, with a distinct sub-culture recognised by shared history, social life and sense of identity, united and symbolised by fluency in Auslan, the principal means of communication within the Australian deaf community. Auslan is an indigenous Australian language. (Commonwealth of Australia 1991, 20)

Within the space of a few years, the various signing traditions scattered throughout a large continent had a single name and had been declared a national language. For the vast majority of the non-aboriginal Deaf community, a great deal had been achieved, especially given the basic uniformity of sign language use among non-aboriginal deaf people in Australia. This uniformity is a result of the time frame involved and the demographic peculiarities of Australia's settlers. In Britain, regional variations in sign languages are more apparent and are the subject of intensive debate within British Deaf communities, especially, in relation to the degree to which the British Sign Language represented in the BSL dictionary (Brien 1992) and the language used on national television, especially in the program "See Hear," is representative of language use throughout the country. The same situation is true of many other European countries, depending on their size, and is even more apparent in most non-Western countries.

With Auslan formally recognized by the national government, in contrast to the situation in Britain where such formal recognition is still being fought for, the signing Deaf community in Australia felt that natural sign language was beginning to triumph over Signed English and that the ground was set for the development of Auslan-based bilingual education as the formally recognized mode of education for deaf people. The actual effect of the national language policy was less dramatic, although bilingual programs have developed with significant educational success. But does such a nationalist policy even potentially satisfy the linguistic and educational needs of all signing deaf people?

Aid as Imperialism

Among both hearing policymakers and the leaders of Deaf communities, the fact that deaf people share deafness tends to override considerations of cultural and linguistic difference. For many hearing people, the fact that Deaf communities develop a wide range of languages in the same way as hearing people, and that sign languages can be as mutually incomprehensible as hearing languages seems to be subsumed by the medical model of deafness. Deaf people become conceptualized simply as deaf individuals, no matter where they come from, rather than as cultural human beings. For many leaders of Deaf communities at national and international levels, the assertion of deaf unity at the political level glosses over the cultural and linguistic differences, often giving rise to an unconscious linguistic and cultural imperialism on the part of the dominant Deaf communities. This dynamic has been particularly apparent in the spread of Western educational programs throughout Asia, Africa, and the Pacific.

Throughout the former Third World and beyond, Western educators are selling their educational resources as fervently as the West sold fertilizers and dwarf varieties of grain in the 1960s. They sell courses, set up overseas campuses, and provide an endless stream of educational consultants. The education of deaf people has not been exempt from this neocolonial process. Teachers from particular countries who plan to teach deaf students are trained in the West through aid programs and take the national sign languages or manual codes back with them as the basis to develop signing processes for use in their country's schools. In other cases, Deaf and hearing educational experts from the West have simply gone in and used their own sign languages as the language of education, either ignoring or assuming the nonexistence of local sign languages. In other places overseas, educational experts have sat in committees and created national signing systems that are tied to the national spoken languages.

More than thirty years have passed since Theresa Hayter published her devastating critique of Western aid programs, *Aid as Imperialism* (Hayter 1971). But the imperial mentality is as evident as ever in the aid work carried out by Western governments and the World Federation of the Deaf in so-called "developing" countries. Although missionaries in the past introduced the signing conventions of Britain or America or France into the schools they established throughout the colonized world, the aid workers of the postcolonial world have introduced the natural sign languages of the West, claiming to provide deaf people with sign language, as though they did not already have any. In parts of Africa, for example, deaf people are beginning to assert their own linguistic identities by rejecting the American Sign Language introduced by aid workers.[9]

At the same time, deaf aid workers have gone out to recruit deaf people to the Deaf community, to promote a sense of Deaf identity as though that identity must, in all cultural circumstances, override any other identity. Research into non-Western communities containing large numbers of deaf people has shown that this kind of a Deaf identity is often meaningless where kin- and community-based identities are primary and, especially, where sign languages are used readily and naturally by the majority of the community, both deaf and hearing.[10]

Recently, involvement of both sign language experts and educators of deaf people has been increasing with respect to recording and developing national sign languages for use in education. In Indonesia, for example, an international committee developed a system of signed Indonesian.[11] In Thailand, the emergence of sign language dictionaries has a long and complex history involving a progression from collections of signs by teachers of deaf students to the publication of the revised and expanded edition of *The Thai Sign Language Dictionary* in 1990 (The National Association for the Deaf in Thailand 1990, xlvi ff.). These compilations have constantly involved Western experts but have also increasingly involved deaf Thai people. In the latest edition, despite an effort to stress that Thai Sign Language is a language in its own right, completely separate from spoken Thai lexically and syntactically (The National Association for the Deaf in Thailand 1990, xxxii–xxxiv), signs were collected from many parts of Thailand with the apparent assumption that a single Thai Sign Language exists, a national language. Yet current research indicates that American influences on signing among the educated Deaf people in Bangkok are significant (Woodward 1997a) and that wide variations in signing occur among Deaf communities in Thailand as well as throughout Vietnam and Laos (Woodward 1997b).[12]

In South Africa, a committee collected signs from all over the country to construct a *Dictionary of Southern African Signs for Communicating with the Deaf* (Penn 1992). The signs illustrated in these volumes come from at least twelve cultural regions, from twelve distinct communities with distinct natural sign languages, and yet, one of the prefaces to the first volume states,

> A beginning has now been made to record the beauty and diversity of South African Sign Language. . . . Needed as well are studies of the syntax of South African Sign Language in its many forms. . . . This is a formidable challenge, but it is one that the South African Deaf community is more than capable of meeting. (Penn 1992, xi)

The slip from the recognition of the diversity and multilingual nature of South African Deaf communities into a unitary orientation toward "South African Sign Language" and "the South African Deaf community," both in the singular, is symptomatic of the approach taken by governments, linguists, and linguistic rights activists alike.

Deaf people in any country, no matter what linguistic differences exist among them, are faced with a national problem. They are faced with the imposition of national signed systems and with education processes coordinated at a national level. Their response, where an urban and nationally conscious Deaf community exists, is likewise a national response as they oppose signed versions of the national spoken language by asserting the existence of a national sign language. The sign language dictionary has become an emblem of triumph over the dominant hearing spoken language.

In this kind of battle, the international level of activity has also been important, with the World Federation of the Deaf providing strong support to national organizations. But again, the coordination of activities is assumed to be at the national level. So, for example, in relation to the rights of Deaf children to sign language as a first language and to education through sign language, the "Recommendations of the Commission on Sign Language" of the World Congress of the World Federation of the Deaf held in Tokyo in 1991 (World Federation of the Deaf n.d., 50–53) state:

> A. A Sign language should be recognized and treated as the first language of a Deaf child.
>
> a) The Sign language in question must be the national Sign language, that is, the natural Sign language of the adult Deaf community in that region. (World Federation of the Deaf n.d., 50)

The recommendations continue in relation to the education of deaf children:

> B. Deaf children have the right to be educated, particularly with regard to reading and writing, in a bilingual (or multilingual) environment.
>
> a) The national Sign language should be the language of instruction for most academic subjects. (World Federation of the Deaf n.d., 50)

National sign languages are assumed to exist.

Although such a national approach might be appropriate for countries such as Britain and America that have long-established educational systems for deaf people, these kinds of policies need to be critically examined for non-Western countries, for example Indonesia, in which large numbers of geographically dispersed communities generate large numbers of sign languages. We must also note that, in many Western societies, current sign language policies, in focusing exclusively on assumed national sign languages, ignore the sign languages of cultural minorities, especially those of their indigenous inhabitants. For example, in Australia, which has a long history of Deaf education, the acceptance of Auslan as a national sign language ignores the existence of numerous indigenous sign languages. The iron cage of bureaucracy continues to contain—that is, rationalize—policy and practice to suit the wider administrative requirements of the economy and the state.

Linguistic Imperialism at Home and Abroad

The prime concern in this chapter has been to examine what effect the ideology and practice of ethno-nationalism—and, by extension, multinationalism—has had on the framing and realizing of policies toward sign language that has been done by educators, by governments, and by the Deaf communities themselves. In particular, we have been concerned with critically examining the moves by Deaf communities to assert and manifest national sign languages through processes of standardization. In the past, deaf people have been subjected to linguistic imperialism as an aspect of normalization, particularly through the agency of education. Current moves by the urban-based leaders of national Deaf communities appear to be doing the same to Deaf minorities, as the forces of nationalism impose the national sign language as the source of all knowledge and the basis for effective membership in the national Deaf community.

In the process, the differences among the sign languages within nation-states are devalued or ignored. Although the acknowledgment of national sign languages, which are, in fact, natural languages and widespread, involves the realization of linguistic human rights for some and even possibly a majority of the Deaf communities of a nation, they tend to obscure the linguistic complexities of the deaf population. Inevitably, they create minorities within minorities.

Was the Australian government's recognition of Auslan a clear and uncontroversial triumph for minority linguistic rights? Can we assume that Australia has a national sign language? What about the untapped world of Aborigine sign languages? And what about those non-Anglo-Celtic migrants into Australia? A recent study revealed that, for the state of Victoria alone, of the deaf children in segregated schools and segregated facilities within schools, 24 percent came from non-English-speaking background (NESB) families. Thirty-four languages other than English (LOTE) were in use among the families of these NESB students. Among NESB deaf students who were integrated into mainstream schools, thirty-one LOTE were in use (Branson and Miller 1998c).

The process to select appropriate sign languages to act as the regional or national vehicles for the development of bilingual systems of deaf education is, of course, not straightforward. The problem is also not peculiar to sign languages, as Bamgbose's review of the problems selecting languages for education in sub-Saharan Africa shows (Bamgbose 1991). Although, on the surface, a policy of bilingual education appears to acknowledge the linguistic human rights of minority groups, the unintended consequences can be a symbolic violence resulting from national policies that ignore the linguistic and cultural diversity of Deaf communities within national boundaries.

We have also shown how Western Deaf communities and their leaders and organizations can unwittingly become the agents of a cultural and linguistic imperialism over non-Western Deaf communities. Western Deaf people are in danger of imposing on these non-Western deaf people the sort of oppression and alienation that they themselves have had to suffer for so long from hearing "missionaries," religious and secular. Threatened, in part, by the kinds of linguistic imperialism outlined above, many of the natural sign languages of the world are disappearing as quickly and as surely as Western imperialism destroyed the vast majority of aboriginal languages in the lands they colonized.

We have focused here on the achievements of Deaf activists around the world, on their hopes for themselves and for Deaf children, and on their aspirations for deaf people throughout the world. We have also shown how even the oppressed can themselves become oppressors if the complexities of linguistic and cultural rights are not explored carefully. Deaf people have achieved a great deal in the last decade insofar as natural sign languages have received widespread recognition academically and politically and insofar as Deaf communities have been recognized as linguistic minorities rather than as collections of "disabled" individuals.

But the medical model of deafness also remains strong, manifest particularly in the faith of people at large and in investment by governments and private enterprise in the cochlear implant and associated oral-aural educational programs. Medical diagnosis also remains the mechanism by which deaf people are discriminated against. For example, although it is now ideologically incorrect to refuse a prospective immigrant entry to Australia on the basis of their being "deaf" or "disabled," the current regulations provide for the refusal of entry on medical grounds. The "Public Interest Criteria" (criteria 4005) in the Migration Act state that the prospective migrant can enter Australia if he or she is "free of any disease or condition" that would "in the opinion of a Commonwealth medical officer" require care or treatment of various kinds or would result in the person becoming "a significant charge on public funds." The criteria also contain an additional clause, with more than a hint of eugenics, that states that the applicant for entry must be

> found to be free from any disease or condition that, if offspring were produced, would, in the opinion of a Commonwealth medical officer, result in the offspring being affected by a disease or condition referred to in clause 4005. (Commonwealth of Australia 1993, 478)

A recent newspaper report documents how, sixteen years ago, a Malaysian couple and their children migrated to Australia. Under the family reunion program, other members of their family have joined them. The couple have also sponsored children of their own siblings to come to Australia for their education. But one brother has consistently been refused permission to migrate to Australia. Why? Because he is, as the article put it "a deaf mute" ("It's All in the Family, They Say" 1996). Medicine remains the profession through which discrimination is legitimized. The concept of "pathology" continues to ensure that "normality" is central to the conceptualization of humanity. Bureaucracy continues to provide the framework and process through which people are labeled "disabled" and through which discrimination is rationalized. Deaf people are still damned for their difference.

What then are the limits that are imposed on the celebration of difference by democratic societies oriented, as in the last instance, not to the realization of human rights by means of equality of opportunity and individual rights before the law, but to the accumulation of capital?

The Limits to Change

"To err is human, to persist in error is diabolical."

—Canguilhem 1988a, ix

Scientists, professionals, and administrators have developed and promoted a view of humanity that is based on a fundamental distinction between the able-bodied and the disabled, between the normal and the pathological. Their assumption, an erroneous one, has been that these classifications are either common sense or scientific. The error is one that has disabled and oppressed countless people and has doomed a portion of the population to be ostracized as less than human, as beyond the pale.

The celebration rather than the damnation of difference requires that differences be accommodated and that time, energy, and expense be distributed according to human need when equalizing access to economic, political, cultural, linguistic, spiritual, and educational resources. However, that kind of orientation runs counter to the calculated use of labor power in the interest of profit. It runs counter to an egalitarian individualism based on competition among like units of humanity in the pursuit of success and on the pursuit of individuated, exclusive achievement linked to a sense of honor that lies in the individual attainment of riches.

It challenges not only the imagery that sets the standards of acceptable or, at least, desirable humanity through advertisements, daytime serial dramas, and the imagery of popular culture but also the economic system that uses this imagery and that feeds off the desire to be a beautiful, "able-bodied," fast-moving competitor on the playing field of life.

As we enter the new millennium, government-based policies associated with "the disabled" continue to focus on transforming "disabled" people's way of life by means of "integration," "normalization," and "community care." But as the exploration of mainstreaming practices showed, policy is far too quickly defused of its radical purpose in practice. The administrative processes combined with expertise that is exercised through established professions subvert the radical intent of inspired policy; thus, despite transformations in the treatment and even classification of "the disabled," the cosmology remains essentially unaltered. The dyadic division of the population into "normal" and "pathological," the "able-bodied" and the "disabled," remains. Why does this subversion take place? Does it happen because the bureaucracy ultimately serves the interests of an economy that sets the limits to innovation? Does the economy set limits to ideological and political innovation? Does it depend on the creation of an "able-bodied" workforce and, thus, on the sociocultural construction of "the disabled"?

"Economic Man" and the Damnation of Difference

What ultimately lies in the way of the celebration of difference, is *homo oeconomicus*, economic man. Economic man has no need for "others" except insofar as they act as foils for himself. The "others" who define his normality and his masculinity are but negative shadows, silences that lie behind the confident assertions of his sexuality, his sanity, his reasonableness, his self-discipline, his intelligence, his able-bodiedness. These "others" are constructed as other than the sexuality, the sanity, the reason, the intelligence that characterizes economic man. Just as female sexuality is constructed as a negativity against the positive value accorded male sexuality, so too is the person judged "disabled" constructed as a negativity in terms that give *homo oeconomicus* form and value. To what degree can a society subvert and redefine dominant practices and associated discursive processes by transforming those practices and processes?[13]

Today, the call for radical, even revolutionary, change is unfashionable. The heady days of the late 1960s and 1970s are long past, the

Berlin Wall has gone, and China is a prime site for capitalist investment. World capitalism is triumphant and tends to be accepted as the inevitable way of the world. The changes called for by radicals in the West are essentially cosmetic, which is not to say that they are not important to the quality of life but, rather, to point out that they do not demand fundamental structural change. They do not seek to transform the economic system but only to tinker with the complexion of its labor force—a higher proportion of women here, more blacks there, disabled workers where they were not before. The economy and its ideological complexion remain as before and, as before, demand normalization through discipline; through the embodiment and institutionalization of unreason or insanity; and through the diagnosis, embodiment, and technological treatment of the pathological.

Whoever, in fact, embodies unreason or pathology may change, but these concepts must be embodied. If anti-racist movements render the discrimination against the black population unworkable, then other categories will emerge to ensure that a supply of cheap itinerate labor is available. The "disabled," women, migrants, the uneducated, and the very young are all, as they have been throughout history, potential candidates.

Western societies, therefore, twist and turn in complex ways as they work through the contradictory expressions that are generated with the coexistence of an exploitative mode of production and the ideologies of equality and individualism. In 1939 when eugenicist fascism was at its height and Stalin was in control in Russia, E. M. Forster wrote:

> Two cheers for Democracy: one because it admits variety and two because it admits criticism. Two cheers are quite enough: there is no occasion to give three. Only Love the Beloved Republic deserves that. (Forster 1965, 78)

Ongoing criticism of society's discriminatory processes depends on carefully analyzing the facts through a sociological imagination that questions the most taken-for-granted premises on which our cultural constructs are based. True, Western democracies "admit variety," but they do so within classificatory frameworks that, despite apparent and even tangible improvements in the quality of life, continue to disable and oppress. The concept of "the disabled" remains an ideological construct against which the "normal" workforce is constructed. The "disabled" fight for access to resources and gain some ground—ramps, lifts, note-takers, toilet facilities—and achieve some concessions, even legislation, but they remain "disabled." The classification and education of deaf people continues to be formed and transformed by the ideological transformations of the wider society.

Notes

1. For a description of the march, see the editorial "BSL March: Its Historical Significance: (1999).

2. Namely, Gallaudet University in Washington, D.C., and the National Technical Institute for the Deaf at Rochester Institute of Technology, Rochester, New York.

3. Note that, today, these "communities" are essentially communities of adults who come together as adults. These communities contrast sharply with the communities of the nineteenth century that were firmly grounded in school-based communities of children and adolescents.

4. An earlier version of this discussion was published in the *Journal of Sociolinguistics* (Branson and Miller 1998a).

5. The survey did not discuss the presence of a range of specialist dictionaries such as dictionaries of technical signs, gay signs, and so on, but one should note that these specialist dictionaries are also national dictionaries.

6. See Edwards (1985, 27ff.) and Fishman (1973, 55ff.).

7. For a discussion of the fundamental link between the educational use of minority languages and human rights, see *The Hague Recommendations Regarding the Educational Rights of National Minorities* (Foundation on Inter-Ethnic Relations 1996).

8. These differences are, for the most part, relatively minor lexical differences. As a nonliterate language, Auslan has existed, of course, only in its practice, through face-to-face interaction, until the recent effect of videos, television, and the graphic representation of signing in dictionaries.

9. Personal discussions with delegates at the International Conference of Teachers of the Deaf in Tel Aviv in 1995.

10. See material for Balinese communities in Branson, Miller, and Marsaja (1996, 1999).

11. The sources of the 1,904 signs included in the dictionary are outlined in the foreword:

> This Indonesian Language Sign [Gesture] System Dictionary [Kamus Sistem Isyarat Bahasa Indonesia] contains 1904 signs including signs for affixes and numerals. The data for the Indonesian Language Sign System Dictionary was collected from a number of resources, such as the Sign Dictionary developed by the Institute for the Development of Total Communication, Zinnia Educational Foundation, Jakarta, the Dictionary of Indonesian Language Signs developed by the Working Party on Special Education (KKPLB), IKIP Jakarta, the Sign Dictionary developed by the Karya Mulya

> Foundation, Surabaya, American Sign Language (ASL), British Sign Language, Sign for Singapore, plus signs developed by our own Dictionary Writing Team. The word list for the Dictionary was taken from the Indonesian language syllabus for the Elementary School. (Departemen Pendidikan dan Kebudayaan 1994, v)

12. The fact that such wide variation can be expected in non-Western environments such as Thailand is also supported by recent research on sign language use in north Bali, Indonesia, where significant variations were found in the sign languages that were used, even within a region of north Bali (Branson, Miller, and Marsaja 1999).

13. By posing these questions, we are back to the central questions of nineteenth- and early twentieth-century philosophy and political economy, to the Gramscian confrontation with the role of the intellectual and to Rosa Luxemburg's advocating for reform as an avenue to the revolutionary transformation of society.

Appendix

The 1881 Survey of Methods Used in British Schools for the Deaf

In 1881, the *American Annals of the Deaf and Dumb* published the results of a survey of the methods used in British schools for the deaf (Fay 1881). The results give an interesting overview of the British situation at the time of the Milan Congress and on the eve of The Royal Commission on the Conditions and Education of the Deaf and Blind. In listing the responses to their questions, Fay indicates the way in which classifications of the methods used have been interpreted. He admits to "careless phrasing" of their questions, which resulted in some confusion about the way the "combined method" was interpreted. From the description of results, we can derive the following table (see table 1). Results were not received from Brighton and Exeter, but knowledge of these schools from other sources enables us to include them in the table. The fourth category of "combined" was omitted from the table because it did not apply to any institutions. The three columns for the combined method refer respectively to the three variants outlined by Fay as follows (see also chapter 6):

> By the "manual" method is meant the course of instruction which employs the sign language, the manual alphabet, and writing as the chief means in the education of the deaf, and has facility in the comprehension and use of written language as its principal object. . . .
>
> By the "oral" method is meant that in which signs are used as little as possible; the manual alphabet is discarded altogether, and articulation and lip-reading, together with writing, are made the chief means as well as the end of instruction. . . .

Table 1.
Teaching Methods Used in British Schools—1881

School	Manual	Oral	Combined		
			1	2	3
Aberdeen	√				
Bath	√			√	
Belfast	√			√	
Boston Spa			√		
Brighton	√				
Bristol	√			[√]	
Doncaster	√			√	√
Dublin (St Joseph's)	√				
Dublin (St Mary's)	√				
Dublin (Claremont)	√			[√]	
Edgbaston—large no. of "deaf-mutes" as staff members	√		√		
Edinburgh (Institute)	√			√	
Edinburgh (Donaldson's Hospital)	√			√	
Exeter (to 1877)	√			?	
Glasgow				√??	
Hull	√				
Llandaff	√				
Liverpool				√	
London (Old Kent Road)			√		
London—Jews Home		√			
London—Association for Oral Instruction		√			
London—Miss Hull		√			
London—Soc. for Diffusion of German System		√			
London School Board—Assoc. for Oral Instr.		√			
London School Board—Stainer			√	√	
Manchester				√?	
Margate				√	
Newcastle-on-Tyne	√			√	
Northampton—Arnold		√			
Swansea	√			√	

> The "combined" method is not so easy to define, as the term is employed indiscriminately with reference to several distinct methods, such as (1) the free use of both signs and articulation, with the same pupils and the same teachers throughout their course of instruction; (2) the general instruction of all pupils is by means of the manual method, with the special training of a part of them in articulation and lip-reading as an accomplishment; (3) the instruction of some pupils by the manual method and others by the oral method in the same institution; (4) though this is rather a combined *system*—the employment of the manual method and the oral method in separate schools under the same general management, pupils being sent to one establishment or the other as seems best with regard to each individual case. (Fay 1881, 188)

The results are particularly interesting because they reveal an overwhelming preference for the manual method, with articulation simply seen as an accomplishment available to those with aptitude for speech. Pure oralism is confined to private schools and those controlled by the Association for Oral Instruction. The teachers and benefactors from these private schools plus Stainer from the London School Board and Elliott from Margate are the group that "represented" Britain at the Congress of Teachers of the Deaf in Milan in 1880. If we take the number of schools teaching solely or primarily by the manual method—where, if articulation is taught at all, it is as an additional skill to those with the necessary aptitude—as one category and pure oralism and the combination of oralism and manualism as the other two possibilities, a pie graph of the distribution of schools looks like what is shown in figure 1.

This pie graph is based on the number of schools, not the number of pupils. Were the number of pupils taken into account, the manual slice would be much more dominant.

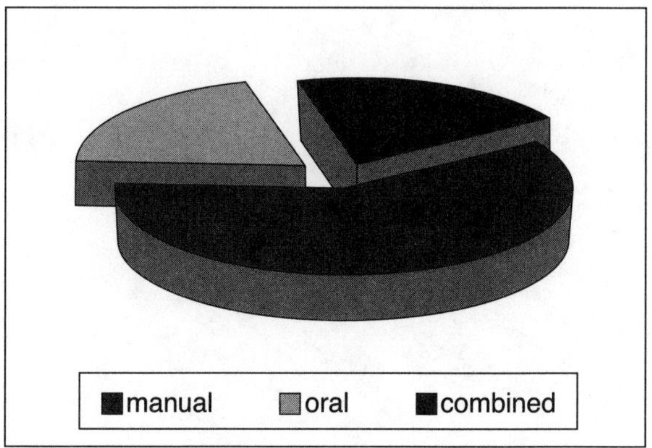

Figure 1. U.K. Teaching Methods—1881

Bibliography

Abberley, Paul. "The Concept of Oppression and the Development of a Social Theory of Disability." *Disability, Handicap, and Society* 2, no. 1 (1987): 5–19.

Abraham, Ernest. "The Limitations of the Pure Oral Method." *The British Deaf Monthly* 8, no. 96 (October 1899): 259–61.

Ahern, G. *Sun at Midnight: The Rudolf Steiner Movement and the Western Esoteric Tradition*. Wellingborough, England: Aquarian Press, 1984.

Ahlgren, Inge. "Sign Language in Deaf Education." In *Sign Language Research and Application: Proceedings of the International Congress, Hamburg, 1990*, edited by Siegmund Prillwitz and Tomas Vollhaber, 91–96. Hamburg: Signum Press, 1990.

Allen, Thomas E., and Scott R. Schoem. "Educating Deaf and Hard-of-Hearing Youth: What Works Best?" Paper presented at the Combined Otolaryngological Spring Meeting of the American Academy of Otolaryngology, Scottsdale, Ariz., 14 May 1997.

Anderson, Benedict. *Imagined Communities: Reflections on the Origin and Spread of Nationalism*. London: Verso, 1991.

Anderson, Perry. *Passages from Antiquity to Feudalism*. London: New Left Books, 1974.

Angell, R. "Science, Sociology, and Education," *Journal of Educational Sociology* 1, no. 1 (1928).

Anthony, David. "Seeing Essential English." In *Recent Developments in Manual English*, edited by Gerilee Gustason and James C. Woodward. Washington, D.C.: Department of Education, Gallaudet College, 1973.

Apple, Michael W. *Ideology and Curriculum*. London: Routledge and Kegan Paul, 1973.

———. *Education and Power*. London: Routledge and Kegan Paul, 1982.

———. *Teachers and Texts: A Political Economy of Class and Gender Relations in Education*. London: Routledge and Kegan Paul, 1986.

Ariès, Philippe. *Centuries of Childhood*, London: Jonathon Cape, 1962.

Aristotle. *The Works of Aristotle*. Translated by D'Arcy Wentworth Thompson. Oxford: Clarendon, 1910.

Arnold, David. "Man's Ascent in Epidemic Leaps." *The Times Higher Education Supplement* (16 January 1998): 24.

Arnold, Thomas. *A Method of Teaching the Deaf and Dumb Speech, Lip-Reading, and Language*. London: Smith, Elder, 1881.

———. *Education of Deaf Mutes: A Manual for Teachers*. Vol. 1. London: Wertheimer, Lea, 1888.

———. *Education of Deaf Mutes: A Manual for Teachers*, Vol. 2. London: Wertheimer, Lea, 1891.

———. "Reminiscences of Forty Years." In *The History of the Church of Doddridge*, edited by Thomas Arnold and J. J. Cooper. Kettering, England: Northamptonshire Printing and Publishing, 1895.

Arnold, Thomas, David Buxton, William Stainer, Susanna Hull, and John Ackers. "A Protest." *American Annals of the Deaf and Dumb* 26, no. 2 (1881): 138–39.

Arnot, Hugo. *The History of Edinburgh from the Earliest Accounts to the Present Time*. London: Paternoster-Row, 1788.

Aron, Raymond. *Main Currents in Sociological Thought*. Vol. 2. Harmondsworth, England: Penguin, 1970.

Arthur, Murphy. *The Life of David Garrick*. Vol. 1. London: J. Wright, 1801.

Atkinson, Alexander. *Memoirs of My Youth*. Newcastle-on-Tyne, England: John W. Swanston, 1865.

Australian College of Education. *Some Aspects of the Education of Handicapped Children in Australia*. Carlton, Victoria: Australian College of Education, 1971.

Baker, Charles. *The Education of the Senses, as Exhibited in the Instruction of the Blind, and the Deaf and Dumb*. London: Taylor and Walton, 1837.

———. *Contributions to the Publications of the Society for the Diffusion of Useful Knowledge and the Central Society of Education*. Privately printed, 1842.

Baker, Colin. *Key Issues in Bilingualism and Bilingual Education*. Clevedon, England: Multilingual Matters, 1988.

Baker, Henry. Letters. Farrar Deaf Education Collection. John Rylands Library, University of Manchester, Deansgate, England.

———. Papers. Farrar Deaf Education Collection. John Rylands Library, University of Manchester, Deansgate, England.

Baker, Rob, and Dennis Child. "Communication Approaches Used in Schools for the Deaf in the U.K.: A Follow-up Study." *Journal of the British Association of Teachers of the Deaf* 17, no. 2 (1993): 36–47.

Baker, Thomas. "Biographical Sketch of the Late Charles Baker, Ph.D." *American Annals of the Deaf and Dumb* 20, no. 4 (October 1875): 202–11.

Bamgbose, Ayo. *Language and the Nation: The Language Question in Sub-Saharan Africa*. Edinburgh: Edinburgh University Press, 1991.

Banham, Debby, ed. *Monasteriales Indicia: The Anglo-Saxon Monastic Sign Language*. Pinner, England: Anglo-Saxon Books, 1991.

Bannister, John. "Presidential Address by John Bannister on His Inauguration as Eighth President of the British Association of Teachers of the Deaf." *Journal of the British Association of Teachers of the Deaf* 16, no. 1 (1992): 1.

Barham, Peter. *Closing the Asylum: The Mental Patient in Modern Society*. Harmondsworth, England: Penguin, 1992.

Barrett, Michèle. *Women's Oppression Today*. London: Verso, 1980.

Barrett, Michèle, and Mary McIntosh. *The Anti-Social Family*. London: New Left Books, 1982.

Barton, Len, ed. *Integration: Myth or Reality*? Brighton, England: Falmer, 1989.

Barton, Len, and Sally Tomlinson. "The Politics of Integration in England." In *Special Education and Social Interests*, edited by Len Barton and Sally Tomlinson. London: Croom Helm, 1984.

Bateman, F. *The Idiot: His Place in Creation and His Claims on Society*. Norwich, England: Jarrold and Sons, 1897.

Baumann, Bommi. *How It All Began: The Personal Account of a West German Urban Guerrilla*. Vancouver, B.C.: Pulp Press, 1977.

Baynton, Douglas C. *Forbidden Signs: American Culture and the Campaign against Sign Language*. Chicago: University of Chicago Press, 1996.

Bazot, A. M. *Eloge historique de L'Abbé de L'Epée, fondateur de l'Institution des Sourds-Muets*. Paris: Barba Libraire, 1819.

Beaver, Patrick. *A Tower of Strength: Two Hundred Years of the Royal School for Deaf Children*. Sussex, England: Book Guild, 1992.

Bébian, Roch-Ambroise-Auguste. *Essai sur les Sourds-Muets et sur le Langage Naturel ou Introduction a une Classifiscation Naturelle des Idées avec Leur Signes Propres*. Paris: J. G. Dentu, 1817.

———. *Mimographie, ou Essai d'Écriture Mimique Propre a Régulariser le Langage des Sourds-Muets*. Paris: Chez Louis Colas, 1825.

———. *Manuel d'Enseignement Pratique des Sourds-Muets; Tome 1. Modeles d'Exercises*. Paris: Chez Mequignon, 1827.

Bede, Venerable. *The History of the Church of Englande*. Translated by Thomas Stapleton. Antwerp: John Laet, 1565.

Beier, A. L. *Masterless Men: The Vagrancy Problem in England 1560–1640*. London: Methuen, 1985.

Bell, Alexander Graham. "The Formation of a Deaf Variety of the Human Race." *American Annals of the Deaf and Dumb* 29 (1884a): 70–77.

———. *Memoir upon the Formation of a Deaf Variety of the Human Race*. Washington, D.C.: Government Printing Office, 1884b.

———. "Historical Notes Concerning the Teaching of Speech to the Deaf. Chapter V, Braidwood's Institution for the Education of the Deaf and Dumb, at Cobbs, Va." *Volta Review* 2, no. 4 (October 1900a): 385–409.

———. "Historical Notes Concerning the Teaching of Speech to the Deaf. Chapter VI, The Manchester School." *Volta Review* 2, no. 5 (December 1900b): 33–68.

———. "How to Improve the Human Race." *Journal of Heredity* 5 (1914): 1–7.

Bender, Ruth. *The Conquest of Deafness*. Cleveland: Case Western Reserve University, 1960.

Berg, Otto B. *A Missionary Chronicle: Being a History of the Ministry to the Deaf in the Episcopal Church (1850–1980)*. Hollywood, Md.: St. Mary's Press, 1984.

Berger, Peter L. *The Sacred Canopy: Elements of a Sociological Theory of Religion*. New York: Doubleday Anchor, 1969.

Berman, Marshall. *All That Is Solid Melts into Air: The Experience of Modernity*. New York: Viking, 1990.

Bernal, Brian, and Jennifer Toms. "Life as a Pupil at the Victorian School for Deaf Children in the 1940s and 1950s." In *Collage: Works on International Deaf History*, edited by Renate Fischer and Tomas Vollhaber. Hamburg: Signum Press, 1996.

Bernstein, Basil. *Class, Codes, and Control*. London: Routledge and Kegan Paul, 1971.

Berthier, Ferdinand. *L'Abbé de l'Épée, Sa Vie, Son Apostolat, Ses Travaux, Sa Lutte et Ses Succès*. Paris: Michel Lévy Frères, 1852.

Berthier, Ferdinand, ed. "L'Abbé de L'Epée 1712–1789." Pamphlet. Farrar Collection. John Rylands University Library, Deansgate, Manchester, circa 1870.

Biesold, Horst. *Crying Hands: Eugenics and Deaf People in Nazi Germany*. Washington, D.C.: Gallaudet University Press, 1999.

Binet, Alfred, and Theodore Simon. "Application des Méthodes Nouvelles au Diagnostic du Niveau Intellectuel chez des Infants Normaux et Anormaux d'Hospice et d'École Primaire." *L'Année Psychologique* 11 (1905): 245–66.

Bisseret, Noelle. *Education, Class Language, and Ideology*. London: Routledge and Kegan Paul, 1979.

Blaxter, Mildred. *The Meaning of Disability: A Sociological Study of Impairment*. London: Heineman, 1976.

Bogdan, Robert. *Freak Show*. Chicago: University of Chicago Press, 1988.

Bolling, William. Letters. Gallaudet University Archives, Washington, D.C.

Bonet, Juan Pablo. *Reduccion de las Letras, y arte para enseñar á hablar los mudos*. Madrid, 1620.

———. *Simplification of the Letters of the Alphabet and Method of Teaching Deaf-Mutes to Speak*. Translated by H. N. Dixon with an introduction by Abraham Farrar. London: Hazell, Watson, and Viney, 1890.

Bornstein, Harry. "Signed English, an Aid to English Language Development." In *Recent Developments in Manual English*, edited by Gerilee Gustason and James C. Woodward. Washington, D.C.: Department of Education, Gallaudet College, 1973.

Boswell, John. *The Kindness of Strangers: The Abandonment of Children in Western Europe from Late Antiquity to the Renaissance*. New York: Vintage, 1990.

Bouilly, Jean-Nicolas. *L'Abbé de L'Épée, Comédie Historique en Cinq Actes et en Prose*. Paris: Chez André, 1800.

———. *The Deaf and Dumb; or The Abbé de L'Épée, an Historical Play in Five Acts*. London: T. N. Longman and O. Rees, 1801a.

———. *Deaf and Dumb: or, The Orphan Protected: An Historical Drama in Five Acts*. Theatre Royal. London: J. D. Dewick, 1801b.

———. *Deaf and Dumb; or, The Orphan. An Historical Drama in Five Acts*. Translated by Benjamin Thompson. London: Verna and Hood, 1803.

———. *Deaf and Dumb: or, The Orphan Protected: An Historical Drama in Five Acts*. New York: Dramatic-Repository, Shakspeare-Gallery, 1817.

Bourdieu, Pierre. "Cultural Reproduction and Social Reproduction." In *Power and Ideology in Education*, edited by J. Karabel and A. H. Halsey. New York: Oxford University Press, 1977a.

———. *Outline of a Theory of Practice*. London: Cambridge University Press, 1977b.

———. *Le Sens Pratique*. Paris: Les Editions de Minuit, 1980.

———. *Ce Que Parler Veut Dire*. Paris: Fayard, 1982.

———. *Distinction: A Social Critique of the Judgement of Taste*. Cambridge, Mass.: Harvard University Press, 1984.

———. *La Noblesse d'Etat: Grandes Ecoles et Esprit de Corps*. Paris: Les Editions de Minuit, 1989.

———. *Language and Symbolic Power*. Cambridge: Polity Press, 1991.

Bourdieu, Pierre, and Jean-Claude Passeron. *Reproduction in Education, Society, and Culture*. London: Sage, 1977.

Bouvet, Danielle. *The Path to Language: Bilingual Education for Deaf Children*. Clevedon, England: Multilingual Matters, 1990.

Bowles, Samuel, and Herbert Gintis. *Schooling in Capitalist America: Educational Reform and the Contradictions of Economic Life*. London: Routledge and Kegan Paul, 1976.

Boyce, Anthony J., and Elaine Lavery. "Miss Mary Hare." *Deaf History Journal* 1, no. 2 (August 1997): 11–17.

———. *The Lady in Green: The Biography of Mary Hare*. Feltham, England: British Deaf History Society Publications, 1999.

Bragg, Bernard. *Lessons in Laughter: The Autobiography of a Deaf Actor*. Washington, D.C.: Gallaudet University Press, 1989.

Braidwood, Thomas. Letter. *Scots Magazine* (July 1769): 342.

———. Letters. Volta Bureau Library Archives. A. G. Bell Association for the Deaf and Hard of Hearing, Washington, D.C.

Branson, Jan. "An Action Plan for Equality of Opportunity and Social Justice for Deaf Students in Victorian Government Schools." In *Directions for the Future—Education for Students Who Are Deaf in Victorian Government Schools*, by Implementation Task Force. Victoria, Australia: Ministry of Education, 1991a.

———. "The Rationale for the Establishment of a Bilingual System of Education." In *Directions for the Future—Education for Students Who Are Deaf in Victorian Government Schools*, by Implementation Task Force. Victoria, Australia: Ministry of Education, 1991b.

Branson, Jan, and Don Miller. "Feminism and Class Struggle." *Arena* (1977): 47–48.

———. *Class, Sex, and Education in Capitalist Society: Culture, Ideology, and the Reproduction of Inequality in Australia.* Melbourne: Longman-Sorrett, 1979.

———. "Beyond Integration Policy: The Deconstruction of Disability." In *Integration: Myth or Reality*? edited by Len Barton. London: Falmer, 1989a.

———. "Pollution in Paradise: Hinduism and the Subordination of Women in Bali." In *Creating Indonesian Culture*, edited by P. Alexander. Sydney: Oceania Publications, 1989b.

———. "Sign Language and the Control of Deaf Education." *Australian Hearing and Deafness Review* (January 1990).

———. "Normalization and the Socio-Cultural Construction of 'Disabilities': Towards an Understanding of Schooling, Discipline, and the Integration Programme." In *Discipline in the Integrated Classroom*, edited by Malcolm Lovegrove and Ramon Lewis. Melbourne: Longman Cheshire. 1991.

———. "Sign Language, the Deaf, and the Epistemic Violence of Mainstreaming." *Language and Education* 7, no. 1 (1993): 21–41.

———. "Sign Language and the Discursive Construction of Power over the Deaf through Education." In *Discourse and Power in Educational Organizations*, edited by D. Corson. Cresskill, N.J.: Hampton Press, 1995a.

———. *The Story of Betty Steel: Deaf Convict and Pioneer.* Sydney: Deafness Resources, 1995b.

———. "Frederick John Rose: An Australian Pioneer." In *Collage: Works on International Deaf History*, edited by Renate Fischer and Tomas Vollhaber. Hamburg: Signum Press, 1996a.

———. "Writing Deaf Subaltern History: Is It Myth, Is It History, Is It Genealogy? Is It All, or Is It None?" In *Collage: Works on International Deaf History*, edited by Renate Fischer and Tomas Vollhaber. Hamburg: Signum Press, 1996b.

———. "Nationalism and the Linguistic Rights of Deaf Communities: Linguistic Imperialism and the Recognition and Development of Sign Languages." *Journal of Sociolinguistics* 2, no. 1 (February 1998a): 3–34.

———. "Abraham Farrar, Donor of the 'Farrar Collection' of Books on the Education of the Deaf and Cognate Subjects in the John Rylands University Library of Manchester, Deansgate." *Bulletin of the John Rylands University Library of Manchester* (spring 1998b): 173–96.

———. "Achieving Human Rights: Educating Deaf Immigrant Students from Non-English Speaking Families in Australia." In *Issues Unresolved: New*

Perspectives on Language and Deaf Education, edited by A. Weisel. Washington, D.C.: Gallaudet University Press, 1998c.

Branson, Jan, Don Miller, and K. R. Branson. "An Obstacle Race: A Case Study of a Child's Schooling in Australia and England." *Disability, Handicap, and Society* 3, no. 2 (1988): 101–18.

Branson, Jan, Don Miller, and I. Gede Marsaja. "Everybody Here Speaks Sign Language Too: A Deaf Village in Bali, Indonesia—An Initial Report." In *Multicultural Aspects of Sociolinguistics of Deaf Communities*, edited by Ceil Lucas. Sociolinguistics in Deaf Communities Series, vol. 2. Washington, D.C.: Gallaudet University Press, 1996.

———. "Sign Languages as a Natural Part of the Linguistic Mosaic: The Impact of Deaf People on Discourse Forms in North Bali, Indonesia." In *Storytelling and Conversation: Discourse in Deaf Communities*, edited by Elizabeth Winston. Sociolinguistics in Deaf Communities Series, vol. 5. Washington, D.C.: Gallaudet University Press, 1999.

Branson, Jan, Don Miller, and Julie McLeod. "The Integration of the So-Called 'Disabled' into Mainstream Education: Beyond the Add-on Principle." In *Addressing Behaviour Problems in Australian Schools*, edited by C. Szaday. Melbourne: Australian Council for Educational Research, 1989.

Branson, Jan, Jennifer Toms, Brian Bernal, and Don Miller. "Understanding Fingerspelling in a Linguistic Context." In *Sign Language Research, 1994*, edited by Heleen Bos and Trude Schermer. Hamburg: Signum Press, 1995.

"A Brief historical sketch of the origins and progress of the Glasgow Deaf and Dumb Institution founded January 1819." London: John Smith and Co., 1835.

Brien, David, ed. *Dictionary of British Sign Language/English*. London: Faber and Faber, 1992.

Brightman, Alan J., ed. *Ordinary Moments: The Disabled Experience*. Baltimore: University Park Press, 1984.

Brill, Richard. *International Congresses on Education of the Deaf: An Analytical History, 1878–1980*. Washington, D.C.: Gallaudet University Press, 1984.

British Association for the Advancement of Science. "Report of the Committee Appointed to Consider and Report on the German and Other Systems of Teaching the Deaf to Speak." Report of the Fiftieth Meeting of the British Association for the Advancement of Science, Swansea 1880. London: John Murray, 1880.

British Broadcasting Corporation. *Pictures in the Mind*. 1988. Videocassette.

The British Deaf Monthly 6, no. 68 (1897): 179.

Brown, Peter R. *Banton*. Feltham, England: British Deaf History Society Publications, 1994.

———. "Deaf History." *British Deaf News* (December 1997): 7.

"BSL March: Its Historical Significance." *Deaf History Journal* 3, no. 1 (August 1999).

Buckley, S., and G. Bird. *Meeting the Educational Needs of Children with Down Syndrome*. Down Syndrome Educational Trust: Hampshire, England, 1994.

Bulwer John. *Chirologia or the Natural Language of the Hand. . . .* London: Harper, 1644.

———. *Philocophus: or the Deafe and Dumbe Man's Friend. . . .* London: Humphrey and Mosley, 1648.

Busfield, Joan. *Managing Madness: Changing Ideas and Practice*. London: Unwin Hyman, 1989.

Buxton, David. "On the Marriage and Intermarriage of the Deaf and Dumb." An offprint sent to Bell at the Volta Bureau by the author. Liverpool: W. Fearnall, 1857.

———. "Dr. Buxton on the Education of the Deaf and Dumb." *The Deaf and Dumb Herald and Public Intelligencer* 1, no. 7 (October 1876): 98–100.

———. "Notes of Progress in the Education of the Deaf." A paper read at the education department of the National Association for the Promotion of Social Science at the Twenty-Sixth Annual Congress, Nottingham, 22 September, 1882. London: W. H. Allen, 1882.

———. "Speech and Lip-Reading for the Deaf: A Teacher's Testimony to the 'German' System." Paper presented at the International Congress on the Education of the Deaf, Milan, September, 1880.

Caldwell, Malcolm. *The Wealth of Some Nations*. London: Zed Press, 1977.

Callinicos, Alex. *Against Postmodernism: A Marxist Critique*. Cambridge: Polity Press, 1989.

Camporesi, Piero. *Bread of Dreams: Food and Fantasy in Early Modern Europe*. Cambridge: Polity Press, 1989.

Canguilhem, George. *Ideology and Rationality in the History of the Life Sciences*. Cambridge, Mass.: MIT Press, 1988a.

———. *The Normal and the Pathological*. Cambridge, Mass.: MIT Press, 1988b.

Canter, Lee, and Marlene Canter. *Assertive Discipline: A Take Charge Approach for Today's Educators*. Santa Monica: Canter, 1976.

Capra, Franz. *The Turning Point: Science, Society, and the Rising Culture*. Toronto: Bantam, 1983.

Carew, Richard. *The Survey of Cornwall*, London: Simon Stafford for John Jaggard, 1602.

Castells, Manuel. *The Power of Identity*. Information Age, vol. 2. Malden, Mass.: Blackwell, 1997.

Child, Dennis. "A Survey of Communication Approaches Used in Schools for the Deaf in the U.K." *Journal of the British Association of Teachers of the Deaf* 15, no. 1 (1991): 20–24.

Cohen, Joshua, and Joel Rogers. *On Democracy: Toward a Transformation of American Society*. London: Penguin, 1983.

Comaroff, John L. "Ethnicity, Nationalism, and the Politics of Difference in an Age of Revolution." In *Perspectives on Nationalism and War*, edited by John L. Comaroff and Paul C. Stern. Luxembourg: Gordon and Breach, 1995.

Commonwealth of Australia. *The Language of Australia: Discussion Paper on an Australian Literacy and Language Policy for the 1990s.* Canberra: Australian Government Publishing Service, 1990.

———. *Australia's Language: The Australian Language and Literacy Policy.* Canberra: Australian Government Publishing Service, 1991a.

———. *Companion Volume to the Policy Paper* Australia's Language: The Australian Language and Literacy Policy. Canberra: Australian Government Publishing Service, 1991b.

———. *Migration (1993) Regulations.* Canberra: Australian Government Publishing Service, 1993.

Commonwealth Schools Commission. *The National Policy for the Education of Girls in Australian Schools.* Canberra: Commonwealth Schools Commission, 1987.

Conrad, R. *The Deaf School Child.* London: Harper and Row, 1979.

Corker, Mairian. *Deaf Transitions.* London: Jessica Kingsley, 1996.

———. *Deaf and Disabled or Deafness Disabled? Towards a Human Rights Perspective.* Buckingham: Open University Press, 1997.

Corson, Harvey. "Comparing Deaf Children of Oral Deaf Parents and Deaf Parents Using Manual Communication with Deaf Children of Hearing Parents on Academic, Social, and Communicative Functioning." Ph.D. diss., University of Cincinnati, 1973.

Coulton, George Gordon. *Social Life in Britain from the Conquest to the Reformation.* Cambridge: Cambridge University Press, 1919.

Cranefield, Paul F. "A Seventeenth-Century View of Mental Deficiency and Schizophrenia—Thomas Willis on Stupidity or Foolishness." *Bulletin of the History of Medicine* 35 (1961): 291–316.

Crickmore, Barbara. L. *Education of the Deaf and Hearing Impaired: A Brief History.* 2d ed. Mayfield, Australia: Education Management Systems, 1995.

Crocker, Lester G. Introduction to *The Blackwell Companion to the Enlightenment*, edited by John W. Yolton, Roy Porter, Pat Rogers, and Barbara Maria Stafford. Oxford: Blackwell, 1995.

Crossley, Rosemary, and Annie McDonald. *Annie's Coming Out.* Ringwood, Australia: Penguin, 1979.

Crystal, David. *The Cambridge Encyclopedia of Language.* Cambridge: Cambridge University Press, 1987.

Cummins, Jim. *Bilingualism and Special Education: Issues in Assessment and Pedagogy.* Clevedon, England: Multilingual Matters, 1984.

Curtis, John Harrison. *An Essay on the Deaf and Dumb; Shewing the Necessity of Medical Treatment in Early Infancy With Observations on Congenital Deafness.* London: Longman, Rees, Orme, Brown and Green, 1829.

———. *A Treatise on the Physiology and Pathology of the Ear*. 6th ed. London: Longman, Rees, Orme, Brown and Green, 1836.

———. *Advice to the Deaf. The Present State of Aural Surgery*. 6th ed. London: Whittaker; Paris: Galignani, 1846.

Dalgarno, George. *Ars Signorum, Vulgo Character Universalis et Lingua Philosophica. . . .* London: Hayes, 1661.

———. *Didascalocophus or the Deaf and Dumb Mans Tutor. . . .* Oxford: Theatre, 1680.

Darwin, Charles Robert. *On the Origin of Species by Means of Natural Selection, or the Preservation of Favoured Races in the Struggle for Life. . . .* London: John Murray, 1859.

Davis, Lennard J. *Enforcing Normalcy: Disability, Deafness, and the Body*. London: Verso, 1995.

Davis, Mike. "Urban Renaissance and the Spirit of Postmodernism." *New Left Review* 151 (1985): 106–13.

———. *City of Quartz: Excavating the Future in Los Angeles*. London: Verso, 1990.

Day, George, E. "On the Late Efforts in France and Other Parts of Europe to Restore the Deaf and Dumb to Hearing." *Silliman's American Journal* (July 1835): 301–23.

De Gérando, Baron Joseph-Marie. *De L'Éducation des Sourds-Muets de Naissance*. Vol. 1. Paris: Chez Méquignon L'Ainé Père, 1827a.

———. *De L'Éducation des Sourds-Muets de Naissance*. Vol. 2. Paris: Chez Méquignon L'Ainé Père, 1827b.

The Deaf-Mutes Journal 5, no. 43 (October 1876).

Deegan, Mary Jo, and Nancy A. Brooks, eds. *Women and Disability: The Double Handicap*. New Brunswick, N.J.: Transaction Books, 1985.

Defoe, Daniel. *The Dumb philosopher or great Britain's Wonder*. London: Thos. Bickerton, 1717.

———. *The History of the Life and Adventures of Mr Duncan Campbell*. London: E. Curll, 1720.

Departemen Pendidikan dan Kebudayaan. *Kamus sistem isyarat Bahasa Indonesia*. Edisi pertama. Jakarta: Departemen Pendidikan dan Kebudayaan, 1994.

Derrida, Jacques. *Of Grammatology*. Translated by G. C. Spivak. Baltimore: John Hopkins University Press, 1976.

———. "Choreographics: Interview with Christie V. McDonald." *Diacritics* 12, no. 2 (1982): 66–76.

deVilliers, Jill. "A Longitudinal Study of Language Development in Young Oral Deaf Children." Typescript, Smith College, 1988.

Dexter, T. F. G. *The Pagan Origin of Fairs*. Cornwall: New Knowledge Press, 1934.

Diderot, Denis. *Lettre Sur Les Sourds et Muets*. 2 vols. Paris, 1751.

Digby, Kenelm. *Two Treatises: In one of which The Nature Of Bodies, In the other, The Nature of Man's Soul is looked into: In way of discovery of the Immortality of Reasonable Souls*. London, 1645.

Doerner, Klaus. *Madness and the Bourgeoisie: A Social History of Insanity and Psychiatry*. Oxford: Blackwell, 1981.

Down, John Langdon. *On Some of the Mental Affections of Childhood and Youth*. Classics in Developmental Medicine, no. 5. London: Mac Keith, 1990.

Draper, Amos G. "Report of Professor Draper on the International Congress of Deaf Mutes in Paris." In *Thirty-second Annual Report of the Columbia Institution for the Deaf and Dumb to the Secretary of the Interior*. Washington, D.C.: Government Printing Office, 1889.

Dreyfus, Hubert L., and Paul Rabinow. *Michel Foucault: Beyond Structuralism and Hermeneutics*. Brighton, England: Harvester Press, 1982.

Dumont, Louis. *Homo Hierarchicus: The Caste System and Its Implications*. Chicago: University of Chicago Press, 1980.

———. *Essays on Individualism: Modern Ideology in Anthropological Perspective*. Chicago: University of Chicago Press, 1986.

Duncan, P., and W. Millard. *A Manual for the Classification, Training, and Education of the Feeble-Minded, Imbecile, and Idiotic*. London: Longmans, Green, 1866.

Durkheim, Émile. *The Division of Labor in Society*. Urbana, Ill.: Free Press, 1947.

Du Verney, Guichard Joseph. *A Treatise of the Organ of Hearing: Containing The Structure, the Uses, and The Diseases of All the Parts of the Ear*. Paris: Chez Estienne Michallet, 1737.

Eco, Umberto. *The Name of the Rose*. London: Picador, 1984.

———. *The Search for the Perfect Language*. Oxford: Blackwell, 1995.

Education Department of Victoria. *School Disciplinary Procedures 1985*. Melbourne: Education Department of Victoria, 1985.

Edwards, John. *Language, Society, and Identity*. Oxford: Blackwell, 1985.

Elliott, Richard. "Reminiscences of a Retired Educator." *Volta Review* 12 (1911): 13.

Eriksson, Per. *The History of Deaf People: A Source Book*. Örebro, Sweden: Daufr, 1998.

Evans, Lionel. *Total Communication, Structure, and Strategy*. Washington, D.C.: Gallaudet University Press, 1982.

Evans, Lionel, and Doin Hicks. "Getting on Terms with Total Communication." In *The Education of the Deaf: Current Perspectives*, edited by I. G. Taylor. Vol. 1. London: Croom Helm, 1988.

Evans, Richard J. *The German Underworld: Deviants and Outcasts in German History*. London: Routledge, 1988.

Ewoldt, Carolyn. *Mainstreaming the Hearing Impaired Child: Process Not Goal*. ERIC Document Reproduction Service No. ED 168 275, 1979.

Farrar, Abraham. "Speech for the Deaf and Dumb." *Sunday Magazine* (December 1883).

———. *Arnold on the Education of the Deaf: A Manual for Teachers*. London: Simpkin, Marshall, 1901.

———. "My Story." *Magazine of the Spring Hill School for the Deaf* (December 1937).

Farrell, Gabriel. *The Story of Blindness*. Cambridge, Mass.: Harvard University Press, 1956.

Fay, Edward A. "The Methods of the British Schools." *American Annals of the Deaf and Dumb* 26, no. 3 (1881): 182.

———. "The Examination of Teachers in England." *American Annals of the Deaf and Dumb* 30, no. 3 (1885): 173–74.

———. "The Instruction of the Deaf." *Science* 17 (1891): 421.

Finkelstein, V. "'We' Are Not Disabled, 'You' Are." In *Constructing Deafness*, edited by Susan Gregory and G. M. Hartley. London: Pinter, 1991.

Fishman, Joshua A. *Language and Nationalism: Two Integrative Essays*. Rowley, Mass.: Newbury House, 1973.

Fletcher, L. "Deafness: The Treatment." In *Being Deaf: The Experience of Deafness*, edited by George Taylor and Juliet Bishop. London: Pinter, 1991.

Forster, E. M. *Two Cheers for Democracy*. Harmondsworth, England: Penguin, 1965.

Foucault, Michel. *Madness and Civilization*. New York: Vintage, 1973.

———. *The Birth of the Clinic*. New York: Vintage, 1975.

———. *Discipline and Punish: The Birth of the Prison*. London: Peregrine, 1979.

Foundation on Inter-Ethnic Relations. *The Hague Recommendations Regarding the Education Rights of National Minorities*. The Hague: Foundation on Inter-Ethnic Relations, 1996.

Fournié, Edouard le. *Physiologie et Instruction Du Sourd-Muet D'après La Physiologie des Divers Langages*. Paris: Adrien Delahaye, 1868.

Fox, Richard W., and James T. Kloppenberg, eds. *Companion to American Thought*. Oxford: Blackwell, 1995.

Friedlander, Henry. *The Origins of Nazi Genocide: From Euthanasia to the Final Solution*. Chapel Hill: University of North Carolina Press, 1995.

———. Introduction to *Crying Hands: Eugenics and Deaf People in Nazi Germany*, by Horst Biesold. Washington, D.C.: Gallaudet University Press, 1999.

Friere, Paulo. *Cultural Action for Freedom*. Harmondsworth, England: Penguin, 1972a.

———. *Pedagogy of the Oppressed*. Harmondsworth, England: Penguin, 1972b.

Fulcher, Gillian. "Australian Policies on Special Education: Towards a Sociological Account." *Disability, Handicap, and Society* 1, no. 1 (1986): 19–52.

———. "Integration: Inclusion or Exclusion?" In *Discipline and Schools: A Curriculum Perspective*, edited by R. Slee. South Melbourne: Macmillan, 1988.

———. *Disabling Policies? Comparative Approaches to Educational Policy and Disability*. London: Falmer, 1989.

Gallaudet, Edward Miner. "Report of the President on the Systems of Deaf-Mute Instruction Pursued in Europe." *Tenth Annual Report of the Columbia Institution for the Deaf and Dumb for the Year Ending June 30, 1867*. Washington, D.C.: Government Printing Office, 1867.

———. "Deaf-Mute Instruction in Great Britain and Ireland." *American Annals of the Deaf and Dumb* 20, no. 2 (1875): 154–61.

———. "The Milan Convention." *American Annals of the Deaf and Dumb* 26, no. 1 (1881): 1–16.

Gannon, Jack R. *The Week the World Heard Gallaudet*. Washington, D.C.: Gallaudet University Press, 1989.

Gellner, Ernest. *Language and Solitude: Wittgenstein, Malinowski, and the Habsburg Dilemma*. Cambridge: Cambridge University Press, 1998.

Genesee, Fred. *Learning through Two Languages*. Cambridge: Newbury House, 1987.

Gerth, H. H., and C. Wright Mills, eds. *From Max Weber*. New York: Oxford University Press, 1946.

Giddens, Anthony. *Capitalism and Modern Social Theory: An Analysis of the Writings of Marx, Durkheim, and Max Weber*. Cambridge: Cambridge University Press, 1971.

———. *Politics and Sociology in the Thought of Max Weber*. London: Macmillan, 1972.

———. *The Class Structure of the Advanced Societies*. London: Hutchinson University Library, 1973.

Gilby, F. G. W. Memoirs. Royal National Institute for the Deaf Library Collection, London.

Gilman, Sander L. *Difference and Pathology: Stereotypes of Sexuality, Race, and Madness*. Ithaca, N.Y.: Cornell University Press, 1985.

———. *Inscribing the Other*. Lincoln: University of Nebraska Press, 1991a.

———. *The Jew's Body*. New York: Routledge, 1991b.

———. *Health and Illness: Images of Difference*. London: Reaktion Books, 1995.

Gilmore, Myron P. *The World of Humanism: 1453–1517*. New York: Harper Torchbooks, 1962.

Glasser, William. *Schools without Failure*. New York: Harper and Row, 1969.

Goddard, Henry. "Mental Tests and the Immigrant." *Journal of Delinquency* 2 (1917): 243–77.

Goffman, Erving. *Asylums*. Harmondsworth, England: Penguin, 1961.

Gordon, Thomas. *T.E.T.: Teacher Effectiveness Training*. New York: New American Library, 1975.

Gould, Stephen J. *The Mismeasure of Man*. London: Penguin, 1984.

———. *An Urchin in the Storm*. London: Penguin, 1990.

Grant, Brian. "Francis Maginn, 1861–1918." In *Looking Back. A Reader on the History of Deaf Communities and their Sign Languages*, edited by Renate Fischer and Harlan Lane. International Studies on Sign Language and Communication of the Deaf, no. 20. Hamburg: Signum Press, 1993.

Gray, David E. "The Hearing Impaired, Unequal Opportunities, and the National Curriculum." *Journal of the British Association of Teachers of the Deaf* 17, no. 5 (1993): 117–23.

Green, Edward J. *Breaking the Silence: The Education of the Deaf in Ireland, 1816–1996*. Dublin: Irish Deaf Society, 1997.

Green, Francis. *Vox Ocula Sugjecta; a dissertation on the Most Curious and Important Art of Imparting speech, and the knowledge of Language, to the naturally Deaf and (consequently) Dumb*. London: Benjamin White, 1783.

Gregory, Susan, and Juliet Bishop. "The Integration of Deaf Children into Ordinary Schools: A Research Report." *Journal of the British Association of Teachers of the Deaf* 13, no. 1 (1989): 1–6.

Gregory, Susan, and G. M. Hartley, eds. *Constructing Deafness*. London: Pinter, 1991.

Griffey, N. "From a Pure Manual Method via the Combined Method to the Oral-Auditory Technique: Educating Profoundly Deaf Children: Experience in Thirty Years Teaching Deaf Children." Appendix D to *Breaking the Silence: The Education of the Deaf in Ireland, 1816–1996*, by Edward J. Green. Dublin: Irish Deaf Society, 1997.

Groce, Nora Ellen. *Everyone Here Spoke Sign Language: Hereditary Deafness on Martha's Vineyard*. Cambridge, Mass.: Harvard University Press, 1985.

Gustason, Gerilee. "Signing Exact English." In *Recent Developments in Manual English*, edited by Gerilee Gustason and James C. Woodward. Washington, D.C.: Department of Education, Gallaudet College, 1973.

Hanna, William A. *Bali Profile: Peoples, Events, Circumstances, 1001–1976*. New York: American Universities Field Staff, 1976.

Hansen, B. "Trends in the Progress towards Bilingual Education for Deaf Children in Denmark." Copenhagen: Døves Center for Total Communication, 1989.

———. "The Development towards Acceptance of Sign Language in Denmark." Copenhagen: Døves Center for Total Communication, 1991.

Hansen, Brita, and R. Kjaer-Sorensen. *The Sign Language of Deaf Children in Denmark*. Copenhagen: The School for the Deaf, 1976.

Hanson, Olaf. Papers and newspaper clippings, 1891–1909. Gallaudet University Archives, Washington, D.C.

Harding, Sandra. *The Science Question in Feminism*. Milton Keynes, England: Open University, 1986.

Harley, Brigit. *Age in Second Language Acquisition*. San Diego: College-Hill Press, 1986.

Harris, Jennifer. *The Cultural Meaning of Deafness*. Aldershot, England: Avebury, 1995a.

Harris, Roy. *The Language Makers*. London: Duckworth, 1980.

———. "Language." In *The Blackwell Companion to the Enlightenment*, edited by John W. Yolton, Roy Porter, Pat Rogers, and Barbara Maria Stafford. Oxford: Blackwell, 1995b.

Hartmann, Arthur. *Deafmutism and the Education of Deaf-Mutes by Lip-Reading and Articulation*. Translated and enlarged by James Patterson Cassells, M.D. London: Tindall and Cox, 1881.

Harvey, David. *The Urban Experience*. Oxford: Blackwell, 1989.

———. *The Condition of Postmodernity: An Enquiry into the Origins of Cultural Change*. Oxford: Blackwell, 1990.

Hawkesworth, M. E. "Knowers, Knowing, Known: Feminist Theory and Claims of Truth." *Signs: Journal of Women in Culture and Society* 14, no. 3 (1989): 533–57.

Hay, John, and Raymond Lee. "Thomas Braidwood: A Hackney Pioneer." *Hackney Terrier: The Friends of Hackney Archives Newsletter* 33 (Winter 1994): 2–4.

———. *A Pictorial History of the Evolution of the British Manual Alphabet*. Feltham, England: British Deaf History Society Publications, 1994.

Hayter, Theresa. *Aid as Imperialism*. Harmondsworth, England: Penguin, 1971.

Hazard, Paul. *The European Mind, 1680–1715*. Harmondsworth, England: Penguin, 1973.

Heddell, F. *Accident of Birth: Aspects of Mental Handicap*. London: BBC Publishers, 1980.

Hilton, Rodney. "Warriors and Peasants." *New Left Review* 83 (1973): 83–94.

Hirst, Paul Q., and Penny Woolley. *Social Relations and Human Attributes*. London: Tavistock, 1982.

Hobsbawm, Eric J. *Nations and Nationalism Since 1780: Programme, Myth, Reality*. Cambridge: Cambridge University Press, 1990.

Hobsbawm, Eric, and G. Rude. *Captain Swing*. London: Lawrence and Wishart, 1969.

Hodgson, Kenneth, W. *The Deaf and Their Problems: A Study in Special Education*. London: Watts, 1953.

Holder, William. *Elements of Speech: An Essay of Enquiry into The Natural Production of Letters: with an Appendix Concerning Persons Deaf and Dumb*. London, 1669.

———. *A Supplement to the Philosophical Transactions of The Royal Society July 1670. With some Reflections on Dr. John Wallis, his LETTER There Inserted*. London: Henry Brome, 1678.

———. "A Discourse Concerning Time, With Application of The Natural Day, and Lunar Month, and Solar Year, as Natural." London: Heptinstall, 1694.

Howard, James. Letter to the *Sunday Magazine* (December 1883).

Hull, Susanna E. "Do Persons Born Deaf Differ Mentally from Others Who Have the Power of Hearing?" *American Annals of the Deaf* 22, no. 4 (October 1877): 234–40.

———. "The International Congress: A Reply." *American Annals of the Deaf and Dumb* 26, no. 2 (April 1881a): 93–98.

———. "Instruction of Deaf-Mutes." *Education* 1 (1881b): 286–93.

Illich, Ivan. *Celebration of Awareness: A Call for Institutional Revolution*. Harmondsworth, England: Penguin, 1973.

"In the Interests of Deaf Children." *Teacher of the Deaf* 59 no. 349 (1961): 20–23.

Ingstad, Benedicte, and Susan Reynolds Whyte, eds. *Disability and Culture*. Berkeley: University of California Press, 1995.

Israelite, Neita, Carolyn Ewoldt, Robert Hoffmeister, and J. Greenwald. "A Review of the Literature on the Effective Use of Native Sign Language on the Acquisition of a Majority Language by Hearing Impaired Students." Draft of final report, 1989.

Itard, Jean Marc Gaspard. "Rapport fait à son excellence le Ministre de l'Interieur sur le Sauvage de l'Aveyron." Paris (circa 1806). Bound in the back of *Essai sur les Sourds-Muets et sur le langage naturel ou introduction a une classification naturelle des idées avec leur signes propres*, A. Bébian. Paris: J. G. Dentu, 1817.

———. *The Wild Boy of Aveyron*. Translated by George and Muriel Humphrey. New York: Century Company, 1932.

"It's All in the Family, They Say." *The Age* (4 July 1996): 1.

Jackson, H., ed. *The Anatomy of Melancholy*. 3 vols. London: Dent, 1968.

Jacoby, Henry. *The Bureaucratisation of the World*. Berkeley: University of California Press, 1973.

Jahoda, Gustav. *Images of Savages: Ancient Roots of Modern Prejudice in Western Culture*. London: Routledge, 1999.

Jameson, Frederick. "Postmodernism, or The Cultural Logic of Late Capitalism." *New Left Review* 146 (1984): 53–93.

Jamieson, Dale. "Singer and the Practical Ethics Movement." In *Singer and His Critics*, edited by Dale Jamieson. Oxford: Blackwell, 1999.

Jeanes, Ray C., and B. E. Reynolds. *Dictionary of Australasian Signs for Communication with the Deaf*. Melbourne: Victorian School for Deaf Children, 1982.

Jeanes, Ray C., B. E. Reynolds, and B. C. Coleman. *Dictionary of Australasian Signs for Communication with the Deaf*. 2d ed. Melbourne: Victorian School for Deaf Children, 1989.

Jenkinson, J. C. *School and Disability: Research and Practice in Integration*. Melbourne: Australian Council for Educational Research, 1987.

Jensen, Arthur. "The Nature of Black-White Difference on Various Psychometric Tests: Spearman's Hypothesis." *The Behavioural and Brain Sciences* 8 (1985): 193–263.

Johnson, Robert C. "Inside a Bilingual Program for Deaf Students." *Research at Gallaudet* (Spring 1999): 1, 4–6.

Johnson, Robert E. "Sign Language and the Concept of Deafness in a Traditional Yucatec Mayan Village." In *The Deaf Way: Perspectives from the International Conference on Deaf Culture*, edited by Carol Erting, Robert C. Johnson, Dorothy L. Smith, and Bruce D. Snider. Washington, D.C.: Gallaudet University Press, 1994.

Johnson, Robert E., and Carol J. Erting. "Ethnicity and Socialization in a Classroom for Deaf Children." In *The Sociolinguistics of the Deaf Community*, edited by Ceil Lucas. New York: Academic Press, 1990.

Johnson, Robert E., Scott K. Liddell, and Carol J. Erting. "Unlocking the Curriculum: Principles for Achieving Access in Deaf Education." Gallaudet Research Institute Working Paper 89-3. Washington, D.C.: Gallaudet University, 1989.

Johnson, Samuel. *A Dictionary of the English Language*. Vol. 1. London: Knapton, Longman, Hitch and Hawes, Millar and R. and J. Dodsley, 1755.

———. *A Journey to the Western Islands of Scotland*. London: Strahan and Cadell, 1775.

Johnson, Samuel, and James Boswell. *Johnson's Journey to the Western Islands of Scotland and Boswell's Journal of a Tour to the Hebrides with Samuel Johnson*. Edited by R. W. Chapman. London: Oxford University Press, 1924.

Johnston, Trevor. *Auslan Dictionary: A Dictionary of the Sign Language of the Australian Deaf Community*. Sydney: Deafness Resources Australia, 1989.

———. "Autonomy and Integrity in Sign Languages." *Signpost* (spring 1991): 2–5.

Jordan, I. King. "Communication Methods Used at Schools for the Deaf and Partially Hearing Children and at Units for Partially Hearing Children in the United Kingdom." *American Annals of the Deaf* 127, no. 7 (1982): 811–15.

Kanner, Leo. *A History of the Care and Study of the Mentally Retarded*. Springfield, Ill.: Charles C. Thomas, 1964.

Karacostas, Alexis. "Fragments of *Glottophagia*: Ferdinand Berthier and the Birth of the Deaf Movement in France." In *Looking Back: A Reader on the History of Deaf Communities and their Sign Languages*, edited by Renate Fischer and Harlan Lane. Hamburg: Signum Press, 1993.

Karchmer, Michael A., and Thomas E. Allen. "The Functional Assessment of Deaf and Hard of Hearing Students." *American Annals of the Deaf* 144, no. 2 (1999): 68–77.

Kerr Love, James. *Deaf Mutism, A Clinical and Pathological Study with Chapters on the Education and Training of Deaf Mutes by W. H. Addison, Principal of the Glasgow Deaf and Dumb Institution*. Glasgow: James MacLehose, 1896.

Kevles, Daniel. *In the Name of Eugenics: Genetics and the Uses of Human Heredity*. Berkeley: University of California Press, 1985.

Kinniburgh, Robert, ed. *The Edinburgh Messenger: A Record of Intelligence Regarding the Deaf and Dumb*. Vol. 2. Edinburgh: Edinburgh Institution, 1847.

Kirp, David L. "Professionalization as a Policy Choice: British Special Education in Comparative Perspective." In *Special Education Policies: Their History, Implementation, and Finance*, edited by Jay C. Chambers and William T. Hartman. Philadelphia: Temple University Press, 1983.

Kloppenberg, James T. "The American Enlightenment." In *The Blackwell Companion to the Enlightenment*, edited by John W. Yolton, Roy Porter, Pat Rogers, and Barbara Maria Stafford. Oxford: Blackwell, 1995.

Kuhn, Annette, and AnnMarie Wolpe, eds. *Feminism and Materialism: Women and Modes of Production*. London: Routledge and Kegan Paul, 1978.

Kumar, Krishan. *Prophesy and Progress*. Harmondsworth, England: Penguin, 1978.

Kumar, Krishan, ed. *Revolution, The Theory and Practice of a European Idea*. London: Weidenfeld and Nicholson, 1971.

Kyle, Jim G., and Bencie Woll. *Sign Language: The Study of Deaf People and Their Language*. Cambridge: Cambridge University Press, 1985.

La Barre, Weston. *The Peyote Cult*. Hamden, Conn.: Shoe String Press, 1964.

La Follette, Marcel C. *Making Science Our Own: Public Images of Science, 1910–1955*. Chicago: Chicago University Press, 1990.

Ladd, Paddy. "Making Plans for Nigel: The Erosion of Identity by Mainstreaming." In *Being Deaf: The Experience of Deafness*, edited by George Taylor and Juliet Bishop. London: Pinter, 1991.

———. "Deaf People, Disabled People, and the Future." *British Deaf News* 26, no. 12 (December 1995): 6–9.

Lane, Harlan. *The Wild Boy of Aveyron*. Cambridge, Mass.: Harvard University Press, 1976.

———. *When the Mind Hears. A History of the Deaf*. New York: Random House, 1984.

———. *When the Mind Hears: A History of the Deaf*. Harmondsworth, England: Penguin, 1988.

———. *The Mask of Benevolence: Disabling the Deaf Community*. New York: Knopf, 1992.

Lane, Harlan, Robert Hoffmeister, and Ben Bahan. *A Journey into the Deaf World*. San Diego: DawnSignPress, 1996.

Lang, Harry G., and Bonnie Meath-Lang. *Deaf Persons in the Arts and Sciences: A Biographical Dictionary*. Westport, Conn.: Greenwood Press, 1995.

Latham, Robert, and William Matthews, eds. *The Diary of Samuel Pepys: A New and Complete Transcription*. Vol. 5. London: Bell, 1982.

Leach, Edmund. *Social Anthropology*. Oxford: Oxford University Press, 1982.

Lee, Raymond. "A Mother and Her Son." *British Deaf News* (June 1997): 7.

———. "Deaf History." *British Deaf News* (March 1998): 7.

———. *John William Lowe*. Feltham, England: British Deaf History Society Publications, 1999.

Lee, Raymond, and John A. Hay. *Bermondsey 1792*. Feltham, England: British Deaf History Society Publications, n.d.

Lenin, Vladimir I. *The State and Revolution*. Moscow: Progress Publishers, 1975.

Lenoir, Alphonse. *Faits Divers, Pensées Diverses, et Quelques Réponses de Sourds-Muets Précédés D'une Gravure Représentant Leur Alphabet Manuel*. Paris: Rue Racine, 1850.

Lettsom, John Coakley. *Hints Designed to Promote Beneficence, Temperance, and Medical Science*. 3 vols. London: J. Manman, 1801.

Lewis, John. "The Development of Remedial Education in Victoria, 1910–1940." Master's thesis, La Trobe University, 1983.

———. "Removing the Grit: The Development of Special Education in Victoria, 1887–1947." Ph.D. diss., La Trobe University, 1989.

Lewis, M. *Managing Madness: Psychiatry and Society in Australia, 1788–1980*. Canberra: Australian Government Publishing Service, 1988.

Lewis, M. M. *Report into the Place of Finger-Spelling and Signing in the Education of the Deaf*. London: Her Majesty's Stationery Office, 1968.

Lindsey, Mary P. *Dictionary of Mental Handicap*. London: Routledge, 1989.

Littlewood, Robert, and Michael Lipsedge. *Aliens and Alienists: Ethnic Minorities and Psychiatry*. London: Unwin Hyman, 1989.

Llwellyn-Jones, W. "Bilingualism and the Education of Deaf Children." In *Constructing Deafness*, edited by Susan Gregory and G. M. Hartley. London: Pinter, 1991.

Lo Bianco, Joe. *National Policy on Languages*. Canberra: Australian Government Publishing Service, 1987.

Locke, John. "A New Method of Making Common-Place-Books." London: J. Geenwood, 1706.

Lou, Mimi W. "The History of the Education of the Deaf in the United States." In *Language Learning and Deafness*, edited by Michael Strong. Cambridge: Cambridge University Press, 1988.

Lovegrove, Malcolm, Ray Lewis, and Eva Burman. *You Can't Make Me! Developing Effective Classroom Discipline*. Bundoora, Australia: La Trobe University Press, 1989.

Lowe, A. "The Historical Development of Oral Education of Deaf Children Seen From the German Point of View." *Journal of the British Association of Teachers of the Deaf* 15, no. 3 (1991): 69–75.

Lucas, Ceil, ed. *The Sociolinguistics of the Deaf Community*. San Diego: Academic Press, 1989.

———. *Sign Language Research: Theoretical Issues*. Washington, D.C.: Gallaudet University Press, 1990.

Luetke-Stahlman, Barbara. "Building a Language Base in Hearing-Impaired Students." *American Annals of the Deaf* 131, no. 3 (1986): 220–28.

Luxemburg, Rosa. "Social Reform or Revolution." In *Selected Political Writings*. New York: Monthly Review Press, 1971.

Lynas, Wendy. "Choosing between Communication Options in the Education of Deaf Children." *Journal of the British Association of Teachers of the Deaf* 18, no. 5 (1994): 141–53.

Lysons, C. K. "United Kingdom." In Vol. 2 of *Gallaudet Encyclopedia of Deaf People and Deafness*, edited by John Vickrey Van Cleve. New York: McGraw-Hill, 1987.

MacDonald, Michael. *Mystical Bedlam: Madness, Anxiety and Healing in Seventeenth-Century England*. Cambridge: Cambridge University Press, 1981.

Mackay, James. *Sounds Out of Silence: A Life of Alexander Graham Bell*. Edinburgh: Mainstream, 1997.

Mackenzie, Catherine. *Alexander Graham Bell: The Man Who Contracted Space*. New York: Grosset and Dunlap, 1928.

Malinowski, Bronislaw. "The Problem of Meaning in Primitive Language." In *The Meaning of Meaning: A Study of the Influence of Language upon Thought and the Science of Symbolism*, edited by C. K. Ogden and I. A. Richards. London: Routledge and Kegan Paul, 1960.

Mandel, Ernest. *Marxist Economic Theory*. London: Methuen, 1968.

Manganaro, Marc, ed. *Modernist Anthropology: From Fieldwork to Text*. Princeton: Princeton University Press, 1990.

Mann, Edwin John. *The Deaf and Dumb: or, A Collection of Articles relating to the Condition of Deaf Mutes; Their Education and the Principal Asylums Devoted to their Instruction*. Boston: D. K. Hitchcock, 1836.

Marcuse, Herbert. *One Dimensional Man*. London: Routledge and Kegan Paul, 1964.

Marsaja, I Gede. "Language Choice and Code-Switching in the Classroom: An Ethnographic Study of the Use of Balinese and Indonesian by a Third Grade Class Teacher and Children in Mathematics Classes at an Elementary School in Singaraja, Bali, Indonesia." Master's thesis, La Trobe University, 1996.

Marx, Karl, and Frederich Engels. *The German Ideology*. Moscow: Progress Publishers, 1968.

———. *The Holy Family, or Critique of Critical Criticism, against Bruno Bauer and Company*. Moscow: Progress Publishers, 1975.

Mason, C. "School Experiences." In *Being Deaf: The Experience of Deafness*, edited by George Taylor and Juliet Bishop. London: Pinter, 1991.

McCall, Andrew. *The Medieval Underworld*. London: H. Hamilton, 1979.

McLellan, David. *Simone Weil: Utopian Pessimist*. London: Macmillan, 1989.

McLoughlin, M. G. *A History of the Education of the Deaf in England*. Liverpool: G. M. McLoughlin, 1987.

Meadow, Kathryn. "Early Manual Communication in Relation to the Deaf Child's Intellectual, Social, and Communicative Functioning." *American Annals of the Deaf* 113 (1968): 29–41.

Mercer, Jan, and Donald B. Miller. "Liberation: Reform or Revolution?" In *The Other Half: Women in Australian Society*, edited by Jan Mercer. Ringwood, Australia: Penguin, 1975.

Merchant, Carolyn. *The Death of Nature: Women, Ecology and the Scientific Revolution*. San Francisco: Harper and Row, 1980.

Merrill, Edward C. "Universal Rights and Progress in Education of the Deaf." *Gallaudet Today* (Fall 1975).

Merrington, John. "Town and Country in the Transition to Capitalism." *New Left Review* 93 (1975): 71–92.

Midelfort, H. C. E. "Madness and Civilization in Early Modern Europe: A Reappraisal of Michel Foucault." In *After the Reformation: Essays in Honour of J. H. Hexter*, edited by B. Malament. Philadelphia: University of Pennsylvania Press, 1980.

Miller, Donald B. "Hinduism in Perspective: India and Bali Compared." *Review of Indonesian and Malaysian Affairs* (December 1983): 36–64.

———. "Louis Dumont." In *Social Theory: A Guide to Central Thinkers*, edited by P. Beilharz. Sydney: Allen and Unwin, 1991.

Miller, Donald B., ed. *Peasants and Politics: Grass Roots Reaction to Change in Asia*. London: Edward Arnold; and New York: St. Martin's Press, 1978.

Miller, Donald, and Jan Branson. "Pierre Bourdieu." In *Social Theory: A Guide to Central Thinkers*, edited by P. Beilharz. Sydney: Allen and Unwin, 1991.

Mills, C. Wright. *The Sociological Imagination*. Harmondsworth, England: Penguin, 1970.

Mirzoeff, Nicholas. *Silent Poetry: Deafness, Sign, and Visual Culture in Modern France*. Princeton: Princeton University Press, 1995.

Mitchell, David, and Sharon L. Snyder, eds. *The Body and Physical Difference: Discourses of Disability*. Ann Arbor: University of Michigan Press, 1997.

Moi, Tonil. *Sexual-Textual Politics*. London: Methuen, 1985.

Mollat, Michel. *The Poor in the Middle Ages: An Essay in Social History*. New Haven, Conn.: Yale University Press, 1986.

Monboddo, Lord James Burnett. *Of the Origin and Progress of Language*. Vol. 1. Edinburgh: Kincaid and Creech; and London: Cadell, 1773.

Montgomery, George. "Bionic Miracle or Megabuck Acupuncture? The Need for a Broader Context in the Evaluation of Cochlear Implants." In *Perspectives on Deafness*, edited by Mervin D. Garretson. A Deaf American Monograph, vol. 41. Silver Spring, Md.: NAD, 1991.

———. *Silent Destiny*. Edinburgh: Scottish Workshop Publications, 1997.

Montgomery, George, ed. *The Integration and Disintegration of the Deaf in Society*. Edinburgh: Scottish Workshop Publications, 1981.

Moore, Henrietta L. *Feminism and Anthropology* Cambridge: Polity Press, 1988.

Moores, Donald F. *Educating the Deaf: Psychology, Principles, and Practices.* Boston: Houghton Mifflin, 1978.

Mühlhäusler, Peter. *Linguistic Ecology: Language Change and Linguistic Imperialism in the Pacific Region.* London: Routledge, 1996.

Mundin, E. L. "Oralism and Its Critics: Why Not a New Approach?" *The Teacher of the Deaf* 47, no. 277 (February 1949): 7–18.

Murphy, Elaine. *After the Asylums: Community Care for People with Mental Illness.* London: Faber and Faber, 1991.

Murphy, Robert F. *The Silent Body.* New York: Henry Holt, 1987.

———. "Encounters: The Body Silent in America." In *Disability and Culture,* edited by Benedicte Ingstad and Susan Reynolds Whyte. Berkeley: University of California Press, 1995.

Musgrave, Peter, and Robert Selleck, eds. *Alternative Schools.* Sydney: Wiley, 1975.

The National Association of the Deaf in Thailand. *The Thai Sign Language Dictionary.* Bangkok: The National Association of the Deaf in Thailand, 1990.

Newsletter of the British Deaf and Dumb Association (1901): 10.

Office of the Director-General, Education Department. *Integration in Victorian Education: Report of the Ministerial Review of Educational Services for the Disabled.* Melbourne: Office of the Director-General, Education Department, 1984.

Office of Schools Administration. *A Fair Go for All: Guidelines for a Gender-Inclusive Curriculum.* Melbourne: Victoria Ministry of Education, 1990.

An Old Friend of the Deaf and Dumb. *Observations on the oral system of educating the deaf and dumb suggested by the "International Review" on the subject for the first year of its publication, namely 1885.* Dublin: James Duffy and Sons, 1885.

Oliver, Michael. "Disability and Social Policy: Some Theoretical Issues." *Disability, Handicap, and Society* 1, no. 1 (1986): 5–18.

———. *Understanding Disability: From Theory to Practice.* London: Macmillan, 1996.

Olson, David R. *The World on Paper: The Conceptual and Cognitive Implications of Writing and Reading.* Cambridge: Cambridge University Press, 1996.

Ong, Walter. *The Presence of the Word: Some Prolegomena for Cultural and Religious History.* New Haven, Conn.: Yale University Press, 1967.

———. *Orality and Literacy.* London: Methuen, 1982.

Pachter, Henry M. *Paracelsus: Magic Into Science.* New York: Henry Schuman, 1951.

Padden, Carol, and Tom Humphries. *Deaf in America: Voices from a Culture.* Cambridge, Mass.: Harvard University Press, 1988.

Paget, Sir Richard. *Human Speech.* New York: Harcourt Brace, 1932.

Paracelsus. "The Begetting of Fools." Translated by P. Cranefield and W. Federn. *Bulletin of the History of Medicine* 41 (1967): 3–21.

Paul, Peter V., and Dorothy W. Jackson. *Toward a Psychology of Deafness: Theoretical and Empirical Perspectives*. Boston: Allyn and Bacon, 1993.

Peet, Isaac Lewis. "Initial Signs." *American Annals of the Deaf and Dumb* 13, no. 3 (September 1868): 44–57.

Penn, Claire, ed. *Dictionary of Southern African Signs for Communicating with the Deaf*. Johannesburg: Human Sciences Research Council, 1992.

Pennant, Thomas. *A Tour in Scotland and Voyage to the Hebrides, 1771*. Part 2. London: Benjamin White, 1774.

Pernick, Martin S. *The Black Stork: Eugenics and the Death of "Defective" Babies in American Medicine and Motion Pictures Since 1915*. New York: Oxford University Press, 1996.

———. "Defining the Defective: Eugenics, Aesthetics, and Mass Culture in Early-Twentieth-Century America." In *The Body and Physical Difference: Discourses of Disability*, edited by David T. Mitchell and Sharon L. Snyder. Ann Arbor: University of Michigan Press, 1997.

Phillipson, Robert. *Linguistic Imperialism*. Oxford: Oxford University Press, 1992.

Phillipson, Robert, M. Rannut, and Tove Skutnabb-Kangas. Introduction to *Linguistic Human Rights: Overcoming Linguistic Discrimination*, edited by Tove Skutnabb-Kangas and Robert Phillipson. Berlin: Mouton de Gruyter, 1994.

Plann, Susan. *A Silent Majority: Deaf Education in Spain, 1550–1835*. Berkeley: University of California Press, 1997.

Poizner, Howard, Edward S. Klima, and Ursula Bellugi. *What the Hands Reveal about the Brain*. Cambridge, Mass.: MIT Press, 1987.

Porter, Roy. *Mind Forg'd Manacles*. Cambridge, Mass.: Harvard University Press, 1987.

———. *The Greatest Benefit to Mankind: A Medical History of Humanity from Antiquity to the Present*. London: Harper Collins, 1997.

Postman, Neil. *Technopoly: The Surrender of Culture to Technology*. New York: Vintage, 1993.

Postman, Neil, and Charles Weingartner. *Teaching as a Subversive Activity*. Harmondsworth, England: Penguin, 1971.

Power, Des, and Merv Hyde. "The Use of Australian Sign Language by Deaf People." Research Reports 1. Queensland, Australia: Centre for Deafness Studies and Research, Griffith University, 1991.

Powers, Stephen. "A Survey of Secondary Units for Hearing-Impaired Children, Part 1." *Journal of the British Association of Teachers of the Deaf* 14, no. 3 (1990): 69–79.

Powers, Stephen, Susan Gregory, and Ernst Thoutenhoofd. "The Educational Achievements of Deaf Children: A Literature Review Executive Summary." *Deafness and Education International* 1, no. 1 (1999): 1–9.

Principals of the Institutions for the Deaf and Dumb. *Transactions of the First and Second Conferences*. London: Varty and Owen, 1852.

Pritchard, David G. "The Development of Schools for Handicapped Children in England during the Nineteenth Century." *History of Education Quarterly* 3, no. 4 (1963): 215.

Proceedings of the Conference of Headmasters of Institutions and of Other Workers for the Education of the Deaf and Dumb, London, June 22–24, 1881. London: W. H. Allen, 1881.

Proceedings of the Conference of Headmasters of Institutions and of Other Workers for the Education of the Deaf and Dumb, held at Royal Association in Aid of Deaf and Dumb, St. Saviours, Oxford St., London, January 8–10, 1890. London: W. H. Allen, 1890.

Redner, Harry. *The Ends of Science: An Essay in Scientific Authority*. Boulder, Colo.: Westview Press, 1987.

Rée, Jonathan. *I See a Voice: Language, Deafness, and the Senses—A Philosophical History*. London: Harper Collins, 1999.

Society for Training Teachers of the Deaf and for the Diffusion of the German System. "Report of the proceedings of the International congress of the Deaf, held at Milan September 6–11th 1880 with an appendix containing papers written for the Congress by Members of the Society for Training Teachers of the Deaf and the diffusion of the 'German' system in the United Kingdom." London: W. H. Allen, 1880.

Richardson, Ken, and David Spears, eds. *Race, Culture, and Intelligence*. London: Penguin, 1972.

Rijnberk, Gérard van. *Le langage par signes chez les moines*. Amsterdam: n.p., 1954.

Ringland, John, and John Gelston. "Report of Deputation to British Institutions for the Deaf and Dumb." Dublin: James Charles, 1856.

Robins, Joseph. *Fools and Mad: A History of the Insane in Ireland*. Dublin: Institute of Public Administration, 1986.

Robinson, Kathy. *Children of Silence*. Harmondsworth, England: Penguin, 1991.

Rodda, Michael, and Carl Grove. *Language, Cognition, and Deafness*. Hillsdale, N.J.: Erlbaum, 1987.

Rosen, George. *Madness in Society*. London: Routledge and Kegan Paul, 1968.

Rubin, Jerry. *Do It! Scenarios of the Revolution*. New York: Simon and Schuster, 1970.

Ryan, J. "IQ—The Illusion of Objectivity." In *Race, Culture, and Intelligence*, edited by K. Richardson and D. Spears. Harmondsworth, England: Penguin, 1972.

———. "The Production and Management of Stupidity: The Involvement of Medicine and Psychology." In *Studies in Everyday Medical Life*, edited by D. Robinson and M. Wadsworth. Oxford: Martin Robertson, 1977.

Ryan, J., and F. Thomas. *The Politics of Mental Handicap*. Harmondsworth, England: Penguin, 1980.

———. *The Politics of Mental Handicap*. Rev. ed. London: Free Association Books, 1987.

Sacks, Oliver. "Mysteries of the Deaf." *New York Review of Books* (27 March 1986): 23–33.

———. "The Revolution of the Deaf." *New York Review of Books* (2 June 1988): 23.

———. *Seeing Voices: A Journey into the World of the Deaf*. Los Angeles: University of California Press, 1989.

———. "The Last Hippie." *New York Review of Books*. 39, no. 6 (26 March 1992): 53+.

Safford, Philip L., and Elizabeth J. Safford. *A History of Childhood and Disability*. New York: Teachers College Press, 1996.

Saint-Loup, Aude de. "Images of the Deaf in Medieval Western Europe." In *Looking Back: A Reader on the History of Deaf Communities and their Sign Languages*, edited by Renate Fischer and Harlan Lane. Hamburg: Signum Press, 1993.

Saisselin, R. G. "Philosophes." In *The Blackwell Companion to the Enlightenment*, edited by John W. Yolton, Roy Porter, Pat Rogers, and Barbara Maria Stafford. Oxford: Blackwell, 1995.

Santitrakool, N. *Sign Exact Thai and English*. Bangkok: Thamasat University Press, 1979.

Schwartz, Barry N., ed. *Affirmative Education*. Englewood Cliffs, N.J.: Prentice Hall, 1972.

Scott, Joseph F. *The Mathematical Work of John Wallis, D.D., F.R.S. (1616–1703)*. London: Taylor and Francis, 1938.

Scott, William R. *The Deaf and Dumb: Their Position in Society, and the Principles of Their Education Considered*. London: Joseph Graham, 1841.

———. *The Deaf and Dumb: Their Education and Social Position*. 2d ed. London: Bell and Daldy, 1870.

Scull, Andrew. *Museums of Madness: Social Organization of Insanity in Nineteenth Century England*. London: Allen Lane, 1979.

Séguillon, Didier. "Deaf Education at the National Institute of Paris: A Story of Sound and Fury." In *Collage: Works on International Deaf History*, edited by Renate Fischer and Tomas Vollhaber. Hamburg: Signum Press, 1996.

Sellars, M., and B. Palmer. *The Integration of Hearing-Impaired Pupils in Ordinary Schools in Berkshire*. Reading, England: University of Reading, 1992.

Shahar, Shulamith. *Childhood in the Middle Ages*. London: Routledge, 1990.

Showalter, Elaine. *The Female Malady: Women, Madness, and English Culture*. London: Virago, 1987.

Sibscota, George. *The Deaf and Dumb Man's Discourse*. London, 1670.

Sicard, Roch-Ambroise Cucurron. *Signes des mots, considérés sous le rapport de la syntaxe; A l'usage des sourds-muets*. Paris: Imprimerie de l'Institution des Sourds-Muets, 1808a.

———. *Théorie des signes pour servir d'introduction a l'étude des langues, ou le sens des mots, au lieu d'etre defini est mis en action.* Vol. 1. Paris: Roret [et] Mongie, 1823a.

———. *Théorie des signes pour servir d'introduction a l'étude des langues, ou le sens des mots, au lieu d'etre defini, est mis en action.* Vol. 2. Paris: Roret [et] Mongie, 1823b.

Silberman, Bernard S. *Cages of Reason: The Rise of the Rational State in France, Japan, the United States, and Great Britain.* Chicago: University of Chicago Press, 1993.

Singer, Peter. *Practical Ethics.* 2d ed. Cambridge: Cambridge University Press, 1993.

A Sister of Notre Dame de Namur. *Life of the Venerable Anne of Jesus, 1545–1621: Companion of St. Teresa of Avila.* London: Sands, 1932.

Skutnabb-Kangas, Tove, and Robert Phillipson, eds. *Linguistic Human Rights: Overcoming Linguistic Discrimination.* Berlin: Mouton de Gruyter, 1994.

Sleight, William, et al. "Letter to the Editor." *The School Master* (24 October 1889).

Snell, K. D. M. *Annals of the Labouring Poor, 1660–1900.* New York: Cambridge University Press, 1985.

Spivak, Gayatri C. *In Other Worlds: Essays in Cultural Politics.* New York: Methuen, 1987.

Stedt, Joseph D., and Donald F. Moores. "Manual Codes on English and American Sign Language: Historical Perspectives and Current Realities." In *Manual Communication: Implications for Education*, edited by Harry Bornstein. Washington, D.C.: Gallaudet University Press, 1990.

Stewart, Dugald. *Elements of the Philosophy of the Human Mind.* Vol. 2 of *The Collected Works of Dugald Stewart*, edited by Sir William Hamilton. Edinburgh: Thomas Constable, 1854.

———. *Elements of the Philosophy of the Human Mind.* Vol. 4 of *The Collected Works of Dugald Stewart*, edited by Sir William Hamilton. Edinburgh: Thomas Constable, 1860.

Stokes, W. E. D. *The Right to be Well Born or Horse Breeding in Its Relation to Eugenics.* New York: C. J. O'Brien, 1917.

Stokoe, William. "Tell Me Where Is Grammar Bred? 'Critical Evaluation' or Another Chorus of 'Come Back to Milano.'" In *Constructing Deafness*, edited by Susan Gregory and G. M. Hartley. London: Pinter, 1991.

Strong, Michael, and Elizabeth Charlson. "Simultaneous Communication: Are Teachers Attempting an Impossible Task?" *American Annals of the Deaf* 6 (1987): 376–82.

Stuckless, E. Ross, and Jack Birch. "The Influence of Early Manual Communication on the Linguistic Development of Deaf Children." *American Annals of the Deaf* 106 (1966): 452–60.

Sutton-Spence, Rachel, and Bencie Woll. *The Linguistics of British Sign Language: An Introduction*. Cambridge: Cambridge University Press, 1999.

Tambiah, Stanley J. *Magic, Science, Religion, and the Scope of Rationality*. Cambridge: Cambridge University Press, 1990.

———. *Leveling Crowds: Ethnonationalist Conflicts and Collective Violence in South Asia*, Comparative Studies in Religion and Society, 10. Berkeley: University of California Press, 1996.

Tanner, C. Kenneth, Deborah Jan Vaughn Linscott, and Susan Allan Galis. "Inclusive Education in the United States: Beliefs and Practices among Middle School Principals and Teachers." *Education Policy Analysis Archives* 4, no. 19 (24 December 1996) [electronic journal]. Available from http://epaa.asu.edu/epaa/v4n19.html

Taylor, George, and Juliet Bishop, eds. *Being Deaf: The Experience of Deafness*. London: Pinter, 1991.

Tellings, Agnes. "Cochlear Implants and Deaf Children: The Debate in the United States." *Journal of the British Association of Teachers of the Deaf* 20, no. 1 (1996): 24–31.

Therborn, Goran. *The Ideology of Power and the Power of Ideology*. London: Verso, 1980.

Thomas, Keith. *Man and the Natural World: A History of the Modern Sensibility*. New York: Pantheon, 1983.

Thornton, William. *Cadmus Or A Treatise on the Elements of Written Language; With An Essay on the Mode of Teaching the Surd or Deaf and Consequently Dumb to Speak*. Philadelphia: Aitkin and Son, 1793.

Tomlinson, Sally. *A Sociology of Special Education*. London: Routledge and Kegan Paul, 1982.

———. "Critical Theory and Special Education: Is S/He a Product of Cultural Reproduction, or Is S/He Just Thick?" *CASTME Journal* 7, no. 2 (1987): 33–41.

Tönnies, Ferdinand. *Community and Society*. East Lansing: Michigan State University Press, 1957.

Tooley, Michael. "Abortion and Infanticide." In *Applied Ethics*, edited by Peter Singer. Oxford: Oxford University Press, 1986.

Townsend, John. *Memoirs of the Rev. John Townsend, Founder of the Asylum for the Deaf and Dumb and of the Congregational School*. Boston: Crocker and Brewster; and New York: J. Leavitt, 1831.

Uberoi, Jit Singh. *Science and Culture*. Delhi: Oxford University Press, 1978.

United Kingdom. Parliament. *Report of the Royal Commission on the Blind the Deaf and Dumb of the United Kingdom*. 1889.

———. Parliament. *Report of the Royal Commission on the Blind the Deaf and Dumb of the United Kingdom Reprint from the Quarterly Review for January 1890*. 1890.

Valentine, Phyllis Klein. "American Asylum for the Deaf: A First Experiment in Education, 1817–1880." Ph.D. diss., University of Connecticut, 1993.

Vallesii, Francisci (Valles De Covarrubias, Francis). *Of iis, quae scripta sunt Phisice in libris sacris, sive of sacred Philosophia.* 1587. Reprint, Frankfurt: Typis Wolffgangi Richteri, sumtibus omnium heredum Nicolai Bassaei, 1608.

Van Cleve, John Vickrey. "The Academic Integration of Deaf Children: A Historical Perspective." In *Looking Back: A Reader on the History of Deaf Communities and Their Sign Languages*, edited by Renate Fischer and Harlan Lane. Hamburg: Signum Press, 1993.

Van Cleve, John Vickrey, ed. *Gallaudet Encyclopedia of Deaf People and Deafness.* Washington, D.C.: Gallaudet University Press, 1987.

Van Cleve, John Vickrey, and Barry A. Crouch. *A Place of Their Own: Creating the Deaf Community in America.* Washington, D.C.: Gallaudet University Press, 1989.

Van Uden, Anthony. *Sign Languages of Deaf People and Psycholinguists: A Critical Evaluation.* Lisse, Netherlands: Lisse, Swets, and Zeitlinger, 1986.

Veeser, H. Aram, ed. *The New Historicism.* New York: Routledge, 1990.

Verne, Jules. *Voyage au centre de la Terre.* Paris: n.p., 1864.

Wallin, Lars. "Deaf People and Bilingualism." Stockholm: Institute of Linguistics, University of Stockholm, 1987.

Wallis, John. *Grammatica Linguae Anglicanae: Cui Praefigitur De Loquela Sive de Sonorum Formatione Tractatus Grammatico-physicus.* Oxford: Leon Lichfield, 1653.

———. "Letter to Robert Boyle esq. concerning the said Doctor's Essay of teaching a person Deaf to speak. . . ." *Philosophical Transactions* 5, no. 61 (July 1670).

———. "A defence of the Royal Society, and the Philosophical Transactions, particularly those of 1670." London: Thomas Moore St. Dunstan's Church Fleet Street, 1678.

Walsh, M. "Overview of Indigenous Languages of Australia." In *Language in Australia*, edited by Susan Romaine. Cambridge: Cambridge University Press, 1991.

Wampler, Dennis W. "An Introduction to Linguistics of Visual English." In *Recent Developments in Manual English*, edited by Gerilee Gustason and James C. Woodward. Washington, D.C.: Department of Education Graduate School, Gallaudet College, 1973.

Watson, Joseph. *Instruction of the Deaf and Dumb. . . .* 2 vols. London, 1809.

———. "Course of Lessons Used by Dr. Watson at the Asylum for the Deaf and Dumb, Old Kent Road, London." Manuscript. Baker Collection no. 130, Gallaudet University Library, 1820.

Watts, Sheldon. *Epidemics and History: Disease, Power and Imperialism.* New Haven, Conn.: Yale University Press, 1997.

Weber, Max. *The Protestant Ethic and the Spirit of Capitalism.* Translated by Talcott Parsons. London: Unwin, 1985.

Webster, Alec. "Hearing-Impaired Children and the National Curriculum." *Journal of the British Association of the Teachers of the Deaf* 14, no. 2 (1990).

Weedon, Chris. *Feminist Practice and Poststructuralist Theory*. Oxford: Blackwell, 1987.

Welsford, Enid. *The Fool: His Social and Literary History*. London: Faber and Faber, 1935.

White, Michael. *Isaac Newton: The Last Sorcerer*. Reading, Mass.: Addison Wesley, 1997.

Whyte, Susan Reynolds. "Disability Between Discourse and Experience." In *Disability and Culture*, edited by Benedicte Ingstad and Susan Reynolds Whyte. Berkeley: University of California Press, 1995.

Wilde, Oscar. *Collected Works*. London: Collins, 1966.

Wilde, William R. *Practical Observations on Aural Surgery and the Nature and Treatment of Diseases of the Ear, with Illustrations*. London: John Churchill, 1853.

Wilkins, John. A Discourse concerning A New World and Another Planet. . . . London: John Norton, 1640.

———. *Mercury, or the secret and swift messenger: showing how a man may with privacy and speed communicate his thoughts to a friend at any distance*. London: I. Norton, 1641.

———. *An Essay Towards a Real Character and A Philosophical Language*. London: Gellibrand and Martyn printer to the Royal Society, 1668.

Wilkinson, W. "List of Schools, Units, Clinics, and Services for the Child with Impaired Hearing." *Teacher of the Deaf* 59, no. 353 (1961): 231.

Williams, B. R. "The Education of the Deaf: Past, Present, and Future." *Journal of Rehabilitation of the Deaf* 19, nos. 1–3 (1985).

Williams, Paul V. A. *The Fool and the Trickster: Studies in Honour of Enid Welsford*. Cambridge: Cambridge University Press, 1979.

Williams, Raymond. *The Long Revolution*. Harmondsworth, England: Penguin, 1965.

Willis, Paul E. *Learning to Labour: How Working Class Kids Get Working Class Jobs*. Farnborough, England: Saxon House, 1977.

Wilson, Colin. *Rudolf Steiner: The Man and His Vision*. Wellingborough, England: Aquarian Press, 1985.

Winzer, Margret. *The History of Special Education: From Isolation to Integration*. Washington, D.C.: Gallaudet University Press, 1993.

Wood, Anthony A. *Athenœ Oxonienses*. . . . Vol. 1. London: F. C. and J. Rivington et al., 1813.

Woodford, Doreen E. "Some Aspects of Finger-Spelling as Seen in Schools for the Deaf at the Present Time." *The Teacher of the Deaf* 71, no. 419 (May 1973): 188–201.

Woodward, James C. "Manual English, A Problem in Language Standardization and Planning." In *Recent Developments in Manual English*, edited by Gerilee Gustason and James C. Woodward. Washington, D.C.: Department of Education, Gallaudet College, 1973.

———. "The Influence of ASL on Thai Sign Language." Paper presented at the First Australasian Deaf Studies Conference, La Trobe University, Australia, 1997a.

——— "Sign Language Varieties in Thailand and Vietnam." Paper presented at the First Australasian Deaf Studies Conference, La Trobe University, Australia, 1997b.

Woolley, Margaret. "Rights for All." *British Deaf News* 26, no. 12 (December 1995): 3.

World Federation of the Deaf. "Proceedings of Eleventh World Congress of the World Federation of the Deaf." Tokyo, Japan, 2–11 July 1991. Tokyo: World Federation of the Deaf, n.d.

World Federation of the Deaf, Scientific Commission on Sign Language. *Report on the Status of Sign Language*. Helsinki: World Federation of the Deaf, 1993.

Wrigley, Owen. *The Politics of Deafness*. Washington, D.C.: Gallaudet University Press, 1996.

Yates, Lynn. "Australian Research on Gender and Education, 1975–85." In *Australian Education: A Review of Recent Research*, edited by J. Keeves. Canberra: Allen and Unwin; Canberra: Australian Academy of Social Sciences, 1987a.

———. "Curriculum Theory and Non-Sexist Education: A Discussion of Curriculum Theory, Feminist Theory, and Victorian Education Policy and Practice 1975–1985." Ph.D. diss., La Trobe University, Australia, 1987b.

Yellon, Evan, ed. *The Albion Magazine: A Bi-Monthly Magazine-Review Published on Behalf of the Deaf*. Vol. 1. London: Yellon, Williams, 1908.

Young, Iris M. *Justice and the Politics of Difference*. Princeton: Princeton University Press, 1990.

Young, Michael F. D., ed. *Knowledge and Control: New Directions for the Sociology of Education*. London: Collier-Macmillan, 1971.

Young, Robert. *White Mythologies*. London: Routledge, 1990.

Zillman, Felix. *Saint Augustine and the Education of the Deaf*. Translated by S. Klopfer. Parts 1–4 first published in *Our Young People—The Deaf-Mutes' Friend* 41, no. 11, 12 (n.d.); 42, no. 1, 2 (n.d.).

Znaniecki, Florian. "The Scientific Function of Sociology." *Educational Theory* 1, no. 2 (1951): 69–78.

Index

aborigines, rights of, 242
abortion of potentially disabled babies, 32
Abraham, Ernest, 168
"Academy for the Deaf and Dumb," 104
Africa: rejection of ASL in, 244; South African Sign Language, 245; sub-Saharan, 247
African American deaf students, 29
Agricola of Heidelberg, 68
Agung, Dewa, xi
Ahlgren, Inge, 222
aid as imperialism, 243–46
The Albion Magazine, 200–1
alienation of deaf people, 148–77. *See also* eugenics; oralism
alphabets. *See* manual alphabets
American Breeders Society, 29
American deaf education: bilingual programs, 222; Braidwoods and, 134–37; cost of, 190; deaf teachers, 199; first school for the deaf, 136–37; higher education, 142–43; institutionalization of teacher training, 199; IQ testing, 51; methodological signs, development of, 137–39, 159; natural sign language, 155–62; nineteenth century, 132–36; oralism, 183 (*see also* oralism); rival schools, 137–38; women trainees for oral method in, 197
American Eugenics Society, 29
American Sign Language (ASL), 220, 244
ancient attitudes toward deaf people and sign language, 67
Anderson, Ben, 236
animals, marginalization and classification of, 23–25
Anne of Jesus, 14
Anthony, David, 213
apprenticeship system to train teachers of the deaf, 194–96
Ariès, Philippe, 191–92
Aristotle, 87
Arnold, Thomas, 163, 164–68, 196
Arnot, Hugo, 102
articulation. *See* oralism; speech
ASL. *See* American Sign Language
Association for the Oral Instruction of the Deaf and Dumb and Training College for Teachers, 196–97
Asylum for the Support and Education of the Deaf and Dumb Children of the Poor (London), 41, 124–25
asylums, 36, 49, 104, 105, 122
Atkinson, Joseph, 141
audiometry, 201, 204–5, 206
audiphone, 200, 201
aural surgery. *See* surgery
Australia: Auslan, 227, 240–43, 247; combined method versus oralism, 185; deaf teachers in, 143; diagnosing and classifying children in, 46; hospitals for severely disabled children, 49; immigrants, refusal to let enter, 248; institutionalizing deaf as mentally retarded, 48; IQ testing, 51; mainstreaming, 52–54; manual alphabets, 81; oralism, 206–7; Princess Elizabeth

Australia *(continued)*
kindergarten, 207; "Public Interest Criteria" of Migration Act, 248–49; teacher training, 178, 206
Australian Nucleus-22 implant, 227
automata, 23, 24

Bacon, Francis, 16, 17, 22, 67
Baker, Charles, 130, 156, 158, 159, 188, 195–96
Baker, Henry, 93, 96–100, 104, 156
Baker, William, 97–98
Bali, Indonesia, xi, 6
Ballestra, abbé, 166
Bamgbose, Ayo, 247
Banham, Debby, 62
Barker, Charles, 162–64
Barland, James, 140–41
Battie, William, 40
Baynton, Douglas C., 133
Bazot, A.M., 107
BDA. *See* British Deaf Association
BDDA. *See* British Deaf and Dumb Association
beauty map, 29
Bébian, Roch-Ambroise-Auguste, 158, 159
Bede, 68
Bedlam, xiv, 21, 23
begging, 7
Bell, Alexander Graham: day schools favored by, 192; development of hearing equipment, 200, 201; development of technology to test hearing, 175, 201; goal to promote the "wellborn," 30–31; against marriage between deaf people, 152–53; Royal Commission appearance by, 181; teacher training, preference for women, 199; views of, 152–53, 184
Berger, Peter L., 14
Berman, Marshall, 23
Bernal, Brian, 207
Berthier, Ferdinand, 144, 159
Bethlehem Royal Hospital, 21
Biesold, Horst, 153
bilingualism in deaf education, 220–24, 247
Binet, Alfred, 47
Binet Scale, 47
Bingham, H.B., 195
Bird, G., 53–54
Birmingham school, 129, 158–59
Bishop, Juliet, 218–19
Blake, William, 18
boarding schools, 191
body snatchers, 39
Bolling, Thomas, 102, 103
Bone, Edward, 61
Bonet, Juan Pablo, 69, 76
Boswell, John, 5
Bourdieu, Pierre, 44–45, 60, 214
Boyle, Robert, 19, 20, 79, 84, 101
Braidwood, Isabella, 134, 135, 194
Braidwood, John, 101, 111, 134–37, 156, 159, 194–95
Braidwood, Thomas, 100–4, 110, 111, 135, 156, 159, 194–95
Braidwood heritage, 179, 194, 195–96
Britain: boarding schools, 191; committee to review educational provisions for handicapped children, 50; compared to France, 92, 112–13, 129, 144, 156; compulsory medical services in schools, 189; eighteenth century, 87–88; English as language used throughout British Empire, 124; fifteenth century, 13–14; funding of schools, 187–88; historical use of sign language, 61–62; IQ testing, 51; manual alphabets, 63, 81; National Curriculum, 219; public schools, 191; regional sign language variations, 243; seventeenth century, 66–90; wars in twentieth century, 187–88. *See also* British deaf education
British Deaf and Dumb Association (BDDA), 127, 185
British Deaf Association (BDA), 189, 211, 214, 220, 221, 238
British deaf education, 79–84, 124–32, 162–68, 181–96; apprenticeship system to train teachers, 194–96; bilingual programs, 222; books and printed material in schools, 157; British philosophers' involvement with, 76–77; catechism, teaching of, 126; combined method employed in, 182–87; complexity of linguistic environment in deaf schools, 161; day

schools, 191–93; deaf principals and teachers, 140–41; disabling consequences of, 187–91; English as language of education, 189; Fay survey of methods, 161–62, 183, 255–58; first half of nineteenth century, 124–30; funding for, 188–90; higher education, 203; influences on, 123, 179; late-nineteenth century, 179; l'Epée's influence on, 110–11; mainstreaming, 217–20; medical research and, 130–32; missionary orientation of, 130–32; mix of methods in use in 1960s, 211; natural sign language, 155–62; neglect of, 189–91;"one-third clause," 188; oralism, 181–83, 192, 210 (*see also* oralism; pure oralism); partially deaf/ hearing, 203–4, 217; as private enterprise, 96, 100–1; pure oralism, 162–68, 185; rebellion at Birmingham school, 158–59; residential schools, 191–93; Royal Commission on the Conditions and Education of the Deaf and Blind, 180–82; school for poor and deaf students, 110–13; sign language, 156–59, 184; teacher training for, 127–28, 193–96; Total Communication, 214–17; Wallis and tradition of deaf education, 79–84; wealthy students, 127
British Enlightenment, 67, 86
British National Deaf Conference, 185
British Sign Language (BSL): bilingual program, 222; earliest comprehensive linguistic analysis of, 158; evolution of, 130; importance of use in education, 213; march to recognize (1999), 233; natural sign language, in tradition of, 157; regional variations in, 243; Scott and, 158
British Sign Language Dictionary, 238, 243
brute, 23
BSL. *See* British Sign Language
bubonic plague, 6
Buckley, S., 53–54
Bulwer, John, 76–79
bureaucratization and education of deaf people in twentieth century, 42–43, 51, 178–202
Burke, John, 212
Burns, Matthew, 127, 140, 141, 144
Burwood Park School, 191, 203, 204
Buxton, David, 152, 155, 171–75, 188, 194, 197

Cabra schools, 180
CACDP (Council for the Advancement of Communication with Deaf People), 238
cadavers, dissection of, 38–39
Calvinism, 15
Campbell, Duncan, 93–96
capitalism, 8, 9, 20
Capra, Franz, 19
Cartesian duality of body and mind, 24–25, 38, 39
Catechism, teaching of, 126
Cattermole, Mary Ann, 141
certification of teachers of deaf, 179, 196–98
Chidely, E. J., 195
Child, Dennis, 215
churches. *See* religion
Cibber, Caius Gabriel, xiv
The Circle of Knowledge (Baker), 163
classificatory schemes for nature, 22
Clerc, Laurent, 135–36, 137, 144, 149, 159, 160
clinical gaze: on deaf, 114–18, 130–32; defining contour of humanity, 34; as diagnostic approach, 46–48; linked with schools after WWII, 205–6; on those diagnosed pathological, 33, 40
cochlear implants, 224–29
coeducational classes, 152
Cogswell, Mason, 133
College of Teachers of the Deaf, 198
colonial intervention, 27–28
Columbia Institution for the Deaf (Gallaudet College), 184
combined method, 161, 175, 181, 182–87, 210, 214–17, 257
Comité des Sourds-Muets, 144
communication, uniformity of, 8
compulsory education, 42, 50, 179, 189, 191
Comte, Auguste, 37
Condillac, Etienne Bonnot de, 86

Conference of Headmasters of Institutions and of Other Workers for the Education of the Deaf and Dumb, 188, 197, 198
congenital disabilities, elimination of, 31–34. *See also* Eugenics
Conrad, R., 213, 220
Cooper, Astley, 39, 113, 225
Copernicus, 16–18
Cornett, R. Orin, 212
Council for the Advancement of Communication with Deaf People (CACDP), 238
Creasy, John, 135
Crickmore, Barbara, 123
Cronke, Dickory, 93–96
Crossley, Rosemary, 49
Cued Speech, 212
cultural construction of pathological humanity, 37–38
cure, attempts to find, 113–14. *See also* Surgery
Curtis, John Harrison, 131

dactylology, 163
Dalgarno, George, 67, 78, 84–85, 87, 92
Darwin, Charles, 26–27, 29–30, 150
Darwinism, 150–51
day schools, 191–93
deaf-alphabets. *See* Manual alphabets
deaf and deafness: ancient and medieval attitudes toward, 67–69; as category of humanity, in view of philosophers, 86–88; classified as disabled, x–xi, xiii, 59–60, 87, 139, 149, 178, 187–91; degree of deafness, 50–51, 175; institutionalization, 48, 190; stigma of, 31; surgical treatment of (*see* surgery); technology to permit hearing, 200–2
The Deaf and Dumb: Their Education and Social Position (Scott), 158
deaf children:education of (*see* American deaf education; British deaf education; deaf education); institutionalization of, 190; killing under Nazi regime, 32, 153–54
Deaf community: development of, 143–45, 234; international Deaf community, 235–36; nationalism and, 238–40; recruiting efforts of, 244; threat posed by, 152–53
deaf education: alliance with surgical experimentation, 131–32; in America (*see* American deaf education); apprenticeship system to train teachers of the deaf, 194–96; audiometers used in, 201, 204–5, 206; bilingualism in, 220–24, 247; in Britain (*see* British deaf education); bureaucratization in twentieth century, 178–202; coeducational classes, 152; compulsory secondary education, 42, 50, 189, 191; confinement of deaf people, 121–47; Dalgarno's orientation toward, 85; day schools, 191–93; deaf teachers (*see* deaf teachers); deinstitutionlization, 217–20; diagnostic professionals' increasing role, 49–51; disabling process of formal education, 46–49; in eighteenth century, 91–120; English language acquisition, 186; fifteenth century, 68–69; in France (*see* France); hearing aids, use of, 200; language proficiency and, 50–51; l'Epée's influence on, 110–11; mainstreaming, 217–20; monasteries, 62 (*see also* monastic sign languages); natural sign language, 154–62; neglect of, 189–90; nineteenth century, 121–47; philosophical issues in, 77–79; as private enterprise, 96, 100–1; professionalism and depersonalization of disabilities, 43–46; pure oralism, 173–75 (*see also* pure oralism); school as clinic, 205–7; science and, 96, 99; secondary education, 191; segregated, 48–49, 221; sign language banned, 209 (*see also* pure oralism); in Spain, 68–69; in Sweden, 221–22; as therapy, 200–2; twentieth century, 178–202; vocationally oriented schooling, 180; Western aid programs and, 243–46; World War I's effect, 190
deaf identity, xiii–xvi, 154, 160, 161, 233–34, 244
deaf marriage, 61, 151–53, 180
deaf-mute, 25
Deaf pride, 233–34

deaf teachers, 43, 135, 139–45, 153, 154, 199
de Carrión, Manuel Ramirez, 68–69
de Castro, Pedro, 68–69
Defoe, Daniel, 70, 93–96, 100
de Fontenay, Saboureux, 86, 104–5
De Gérando, Joseph Marie, 115–17, 138, 150, 159
deinstitutionalization, 51–52. *See also* mainstreaming
Democracy, birth of, 10–11
Denmark, use of national sign language, 223
Depression of 1890s, 186
Descartes, René, 18–19, 23–25, 38–39, 71
de Velasco, Luis, 76
dictionaries, 71, 238, 243, 244–45
Dictionary of Southern African Signs for Communicating with the Deaf, 245
Diderot, Denis, 86
difference: concept of, xiv (*see also* normalization); impediments to celebration of, 250–51
Digby, Kenelm, 75–76, 85
Disability Discrimination Act of 1995, 221
disabled: able-bodied versus, 7, 249–50; agents of disabling process, 154; alliances with disability rights movements, xiv; bureaucratization, 189; call for social change, 250–52; cultural construction of concept, 9; cultural minorities, 235; deaf classified as, x–xi, xiii, 59–60, 87, 139, 149, 178, 187–91; defining, xiii–xvi; disabling practices, xi, 46–49, 51–52, 154, 160; feudal period, 6–7; government policies, 249–50; grouping of "handicapped" people, 149; immigrants refused entry into Australia, 248; isolation and marginalization of people deemed, 8–9, 23–24; limits to change society's treatment of, 249–50; mainstreaming of, 52–54, 217–20; Nazi killing of, 32–33, 49, 153–54; in non-Western cultures, xi; normalization, 49–51; professionalism and depersonalization of disabilities, 43–46; sterilization of, 32–33
discrimination: call for social change, 250–52; linguistic imperialism as, 124; normalization as form of, 52, 54; overview of sociological history of, 59–64; teachers, parents, educational administrators as agents of, 60
doctors. *See* Surgery
Down, John Langdon, 45–46
Down's syndrome, 46, 54
Dryden, John, 70
Drysdale, Mr., 140, 141
duality of mind and body, 25, 38
"dumb," meaning of, 48
Dundee Association for the Education of the Deaf and Dumb, 140, 142
Dundee school, 140
Du Puget, Louis, 159, 196

Ealing College, 198
education. *See* deaf education; schools
Education Act of 1870, 42, 217
Education Act of 1902, 189
Education Act of 1907, 189
Education Act of 1941, 214
Education Act of 1944, 50, 191, 210
Education Act of 1985, 218
Education Reform Act of 1989, 219
egalitarianism, 10
Eicholz committees, 189–90, 204–5
eighteenth century: Britain, 87–88; deaf education, 91–120; new consciousness of language, 71
Elementary Education Act of 1870, 167
Elliott, Richard, 152, 162, 171–72, 188, 195, 198
English Board of Control, 47
English language: acquisition in deaf education, 186; as language of education, 189; literacy and, 123–24. *See also* Written language
Erasmus, 15
Essay towards a Real Character, 72
ethno-nationalism and linguistic imperialism, 233–53
eugenics, 29–34, 49, 151–54; defined, 29; Nazism and elimination of congenital disabilities, 32–34; support by medical diagnosis, 154
euthanasia, 32–34, 153
evolutionism, 26–29, 150–54

Ewing, Alexander, 205–6
experimentation by surgeons, 41, 113–14, 115, 130
family life; effect of day schools, 191–92; evolution of, 8–9
Farrar, Abraham, 164–68, 197, 208, 225, 229
Fay, Edward: marriage of deaf people, views on, 151–52; survey of methods by, 161–62, 183, 255–58; teaching method favored by, 184
Federation of Deaf People, 233
feebleminded, 45, 47, 48–49, 51
feminization of teaching, 170, 197, 198–200
Ferrers, Benjamin, 61
feudalism, 4–7, 10
fifteenth century, 13–14, 68–69
fingerspelling: in American schools, 138; in antiquity, 74–75; Baker's views on, 163; in British schools, 157, 160, 184, 211; Dalgarno as advocate for use of, 85; Watson's students using, 129. *See also* manual alphabets; sign language;
Fitzroy Square College, 198
Fludd, Robert, 16, 18
Forester, Jane, 100
Forster, E.M., 251
Foucault, Michael, x, xiv, 21, 106, 122
fourteenth century, 70
France: compared to Britain, 92, 112–13, 129, 144, 156; deaf education, 41, 104–9, 114; medical experimentation in, 113–14; natural sign language in, 155–62; oralism, 117, 159; Paris school for the deaf, 114–15, 117; sign language and search for perfect language in, 86. *See also* L'Epée, Charles Michel de
French Enlightenment, 67, 86, 104–9
French method, 123
Friedlander, Henry, 32–33
Friere, Paulo, 52
funding of schools in Britain, 187–90

Galileo, Galilei, 17–18
Gallaudet, Edward Miner: combined method advocated by, 181, 182–87; Royal Commission and opposition to oralism, 171, 181–85; teacher training, 199
Gallaudet, Thomas: Braidwoods and, 134–36; in Britain, 133–36; Clerc and, 137; French method and, 135–36; Hartford school, 137; in Paris, 137; Sicard and, 135; Watson and, 135
Gallaudet College, 184, 199
Gallaudet University, 142–43, 213
Galton, Francis, 29–30, 47
German oral method, 110, 123
gestures, 73–74, 77–78, 87, 150. *See also* sign language
Gilby, F.W.G., 172, 173–75, 193
Gildart, John, 99
Glendonald (Australia), 206–7
God, 13–14 (*see also* religion); Descartes' views on, 18–19
Goddard, Henry, 31–32, 47–48
Goethe, Johann Wolfgang, 18
Goffman, Erving, 49
Goodricke, John, 102, 103
Grant, Brian, 185
Green, Charles, 101–3, 110
Green, Francis, 101, 110
Greenaway, E. S., 212
Gregory, Susan, 218–19, 223
Gwillym, William, 99

Haiselden, Harry, 33–34
Hanson, Olaf, 184–85
Harris, Jennifer, 209
Hayter, Theresa, 244
hearing aids, 200–1, 205
hearing loss, 50–51, 175; technology to overcome, 200–2. *See also* Deaf and deafness
hereditary diseases, 30–34
higher education of deaf, 142–43
Hobbes, Thomas, 8, 20, 22, 25–26, 39, 67
Hockenhull, F., 213
Hodges, John, 99
Hodgson, Kenneth, xii, 190
Holder, William, 78, 82–84, 104
Homo oeconomicus, 250
Hooke, Robert, 21
Howard, James, 166
Hull, Susanna, 150–51, 169–70, 197, 198

human rights: battle for rights of deaf people, 233–53; ideological focus of Western countries, 209; post war era, 49–51; rise of movements for, 186
Hunter, William, 135, 139

"idiot," meaning of, 47, 48
Illich, Ivan, 52
immigrants: eugenics screening, 31–32; IQ testing of, 47–48; refusal of entry into Australia, 248
imperialism: ; aid as, 243–46; effect of, 9, 186; hereditary superiority of British and, 44–45; as symbolic violence, 234–35. *See also* Linguistic imperialism
inclusion. *See* mainstreaming
India, xi, 9, 124
individualism, 9, 10, 26
individuation of deaf people, 148–77
individuation of religion, 15
Indonesia, xi, 244
industrial development, 186
initialized signs, 62, 138, 159–60
insanity. *See* madness
institutionalization of deaf, 48, 190. *See also* Asylums
integration. *See* mainstreaming
intelligence quotient (IQ) testing, 45–48, 50–51
international Deaf community, 235–36
Invisible College, 19, 72. *See also* Royal Society of London
Ireland, schools for deaf, 129, 144. *See also* British deaf education
Irish Sign Language, 212
Irish system of Signed English, 212
Itard, Jean-Marc, 41, 113, 115, 116, 131, 159

Jacoby, Henry, 193
Jahoda, Gustav, 28
Jamet, Pierre, 212
Jeffreys, Mary, 99
Jennings, Isabel, 197
Jews, persecution and extermination in Nazi Germany, 33, 153
Jews' Deaf and Dumb Home, 196
Johnson, Robert C., 222
Johnson, Samuel, 102, 103, 143, 185
Jones, James, 198
Jordan, I. King, 215

Kempe, John, 61
Kepler, Johannes, 17
Kettlewell, A. W., 210
Kingham, John, 196
Kinniburgh, Robert, 130, 134, 141, 143, 156, 195
Kinsey, Arthur, 171, 197
Kirkpatrick, John, 134, 136–37, 159

La Barre, Weston, 62
Ladd, Paddy, 206, 208
Lane, Harlan, 224–26
language: defining of humanity by use of, 24–25; evolution of, 70, 71, 150; key to achieving Descartes' ideals, 71; literacy and education of masses, 123–24; national languages, 70–71, 236–37; perfect language, search for, 71–72; prior to formal education, 63; proficiency as education, 50–51; rationality and, 70–72; systematization of grammar and spelling, 70–71; universal language, search for, 66–90; Wilkins' observations about, 73–75. *See also* national sign languages; natural sign languages; sign language
Laos, 245
Law for the Prevention of Offspring with Hereditary Diseases (Germany), 32
Leibnitz, Gottfried Wilhelm, 92
L'Epée, Charles Michel de: analysis of, 155; Bébian and, 158; biography, 106–7; criticism by Baker, 163; De Gérando's relationship to, 116; influence of, 10, 110–11; methodological signs and, 63, 107, 159; myth about, 105, 107–9; natural sign language and, 155, 156, 159; sign language and, 106–7, 150; two-handed alphabet, 63; universal language and, 86
leprosy, 28
Lettsom, John Coakley, 132
Lewis, M.M., 211
"The Limitations of the Pure Oral Method" (Abraham), 168

linguistic imperialism, 246–49; ethnonationalism and, 233–53; factor in disabling deaf, 160
"linguistic mosaic" of pre-Renaissance world, 70
linguistic rights: deaf struggle for, 238–40; international Deaf community, 235–36
linguistics, birth of, 72
Linguistics of Visual English (LOVE), 213
lipreading, 82, 85, 183. *See also* oralism
literacy and English language, 123–24
Locke, John: De Gérando's regard for, 116; empiricist focus of, 39; equality of individuals at birth, 25–26, 92; Invisible College member, 19; rational society advocated by, 22; scientism and, 20; semiotics, 72; view of individual, 8
LOVE (Linguistics of Visual English), 213
Lynas, Wendy, 215, 223

MacDonald, Annie, 49
madness, 36, 40, 44, 45, 114. *See also* Bedlam
Maginn, Francis, 127, 144, 181, 185, 214
mainstreaming of deaf students, 52–54, 217–20
Mann, Edwin, 138
manual alphabets, 60–63; America, 63; Australia, use today, 81; Baker and, 163; Britain, use in, 62, 81; Dalgarno's design of, 85; designed to serve need of hearing, 62; history of, 60–63; Holder and, 83; linguistic potential of, 76; one-handed alphabets, 62–63, 130; pictorial representation of, 93, 95; Scott and, 158; two-handed alphabets, 62–63, 129–30; Wallis' use of, 63, 81, 93–95; Willkins' alphabet on the hand and, 75. *See also* fingerspelling; sign language
manual communication. *See* sign language
manualist heritage in America, 179
marriage: between deaf persons, 61, 151–53, 180; of disabled person prohibited, 32–33
Mary Hare Grammar School, 191, 203, 204, 210, 220
Mason, Henry Cox, 111, 125
Massieu, Jean, 135, 144
McKenzie, Francis Humberstone, 103
medicalization of deafness, 114–18
medical researchers, 113–14, 115, 130–31. *See also* Surgery
Ménière, Prosper, 117
Mental Deficiency Bill, 190
mentally retarded or defective, 45–47, 190
methodological signs, 63, 107, 137–39, 155, 157–60
Middle Ages, 4–6, 28, 62, 67–70
Migration Act (Australia), 248
Milan Congress of Teachers of the Deaf, 168–73; adoption of pure oralism and rejection of sign languages, 154, 168–73; British representatives at, 162; consequences of, 43, 154, 168–73, 181–82; formal teacher training advocated by, 197; response to in Britain and America, 179
Mills, C. Wright, x, 229
Mirzoeff, Nicholas, 66, 155
missionaries. *See* religion
monarchies, 10, 20–21
monastic sign languages, 5, 62, 68
Monboddo, Lord, 102
Montgomery, George, 225
Moores, Donald F., 183
moral therapy movement, 40–42, 148
Mundin, E. L., 210
Murphy, Robert F., 31

National Association for the Oral Instruction of the Deaf, 198
National Deaf Children's Society, 211
National Deaf Mute College, 142–43. *See also* Gallaudet University
nationalism and deaf struggle for linguistic rights, 238–40
national languages, 70–71, 236–37
national sign languages: Auslan, 227, 240–43, 247; bilingualism in deaf education, 220–24; dictionaries, 238, 244–45; education and, 246; ethnonationalism and linguistic imperialism, 233–53; regional variations, 242; World Federation of the Deaf recommendations, 245–46

National Training College for Teachers, 198
National Union of the Deaf, 221
native sign languages, 220–24; Bali, xi, 6. *See also* national sign languages; natural sign languages; sign language
natural alphabet of Holder, 82
natural sign languages: in America, 155–62; Bébian and, 158; Braidwood and, 103; in Britain, 61–62, 127, 155–62, 184; deaf education and, 154–62; devaluation of, 161; disappearing from education, 186; in France, 155–62; history of, 60–61; l'Epée's views on, 86; in nineteenth century education, 129; rejection of, 59; two-handed alphabets, 62–63, 129–30; Watson and, 156–57. *See also* national sign languages; native sign languages; sign language
Nazi Germany, 29, 32–34, 49, 153–54
Neale, A. S., 52
New Sign Language, 212
Newton, Isaac, 18, 19–20
nineteenth century: confinement of deaf children, 121–47; deaf education in Britain, 124–30; late-nineteenth century, 148–77, 179; teacher training in schools for deaf children in Britain, 193–96
normality, ideology of, 37, 117, 187
normalization: deaf education to achieve, 131, 187; as form of discrimination, 52, 54, 251; nineteenth century desire for, 41; "normalize," first appearance in dictionary, 37; therapy and human rights, 49–51

oblates, 5, 62
Old Kent Road school, 125, 126, 141, 142, 152, 194
one-handed alphabets, 62–63, 130, 160
"one-third clause," 188
Ong, Walter, 61, 63
"On the Marriage and Intermarriage of the Deaf and Dumb" (Buxton), 152
oralism, xii, 148–77, 203; alienation process and, 186; Australia, 206–7; Ballestra and, 166; Britain, 181–82, 192, 210; cochlear implants and, 228–29; combined method (*see* combined method); Elliot and, 171–72; experience in class, 209; Fay survey, 161–62, 183, 255–58; hollow triumph of, 201–2; move to, 150–51; Tarra's resolution, 154, 168; triumph of, 151; in twentieth century, 203, 208–9. *See also* Milan Congress of Teachers of the Deaf; pure oralism; speech
The Origin of the Species (Darwin), 26

Paget, Richard, 209, 211–12
Paget-Gorman system, 212
Paracelsus, 16–18, 21
parlor pupils, 127, 129
partial hearing/deaf, 203–5, 217–18
Pasch of Brandenburg, 68
pathology: cultural construction of normality, 37–38; deafness as pathological syndrome, 149; diagnosis of, 38–40; normalization of, 40–42
Patterson, Andrew, 195
Pattison, Thomas, 141, 143
Peet, Harvey, 159–60
Peet, Isaac Lewis, 138, 159
Pennant, Thomas, 102
Pepys, Samuel, 61, 78
Pereire, Jacob Rodriguez, 86, 104–5
perfect language, search for, 66–90, 150
Pernick, Martin S., 34
Phillipson, Robert, xiii, 237
pillaging of foreign countries, 9
Plann, Susan, 69
Ploetz, Alfred, 29
Ponce de León, Pedro, 68–69
poor laws, 7
Popham, Alexander, 81, 82, 93
Porter, Roy, 42
Porteus, Stanley D., 48
Porteus Maze Test, 48
positivism, 37
Postman, Neil, 52, 149
poverty, 6–7
Powers, Stephen, 215–16, 223
Princess Elizabeth kindergarten (Australia), 207
professionalism, 43–46, 88, 113, 148–49, 178
Protestant Reformation, 15
psychiatry, 45
"Public Interest Criteria" of Migration Act (Australia), 248–49

public schools. *See* schools
pure oralism, 173–75; in Britain, 162–68; opposition to, 185; Paget's system opposed by, 212; Royal Commission report on, 180–82. *See also* oralism

racial identity, 28
Rannut, M., 237
religion: catechism, teaching of, 126; Churches for the Deaf, 145; history of Western religion, 5, 6, 13–16; medieval attitudes toward deaf people and sign language, 67–69; missionary orientation of deaf education,130–32; sign language used in, 173, 175; teachers of deaf also serving as missionaries, 196
residential schools, 191–92
Rhind, Charles, 194, 196
The Right to be Well Born or Horse Breeding in Relation to Eugenics (Stokes), 30
Rochester Method, 212
Rose, Frederick John, 144–45
Rothschild, Baroness Mayer de, 162, 196
Royal Commission on the Conditions and Education of the Deaf and Blind, 180–82, 185, 197
Royal School for the Deaf at Margate, 200
Royal Society of London, 18, 19–21, 67, 72
Ruffel, Ralph, 61

St. Augustine, 67–68
St. Jerome, 5, 62
St. John Ackers, B., 162, 172, 175, 197, 198
St. John of Beverley, 68, 69
St. Luke's, 36
St. Mark's Ophthalmic Hospital, 132
St. Mary's School for the Deaf, 212
School for the Deaf in Derby, England, 222
schools: admission of children with multiple disabilities, 51; alternative, 209–10; in America (*see* American deaf education); audiometers, 201; in Australia, 46, 206–7; bilingualism in deaf education, 220–24; in Britain (*see* British deaf education); bureaucracy and, 42–43; as clinic, 205–7; clinical gaze and, 205; compulsory education, 42, 50, 179, 189, 191; conferences for principals, 188; disabling process of formal education, 46–49; Ewing-style, 206; French school for deaf and poor, 105; funding in Britain, 187–88; missionary orientation in Britain, 130; for partially deaf, 204; public education, 121–24; segregated, 48–49, 221; vocationally oriented, 180. *See also* deaf education; mainstreaming of deaf students; teacher training; *specific school by name*
science, 13–35; battle of and emergence of new philosophy, 16–19; evolution of ideology from religion to, 14–16; mechanistic science, 18; normality defined by, 37–38; ordering of nature and humanity by, 22–29; penetration of daily life by, 21–22. *See also* eugenics; evolutionism
scientism, 16–17
Scotland, deaf schools in, 140–41. *See also* British deaf education
Scott, W.R., 158, 163
Scriptures, 13. *See also* religion
SEE 2 (Signing Exact English), 213
SEE 1 (Seeing Essential English), 212, 213
"See Hear" (television program), 243
Seeing Essential English (SEE 1), 212, 213
segregation; of the "deaf," views of British philosophers, 78; of "defectives," 48–49; mainstreaming and retreat from, 51–54; schools, 48–49, 221; special education, 48–49
Séguillon, Didier, 117
seventeenth century in Britain, 66–90
Sheriff, Alexander, 100
Sheriff, Charles, 100–1, 103
Sicard, Roch-Ambroise-Cucurron: Gallaudet meeting with, 135; head of Paris school and successor of l'Epée, 113; relationship to De Gérando, 116; sign language, views on, 150, 156; Watson and, 157

sideshows, 28
Signed Danish, 213
Signed English, 209–14
Signed German, 213
Signed Indonesian (SIBI), 213
Signed Swedish, 213
Signed Thai, 213
Signing Exact English (SEE 2), 213
sign language: ancient and medieval attitudes toward, 67–69; Baker's use of, 100; Bali, xi, 6; ban on use of, 209 (*see also* pure oralism); Braidwood's pupils using, 102–3; in British schools, 184. *See also* British deaf education; British system, 156–59; Columbia Institution and, 184; combined method, 182–87 (*see also* combined method); De Gérando's view of, 115–16; devaluation of, 150–51; dictionaries, 238, 244–45; education of deaf people and, 79–84 (*see also* deaf education); Fay survey of methods, 161–62, 183, 255–58; in France, 86; Gallaudet University system, 213; historical overview, 60–64; l'Epée and, 106–7; monastic, 5, 62, 68; non-Western, 61; oath as witness using, 61; oralism versus, 173–75, 182–87; pressure to reconsider use, 211; religion and, 173, 175; St. Augustine and, 67–68; Scott and, 158, 163; seventeenth century in Britain, 66–90; Signed English, 209–14; signed international languages, 213; sixteenth century, 61–62; South African Sign Language, 245; speech used with, 212; Victorian society's views on, 28; Watson and, 156–57; World Federation of Deaf resolution, 235–36. *See also* fingerspelling; manual alphabets; methodological signs; national sign languages; native sign languages; natural sign languages
Silberman, Bernard S., 193–94
Simon, Théodore, 47
Skutnabb-Kangas, Tove, xii, xiii, 237
Smith, Samuel, 196
Social Darwinism, 27
Society for Racial Hygiene, 29
sound. *See* speech
South African Sign Language, 245
Spain, 68–69, 76
special education, 48–49, 149. *See also* segregation
species, ordering of, 22
speech, 77–78, 210, 212; British schools promoting in nineteenth century, 125–27; combined oral-manual approach, 183–84 (*see also* combined method); Holder's views on, 82–84; parlor pupils' education focused on, 127, 129; versus signs and gestures, 87; sound, nature of, 75; Wallis' views on deaf and possibility of speaking, 79, 81; Wilkins' views on deaf and possibility of speaking, 73–74. *See also* Milan Congress of Teachers of the Deaf; oralism
speech therapy, 205, 206
sports, 45
Spring Hill School, 190, 203
Stainer, William, 162, 167, 171–73, 195, 198, 217
Stanford Revision of the Binet Scale, 48
Steiner, Rudolph, 18
sterilization, 32–33, 153
Stewart, Dugald, 103
Stokes, W.E.D., 30
surgery, 41, 113–14, 130–31, 224–29
survival of the fittest, 29
Svirsky, Mario, 227
Sweden: education policy in, 221–22; national sign language in, 223
Swift, Jonathan, 71
symbolic violence: imperialism and, 234–35; of Total Communication, 185

Tarra, abbé, 154, 168
The Teacher of the Deaf (British journal), 198, 210–11
teacher training: in America, 199; apprenticeship system, 194–96; in Australia, 178, 206; in Britain, 127–28, 193–94; bureaucracy and, 42–43; certification of teachers of the deaf, 179, 196–98; feminization of teaching. *See* Women; fluent linguistic skills required, 222; Gallaudet and, 199; method, 134–35; professionalism and,

teacher training *(continued)*
43–46, 148–49; signed forms taught to, 223; speech therapy and use of acoustic equipment, 205. *See also* deaf education; deaf teachers
technology to counter hearing loss, 200–2
Technopoly, 149
Tellings, Agnes, 225–26
Terman, Lewis Madison, 48
Thai Sign language, 244–45
The Thai Sign Language Dictionary, 244–45
Thomas, Keith, 23
Thorton, Henry, 111
Thoutenhoofd, Ernst, 223
Tillinghast, David, 144
Tillinghast, Joseph, 144, 185
Toms, Jennifer, 207
Total Communication, 185, 214–17, 223
Tower of Babel, 71
Townsend, John, 111–12, 125, 139
Training College for Teachers of the Deaf, 197
Tuileries, 21
Turner, Joseph, 141
twentieth century: deaf education in, 178–202; denial of deafness in, 203–32
two-handed alphabets, 62–63, 129–30
Tylor, Edward, 150

Ulrich of Cluny, 5
uniformity of communication, 8
United Kingdom. *See* Britain
United States. *See* American deaf education
universal language, search for, 66–90
"Unlocking the Curriculum," 220

Van Praagh, William, 196
Venerable Bede, 68
Victorian School for Deaf Children in Melbourne (VCDC), 207
Victorian society, 28
Vietnam, 245

Wallis, John: Baker and, 100; British tradition of deaf education set by, 79–84; development of British sign system, 156; manual alphabet used by, 63, 81, 93–94; methods transformed by Baker and Braidwood, 104; pictorial representation of manual alphabet, 93, 95; Royal Society and, 19–20; sign language and, 63, 79–84; speech taught to deaf, views on, 79, 81
Wampler, Dennis W., 213
Warnock, Mary, 50
Wars in twentieth century and Britain, 187–88, 190
Watson, Alexander, 194
Watson, James, 194
Watson, Joseph: apprenticeship system used by, 194; Braidwood's relationship with, 100–3; deaf teachers and, 139; Gallaudet and, 135; sign language and, 156–57; teacher at school for deaf and poor, 112; teaching methods of, 127–29, 134
Watson, Samuel, 143
Watson, Thomas, 194
Weald in Kent, 6
Western aid programs, effect of, 243–46
Whaley, Daniel, 79, 81
wild boy of Aveyron, 24, 41, 115
Wilde, William, 132
Wilkins, John, 19, 67, 72–75, 78, 84
Winzer, Margret, 149
wolf children, 24. *See also* wild boy of Aveyron
women: family as realm of, 9; feminization of teaching, 170, 197, 198–200; first female teacher at Old Kent School, 141; trainees for oral method in America, 197
Woodward, James C., 215
World Deaf Games, 238
World Federation of the Deaf, 235, 238, 244, 245–46
Wren, Christopher, 19
written language: Baker's emphasis on, 163; Braidwood's views on, 101; British emphasis on, 157, 160; in France, 160; Holder's views on, 83; in pre-Renaissance world, 70; Wallis teaching to deaf students, 80–81; Watson teaching to deaf students, 128–29

York Retreat, 40–41

zoos, development of, 23